CW00689953

PSYCHOANALYSIS, MIND AND ART

Aristotelian Society Series

Aristotelian Society Monographs Committee:
Martin Davies (Monographs Editor); Thomas Baldwin;
Jennifer Hornsby; Mark Sainsbury; Anthony Savile

Psychoanalysis, Mind and Art

Perspectives on Richard Wollheim

Edited by
Jim Hopkins and Anthony Savile

BLACKWELL
Oxford UK & Cambridge USA

Copyright © Basil Blackwell Ltd 1992
First published 1992

Blackwell Publishers
108 Cowley Road
Oxford OX4 1JF
UK

238 Main Street, Suite 501
Cambridge, Massachusetts 02142
USA

All rights reserved. Except for the quotation of short
passages for the purposes of criticism and review, no
part may be reproduced, stored in a retrieval system, or
transmitted, in any form or by any means, electronic,
mechanical, photocopying, recording or otherwise, without
the prior permission of the publisher.

Except in the United States of America, this book is sold subject
to the condition that it shall not, by way of trade or otherwise,
be lent, resold, hired out, or otherwise circulated without the
publisher's prior consent in any form of binding or cover other
than that in which it is published and without a similar
condition including this condition being imposed on the
subsequent purchaser.

British Library Cataloguing in Publication Data

A CIP catalogue record for this book is available from the British Library.

Library of Congress Cataloging-in-Publication Data

Psychoanalysis, mind, and art; perspectives on Richard Wollheim/
edited by Jim Hopkins and Anthony Savile.
p. cm.—(Aristotelian Society series; v. 11)
Includes bibliographical references and index.
ISBN 0–631–17571–7 (alk. paper)
1. Psychoanalysis. 2. Art—Psychology. 3. Philosophy of mind.
4. Wollheim, Richard, 1923– . 5. Hopkins, James. 6. Savile,
Anthony. I. Series.
BF173.P776 1992
150. 19′5–dc20   91–46360   CIP

Typeset in 10 on 12 Plantin by Pure Tech Corporation,
Pondicherry, India

Printed in Great Britain by T.J. Press Ltd, Padstow, Cornwall

This book is printed on acid-free paper

Contents

Part III: Art and Vision

Part IV: Memory and Motive

Preface

Richard Wollheim is one of the few philosophers in the analytic tradition to have engaged in detail with questions as to why events in life mean what they do and how such significance informs works of art. He is a leading philosophical authority on both psychoanalysis and painting, and even the inclusive title we have given to this collection does not do justice to the variety, connectedness, and freedom from academic convention of his contributions to philosophical thought. These qualities, fortunately, are at least partly mirrored in the essays. Almost all are concerned with the mind, and the majority with psychoanalysis or art. But they have further links, which we have indicated by part titles. We have also appended a select bibliography of Wollheim's publications.

The editors are responsible for inessential details of some references. Citations of *The Standard Edition of the Complete Psychological Works of Sigmund Freud* (Hogarth, London, 1966) are by volume and page, in parentheses after quotation. A similar economy has been adopted where convenient for other references, and those to Wollheim's books are by date to the bibliography.

It was suggested that royalties from this book might go to an educational or charitable cause, and we should like to express our gratitude to the contributors for agreeing to this.

J.H. A.B.S.

Part I

Psychoanalysis, Values, and Politics

1

Psychoanalysis, Interpretation, and Science

JIM HOPKINS

Since this is a volume for Richard Wollheim, I should like to say something about working with him. We gave a series of seminars on philosophy and psychoanalysis together for a number of years while he was in London. Many of our colleagues were from the department Richard had built, and were particularly able and enthusiastic. And I had the opportunity to learn from a pioneer in our subject, whose knowledge was unrivalled, and who conveyed what he knew with a subtlety and wit which made learning a particular pleasure. It was one of the most rewarding experiences of my academic life.

One of the many things that made an impression on me was Richard's ability to use interpretive descriptions. In his presence, or reading his work, there could be no doubt that such thinking was philosophically informative. And although the illumination given by interpretive thought may derive from a particular way of seeing things, the capacity to give information in this way is not unique, and that needed to receive it, fortunately, is spread wider still. Hence, very many instances make us aware of the value of interpretation, and it seems a basic and pervasive source of understanding.

This suggests questions as to how interpretation relates to other sources of knowledge, and particularly to science; and these have often focused on the work of Freud. Psychoanalysis, as Freud envisaged it, was to be an interpretive science. But it is natural to wonder how far a discipline can be interpretive and also scientific, or objective. This is a larger topic than can be treated here, but I should like to sketch some lines of thought which contribute to an overall view.[1]

I

Let us begin with cases in which to interpret something is to understand or specify its meaning.[2] Here interpretation seems a purely
hermeneutic or semantic process. The paradigm objects of such interpretation are linguistic – things like utterances, inscriptions, or
texts – and the abilities we employ in it are familiar and striking, and
show most clearly in our understanding of language. In particular,
human beings seem naturally able to understand novel sentences in
unlimited number, readily and without effort, provided these are
composed of familiar words in grammatical patterns.

This evidently involves abilities which are both syntactic (concerned
with relations of symbol to symbol) and semantic (concerned with
relations of symbol to thing symbolized). Thus understanding words
involves relating them to one another to form sentences and also
relating them to things they designate. Someone who understands a
noun-phrase, for example, not only knows how to combine it with
verb-phrases to form sentences, but also (at least often) knows that it
is supposed to stand for a certain person, place, or thing; knows how
to identify such things; to communicate with people who can tell him
or her about them; and so forth. And again, someone who understands a descriptive word or phrase will know that it is true of certain
objects, will often be able to recognize the properties with which the
description is correlated, communicate with others who can, and so
forth.

Similarly, understanding sentences involves relating them to one
another and also to the world. A speaker who understands a particular
indicative sentence, for example, knows many relations of implication
which hold between that sentence and other sentences, pairs of sentences, and so on. That is, for many sequences of sentences[3] 'S_1' to
'S_{n+1}', a speaker knows something of the form

If 'S_1', 'S_2', . . . 'S_n' are true, so is 'S_{n+1}'.

The importance of such sequences is not merely linguistic; they also
serve as patterns for thinking. Thus someone who understands English will know, for example, that if both 'If cricket is a game, cricket
is good' and 'Cricket is a game' are true, then so is 'Cricket is good'.
More generally, a speaker will recognize that this sort of connection
holds for all instances of the same pattern (here, say, the pattern: if
S_1; S_2; S_1; so S_2) And such patterns will describe transitions, from

sentence to sentence or thought to thought, which speakers acknowledge as cogent.

Also, a speaker who understands an indicative sentence commonly knows the circumstances which would render that sentence true. Thus a speaker of English will know that 'Snow is white' is true just if snow is white, that 'Grass is green' is true just if grass is green, that 'Dogs bark' is true just if dogs bark, and so on, without end. (This may seem so obvious as to go without saying; but this is because we are taking examples from a language we understand. We could not list truths this way for a language unknown to us, and this indicates that linguistic understanding and knowledge of such truths are connected.) So for each sentence 'S' that a speaker is able to understand, he or she will also know something of the form

'S' is true just if S.

This pattern, like the previous one, evidently has indefinitely many instances; and very many of these reflect abilities to link sentences with the world – that is, with the actual objects or situations which the sentences could be used to describe, and which would render them true or false. Thus suppose someone utters, say, 'This snow is white', in order to say of a particular chunk of snow that it is white. A person who understands the sentence will know the kind of thing that would make it true, and in consequence will know how to relate the utterance to its worldly context, and (in many cases at least) how to determine whether it is true or false. So an understander will be able to recognize the particular snow in question as verifying the utterance, and would in the absence of anything appropriate be able to judge it false. Here the white snow spoken of is something of the sort which corresponds to the sentence if it is true. And in understanding language, it seems, we are able to grasp indefinitely many potential correspondence relations of this kind, which enable us to use language as a means of communication about the world.[4]

There is clearly much more to be said about what speakers know about their words and sentences, but this may serve to start our sketch. In considering interpretation, we can usefully focus on these relations between words and things and between sentences and the events or situations which render them true. These seem central to meaning for (among others) two reasons.

First, the possession of meaning by words and sentences seems one manifestation of the broader phenomenon of representation. To specify the meaning of words and sentences seems to be to characte/

their capacity to represent how things are in the world. But to be a representation seems to be to stand in relation to something: namely, that which is represented. So it is natural to hold that, in describing relations of words to things and sentences to situations, we are elucidating meaning by relating representations to what they represent.

Secondly, stating the referents of words or the truth-conditions of sentences already seems a way of saying what they mean. Thus we could use the specifications of truth-conditions above to interpret 'Snow is white' as meaning that snow is white, 'Grass is green' as meaning that grass is green, and so on; and this would be correct. Again, if someone wants to know what a name or a descriptive word means, we can often explain this by specifying (or providing some other means of acquaintance with) the object for which the name stands, the property or relation correlated with the description, and so forth.

Our everyday interpretation of language proceeds spontaneously and without reflection. The same process, however, can be mediated (or partly replaced) by explicit hypotheses or theory, as in the case of someone who uses a dictionary or a grammar in a foreign country to help with understanding what people are saying. We can call this *theoretical* interpretation; and since it involves explicit formulations about language which can be tested in practice, we can use it to cast light on what we ordinarily do naturally. In particular, where we can interpret the same things both naturally and by means of theory, we may be able to regard the theory as specifying some of the information we bring to bear in unreflective practice.[5]

Now our ability to understand sentences on the basis of their words and the way they are put together has suggested to many that human beings must somehow grasp or otherwise embody a system of rules in accord with which this task is accomplished. These would be rules by which we relate language to the world and also, it seems, in accord with which we think. Such a vision inspired Wittgenstein's *Tractatus Logico-Philosophicus*, in which he gave an account of language and representation which was a precursor of many modern views. Wittgenstein thought that our ability to understand sentences showed that they were what he called 'pictures' of reality, by which he meant that they were representations which were both *compositional* and *referential*. And although his ideas here are not unfamiliar, they are relevant enough to our purposes to merit some spelling out.

Wittgenstein argued that in very many cases we can find what we may call systematic element – element: combination – combination correlations, as between representations and the things or reality they represent. As examples he cited, in addition to language, alphabetic notation considered as describing sounds; hieroglyphics; musical notation; maps, blueprints, and models; and even information-bearing mechanical structures such as the groove on a gramophone record, the roll in a player piano, or the system of holes in the cards of a programmable loom.[6] (This was before the prominence of the computer metaphor.)

In each of these cases, Wittgenstein held, we can regard *both* the representations *and* the things they represent as composed of elements which are combined in certain ways. This means that the elements which figure in the representations can be correlated with elements in the represented reality in such a way that the modes of combination in the representations map on to those in the reality. Such element – element: combination – combination correlations enable representations to carry information about what they represent in a particular way.[7] And given such a system of correlations, a combination of symbolic elements can be used because it represents reality accurately; that is, because this combination of symbolic elements is mapped with a combination in reality which actually obtains.

Wittgenstein took human language to be a system of this kind, in which the combinations of symbols which we regarded as grammatical sentences had been naturally constrained (by inbuilt rules of combination and projection) to map ways in which objects, properties, and relations might be combined in the situations we encountered in reality. And his view seems to have been that we naturally *embodied* such rules – that they were 'part of the human organism' – so that we actually knew little about them apart from the connections between words and things on the one hand and sentences and situations on the other, which were the socially salient aspects of their input and output. Thus, as he says:

> Man possesses the ability to construct languages capable of expressing every sense, without having any idea how each word has meaning or what its meaning is – just as people speak without knowing how the individual sounds are produced. Everyday language is a part of the human organism and no less complicated than it.[8]

Wittgenstein thought that the philosophical clarification of thoughts should make such elements, combinations, and 'rules of projection' manifest. Although he did not think of this as a matter for empirical theory, much contemporary research can be seen in terms of this task.

To describe representations in such a system, we must be able to survey relations among representing elements themselves, and so, in the case of language, the 'rules of combination' in accord with which sentences are made up of words. As is familiar, linguists like Chomsky have tried to specify such rules fully and precisely, and have found them to be complex and abstract. Such work provides a detailed explication of this aspect of our practical mastery of language. And explications of this kind can suggest descriptions of computational mechanisms for performing such tasks, and hence hypotheses as to the working of the mind or brain.

Describing the 'rules of projection' which relate human language to the world requires specifying the referents of words and the ways these determine the truth-conditions of sentences. Despite a number of differences, touched on below, this is closely connected with another contemporary project, first advocated by Donald Davidson: that of setting out a *theory of truth*[9] for a language we wish to understand in a theoretical way.

Such a theory, again, provides a description of a language which is compositional and referential. Applied to a particular sentence of the language for which it has been devised, the axioms of a (properly constrained) theory of truth would take as input the subsentential expressions making it up, the way they are put together, and the way they are related to objects,[10] and would yield, as output, conditionals like '"Snow is white" is true if and only if snow is white', covering each sentence of the language. Such conditionals would state, for each sentence, the conditions in which it is true. We have just noted that such conditionals can be seen as describing semantic knowledge a speaker has about the sentences of his or her language, and that stating the truth-conditions of sentences is a way of interpreting them. In light of these and other considerations, Davidson has urged that such a theory could be used for the theoretical interpretation of natural language, and hence to cast light on linguistic meaning itself.

A theory of the kind we are considering regiments information about the structure of sentences and the connections between words and things in such a way that this suffices for interpretation. (Also, such a theory can be used to specify something like a manual of translation between the language of the theory and the language to which it is applied.) Hence, in so far as meaning is what interpretation reveals or what sentences and their translations have in common, it seems, once more, that there is reason to regard the information thus regimented as constitutive of meaning. This also accords with the later Wittgenstein's conception of meaning as use. Wittgenstein stressed that the meanings of words and sentences are fixed by such public features of their use (including ostensive definitions) as an explorer in an unknown country could employ to interpret the language of a people quite strange to him. (Cf. *Investigations* §§32 and 206, and his repeated arguments that there could be no such thing as an uninterpretable language.) Davidson envisages a theory of truth being used in precisely this way; that is, for what, following Quine, he calls 'radical interpretation'. So the information regimented by such a theory as Davidson envisages is precisely that which would relate use, as the later Wittgenstein conceived it, to the more traditional sorts of specifications of meaning which Wittgenstein himself employed in his earlier work.

Compositional or combinatory semantic theories are well known, and have been studied in detail. Also, their use in theoretical interpretation is well established. They can serve to interpret codes, artificial languages, and natural language itself. They provide theories which are both rigorous and powerful, yielding an unlimited number of theorems for interpreting complex symbols on the basis of lists of axioms which are finite and precisely specified. So it seems that we can regard the process of constructing and testing such a theory – and hence that of finding and articulating meaning – as analogous to that in other explanatory enterprises, and hence, in a broad sense, as scientific.

Alan Turing stressed the analogy for a particularly clear case, arguing that 'There is a remarkably close parallel between the problems of the physicist and the cryptographer. The system on which a message is enciphered corresponds to the laws of the universe, the intercepted messages to the evidence available, and the keys for a day or a message to important constants which have to be determined.'[11] Apart from some points about the role of law to be noted below, there seems no objection to regarding theoretical interpretation in something like this way generally. In this perspective, questions as to the detail of semantic theories – for example, regarding whether a theory should include explicit reference to properties as correlated with predicates or facts or situations as correlated with sentences–are to be settled ultimately by reference to their role in science taken as a whole.

Scientific theories seem is general to be supported by their capacity to explain the data they cover, so that when we judge that a theory is confirmed, we are making an inference to the truth, or acceptability, of our best explanatory hypothesis.[12] On this account, we support a scientific theory by showing that it explains certain things well, and better than any other; but there can be no guarantee that some further theory may not do better, and so nothing like final scientific proof. In practice we would take an interpretive theory as confirmed by success in making sense of the utterances or text to which it is applied – as in the case, say, of interpretations of coded German broadcasts. Confirmation of this kind can also be regarded as an instance of inference to the best (psychological) explanation, where what is explained is the production of the symbols which are being interpreted (in the case of Turing's group, the production of certain strings of code) and the explanatory hypothesis is that they were produced intentionally, in order to represent things as the theory specifies (produced, for example, to say *these* things, to communicate this information, these orders, and so on.).

The interpretation of human texts or utterances is also perforce that of the linguistic activities of persons. So the best interpretation of an utterance or text will represent the meaning to be assigned to it as enjoying the best possible fit with the motives – and hence with the actions, surroundings, and lives – of those who promulgated it. For this reason, we must see the application of an interpretive theory as part of an overall project of understanding both language and action. Still, within this context a particular interpretive theory can be strongly confirmed apart from detailed considerations about action, simply by its capacity to render text coherent.

This is because the interpretation of a text subjects it to the constraints of order which are essential for meaning, and these may be rigorous enough in practice to support a particular interpretation and to rule out all natural alternatives. What we are calling 'text' can be taken to consist of strings of symbols which, prior to interpretation, would seem to enjoy unlimited possibilities of combination. Under interpretation, these strings, first, must fit a grammar which restricts their combinations radically, to those of legitimate words and sentences; and secondly, these combinations must also meet the further condition that they cohere, each with all the others, as parts of an intelligible sequence. Unordered strings do not satisfy such conditions. And although here, as elsewhere, a theory may be underdetermined by the data it is used to explain, in practice a theory which makes good sense of a testing stretch of text will often lack rivals which propose seriously different interpretations.

Some of the principles at work in this can be seen clearly in simple but characteristic cases. Thus consider codes which map numbers on to letters of the alphabet. For example, we may take

```
1   2   3       4   5   6   7   8       9   10  11  12  13
T   h   e       q   u   i   c   k       b   r   o   w   n
14  11  15      16  5   17  18  3       19      11  20  3   10
f   o   x       j   u   m   p   e   d       o   v   e   r
1   2   3       21  22  23  24          19  11  25      22
t   h   e       l   a   z   y           d   o   g       A
17  11  17  3   13  1           12  3   13  1       9   24
m   o   m   e   n   t           w   e   n   t       b   y
9   5   1       1   2   3           19  11  25      19  6   19
b   u   t       t   h   e           d   o   g       d   i   d
13  11  1       26  1   6   10      22  1       22  21  21
n   o   t       s   t   i   r       a   t       a   l   l
```

Strings of numbers which can be taken as encoding words and sentences in this way are subject to familiar interpretive constraints. Each string must be so ordered as to yield a word; in addition, each string must be related to others, so that all cohere as parts of an intelligible message. Even in this short example it seems likely that such constraints make it possible to fix on a single good theory, as the reader can verify by trying alternatives. So we see that combinatory interpretive hypotheses can be quite quickly and strongly confirmed in practice, even though they deal with what might seem a daunting number of possibilities. Also, we can see that interpretive confirmation displays a number of characteristic and significant features.

First, confirmation of a particular hypothesis comes only when it is used together with a number of others, and to cover a certain critical amount of material. If we take just a little text – say, the '123' with which the above begins – very many distinct hypotheses will apparently serve equally well to render it coherent. But as more strings are taken into account and hypotheses are framed to cover these as well, alternatives tend to be eliminated, and with increasing rapidity. This suggests that in general the cogency of a good interpretive theory can be recognized only by someone who has applied enough of it, and to enough material. To someone who has not done this, a correct account may seem no better than many incorrect rivals.

This is a consequence of the nature of the theories with which we are concerned or, again, the kind of information or knowledge they embody. Any interpretive theory will, so to speak, spread itself relatively thinly over the material to be interpreted; it will require a distinct hypothesis specifying the referent, or some relation to objects, for each combining symbol, and also a separate hypothesis, or series of hypotheses, bearing on each significant mode of combination. Plainly a theory consisting of so many hypotheses, each relating to potentially distinct data, must be applied as a whole, and to a good range of data, in order for each hypothesis to be tested in use. In this, it is worth noting, interpretive theories differ from paradigms like Newton's, which cover their data by means of just a few laws, all of which may be brought to bear at once in explaining a single event.

Once engaged, however, diverse interpretive hypotheses can work interactively. That is, claims about the referents of symbols can serve in co-ordination with claims about their significant combinations, so as to determine interpretations via various constraints of order simultaneously. Successful interpretive hypotheses can thus lock in on data co-operatively and with some rapidity, as the contribution of each is confirmed by its coherence with others. (Thus in the example above, the interpretation of '123' fixes other occurrences of those symbols, and so constrains further interpretations throughout the text; and that of the first line provides reason for fixing the reference of many numerals on the basis of just one occurrence.) So successful interpretation can yield a relatively full theory, and one which readily makes sense of new strings, with a speed which might seem surprising, given the complexity of both the data and the theory involved.

Secondly, interpretive theories illustrate the possibility that a theory can be entirely satisfactory, but yet predictive only in a delimited way. Confirmation of such a theory enables us to predict that we can use it to make sense of future strings in the same language. But even a theory which we knew to be correct and adequate in all respects would not enable us to predict future strings themselves. This too is in the nature of the case, for an interpretive theory specifies only how strings must be formed if they are to carry information interpretable by that theory. There is no restriction on the infinity of possible messages or on the production of other strings generally.

Here again, owing to the phenomena with which it deals, interpretive theory contrasts with the Newtonian paradigm. We see this also in our own grasp of language, which enables us to understand, but not to predict, what others say (and only if they are vocalizing so as to be understood, and in the right language). Also, this seems to accord with the natural idea that the function of interpretation is to enable us to make use of information provided by others. For this we do not need to predict others' behaviour generally, but rather, only to understand those aspects of it which function to pass on information. Limited as this task is, it is plainly very important.

This links with a third point. Interpretation assigns properties to strings – being generated in accord with certain rules and composed of symbols with certain referents in reality – which are highly theoretic and abstract, and which concern relations with things which may be spatially or temporally very remote from the symbols themselves. Strings will, however, show other, simpler properties of order, which an interpreter may make use of. (Indeed, number-for-letter codes are often unravelled via well-known statistics concerning the frequency of occurrence of various letters and combinations in written English.) But it would be wrong to suppose that an interpretive theory should be assessed in terms of these surface properties, as opposed to its success in yielding interpretations. For the deeper combinatory and referential order which successful interpretation reveals will serve to explain the order (or apparent disorder) which emerges at other levels as resulting from the encoding of the particular message it reveals in the particular system it specifies; but not vice versa.

This can be partly brought out in terms of the example above. Here the sequence '22 23' occurs once, encoding the 'a z' of the word 'lazy'. Since 'a' is a relatively common letter but 'z' not, '22' occurs in other sequences, but '23' does not. Indeed even a much longer message might well contain no other occurrences of 'z', or only occurrences preceded by 'i' (as in 'realize', and the like) but not by 'a'. So, plainly, the combination '22 23', or its interpretation 'a z', might be unique in a considerable stretch of text, and so anomalous by comparison with occurrences of these numerals or letters elsewhere. Still, it is clear that an interpretation which held that '22 23' was a combination with sense and which interpreted it as encoding 'a z' might be correct, and supported in the highest degree. Also, it is clear that this support would be provided in part by '22' and '23' occurring as symbols interpretable by 'a' and 'z' in other combinations. That is, the very same evidential basis, relation to which made the occurrence '22 23' an anomaly, might also render the hypothesis that it encoded 'a z' irresistible.

Since the best interpretation – and one that can be very strongly confirmed – can explain the occurrence of the sequence '22 23' on the hypothesis that it encodes 'a z', it is clear that:

1 It would be a methodological error to argue against this hypothesis on the grounds that 'a' is not usually followed by 'z', nor 'z' usually preceded by 'a', either generally or in this message. That is, it would be a mistake to allow considerations of surface symbol frequency to dominate interpretation in a case in which,

as here, the best interpretation also provides the best explanation of these observed frequencies.

2 It would also be an error to argue against this hypothesis on the grounds that it implies that the production of '22' at this point in the message was a cause of the production of '23' after it, whereas the application to this material of some non-interpretive quantitative method for determining causal connection (say a Millian or Baconian method) does not show evidence of a causal connection between the occurrence of '22' and that of '23'. For, to hold that 'lazy' is the best interpretation of the string in question is to hold that the best account we can give of the intentions (causes) which produced the text includes an intention to encode 'lazy', and hence to encode 'a' followed by 'z' and hence to write '22' followed by '23'. And this does imply that the writing, say, of '22' was a cause of the writing of '23' – in the sense in which the production of one part of a message is among the causes of that of another – despite the failure of non-interpretive methods to bring this out.

A similar point also arises for natural language. As Chomsky has stressed, many of the sentences produced by each of us in speaking our own language are novel, that is, different in one way or another from any produced on any other occasion.[13] Many uttered sentences, therefore, can be regarded as anomalies, whose character is partly owed to the information they serve to communicate. Clearly this does not make their interpretation uncertain. Rather, as with the message above, we recognize that the combinations make sense and that we understand them, and hence that the anomaly is superficial. So it would also be wrong in the case of natural language to allow surface causal or correlational considerations to dominate interpretation. (Consider, for example, the effect of the stipulation that a sentence should not be taken to be true in a particular situation unless it had been used in just that situation before, or often enough to count as a statistically significant indicator of it.)

This point also links with the nature of interpretation and communication. Combinatory strings carry a variety of information precisely by using a variety of symbols and orderings within those permitted by their compositional rules. From any but an interpretive perspective, the variety essential to the encoding of information is apt to seem anomalous, as in the case of 'a z' above or novel sentences generally. So it is essential that the presence of the kind of generative causal order involved in meaning be judged by interpretation, or the relatively full application of a (compositional and referential) semantic theory, rather than by a method which treats of more concrete superficial features. It is a general feature of explanatory theories that they enable us to see that apparent anomalies in observation are in fact aspects of a deeper order; and in the case of interpretive theories, this is the order which sustains meaning. So methods which impose a non-interpretive filter on phenomena with meaning are liable to screen out the very information these phenomena are designed to carry.

II

We have seen that the understanding of language shows a number of distinctive methodological features, which can be related to the kind of theory which makes interpretive information explicit. I want now to argue that psychological understanding is so interwoven with that of language as to share these features. It follows, I think, that commonsense psychology and theories based on it (including Freud's) are liable to systematic mis-evaluation, through methodological judgements which are counterparts to the errors about interpretation just described. Moreover, there seems reason to hold that such mis-evaluation (or at least a bias towards it) is endemic to an established tradition in the philosophy of science.

We have reviewed the fact that people frequently know about the referents of their words and the implications and truth-conditions of their sentences. Let us register this by saying that speakers have knowledge of *semantic connections* which hold for their language, where these include both logical connections and the links of words and sentences to their worldly correspondents (or, as we may say, their *semantic values*).[14] Then we can try to bring out something of the way in which knowledge of semantic connections is bound up with psychological understanding.

As is familiar, we use language in a particular way in articulating[15] the contents of the mind. We have, first, a series of words which we take to describe motives, or mental states or acts – words like 'remember', 'expect', 'imagine', 'believe', 'desire', 'hope', 'fear', 'wish', and a number of others. These, however, do not serve as descriptions on their own; rather, they work by being joined with further phrases or sentences.

Thus we may say that someone desires the death of the King. Here the motive is described by 'desire', and this is supplemented by 'the death of the King'. This latter phrase specifies the desired (type of) event, or, as we also say, the object of desire. Or again, we may say that someone fears that the King is dead. Here description by the word 'fear' is supplemented by 'the King is dead', which describes the feared situation, that is, the object of fear. And we describe the objects of perception, belief, memory, imagination, hope, expectation, and the rest in a similar way. (So the sense of 'object' here is partly grammatical: the object of desire is what is desired; of belief, what is believed; and so on.)

Now it seems that we understand this use of motive-describing expressions as follows: a descriptive phrase or sentence used in this way serves to assign (or specify) a semantic value for the motive or mental state itself. The value, or semantic correlate, is simply that of the articulating phrase or sentence in question. Thus, schematically, the semantic value of a sentence 'S' is the situation which would render 'S' true; and this, on our mode of description, is the situation which would satisfy the desire that S, verify the belief that S, realize the hope or fear that S, and so on. A phrase or sentence used in this way fits its motive like a glove; the relation of the phrase or sentence to the world seems precisely adapted to specify a corresponding relation on the part of the motive. So such description makes explicit the intentionality, or object-directedness, of motives, representing our minds as engaged with the worldly correlates (or potential correlates) of our words, phrases, and sentences.

Linguistic articulation thus provides us with a powerful tool for psychological understanding. It allows us, in effect, to make a double use of natural language: first in describing the world and then in describing the mind in its engagement with the world as described. This in turn enables us to make use of our grasp of semantic connections for describing and understanding the working of motive, and hence in the explanation of behaviour. This has a number of aspects, two of which can be indicated as follows.

First, as is clear, recycling our worldly phrases and sentences in this way allows us to generate from our relatively short list of words for motives an unlimited variety of psychological descriptions, and in such a way that the burden of information in these descriptions is largely borne by the worldly sentences they embed. The single word 'desire', for example, can be combined with any grammatically appropriate phrase or sentence from natural language (including the vocabulary of physical science), so as to yield a description of any thing, property, or situation which might be an object of desire. So, through such embedding of phrases or sentences, we can specify any describable phenomenon which might move us in this particular way. The same, of course, holds for other ways of being moved; for example, the word 'believe' can be combined with any appropriate sentence to describe any situation which might serve to inform our actions; and so on.

Secondly, this mode of description serves to encode the working of motives linguistically. It enables us, that is, to map causal connections which hold as among motives, or as between motives and reality, by semantic connections which hold for the phrases or sentences in terms of which we describe the motives. This in turn renders the knowledge of semantic connections involved in our understanding of language interconvertible in practice with knowledge of the dynamics of motive. So this use of language gives us, in our commonsense psychology, a sort of natural system for the linguistic – or semantic or hermeneutic – representation of psychological causal role.[16]

To bring this out, let us consider the central and relatively clear cases of desire and belief. As is familiar, we describe desires in terms of their objects or conditions of satisfaction; that is, in an instance of 'Jones desires that S', the conditions in which 'S' would be true are those in which the desire would be satisfied. The semantic correlate of 'S' is the object of desire. But this – the desired action or situation – is precisely what we take it that a desire should bring about (that is, cause) if a person acts on it. If Jones desires that he (Jones) goes to Vienna, then this desire, if acted on, should serve to bring about (cause) Jones's going to Vienna. So the description of a desire in terms of its object is at the same time a description of a cause in terms of an effect which that cause should have, if it operates in a certain way.[17]

In this case the semantic encoding of causal role is so simple and direct that we may not even notice it. It shows, however, in the way our understanding of the sentence which specifies the object of desire already tells us how the desire should operate. In understanding the sentence we use to describe the desire, we know the object or situation which the desire should work to secure. Understanding of language, via semantic articulation, secures (partial) grasp of the role of desire in the production of actions.

Something comparable holds for belief. When we articulate a belief by a sentence, we thereby register that the belief is true in the same situations as the sentence. But also, we take it that the situations in which beliefs are true are precisely those which the beliefs are supposed to reflect or be sensitive to. That is, we take it that beliefs should be formed in such a way as to reflect the facts; and this means

that a belief should be causally sensitive to the circumstances in terms
of which it is described. So describing a belief in terms of the conditions in which it would be true is, among other things, a way of
describing an effect in terms of circumstances to which it should be
causally sensitive.[18] Again, grasp of the semantic values of sentences
goes with knowledge of the working of motives, which is so natural
and pervasive that we may not even recognize it for what it is.

These roles come together in the simple patterns we use in explaining actions by reference to their reasons. We may, for example, explain someone's climbing a ladder by saying that he wants to reach a
shelf and believes that he can if he climbs the ladder. We naturally
recognize that such an explanation ascribes to the agent a cogent
reason for wanting to climb the ladder; and we can represent this
formally – for example, in terms of the symbols we have already used
– as follows. The agent

> desires that S_1 (that he reach the shelf)
> believes that if S_2 then S_1 (that if he climbs the ladder, he
> will reach the shelf)

and so

> desires that S_2 (that he climb the ladder).

The pattern by which we thus represent the derivation of the agent's
final desire is comparable to that of a valid argument. In this case the
pattern does not relate truth to truth but, rather, truth to the satisfaction of desire. In a valid argument, the truth of the premisses
guarantees that of the conclusion. Here, by contrast, the truth of an
agent's belief, together with the satisfaction of his derived desire,
guarantees the satisfaction of his initial desire. (Hence the validity of
the practical pattern emerges if it is read from the bottom up.) So the
pattern shows that in forming the desire we want to explain, the agent
has sought rationally to ensure the satisfaction of the desire we cite
in explanation.

Such patterns track the processes by which belief carries the stamp
of reality into the contents of desire, and thence into action. This is
a causal matter, but again, one we trace in terms of semantic connection. Here the transfer of information by which the causes of belief
shape those of action appears as a pattern of transmission of content,
or transfer of semantic value, from motive to motive. The understanding of sentences and their patterns which is part of linguistic
competence enables us at once to grasp this transition and to follow
in it. So in this case, as in others, in processing our linguistic repre-

sentations of an agent's thoughts, we in effect think them again (and without effort), and so locate ourselves with respect to him in the cognitive space we share.

Since desires obtain satisfaction through such connection with reality, implicative patterns of this sort have countless significant and connected instances. We read them on to the sequential bodily movements of others readily and pervasively; and such patterns often reach, more or less in series, from overarching goals through the formation of actual plans down to the details of the strings of movements and manipulations of objects in the immediate environment by which an action or project is implemented. We mark the span of such a series of reasons, as it bears on a whole sequence of bodily movements, by such phrases as 'in order to'; thus we might have registered that our agent above was moving a certain way in order to climb the ladder, in order (say) to reach the shelf, in order to get the gun kept there, in order to confront a prowler, in order to protect his person, family, or property, and so on. Thus we hold that an agent desired that S_{n+1} in order that S_n, desired that S_n in order that S_{n-1}, and so on, up through the order.

Each link in such an ordering represents a part, or aspect, of what an agent does – an element in the flow of his or her behaviour – as at once *goal-directed, information-governed,* and *systematically related in these respects to others*. The goals and information thus specified and related pertain to actual or potential features of the environment, taken as semantic values of the phrases and sentences we use in our description of behaviour and motive alike. The order reflects the way in which each goal is *dominated* by those from which it is derived, in the sense that it owes its place in the order at least in part to the fact that it serves as a way or means to them. So the series consists of specifications of causes (motives) which co-operate in action, each making a particular contribution to the order in action in accord with its place in the order of motive. And finally, since we take each goal as something the agent seeks in preference to others, the 'package' of satisfaction described by the logically linked $S_1 \ldots S_n$ upon which we fix in any particular instance represents a sort of maximum – something like the best the agent thought could be managed in the circumstances. Thus each action or aspect of an action which can be interpreted in this way must fit with all others in the strings in which it figures. And the series of interpretations that we fix in the case of each string must also cohere with those that we fix in others, as an intelligible part of the agent's plans and projects and an expression of his or her values over all.[19]

These requirements for interpretive coherence partly parallel those mentioned in connection with the interpretation of codes above; and since the strings in question are interpreted by sentences related by implication, it is plausible to suppose that further constraints are involved. So although these considerations concern only relatively familiar and superficial features of commonsense psychology, they already suggest that we should regard the explanation of action by motive as similar in important respects to the interpretation of language.

We have seen how commonsense psychology articulates motives by sentences whose semantic connections (with one another and with reality) systematically reflect a range of causal connections (with one another and with reality) which hold for the motives themselves. Commonsense psychology thus supplies, via its use of language, what we might call a *causal semantics* for behaviour: that is, an assignment to elements and sequences in behaviour of (motive-articulating) sentences, and thence an assignment of objects (semantic values).[20] We thus assign to each behaviour or sequence which we interpret a set of interrelated (and so mutually constrained) relations to objects, reflecting the information relating to the environment by which that element of behaviour is driven.

In this perspective the interpretation of both language and behaviour ultimately consists in the fixing of semantic values, so chosen as to reflect causally relevant goals and sources of information. The establishing of such causal/semantic links plainly makes for a form of causal explanation; but it should also be regarded as semantic, in the full sense considered in connection with the hermeneutic interpretation of language in I above. That is, in both cases we understand (interpret) by (1) discerning sequences or strings of elements in behaviour, and (2) assigning to the elements and strings relations or sets of relations to objects. The assignments in both cases are systematic, and interrelated by grammatical or logical patterns in accord with which we take the sequences to be generated; in both cases these patterns require that the assignments to each element in a string cohere with those to all others and that assignments made for one string fit with assignments made for others. In interpreting speech, we assign the objects as it were in causally neutral abstraction, in accord with our conception of meaning; then, in interpreting action, we use these interpreted sentences as templates for assigning the objects again, now as objects of desire, belief, or other motives, and so as specifying systematically related causes. But interpreting speech is also interpreting action, so the circle closes on itself: we can take it to consist throughout in the assignment of values to elements and sequences in behaviour, constrained now by the grammar of language, now by the 'grammar' of action, and so ultimately by both.[21]

It follows, I think, that we should expect the explanation of human behaviour by motive to share the methodological features of the interpretation of language sketched above. So let us return to some of these.

We noted above that many sentences are at once meaningful and novel. So in understanding such sentences, we regularly grasp connections between sentences and their conditions of truth which we do not take as based on simple inductions (inductions not mediated by some complex theory) over past sentences, past pairings of sentence and context, and so forth. And since we also appreciate the new implications of new sentences, the same holds for connections between sentence and sentence. We take it, rather, that our capacity to link sentences with each other and with the world requires to be characterized theoretically, and in terms of the kind of generative structures revealed by, or hypothesized in the course of, interpretation. So if someone were to argue that sentences could not be regarded as having implications or truth-conditions except where these had been established by simple induction, this would be an inductivist fallacy, and one of a particularly destructive kind. For the consequence of adherence to such a fallacy would be the denial of normal understanding of language – the denial of our capacity to interpret one another, as we clearly can.

We can also see that a similar point holds for motives. We constantly form desires and beliefs which are new, in the sense that their articulation requires sentences which are novel; and likewise for the actions to which these motives give rise. So just as it would be a fallacy to hold that semantic connections – linking sentence and sentence or sentence and reality – must be established by simple induction, so it should also be a fallacy to hold that the parallel causal links between motive and motive or motives and their worldly conditions of truth, satisfaction, realization, and so on should have to be established in the same way. And just as adherence to such an inductivist fallacy for language would abrogate linguistic understanding, so adherence to such a fallacy for motive would curtail our natural understanding of action.

Such fallacy would also ignore a flexibility (or creativity) which seems essential to the function of language and action. It is hard to see how our sentences would enable us to communicate and co-operate so fully with respect to our complex and changing world, or how our motives would keep us going so successfully in it, if they lacked the kind of rule-described capacity to adapt to new circumstances which we are considering. Surely, as our discussions of articulation and interpretation imply, we should regard our capacities for forming sentences and motives as closely connected. New sentences would seem to arise from new desires (to say things, to convey new information), and these from new circumstances; so novelty in speech can be seen as an instance of novelty in action. But any rational action will still flow from a series of logical combinations of sententially articulable motives; so this flexibility remains bounded by the system which seems to make it possible.

III

We have seen something of how the commonsense linguistic encoding of causal role turns the full resources of natural language to the service of specifying similarities and differences among motives (causes of behaviour) and the full synthesizing and projective powers of linguistic understanding to grasping the explanatory import of these specifications. As a result, we are in effect naturally able to describe the mind (or brain) as a semantic engine; that is, a device which draws on information from the environment and transforms this into motive with environment-directed conditions of satisfaction.

The achievement implicit in this mode of description seems striking enough to dwell on for a moment. Any psychology which deals with the way living creatures represent and interact with the world must perforce contain both a vocabulary for describing representations and their transformations and one for describing the way in which such representations and the behaviour to which they give rise relate to the world. These are formidable requirements on description, and it is not easy to think of a more simple, direct, or efficient means of meeting them than that already found in common sense.

Articulation enables us to use worldly linguistic representations directly in the explanation of behaviour and to specify the psychological inputs, transformations, and outputs most relevant to understanding in terms of truth, reason, and the satisfaction of desire.[22] Moreover, the parameters thus described – our worldly goals and sources of information – seem central to any understanding of the mind or brain. So our everyday descriptions and their accompanying norms of function marked in terms of meaning and logic already provide a remarkably full and detailed framework for further research (although one which is of course subject to modification and enrichment).[23] It seems that here, as in many other cases, nature has provided a solution to problems of information processing which we do well to understand, acknowledge, and use.

Freud was, so far as I know, the first psychologist not only to employ, but also systematically to extend, this flexible, powerful, and natural system of understanding. I have argued elsewhere that his extension is grounded in a mode of inference which has the potential power, scope, and cogency to give strong support to his basic claims.[24] Such strengths in Freud's reasoning have, however, gone largely unacknowledged in the analytical tradition in philosophy. This, I think, is partly due to methodological assumptions whose flaws we are now in a position at least partly to expose. So I want now to consider these, in light of some of the norms of reason which we take good science to embody.

For this purpose, let us continue to use the idea that scientific theories seek to provide the best explanation for the data they cover, and gain support through their ability to do so. Accordingly, we can represent some connected ideals of scientific objectivity, communication, and rational criticism by the following two principles:

1 An explanatory discipline can be regarded as objective only in so far as the explanations, data, and theory used in it are such that the cogency claimed for them can be appreciated by any rational person who fully understands them.
2 The cogency of an explanatory hypothesis or theory can be properly evaluated only by someone who knows how that hypothesis or theory is used; that is, who understands it, the data it is supposed to explain, and how it does so.

The first of these principles relates objectivity to publicity of evaluation or, what is nearly the same, communicability. To be objective, an explanatory discipline must be *rationally transparent*, in the sense that the data and the theory employed in it and the cogency of the relation of explanation between them are appreciable by anyone sufficiently knowledgeable, thoughtful, and intelligent. The second is closely connected with this, and states that evaluation of a theory or explanation must be *well informed*. According to this principle an evaluator must actually understand the theory in question and know the data it covers, so that he or she can rightly consider the purported explanatory relation between them. Both these ideas seem intuitively plausible; and I think we can see something of their combined working in the success of the physical sciences, which is at once intellectual and social.

As accords with the first principle, the objectivity of physical science is shown by the communication of data and theory, which can be appreciated by anyone competent to understand it. Hence the explanations of physical science can readily be evaluated, more or less at first hand, by a community of people apart from those who devise them. These can reach agreement which is both independent and informed and which, therefore, accords with the second principle. And given this, it is rational, and also in accord with that principle, for people who do not themselves evaluate the theories at first hand to defer to others with greater expertise. (Someone who cannot personally evaluate theory and data about black holes, for example, can best form an opinion by consulting experts; and his deference in this is rational, provided he has good reason to believe that their disciplines are objective, and hence subject in general to evaluation which is well informed.)

Simple and basic as it seems, the requirement of well-informed assessment is opposed by a deep and traditional current in the analytical philosophy of science: that which issues in what we may call 'methodological short-cuts'. These are criteria (characteristically called 'scientific' by their proposers) which are supposed to make it possible to judge a theory or hypothesis in abstraction from particulars of its content, the data it is supposed to explain, or how it explains them. Such short-cuts are meant to enable one to evaluate a theory or explanation definitively, while understanding little of its actual working. So they constitute a sort of philosophical premeditated violation of principles like 2 above.

Thus, according to Popper, for example, corroboration is determined via the application of a single criterion, which is formal or logical: the deductive or predictive power of the theory in relation to the data or observations which it purports to explain. Roughly, a theory counts as scientific only in so far as it entails statements about observations which could falsify it; so in consequence, a theory can genuinely (scientifically) *explain* only phenomena which it could be used to *predict*. Thus theories or explanations which do not yield predictions about the phenomena they explain are no part of science proper, but rather, are metaphysical.

Popper's use of this criterion can be seen in his treatment of Darwin, which is in essentials similar to his celebrated critique of Freud. 'It is important', Popper urges, 'to show that Darwinism [by which he means 'the modern forms' of 'Darwinian theory'] is not a scientific theory, but metaphysical,' and that 'it is metaphysical because it is not testable.' Thus, for example, 'Darwinism does not really *predict* the evolution of variety. It therefore cannot really *explain* it.' Darwin does not offer 'the type of explanation we demand in physics.' For, 'while we can explain a particular eclipse by predicting it, we cannot predict or explain any particular evolutionary change.' Considering the best aspects of Darwinian theory, according to Popper, we can say only that it ' "almost predicts" a great variety of forms of life'; whereas 'in other fields its predictive or explanatory power is still more disappointing. Take "adaptation". At first sight natural selection appears to explain it, and in a way it does, but it is hardly a scientific way.'[25]

Here Popper's criterion enables him to deduce briefly and decisively that Darwin's theories and explanations are only pseudo-scientific, and to do so solely on the basis of predictive power. (And it is clear that the same could have been done, on the same grounds, by someone otherwise entirely ignorant of Darwin's work.) Such a treatment, however, is clearly inadequate. In fact, Darwin's explanations are paradigms of scientific thinking, which should be acknowledged as such on any methodologically unprejudiced account. (I think the same of Freud's, but do not wish to use this in a premiss of the argument.) So Popper's short-cut must be regarded as fallacious.

We should note, however, that Popper was right to assimilate Freud and Darwin and to contrast their work with physics. For both produced accounts of phenomena which had not been explained naturally before and which were similar in structure. (Roughly, Darwin showed that many features of plants and animals could be explained by regarding them as derived, by processes which he was the first to specify, from earlier, sometimes hypothesized forms which had not previously been taken as their origins. The same can be said of Freud, with 'mental life' substituted for 'plants and animals'.) To do this, both had to accomplish what seems the most basic task of explanation: that of exhibiting the data as instances of the generalizations and causal processes which were to provide explanatory information about them. Accordingly, their main work was twofold: on the one hand, they described and specified the new modes of derivation; on the other, they linked the phenomena to these modes by showing repeatedly and in a wide variety of cases that they were as they would be had they been derived as hypothesized.

Popper's short-cut thus applies alike to Darwin and Freud, partly because their research was particularly basic. They worked with new kinds of hypotheses, which did not enjoy the kind of built-in descriptive overlap with the language of observation which we find in physics; so they had to understand and formulate connections between observation and theory case by case. In work of this sort, predictions are often of the delimited kind we saw above in the case of interpretation, in which explanatory success in one instance or area gives grounds for holding that others can be understood in the same way. So both Darwin and Freud claimed support for their hypotheses mainly on the grounds that they served to provide good explanations for the observations they had accumulated and could be relied on to cope with more. And Popper seems to have formulated his criterion precisely to disallow such claims to support in the first place.[26]

So explanatory work like Freud's or Darwin's cannot be dismissed as Popper suggests. Rather, Popper's use of a short-cut criterion to discredit hypotheses in abstraction from their role in explanation is itself to be regarded with suspicion, at least from a rational or scientific point of view. For again, surely, a rational or scientific attitude must involve commitment to fully informed evaluation of hypotheses or explanations. Since this is precisely the process which methodological short-cuts are meant to truncate, there is *prima facie* difficulty in regarding them as respectable. What service could short-cut criteria be relied upon to perform, apart from the perpetuation of judgements made on inadequate grounds?

A further argument may help to bring this out. So far as we have reason to accept a theory if it provides good (best) explanation of the data, then a veridical short-cut would have to exclude the possibility that this is so. To do this, however, the short-cut criterion would somehow have to take account of all the features of theory and data in virtue of which the former could provide good explanation of the latter. (The concepts applied in the criterion should provide something like analyses of our notions of explanation, of what makes one explanation better than another and so on.)[27] But there seems no reason to suppose that any criterion in the short-cut tradition actually does this. So we may expect such criteria to fail in a particular way: they will discount good explanations wrongly, through failing to consider features of explanation which they leave out of account.

This evidently holds for Popper, whose short-cut above requires that all good explanations be assimilable to predictions of particular events. (Cf. his reference to 'a particular eclipse' above and such phrases as 'cannot *predict* . . . so cannot really *explain*', 'predictive or explanatory power', and so on.) This seems a basic mistake: prediction requires certain specific information bearing on the occurrence of events (time and place); but this is clearly only a small part of the information relevant to explanation and understanding generally. (We understand lightning better for knowing that it is an electrical discharge, but this does not enable us to predict the flashes.) And Popper seems to have left predictive information which is less focused on observable particulars out of account. For, as noted above, an interpretive theory, or our own understanding of language, enables us to predict a number of things, but *not* the occurence or observable specifics of the utterances we use it to understand.

We can see similar failures in the neo-Baconian criteria for assessing psychoanalysis recently suggested by Adolph Grunbaum.[28] Grunbaum urges that 'the establishment of a causal connection in psychoanalysis, no less than in "academic psychology" or medicine, has to rely on modes of inquiry that were refined from time-honored canons of causal inference pioneered by Francis Bacon and John Stuart Mill'. And since he argues that motives are causes, the canons are evidently to apply to claims about them.

Among the 'demands for the validation of causal claims' which these canons lay down are 'the sort of controls that are needed to attest *causal relevance*', which can be satisfied in 'experimental or epidemiological findings'. So, according to Grunbaum, since psychoanalysis is 'replete with a host of etiological and other causal hypotheses, Freud's theory is challenged by neo-Baconian inductivism to furnish a collation of positive instances from *both* experimental and control groups, if there are to be inductively *supportive* instances'.

These quotations suggest that only studies which conform to certain patterns – on which, e.g., a claim to causal connection between a putative cause X and effect Y is established quantitatively, by reference to correlations over X's and Y's in various groups – could provide data supporting psychoanalytic claims about motive. This again would provide a radical short-cut, for it would allow the would-be evaluator to dismiss virtually all observations which analysts have argued are best understood on Freudian hypotheses; and hence, again, to dismiss a theory as lacking support despite ignorance or incomprehension of the explanatory work done by it. (I stress that this is *not* a characterization of Grunbaum's own careful argument, which I have discussed in detail elsewhere,[29] but rather of a use to which the criterion he advocates can well be put.) As with the Popperian criterion, such assessment would not be well-informed in the sense required above, and in particular would fail to take account of the ways in which causal hypotheses can be supported by their role in explanation. And clearly such assessment would be liable to the methodological errors discussed towards the end of section I, and might provide analogues of the correlational fallacy about motives described in section II.

Short-cut approaches to serious theory can thus be both anti-rational and prone to fallacy. Also, as we can now see, this should be particularly so where they are applied to interpretive thinking, which embodies the kind of information, or is represented by the kind of theory, described above. The cogency of an interpretive hypothesis (and as opposed to alternatives) can become apparent only when it is applied together with a (generally large) family of others, and to a significant critical mass of material. There is, therefore, always the possibility that an uninformed evaluator will fail to use enough of a theory, or fail to use that theory on enough material, to appreciate its explanatory role in full. (Similarly an evaluator can fail to grasp the delimited nature of interpretive prediction, or seek prematurely to impose a superficial correlational grid.) Such mistakes will naturally be more likely, so far as evaluators regard the use of methodological shortcuts as legitimate means of relieving the frustration of incomplete understanding. So we should expect this tradition to be liable in practice to cut against interpretation, and so to obscure what such thinking might otherwise reveal.

Let us now consider the actual place of psychoanalysis in more detail. From what has been said it might seem that the apparent gulf between interpretation and science could be spanned by the devising of interpretive theory. So let us remind ourselves that interpretation is practical, and that practice shows great and apparently ineliminable gaps that remain. In natural practice we are able to *perceive* meaning in the bodily movements (including vocalization and facial expression) of others. Moreover, we can foresee no substitute for such perception; for it results from the processing of data of which we are frequently unaware and which we can envisage no other means of marshalling or treating. So just as sight provides a basic, ineliminable way of learning how things look, acquaintance with others provides a basic, ineliminable way of learning what they think and feel; and we should expect this to remain so, whatever theories we produce.

Psychoanalytic practice – with its emphasis on free association, full disclosure, and uninhibited expression of feeling – is structured to maximize the analyst's acquaintance with material relevant to understanding the analysand in this way, often over the course of years. Although observations made in this way are real and informative, they are hard to register in full, and impossible to gloss or abbreviate in a way that is fully adequate for communication. (Also, as we have seen, such observations are not connected with the generalizations of the theory which explains them by built-in descriptive links, but rather have to be subsumed anew in each case by interpretive inference. So the terms of the theory do not, in this case, serve so directly to summarize the data they cover.) In consequence, data and theory of this kind cannot be made to travel well; in particular, they are difficult to convey to those who have not made comparable observations.

This restriction is important, since scientific communication ordinarily serves to amplify the voice of reason, by systematically focusing on those inferences in which, as Freud put it, the data speak to one. Hence, in so far as a discipline cannot make such inferences and data readily and fully available, it cannot manifest its objectivity in the way normal for science. A discipline can be fully transparent in principle, but so constrained by the exigencies of actual communication as to seem relatively opaque in practice. In this situation intellectual success within the discipline cannot easily run parallel with fully informed acceptance outside; and those not actively engaged with the full range of data must exercise a kind of trust which is not needed elsewhere. As a result, outsiders, confronted with data which are relatively impoverished and for which they are often well able to frame alternative explanations, will not regard their deference as bound by reason. It thus seems that psychoanalysis can at best be like *science slowed down*, by the need for those considering data and inferences constantly to have recourse to further actual instances of these, as they emerge in practice. Hence, as we observe, criticism of psychoanalysis has often to be set aside as uninformed; but also, advocacy of it cannot carry the authority of fully communicated science.

This flows from the subject itself – from the nature, as it were, of our instruments of mutual understanding – and reflects no fault in the thinking of Freud or his successors. We cannot expect all we learn to be communicable in the same way; and it would be as irrational to confine thought to what can be communicated in a particular way as to use only what came wrapped in plastic. Still, it suggests that the findings of psychoanalysis require to be met not only with the sensitivity to meaning stressed above, but also with a critical alertness, and a willingness to make allowances, appropriate to their interpretive nature. Such complexity of attitude is not required for an approach to normal science.

NOTES

1 This paper continues a discussion of psychoanalysis and methodology
   developed from Wollheim's and my seminars and published in 'Epistemology and Depth Psychology: Critical Notes on *The Foundations of Psychoanalysis*' in Clark and Wright (eds), *Mind, Psychoanalysis, and Science*
   (Blackwell, Oxford, 1988), and 'The Interpretation of Dreams', in J. Neu
   (ed.), *The Cambridge Companion to Freud* (Cambridge University Press,
   Cambridge, 1992). There is also related material in 'Synthesis in the
   Imagination: Psychoanalysis, Infantile Experience, and the Concept of an
   Object', in J. Russell (ed.), *Philosophical Essays in Developmental Psycho-
   logy* (Blackwell, Oxford, 1987) and in my Introduction to *Philosophical
   Essays on Freud*, edited together with Wollheim (Cambridge University
   Press, Cambridge, 1982).

2 The debts in what follows to the work of Wittgenstein and Davidson are,
   I trust, obvious and clearly marked. Also, I was vaguely aware when I
   wrote this material that I had been influenced by Haugeland, *Artificial
   Intelligence, The Very Idea* (MIT Press, Cambridge, Mass., 1985) which I
   had read a few years before. On re-reading ch. 3 of that discussion,
   however, I see that the debt was more pervasive than I had realized.

3 For ease of exposition I am using quotation marks in a way Tarski
   discusses, criticizes, and replaces in the article cited in note 9 below.
   Also, speaking of knowledge of truth-conditions in this way involves a high degree of idealization, which obscures the role of pragma-
   tics, etc.

4 Philosophers disagree about what is encompassed in this relation. Davidson and Strawson, for example, take it that sentences correspond to no
   entities beyond the objects and events referred to by singular terms,
   whereas others assume that predicates may correspond to further entities
   (properties), and that sentences can correspond to facts, situations, or
   states of affairs, which are 'complexes' of objects and properties. Ruth
   Garret Millikan provides a carefully qualified and thoroughly naturalized
   version of such an account in *Language, Thought, and Other Biological
   Categories* (MIT Press, Cambridge, Mass., 1984); and her discussion
   constitutes a powerful argument that some such account is required. I
   take this for granted in much of what follows; but my argument would
   survive reconstrual into any satisfactory account. On these questions, see
   also note 16.

5 This distinction is not sharp, for theory can be more or less explicit and
   also more or less internalized.

6 See for example Wittgenstein, *Tractatus* (Routledge, London, 1961), 2.1–
   3.1413, 4.01–4.041; and *idem, Philosophical Grammar* (Blackwell, Oxford,
   1974,) pp. 69, 104, 187–90.

7 This seems to be part of the claim in *Tractatus*, 4.014.

[8] *Tractatus*, 4.002.

[9] For the original rigorous formulation of the idea of a theory of truth, see A. Tarski, 'The Concept of Truth in Formalized Languages', in *Logic, Semantics, Metamathematics* (Oxford University Press, Oxford, 1956). There is a particularly lucid and readable account of Tarski's work in W. V. Quine, *Philosophy of Logic* (Prentice-Hall, Englewood Cliffs, N. J., 1970). It was Davidson's idea to use such a theory of truth as the basis of a theory of meaning, and this requires subjecting a Tarskian theory to constraints which make it reasonable to regard its theorems as yielding correct interpretations. My remarks about Davidson's project are meant to be introductory and not complete. For the full account, see Davidson, *Inquiries into Truth and Interpretation* (Oxford University Press, Oxford, 1984), and 'The Structure and Content of Truth', *Journal of Philosophy* (January 1990). (For discussion of constraint, see Davidson's 'Reply to Foster' in *Inquiries*.) Also there is a recent discussion of this and a number of related issues in Bjørn Ramberg, *Donald Davidson's Philosophy of Language* (Blackwell, Oxford, 1989).

[10] Tarski's own approach dispenses with the *Tractatus* idea of taking predicates as referring to properties and relations, and also that of regarding sentences as correlated with facts, or 'complexes' of objects and properties. Rather, predicates are related to the objects of which they are true by clauses stating their conditions of satisfaction, and these in turn yield statements of the truth-conditions of sentences. Still, a theorist who thinks it important to acknowledge the role of properties, spatio-temporal 'complexes' of properties and objects, and so on can frame a theory in the Tractarian way. So the question is one upon which further considerations may be brought to bear. (But note that Millikan's *Language, Thought, and Other Biological Categories* provides many qualifications to such Tractarian ideas; see esp. ch. 6.)

[11] I owe this quotation (and my other references to Turing) to Justin Lieber, *Invitation to Cognitive Science* (Blackwell, Oxford, 1991), which appeared just as this essay went to press. Turing's statement is from 'Intelligent Machines', in Meltzer and Mitchie (eds), *Machine Intelligence* (Edinburgh, 1969). Davidson in effect compares his and Turing's views on interpretation in 'Turing's Test', in Said *et al. Modelling the Mind* (Oxford University Press, Oxford 1990).

[12] For a recent discussion of this idea, see P. Lipton, *Inference to the Best Explanation* (Routledge, London, 1991).

[13] Chomsky, 'Review of Skinner's *Verbal Behaviour*, *Language*, 35 (1926–58).

[14] On the view I am taking here, a true sentence, or again a complex description satisfied by something, will have a semantic correlate of its own, apart from the correlates of the words which compose it; whereas a false sentence or an empty description will not. Still, someone who un-

derstands the words which make up a false sentence or an empty description will know (by knowing the correlates of its components) the kind of correlate it would have if it were true or satisfied. This also counts as knowledge pertaining to semantic values.

[15] The term 'articulation' is Wittgenstein's. See for example his *Philosophical Remarks* (Blackwell, Oxford, 1975), p. 70: 'I call only an *articulated* process a thought . . . Salivation, no matter how precisely measured, is *not* what I call expectation.' Russell called such articulated motives 'propositional attitudes' in his Introduction to the *Tractatus*, and this phrase is still in use. But Wittgenstein's intention there was to relate them, as here, to the worldly states of affairs which would render the articulating sentences true, and not via any abstract intermediary.

[16] Although I am arguing for this view on mainly conceptual grounds, it would suggest that mastery of commonsense psychology should more or less come with mastery of language, the final stage being the use of motive-ascribing words themselves. This empirical consequence seems roughly borne out by recent research, which suggests that children of three years are already adept at belief–desire explanation. See H. M. Wellman, *The Child's Theory of Mind* (MIT Press, Cambridge, Mass., 1990).

[17] A number of explications of the 'should', 'certain way', etc. here are possible (optimal functioning, etc.). I think the best is via Millikan's notion of 'proper function'. The proper function of desires is to produce (cause) their conditions of satisfaction, and the accurate mapping by beliefs of the states of affairs they are about is required for this. See Millikan, *Language, Thought and Other Biological Categories*, esp. ch. 6.

[18] This causal sensitivity is of course a highly complex matter. The more straightforward cases would be provided by beliefs formed on the basis of perception or testimony.

[19] To indicate some aspects of this very roughly: we tend to find agents consistent in so far as strings are characteristically headed by S which are similar or cohering in content (meaning); consistency also requires that S should not change in domination relations from string to string, either *vis-à-vis* other S in a string or *vis-à-vis* alternative S which were candidates for places in a string. (Such changes thus form *prima facie* candidates for change of mind.) Also we take it that the values of the S-specified goals in series are discounted in accord with such likelihoods as the agent attaches to the truth of the conditionals linking them.

These and other constraints mean that in commonsense psychology ascriptions are in effect repeatedly and richly cross-checked, both against one another and against behaviour, in the course of developing an account of a person's motives, and hence form, in practice, a mutually interlocking and supporting system. The same holds for psychoanalytic ascriptions, for these mainly ascribe values to an agent's motives on the basis of wish-fulfilling representations (phantasies) caused by those motives, and so yield further and deeper specifications of objects of desire, which are checked both against those which arise in understanding action and also those which arise from the interpretation of other wish-fulfilments. This is discussed in more detail in 'The Interpretation of Dreams', cited in note 1 above, and also in the other papers cited there.

[20] The explanations we give of human action are thus, despite their complexity, ultimately comparable to those we might give of the behaviour of honey-bees, by relating their activities systematically to the parameters by which we interpret the 'language' of their dances.

[21] At a more general level, on this view, interpretation consists in linking structures in language, behaviour, and reality which are salient partly because non-coincidentally related. One sees something of this in the way that Augustine has the infant play the discernible orders in behaviour (including speech) and reality off against one another, so as to interpret the former in terms of the latter, in the passage with which *Philosophical Investigations* begins.

[22] I take perception as encompassed in this mode of description, since to perceive that S is generally to have reason to believe that S which is caused by the semantic value of 'S'.

[23] In particular, commonsense psychology can be taken systematically to describe and relate the kind of phase-spaces – the 'as the world presents itself' space and the 'as my body should be' space – which neurocomputational physiologists hope to use to understand the working of the brain. For description of such work, see P. Churchland, *Neurophilosophy* (MIT Press, Cambridge, Mass., 1986), ch. 10; the quoted phrases occur on p. 428.

[24] I discuss Freud's mode of inference with respect to wish-fulfilment in some detail in 'The Interpretation of Dreams', cited in note 1.

[25] These quotations are from pp. 135–8 of section 37, 'Darwinism as Metaphysics', of Popper's contribution to P. A. Schilpp (ed.), *The Philosophy of Sir Karl Popper* (Open Court, La Satle, Ill., 1974).

[26] See for example his dismissive remarks about explanatory power in the title essay of *Conjectures and Refutations* (Routledge, London, 1963).

[27] Popper should be credited with full awareness of this point, for much of his work can be interpreted as trying to prove that it was so.

[28] Grunbaum, *The Foundations of Psychoanalysis* (University of California Press, Berkeley and Los Angeles, 1984); quotations from pp. 47, 128, 185, 189, 280 respectively.

[29] For a fuller discussion of his argument, which I think flawed by reliance on this criterion, see 'Epistemology and Depth Psychology . . . ' cited in note 1. Footnote 21 of 'The Interpretation of Dreams', also cited there, contains material on Grunbaum, but he has informed me that it miscon-

strues his views on the application of Millian reasoning to motives. Therefore much of the argument of that note, and in particular that of the seventh paragraph, does not apply as intended.

[30] I should like to thank Mark Sainsbury and Gabriel Segal for comments which both suggested improvements and saved me from errors.

2

The Nature and Source of Emotion

SEBASTIAN GARDNER

As we said in the beginning that the act of envy had somewhat in it of witchcraft, so there is no other cure of envy but the cure of witchcraft.
Francis Bacon, 'Of envy'

(1) The aim of this paper is to outline and defend a suggestion about the nature and explanation of emotion. The suggestion is, in brief, that emotion is a kind of mental state which cannot be understood apart from – for the reason that it is derived from – the kind of mental state that psychoanalytic theory refers to as phantasy.[1]

The claim that emotion is derived from phantasy is evidently not a commonsensical idea, and it may sound initially more empirical than conceptual. The first part of the argument therefore consists in an attempt to identify, on philosophical grounds, conceptual pressures that might incline us towards accepting it. The second part of the argument seeks to show, with reference to the developmental theory of Melanie Klein, in what ways psychoanalytic theory supports and promises to fill out the philosophical account of emotion argued to be required.

I will begin with some observations about the concept of emotion in commonsense psychology, and define the precise philosophical problem set by emotion which will lead the enquiry.

(2) We have basic working notions of appropriateness for emotions. An instance of anger may be unwarranted if it lacks grounds or if its strength is out of proportion to the grounds that it has. In a similar vein, we can assess emotions in terms of consistency: if an

individual reacts emotionally in contrary ways to similar situations, then, in the absence of any further belief indicating a relevant difference, he or she may be described as irrational.[2]

Our customary modes of evaluating the rationality of emotions can thus be viewed as deploying a normative framework composed of rules of the form 'If circumstances C obtain, then emotion E is fitting.' These rules are publicly recognized and endorsed, so that an individual may be criticized if E obtains in the absence of C or if its intensity is disproportionate to C. In this way, it is natural to think that the measure of rationality for emotion is closely akin to that for belief: it must fit the facts. Emotion is irrational in so far as it fails to fit the facts.

(3) These commonsensical considerations suggest the philosophical picture of the emotions that I will call the 'rationalistic account'. In respecting the proximity and sensitivity of emotion to belief, the rationalistic account holds that emotions are *direct and sufficient outcomes of complexes of belief*: those beliefs which identify the emotion's kind, cause, and object and reflect its normative framework. These we can call the 'rationalizing beliefs' of emotion. They are explanatory of emotion in the way that reasons are, and share with them a justificatory role.

So in the case of pride, for example, there is, schematically, a belief that an object has value and a belief that one's relation to it is such that one may share in its value. The relevant rule for appropriateness says that pride is warranted in a person who stands in such-and-such a kind of relation to such-and-such a kind of object; it specifies the proper circumstances of pride and functions as a premise, allowing pride to follow as in a sequence of reasoning.

The next philosophical task for the rationalist is to produce a taxonomy of the rationalizing beliefs appropriate to each emotion-kind. Such an enquiry will analyse emotion-kinds in terms of the character (for example, moral or non-moral, self-regarding or other-regarding) of the concepts that enter into its rationalizing beliefs, and will engage with such questions as, for example, the differentiation of guilt from remorse, working on the assumption that such distinctions can be understood in terms of differences in rationalizing beliefs.[3]

The implication of the rationalistic account is that, when E fits C and all other things are equal, having an emotion is *a rational kind of state for a person to be in.*[4]

(4) The problem for the rationalistic account can be stated very simply: *What more is there, then, to emotion than belief?*

The force of this question is best illustrated from within the perspective of what P. F. Strawson calls our 'reactive attitudes'. When we exact an emotion from someone, as we often do, viewing the circumstances C as requiring an emotional response E (perhaps in order to restore a disturbed moral equilibrium), we demand that more should take place than just that the other party should form the relevant rationalizing belief (the belief that C obtains). For example, to reproach someone is to call for guilt to ensue in the person reproached: their merely acknowledging that they have done wrong will not suffice as a response. Some *further* inner event has to take place.

The following example will illustrate the point. Suppose that, questioned as to why I vetoed Jones's application to join my club, I reply that I was angry with Jones.[5] My interlocutor is then free to ask the reasons for my anger (to request a description of C that would warrant E). If I supply these (referring perhaps to Jones's obnoxious political views), then I will have succeeded in explaining my behaviour, even if at the same time I admit that I do not think my reasons for anger were relevant reasons for Jones not to be made a member of the club. If my interlocutor remains uncomprehending, rather than just critical, of my behaviour, then there shortly comes a point at which it would have to be said that my interlocutor is *failing to grasp* what it is to cite anger as an explanation of action. The interlocutor is failing to acknowledge, for example, that anger may give rise to actions which can be *understood* as malicious, but not rationally justified in this way.

The relation of anger to malice is paralleled by the relations of guilt to reparation, melancholy to loss of interest in life, envy to destructiveness, and so on.

This shows that there are specific relations between emotions and desires which are essential to, and constitutive of, each emotion-kind. Creatures whose 'guilt' did not standardly lead them to engage in reparative behaviour or which standardly disposed them to inflict further harm could not be recognized as suffering guilt. A further consequence is that emotions are understood by those who attribute them as *bridging terms* in explanation, with beliefs as input and transitions to desires and dispositions to action as output. These latter connections contribute to the individuation of emotion-kinds, and someone who is blind to them lacks a substantial piece of basic psychological knowledge.

That emotions are accorded such a role entails that they are credited with greater causal powers than their rationalizing beliefs alone possess. This creates a deficiency in the rationalistic account: where do these additional causal powers come from?

A natural attempt to remedy the deficiency is to add a component of *feeling*. So, to exact an emotion from someone is to demand that, in addition to having certain beliefs, he or she feel something.

The introduction of feeling, however, threatens merely to push the problem back a stage. We have as yet no understanding of what 'feeling' means in this context: not any old phenomenal event will do; the feeling must be a manifestation of the relevant kind of emotion.

The challenge facing the rationalist is then to find an adequate description of the feeling-component. It will have to be envisaged either as *qualitative* or as *having content*.

The first option just reproduces the original puzzle: why should some beliefs, on some occasions but not others, give rise to certain qualitative states? And even if this could be explained, purely qualitative states are not the right kind of thing to lead to complex desires and dispositions to action. If it could be explained why the 'quality' of guilt is intelligibly and intrinsically related to reparative behaviour (in the same way as the quality of painfulness is related to aversion behaviour), then the real explanation would inevitably lie *below* the level of quality. This can be confirmed by thinking once again about cases of reactive attitudes: the internal quality of feeling that reproach calls for is of course unpleasurable, but it is necessarily not just a painful sensation. What we want to see happen in the person we reproach is something more complex.

So, if emotions are to explain the relations of input to output which are constitutive of emotion-kinds, the second alternative – emotion as having content – seems clearly necessary. The rationalist, however, lacks any materials with which to unpack this content, other than, ineffectually, as 'the feeling of having the rationalizing belief' or 'the feeling that things are as the rationalizing belief represents them as being'. Such states continue to fail to make the requisite connection with emotion's output.

Nor can the deficiency in the rationalistic account plausibly be compensated for by building the causal powers of emotion into the proposition which is believed; for example, by saying that being proud of x results from believing that x is 'prideworthy'; for then what we have under the name of a belief is really an emotion, disguised in a neologized predicate.

It is hard to see what amplification of the rationalistic account could soak up the causal surplus without transforming it into an account of a wholly different sort.

(5) On the rationalistic account, it is only a contingent fact that emotions have any connection with irrational thought and action; the relation is purely external.[6]

This does not cohere with the fact that the mappings from belief to desire which are involved in, and help to individuate, emotion-kinds are not, in any ordinary sense, rational. Indeed, they are typically irrational, and are best conceptualized as instances of *expression*: we would naturally say that an action such as my blocking Jones's application is explained when it is seen as an expression of emotion, but not that my anger gave me reason to act as I did.

The irrationality of emotion is not just an effect of the typical background connections of emotion (the fact that in being emotional one becomes 'an easy prey to imagination'); nor is it just a concomitant of some wholly general effect of emotion (as if it simply resulted from some inherent power of emotion to interfere with reasoning). Irrationality is implicated in the very possession of the capacity for emotion, and the connections are systematic, irrationality of belief assuming particular forms tailored to each emotion-kind.[7]

The claim that the association of emotion and irrationality is characteristic rather than accidental is of course partly empirical, but not for that reason a mere matter of opinion. Surely, we share an intuition to the effect that, whatever normative frameworks emotions can be surrounded with, the weighty tradition of humanist reflection that regards the 'passions' as fundamentally disruptive has a solid basis. That emotions are *by nature* liable to 'go out of control' is a description readily intelligible in its application as it is not to other kinds of mental state. This gives an oblique indication as to the nature of emotion: it must be a kind of mental state that is *intrinsically at variance* with the truth-directed concerns of belief.[8]

(6) There are, in sum, three interlinked objections to the rationalistic account: it fails to account for the transitional role of emotion in taking us from beliefs to desires; consequently, it fails to individuate emotion-kinds correctly; and it fails to do justice to the frequently distinctively irrational character of the desires to which emotion effects a transition.

The discussion so far leaves us in the following situation. Emotion plays a relatively basic role in psychological explanation. Although its basicness is not as radical as that of purely phenomenal states such as pain, whose role is self-explanatory, there will doubtless come a point in the explanation of emotion at which unanalysable psychological connections will have to be granted.[9] So we *could*, logically, at the present point, postulate psychological laws which do no more than correlate certain beliefs with certain feelings, and these with certain desires. But, to the extent that such laws seem arbitrary and the implied picture of the mind unnecessarily shallow, it is reasonable to look for an account with more explanatory depth.

These considerations determine the general form of a correct explanation of emotion: it must attribute *more content to emotion than can be derived from its rationalizing beliefs alone.*

(7)   As a prelude to investigating psychoanalytic theory, I want to look briefly at Sartre's *Sketch for a Theory of the Emotions*. Sartre's theory aims ambitiously at providing a unified philosophical explanation of all emotion. It has many implausibilities, but gains in interest when seen as pointing in the direction of a psychoanalytic account.

In order to demonstrate the inadequacy of theories of the emotions, such as those of William James and Janet, which identify emotions with physiological events and patterns of behaviour respectively, Sartre makes the objection that neither James's nor Janet's theory makes reference to or is capable of accommodating: the fact that phenomenological changes invariably accompany the advent of an emotion. When an emotion sets in, the part of the world proximate to its object is experienced as acquiring a new organization. Things are assigned distinctive emotional qualities, and the subject's patterns of salience are systematically modified. Sartre takes these features to set the following problem, which the non-phenomenological theories are unable to solve: if, as it seems, emotion characterizes the world significantly, what *is* that significance, and what purpose is served by the onset of emotion?

The notion of emotion as a mode of response to *difficulty* provides the cornerstone of Sartre's theory. Emotion is regarded as a successor to a set of beliefs and desires: the world is presented in the form of a *problem*, to which emotion answers as something akin to a *solution*. Emotion is 'a transformation of the world',[10] and the solution that it offers is wrapped up in its phenomenology.

To ascertain the particular sense in which an emotional transformation eliminates difficulty, analysis is required. With regard to melancholy, for example, 'What it comes to in short, is that I make the world into an affectively neutral reality, a system which is, affectively, in complete equilibrium [. . .] In other words, lacking both the ability and the will to carry out the projects I formerly entertained, I behave in such a manner that the universe requires nothing more from me.'[11] When in melancholy the world is experienced without implications for action, it has been remoulded in a form that is congenial to desire.

It is hard to know how best to express the idea that emotional phenomenology has the character supposed by Sartre. We do not want to equate the phenomenology of emotion with belief, because of the difficulty surrounding the idea that there is a species of belief (somehow 'blurred' or diffused) which can manifest itself only in experiential and apparently non-propositional terms. Yet, if Sartre's theory is on the right track, it suggests that emotions are very much like thoughts: they determine patterns of significance in ways that can be propositionally spelled out. The content of emotional phenomenology may then be defined as a *power to determine phenomenological properties of the objects of thought and experience and, thereby, patterns of behaviour, in such a way as to be reconstructable as a more or less complex thought*. This does justice to the systematic character of the significance spread on to the world by emotion, without our actually having to identify an emotion's phenomenology with a state of belief.

Sartre's theory therefore answers the question, What more is there to emotion than belief?, by assigning a certain content to emotion's phenomenology, whose role it is to respond to desire.

Sartre's theory cannot, however, be accepted as it stands. It assimilates emotion, implausibly, to self-deception, and is incapable of saying why emotion comes about. What for Sartre fundamentally explains emotion is in fact nothing less than a *belief in magic*: 'We try [. . .] to live as though the relations between things and their potentialities were not governed by deterministic processes but by magic.'[12] The existence of this belief, that echoes so strongly what Freud calls the omnipotence belief, has no satisfactory explanation within the parameters of Sartre's own philosophy, or, indeed, in the terms of commonsense psychology.

What may nevertheless be retained from Sartre's account is his view that emotion answers to motivation. That Sartre's account fails because of its inability to explain such a thing as a 'belief in magic' suggests that psychoanalytic theory – as a theory which leans heavily on the attribution of pre-rational, partly non-intentional processes – should be explored next.

(8)   One familiar respect in which the theory of emotion intersects with the philosophy of psychoanalysis is the problem of attributing unconscious emotion, a topic which demands separate treatment, as part of a general theory of unconscious phenomenology. The other respect, which is not familiar, and which I argue for here, with

reference to Klein's theory of envy, is the interest of psychoanalytic explanation in accounting for the existence of emotion-kinds and, by extension, the existence of emotion *per se.*

Klein opens her discussion of envy with a characterization of it in terms of its rationalizing beliefs, together with an identification of the irrational dispositions which it characteristically involves: 'Envy is the angry feeling that another person possesses and enjoys something desirable – the envious impulse being to take it away or to spoil it.'[13] Klein then turns to 'the earliest exclusive relation with the mother', and contrasts the phantasy of the infant identified with greed, the phantasy of 'completely scooping out, sucking dry and devouring the breast', with the more complex phantasy, bound up with projection rather than introjection, which marks envy:

> Envy not only seeks to rob in this way, but also to put badness, primarily bad excrement and bad parts of the self, into the mother and first of all into her breast, in order to spoil and destroy her. In the deepest sense this means destroying her creativeness. This process [. . .] I have elsewhere defined as a destructive aspect of projective identification starting from the beginning of life.

Klein's account of this phantasy may be understood in the following way. Envy originates in the developmental stage which Klein calls the paranoid-schizoid position, when the infant's awareness of the world takes a largely episodic form, marked by a rough distinction of self and other, but not by stable representations of reidentifiable individuals. The first general law that governs the formation of phantasy directs it towards producing an ideal situation in which the distribution of badness and goodness on the 'map' of self and world is such that all goodness is coincident with the ego and all badness external to it. This 'a priori' of phantasy is the basic condition which determines when configurations of psychological states do and do not call for phantastic solutions and what formations of the inner world phantasy should and should not aim to produce.

When to this matrix we add the operation of the life (preservative) and death (destructive) instincts, which are assumed to be either innate or at least directly formed out of bodily experience, envy occurs for the first time. The recognition that some goodness is external means that the world fails to accord with the internal map of an ideal world, and this triggers the operation of the death instincts, in an attempt to 'solve' the problem of external goodness, which is 'destroyed'.

This process is reinforced by another factor, which is the infant's response to its condition of utter dependence. The near impotence, in real terms, of the infant's ego exposes it continually to the insecurity of being vulnerable to frustration by the mother: 'The infant's feelings seem to be that when the breast deprives him, it becomes bad because it keeps the milk, love, and care associated with the good breast all to itself. He hates and envies what he feels to be the mean and grudging breast.'[14] This further motivates the pseudo-solution of envy: by denying that there *is* any goodness external to the ego, the relation of dependence is 'eliminated'.

Going back to the characterization that Klein first gave of envy, there is, it can now be seen, a puzzle created by commonsense's conception of it. This lies in the fact that envy conflicts with the disposition – which binds all rational subjects – to preserve value. Hence the puzzle: *why should* a belief that something is good or desirable, as input, lead to destructive desires as output? This is a further instance of the general question, discussed earlier, as to the nature of the connection between the rationalizing beliefs of an emotion-kind and the states to which it leads. It may now be observed that Klein, by returning to the first historical instance of envy, has succeeded in offering an explanation of why there should be an irrational phenomenon such as envy; this has been done by attaching it in the first instance to infantile and phantastic representation rather than belief.

Overcoming envy is an important part of attaining what Klein calls the depressive position. This involves not the outright elimination of phantastic representation, as might at first be thought, but what should be called a *successful solution* in phantasy, which in this context consists in a secure internalization of a good object. A second emotion-kind, gratitude, marks that achievement:

A full gratification at the breast means that the infant feels he has received from his loved object a unique gift which he wants to keep. This is the basis of gratitude. Gratitude is closely linked with the trust in good figures. This includes first of all the ability to accept and assimilate the loved primal object (not only as a source of food) without envy interfering too much; for greedy internalization disturbs the relation to the object.[15]

The state of gratitude defines a regulative ideal for the emotional life.

(9)   I now want to consider Klein's account in philosophical terms. (For the present I will simply assume that Klein's account of envy

and gratitude can be generalized to other emotions; the extent to which this is correct will be reviewed later.) The central task is to make more precise the relation between the concepts of emotion and phantasy. This is a complex matter; the view I set out is adequate for the purposes of my argument, but no doubt open to improvement.

The relation between phantasy and emotion is obviously not one of identity: even when a phantasy is entertained in exact correspondence with an emotional state, we do not want to say that the emotion just *is* the phantasy. Rather, it is a looser relation of the kind which characteristically results from genetic explanation: the consciously recognized and self-ascribed state of emotion is a *historical descendant* of an earlier kind of state, which is one of phantasy. The philosophical claim is that a state of emotion is fully intelligible only in terms of such an ancestor-state.[16] So, even when an emotion occurs in adult life and is adjudged appropriate, appearing not to indicate any kind of unconscious activity, it remains true that it is at least a derivative of an infantile and phantastic prototype.[17]

This means that there are two levels at which psychoanalytic theory offers explanation of an instance of emotion: it tells us what *kind* of phantasy is its ancestor-state; and it tells us, or may tell us, what *particular* phantasy currently underpins it. The first level has application to all instances of emotion; the second is conditional upon an instance's being unconsciously motivated.

The phenomenology within which Sartre detected elements that looked very much like the products of wish-fulfilment can now be accounted for. Such content can be identified as vestigial representation of the object in phantastic terms, representation which has been worked over by psychological processes in such a way as to bring it into conformity with the conditions of acceptability constraining conscious representation. We can now say, referring back to the formula that an emotion is a thought-like power to determine phenomenological properties, that the thought from which this power is derived is an unconscious, phantastic thought, and that to each emotion-kind there corresponds a particular kind of phantastic thought.

Psychoanalytic theory is able to make room for another important element in our ordinary understanding of emotion, which was obscured by Sartre's view of emotion as a mental action. This is the way in which emotion, despite its intimate connections with desire, is typically experienced by us as *undergone,* rather than *enacted.* The reason why emotion appears passively is that it derives from phantasy, at which level events are neither given to consciousness nor voluntary. Emotion may consequently be likened to an opaque 'perception' of phantasy, this being experienced as, to some degree, external to the perceiver and, for that reason, passively. Representations in phantasy are thus ideal candidates for a sub-class of the items that Spinoza claimed to lie at the origin of emotion and which he calls 'inadequate ideas' and views as directly responsible for the mind's passive states.[18]

The discussion so far has left undecided the exact degree to which the descendant-state, both as a kind and in its individual instances, is in its actual operation either causally independent of or dependent on the present existence or operation of any of its ancestor-states. What should be said about this?

It is not strictly necessary for a philosophical account of emotion to commit itself to a definite view of this matter; and ultimately this is an empirical question. Nevertheless, the options can be sketched. (a) On a weak view, once emotion as a mental kind has evolved, it is, as a kind, autonomous, and its existence is independent of that of phantasy – in which case it would be theoretically possible for emotions to occur in a subject that had been, but was no longer, capable of entertaining phantasies. (b) On a strong view of the relation, by contrast, an actual occurrence in phantasy must contribute causally to each emotional response. Klein's view is that all adult mental life is structured in this way.[19] (c) A mid-way position would have it that, although it is not the case that a phantasy is unconsciously entertained every time an emotion is undergone, an overall, diffuse causal relation between emotion and phantasy must nevertheless persist, and that without an enduring connection to the inner world of phantasy, the capacity for emotional response would wither.

Klein's account of emotional development has some features that might seem to make it innovative of our ordinary understanding of emotions in the way characteristic of a scientific theory. For example, Klein makes a distinction between persecutory and depressive anxiety, the former being due to the threat presented by bad internal objects, the latter an effect of the proximity with aggressive wishes into which good internal objects are brought when the depressive position is worked towards. By making such distinctions, new criteria of identity for emotions, based on novel and amplified conceptions of their causal role, are introduced: emotions are individuated in terms that are not available at the level of ordinary thought, namely, concepts of phantasy.[20]

Although psychoanalytic individuation of emotion-kinds must of course remain *roughly* within the parameters set by our ordinary classification, the important possibility is created that two different instances of emotion may be regarded as exemplifying different emotion-kinds despite an identity of feeling and conscious belief across cases, since this remains compatible with a difference in content at the level of phantasy. The psychoanalytic individuation of emotion-kinds will, then, on some occasions be finer than that of ordinary psychology. In other respects it may be coarser, since some distinctions important at the level of ordinary psychology (for example, between regret and remorse) may not be important at a psychoanalytic level. This is not to say, of course, that psychoanalytic theory denies the reality of ordinary psychological distinctions.

These innovations are closely bound up with psychoanalytic theory's important connections with narrative understanding. As Klein's theory of envy makes clear, emotion-kinds occupy roles in typical sequences, and this permits a relational identification of an emotion in terms of what precedes and what follows it in the model narrative set out in psychoanalytic theory. This contrasts with our pre-psychoanalytic 'atomism' about emotions: we do not ordinarily, at least explicitly, suppose that emotions have a deep organization which interrelates them. To a large extent, we ordinarily take emotions on a one-off basis, seeking immediate environmental cues for each instance of emotion.[21] Psychoanalytic theory improves on this 'shallow' view.

Kleinian theory thus enables the formulation of psychological laws which run deeper than those available in ordinary psychology. This is also shown by psychoanalytic theory's reference to structural conditions of the mind which are not recognized in ordinary psychology – such as capacity or incapacity to tolerate levels of frustration – that function as variables determining the course and upshot of an instance of emotion.[22]

All these features recall other, more familiar cases in which scientific explanation improves on common sense. If we press this analogy, we will be tempted to see the relation of phantasy and emotion as one of real and nominal essence.

However, carrying over in full this model from the context of natural science in which it originates would suggest that what is picked out by 'envy' in commonsense psychology is only an *effect* of an underlying state picked out in psychoanalytic interpretation, and that emotions as identified in ordinary psychology are only epiphenomenal, real causal power attaching to their psychoanalytically identified causes.[23] Such a picture cannot be right if, as the earlier argument tried to make plain, ordinary psychology does not conceive emotion simply as an unstructured feeling or a kind of state defined purely in terms of rationalizing beliefs. If emotion is *already*, prior to psychoanalytic conception, conceived as having a motivational character of its own, then ordinary psychology is already *half-way* to the 'real essence' of emotion. The concepts employed in psychoanalytic understanding of emotion are then not sufficiently distant from those of ordinary psychology for the relation to be one of real to nominal essence; so when psychoanalytic theory tells us 'what envy is', it is not the 'is' of theoretical identification (understood according to scientific realism) that is employed.

(10)   To recapitulate: the relation of emotion and phantasy is not reductive; nor is it one of merely contingent causal explanation.[24] It is a constitutive causal relationship holding between distinct and equally real levels of mind, the precise nature of which depends upon how tight or how loose we think the relation between instances of emotion and events in phantasy should be made. Emotion is formed out of phantasy in such a way that it carries over, incorporating and bearing the imprint of, phantastic thoughts. These are distinct from the conscious thoughts formed out of the rationalizing beliefs of emotion, and they comprise emotion's *constitutive psychological substrate*. Although they continue not to present themselves to consciousness and therefore do not participate in conscious inference-making, they have the power to determine important aspects of experience, thought, and action in a thought-like way.

Because psychoanalytic explanation attempts to provide a depth analysis, it is exposed to the objection that it misidentifies emotion's essential properties.[25] For example, in identifying a necessary substrate of guilt in terms of Freud's theory of the superego, a psychoanalytic account is almost certain to fall short of explaining why it is that guilt necessarily involves conscious thoughts employing specifically moral concepts such as fairness. This may make it seem as if psychoanalytic theory overlooks what is essential to *guilt*.

But this is simply a consequence of the fact that psychoanalytic theory, despite its strong implications for moral psychology,[26] does not provide a conceptual analysis of ordinary moral thought. It follows that there is indeed a sense in which psychoanalytic theory does not provide the whole story of the emotions; but what it omits is only our *manner of conceptualizing* them; and this is something distinct from the matter of why those emotions exist in the first place. If psychoanalytic theory is right about the explanation of guilt, then guilt, as an emotion-kind, does not *come into existence* through the conscious entertaining of moral thoughts. Moral thoughts may instead be accommodated on the psychoanalytic picture by being regarded as essential to our manner of conceptualizing the emotion of guilt. This does not imply that particular manners of conceptualizing emotions are optional or arbitrary or in any way lacking in objective foundation; no doubt, there is a perfectly good explanation, consistent with psychoanalytic theory, of why guilt *has to be* conceptualized in moral terms.[27]

One way of tying up several ideas that have emerged is to say that psychoanalytic theory is principally concerned with identifying *the class of fundamental emotion-kinds that are necessary for any recognizably human psychological constitution.*[28] These may well be very few in number. The fundamental character of envy is a case in point. Envy is a fundamental emotion-kind because it is so intimately connected with the *very phenomenon* of desire; the situation of one who desires is *ex hypothesi* a situation in which goodness is as yet unpossessed and hence recognized as external to the ego. Consequently, it is a situation which stands on the threshold of envy. Envy is a fundamental emotion-kind because it is immanent in desire.

The many further and finer distinctions of emotion-kinds which are not important for psychoanalytic theory, based on the content of the conscious thoughts which are involved in awareness of emotion, are made on grounds that do not engage fundamental features of the human psychological constitution. The psychoanalytic view retains its cutting edge by denying that these mark distinctions of fundamental emotion-kinds and by asserting that emotion-kinds that are not fundamental depend for their existence on those that are.

Further in this vein, one might go on to identify among non-fundamental emotion-kinds a sub-set that are socially constructed. Shame, as experienced in an 'honour culture', is a prime example.[29] For such emotion-kinds, it is not just the case that social norms determine judgements of appropriateness, which is true of all emotions; they are distinguished by being derived from the basic stock of natural emotions only through the addition of certain specifically social conceptions, such that they *could not be felt* without a grasp and internalization of these.[30]

(11) If emotion does have a profoundly irrational aspect, ought we not to try to excise it from our lives?

This would make sense only if it were thought that people should aspire to live in a world stripped of emotional qualities and that they could prise themselves apart from their deepest sources of motivation. We would not know how to begin to act on either of these assumptions.

To bring emotion into close conceptual association with phantasy does not entail the undesirability of emotion. Rather, it suggests the desirability of one's emotional life being structured by, and characteristically manifesting attainment of, the depressive position. The undesirable emotional states that constitute human bondage are those structured by the paranoid-schizoid position. We eventually come to think of the kinds of emotion that we favour as *rational kinds* of mental state, but this involves a confusion. The demand for appropriate emotion can be adequately understood in naturalistic terms; the distinction between Kleinian positions or fundamental psychological structures conjoins with our practical interest in fostering emotion characteristic of the depressive position to provide for the concept of reasonable emotion. In this way, the claims of the rationalistic account, that emotion is a rational kind of state to be in and that the distinction between rational and irrational emotion corresponds to that between 'normal' and 'abnormal' emotion, can be rejected, without it following that there is never such a thing as an appropriate emotion.

All this is to say that, given that we live in, and cannot want not to live in, an emotionally characterized world, what should be aspired to is a condition in which emotion contributes maximally to psychological integration and malforms belief as little as possible.

(12) The disagreement between the psychoanalytic account of emotion and the rationalistic account can be summarized as follows. The rationalistic account holds that the logically primary matrix of emotion is belief, and that emotions which are not warranted by beliefs are deviant phenomena and logically secondary; thus emotion *per se* is a rational kind of state. The psychoanalytic account holds, by contrast, that the logically primary matrix of emotion in adult life is not belief but phantasy; thus emotions which fail to be warranted by beliefs are not deviant phenomena and not logically secondary, and emotion *per se* is not a rational kind of state.

The psychoanalytic account solves the problem which I argued the rationalistic account is unable to do justice to, and explains why it is that the rationalistic account should be mistakenly thought to be true. What the rationalistic account is right about is not the causal explanation of emotion, since this is not in fact a process of syllogistic practical reasoning; what it correctly models is the non-causal, normative relations that constitute the concept of appropriate emotion.

Sartre's characterization of emotion as magical thinking, in the perspective of psychoanalytic theory, comes to this: *Were* we to confront not the rationalizing beliefs of emotions but, instead, their phantasy-derived components or infantile prototypes, we would be able to rationalize the role played by those components or prototypes in our mental life only by adopting a 'belief in magic'. That we would never attempt a justification by appealing to magic marks the limit of the extent to which emotion – and persons in so far as they are subject to emotion – can be regarded as rational.

(13)   In conclusion, I want to make a general point about psychological explanation, suggested by the foregoing. What I wish to point to is not the familiar and much discussed epistemological link between the attribution of emotion and bodily behaviour. It is rather the idea that knowledge of emotion-kinds plays an important role in shaping the attribution of propositional attitudes. Certain patterns of belief and desire cohere with the particular narratives associated with given emotion-kinds. This could be put by saying that there are emotional *schemata*. We need not think of these schemata as *known*, in a strong sense, by the subject. The subject's possession and employment of a schema may be said to consist simply in a propensity for that person to interpret the mental life of others in line with the narrative of a given emotion-kind.[31]

This propensity may be envisaged as determining the attribution of propositional attitudes in a way that may fruitfully be compared with the way in which perception is said by psychologists to be guided by schemata. Perceptual schemata are structures which pre-exist individual perceptions and bear on them in a way that is wholly unlike the way in which a premiss functions in a sequence of reasoning; when a certain organizational threshold is reached, the data of sensory experience elicit a schema which, once cued, determines what the data are grasped as representing. So, pursuing the analogy with perception, the supposition with regard to emotion is that when a certain level of behavioural data and information about mental states is reached – at some point prior to that at which mental states configure in such a way as to make sense *fully* of a person – an emotional schema is elicited, on account of which other beliefs and desires of a more central and explanatory character are attributed. There is, of course, no pretending that this kind of process underpins psychological attribution in all contexts; the claim is just that it has a role to play whenever action involves anything over and above cool instrumentality.

With regard to the origin of emotional schemata, a natural view would be that it is the propensity of one's own mental life to fall in line with emotion-kinds that creates the propensity to so interpret others; the experience, particularly of course the infantile experience, of our own mental lives as exhibiting a certain order causes us to seek to discern the same order in the mental lives of others. But this 'empiricist' view is not obligatory; it may be that the schemata are innate in a strong sense,[32] and that it is in fact their presence in such a form that helps to explain why infantile experience follows the course it does. What in any case is important for the present argument is the role that such schemata can be seen as playing in our knowledge of one another. The hypothesis of such schemata promotes the idea that we stand epistemiologically, to some degree, albeit at a very rudimentary level, in relations of pre-ordained harmony with one another. This thought reduces some of the pressure for thinking that we have to strain to *make* sense of one another.

If there are emotional schemata, then an explanation can be given – in terms other than rationality – for why, with regard to some central cases at least, we attribute the particular beliefs and desires that we do; this is because certain sets and organizations of beliefs and desires accord with, whereas others depart from, the schemata that we are capable of recognizing in a relatively direct fashion in behaviour. There would then be a stratum, of a fully psychological character, intervening between bare behaviour and complex attributions of belief and desire, which would give us reason (of a realist kind, independent of considerations of interpretive methodology) for taking the particular beliefs and desires that we attribute to be correctly in place.[33]

It is worth indicating how this idea may be generalized. If psychoanalytic theory is, even in rough outline, correct, then out of all the possible sets of propositional attitudes, only *some* form recognizable patterns. These are the sets which exhibit the right kind of unconscious background. In this way psychological attribution does not begin or end in a limbo; it is structured from the start by implicit recognition of a universal unconscious base, and only sets of propositional attitudes which manifest our actual unconscious constitutions will be recognizable to, and attributed by, us.

NOTES

[1]　I will be concerned with the Freudian-Kleinian form of psychoanalytic theory presented and defended by Richard Wollheim in *The Thread of Life* (1984). I would like to thank Jim Warren, Jim Hopkins, and Barry Smith for extremely valuable comments and criticism.

[2]   See Ronald de Sousa, 'Self-Deceptive Emotions', in Amélie Oksenberg Rorty (ed.), *Explaining Emotions* (University of California Press, Berkeley, 1980), for an elaboration of a case of this kind.

[3]   See Donald Davidson, 'Hume's Cognitive Theory of Pride', in *Essays on Actions and Events* (Clarendon Press, Oxford, 1980); and Gabriele Taylor, *Pride, Shame and Guilt: Emotions of Self-Assessment* (Oxford University Press, Oxford, 1985), ch. 1. For ease of exposition, my presentation of the rationalistic account fuses Davidson's and Taylor's positions. It may seem that Davidson cannot be an exponent of the rationalistic account, since he holds that 'attitudes' (of approval, prizing, etc.) also figure in the antecedents of emotion (pp. 281–6). These, however, he identifies with *judgements* (pp. 283 and 287), and such evaluative beliefs are not excluded from my statement of the materials of the rationalistic account. It is in any case certain that Davidson holds to the essential rationality of pride (p. 285).

[4]   This claim is developed by Ronald de Sousa in *The Rationality of Emotion* (MIT Press, Cambridge, Mass., 1987); and by Nelson Goodman in 'Art and Inquiry', in *Problems and Projects* (Bobbs-Merrill, New York, 1972), pp. 107–10.

[5]   I owe this example to Jim Hopkins.

[6]   This view is to be found in Bernard Williams, 'Morality and the Emotions', in *Problems of the Self: Philosophical Papers 1956–1972* (Cambridge University Press, Cambridge, 1973), p. 224.

[7]   Franz Alexander, 'The Logic of Emotions and its Dynamic Background', *International Journal of Psychoanalysis*, 16 (1935), pp. 399–413, puts the point that emotions make irrational connections by representing emotions as invalid syllogisms.

[8]   Cf. Brian O'Shaughnessy, *The Will: A Dual Aspect Theory* (2 vols, Cambridge University Press, Cambridge, 1980), vol. 1, p. 21, who doubts whether the having of an emotion can ever itself be described as rational or not.

[9]   See for example Wollheim's discussion of a fundamental law governing aggression in *The Thread of Life*, pp. 206–10.

[10] Sartre, *Sketch for a Theory of the Emotions*, tr. Philip Mairet (Methuen, London, 1971), p. 63.

[11] Ibid., p. 69.

[12] Ibid., p. 63.

[13] Klein, 'Envy and Gratitude' (1957), in *Envy and Gratitude and Other Works 1946–1963, The Writings of Melanie Klein*, vol. 3, ed. Roger E. Money-Kyrle (Hogarth, London, 1975), p. 181.

[14] Ibid., p. 183.

[15] Klein, 'A Study of Envy and Gratitude' (1956), in *The Selected Melanie Klein*, ed. Juliet Mitchell (Penguin, Harmondsworth, 1986), p. 215.

[16] On the role and conditions of legitimacy of genetic explanation in psychoanalytic theory, see Jerome Neu, 'Genetic Explanation in *Totem and Taboo*', in *Freud: A Collection of Critical Essays*, ed. Richard Wollheim

(Anchor/Doubleday, New York, 1974); reprinted as *Philosophers on Freud: New Evaluations* (Aronson, New York, 1977).

[17] Note Wittgenstein's remarks on envy, which seem (rather surprisingly) congruent with Klein's account: 'Envy is a superficial thing – i.e. the colour characteristic of envy does not go down deep – further down passion has a different colour. (*That*, of course, does not make envy any the less real.)' (*Culture and Value*, ed. G. H. von Wright and Heikki Nyman (Blackwell, Oxford, 1980), p. 35e).

[18] Spinoza, *Ethics*, pt III, proposition 3.

[19] Klein, 'Our Adult World and its Roots in Infancy' (1959), in *Envy and Gratitude*.

[20] Donald Meltzer distinguishes as many as six different types of anxiety in *The Psycho-Analytical Process* (Clunie Press, Perthshire, 1967). It is of course a moot point in general where a putative distinction among emotion-kinds should be recast as a distinction among causes for one kind. This difficulty, which tends to make each attempt at a taxonomy of the emotions appear unsatisfyingly arbitrary, stems from the greater range of options that we have for individuating emotions than we do, say, for beliefs.

[21] The idea that there is a buried order to emotional sequences has a further consequence: that order can also be exhibited *across* individuals. Herein lies the warrant for the extension of Kleinian theory to group psychology. See Wilfred R. Bion, *Experiences in Groups and Other Papers* (Tavistock/Routledge, London, 1989).

[22] See for example Klein, 'Some Theoretical Conclusions Regarding the Emotional Life of the Infant' (1952), in *Envy and Gratitude*, pp. 75–6, on what determines the ability to tolerate frustration. Meltzer summarizes the determinants and determining role of the ability to tolerate mental pain in *Sexual States of Mind* (Clunie Press, Strath Tay, 1973), p. 94.

[23] This, it may be noted, is what we would get by conjoining psychoanalytic explanation of emotion with the rationalistic account, or with the view that emotion-terms in commonsense psychology are names of feelings.

[24] Defending the view that there is only a contingent relation between emotion and psychoanalytic explanation, see William Lyons, *Emotion* (Cambridge University Press, Cambridge, 1980), ch. 1.

[25] See David Jones, 'Freud's Theory of Moral Conscience', *Philosophy*, 41 (1966), pp. 34–57. A similar style of objection is employed against psychoanalytic talk of unconscious desire by Roger Scruton in *Sexual Desire: A Philosophical Investigation* (Weidenfeld and Nicolson, London, 1986), p. 203.

[26] See Wollheim, *The Thread of Life*, ch. 7, and *idem*, 'The Good Self and the Bad Self: The Moral Psychology of British Idealism and the English School of Psychoanalysis', in *Rationalism, Empiricism and Idealism: British Academy Lectures on the History of Philosophy*, ed. Anthony Kenny (Clarendon, Oxford, 1986).

27   Nor, of course, does the psychoanalytic account imply that a person's consciously entertaining moral thoughts is causally ineffective in making that person feel guilty.

28   Anthony Kenny, in *Action, Emotion and Will* (Routledge and Kegan Paul, London and Henley, 1972), notes the possibility of asking after the cause of emotions *simpliciter*: 'This would be to ask the question, "why does he have fears?" or "why does he have dislikes?", to which the only answer seems to be: because he is a human being' (p. 74). Psychoanalytic theory can be seen as amplifying Kenny's response.

29   See Taylor, *Pride, Shame and Guilt*, pp. 54–7.

30   Three further limitations on the explanatory scope of the psychoanalytic account presented here should be spelled out. (a) Many of the states that we would perhaps pre-philosophically class as emotions, which involve only a thought with a 'hedonic tone' and have no typical motivational character, are excluded (see Malcolm Budd, *Music and the Emotions: The Philosophical Theories* (Routledge and Kegan Paul, London, 1985), ch. 1). We might call these 'feelings' as opposed to 'emotions'. Gilbert Ryle, *The Concept of Mind* (Penguin, Harmondsworth, 1976), ch. 4, calls them 'agitations', contrasting them with 'inclinations'. (b) The psychoanalytic account presented here does not have direct application to the moral sentiments, conceived as apprehensions of moral qualities of actions and situations; this would require supplementation in terms of a theory of such qualities as achievements of projection (see Wollheim, *Painting as an Art* (1987), pp. 80–4, on expressive perception, and *idem, The Thread of Life*, pp. 213–18). (c) The phenomenon of mood is not catered for here; it, too, seems open to psychoanalytic elucidation, but to establish this would again require further elaboration.

31   These ideas are suggested by Wollheim's discussion of psychological interpretation in *The Thread of Life*, pp. 170–3 and 185–7.

32   See Wollheim, 'The Mind and the Mind's Image of Itself', in *On Art and the Mind*; and *idem*, 'Memory, Experiential Memory, and Personal Identity', in *Perception and Identity*, ed. G. F. Macdonald (Cornell University Press, Ithaca, 1979), p. 232; and Jerry Fodor, *Psychosemantics: The Problem of Meaning in the Philosophy of Mind* (MIT, Cambridge, Mass., 1987), Epilogue.

33   Thus the argument impinges on Davidson's account of minds as entities constituted by interpretive practice governed by the Principle of Charity.

3

Acting on Phantasy and
Acting on Desire

HANNA SEGAL

I consider it an honour to contribute to a *Festschrift* for Richard Wollheim. Wollheim is unique among philosophers in his profound knowledge and understanding of psychoanalysis, which includes the more recent developments. He uses such psychoanalytical concepts as he finds useful to illuminate the broad borderline area of equal interest to psychoanalysts and philosophers, such as theories of knowledge, ethics, and aesthetics.

In *The Thread of Life* (1984) he addresses himself to the subject of the philosophy of life itself, which was the great preoccupation of philosophy in the past, and which I think is sadly neglected by modern philosophy. This, of course, is a layman's complaint.

I have some apprehension about my contribution to this volume, since my knowledge of philosophy is only amateurish and superficial. What I can contribute springs from my own psychoanalytic experience, which enables me to address myself to some of the psychoanalytical concepts which underlie much of Wollheim's work. The concept of unconscious phantasy is central in psychoanalysis, and Wollheim uses this concept in his work on the philosophy of mind. In *The Thread of Life*, he shows how unconscious phantasy enshrining archaic object relationships can dominate our minds and become 'the tyranny of the past' and an obstacle to freedom of choice and to leading a meaningful life.

I want to address myself to the distinction that Wollheim establishes between 'acting on phantasy' and 'acting on desire'. Phantasy can be contrasted with action. Wollheim says that phantasy has a weak relation with action. For, 'unlike desire on the one hand and imagination on the other hand, phantasy is not characteristically motivational: it does not conjoin with belief so that an intention is formed' (p. 143).

However, phantasy often propels to action. Phantasies are acted out. And acting out a phantasy is different from acting on desire. Wollheim shows the practical usefulness of the distinction: for instance, in his paper 'Crime, Punishment and Pale Criminality' (1988). One could say that in this distinction he applies the distinction that Freud made in 'Formulations on the Two Principles of Mental Functioning' between the pleasure–pain principle and the reality principle:

> In the psychology which is founded on psycho-analysis we have become accustomed to taking as our starting-point the unconscious mental processes, with the peculiarities of which we have become acquainted through analysis. We consider these to be the older, primary processes, the residues of a phase of development in which they were the only kind of mental process. The governing purpose obeyed by these primary processes is easy to recognize; it is described as the pleasure – unpleasure principle, or more shortly the pleasure principle. These processes strive towards gaining pleasure; psychical activity draws back from any event which might arouse unpleasure. (Here we have repression.) Our dreams at night and our waking tendency to tear ourselves away from distressing impressions are remnants of the dominance of this principle and proofs of its power. It was only the non-occurrence of the expected satisfaction, the disappointment experienced, that led to the abandonment of this attempt at satisfaction by means of hallucination. Instead of it, the psychical apparatus had to decide to form a conception of the real circumstances in the external world and to endeavour to make a real alteration in them. A new principle of mental functioning was thus introduced; what was presented in the mind was no longer what was agreeable but what was real, even if it happened to be disagreeable. This setting-up of the *reality principle* proved to be a momentous step. (xii. 218–19)

There is a common misconception that acting on the pleasure–pain principle is acting on uninhibited desire. For instance, there is a popular view that sexual crimes are due to lack of inhibition and control of sexual desires. This is very far from being an ascertainable psychological fact.

In Freud's description, the omnipotent mind of the infant, under the sway of the pleasure–pain principle, hallucinates the breast when hungry. The desire disappears, and it is replaced by a hallucination. Thus the need to act to satisfy a desire disappears.

However, in 'Formulations on the Two Principles of Mental Functioning' Freud does not in fact use the concept of phantasy crucial to

Wollheim's distinction. Freud sees phantasy as a late phenomenon after the reality principle has been established:

> With the introduction of the reality principle one species of thought-activity was split off; it was kept free from reality testing and remained subordinated to the pleasure principle alone. This activity is *phantasying*, which begins already in children's play, and later, continued as *day-dreaming*, abandons dependence on real objects. (xii. 222)

What, then, is the hallucinatory wish-fulfilment? Since Freud's time, specifically since Klein and Susan Isaacs,[1] the concept of unconscious phantasy has been extended, and I think Wollheim uses the concept of phantasy in this new way. Klein, and following her, others, went into far more clinical detail about those early processes. In the earliest stages of development, which Klein called the paranoid-schizoid position, the infant is dominated by omnipotence. Whereas Freud thought that phantasy is a late product and did not connect the early hallucinatory wish-fulfilment with phantasy, Klein sees it as a manifestation of phantasy. Every impulse and desire inherently carries with it a phantasy of its own fulfilment.

Also, in 1911, Freud did not take into consideration basic destructive and self-destructive impulses, only libidinal ones. It was only in 1920 that he gave Thanatos a role equal to that of Eros. Klein, whose work started in the 1920s, considered that the omnipotent phantasy is called up by destructive desires as well as by libidinal ones and that the omnipotently produced hallucinatory world consists not only of libidinal objects but also of objects destroyed and destructive. Hence the very young infant swings from states of bliss to states of extreme distress. She also described as one of the most primitive mechanisms that of projective identification. Under the sway of the pleasure–pain principle the infant wants to get rid from inside him or herself of anything that causes distress, such as hunger, anxiety, and anger; and achieves this aim by projecting parts of himself outside and attributing them to an object. Drives are projected and externalized. The love and desire are represented by an ideal breast, which the infant wants to introject and possess. Bad feelings and pain-giving parts of the self are equally projected onto the outside, giving rise to damaged, bad, and persecuting objects. The consequence of the operation of projective identification is a constant blurring of perceptions of reality, both external and internal. The phantasied object obliterates the perceived object, distorting external reality; but the internal reality of one's own needs and desires is equally blurred, since it has become vested in an object. The knowledge of one's desires disappears.

Wollheim comments that phantasy conceals desire. Projective identification, I think, is the mechanism by which it is achieved.

Acting on phantasy is characterized by certain conjoint phenomena:

a misperception of external reality

a misperception of internal reality – for instance, the reality of one's desire

a compulsion to act rather than a choice of action.

I shall return later to the point of the compulsion to act. Because of the importance of the misperception, I shall call what Wollheim calls 'acting on phantasy' 'acting on delusion'. I shall illustrate this by gross examples from known criminal cases, to try to show some of the mental mechanisms at work. I take these particular examples because they display so clearly the psychopathology involved, also to follow Wollheim in applying his ideas to the problem of criminal responsibility.

Many years ago, two small children, a boy and a girl, were found murdered in a wood; and the murderer was never found. Years later a man who was in prison on another charge was undergoing intensive psychoanalytic psychotherapy. He admitted to his psychotherapist that he had killed those children. He had taken them to the wood to play with them, because he thought they were lonely. He felt lonely too. He thought he would make them happy playing, and he would be less lonely himself. However, as he kept them for a long time, they were not amused any more, and as it was getting dark, the little boy began to get frightened and started crying that he wanted to go home. The man took a stone and crushed his skull with it. He did not know why, and because the little girl was a witness, he had to kill her too. That man, as a very small child, had been evacuated during the war. In his foster home he was ill-treated, terrified, and lonely. He was so miserable that at the age of three he consciously and deliberately tried to kill himself by drinking cleaning fluid and eating shoe-polish.

In his analysis it became quickly apparent that the little boy was perceived by the man as though he was himself as a small child, and when he became frightened, lonely, and started to cry, it was as intolerable to the man as was the memory of himself in the same state of mind as the little boy. His suicidal impulse at the age of three became the compulsive murder of the little boy seen as the child himself who had to be killed. A psychoanalytical view would be that the man projected into the child a part of himself that was unbearably painful.

In a more recent murder of this kind, Nielsen, a schizoid, depressed, inadequate homosexual was killing young men just like himself. This was so clear that many commentators with no deep psychoanalytic knowledge noticed that he was killing an image of himself again and again. *Again and again.* The repetition compulsion is unavoidable, because if the aim of the murderer's action is to destroy bad internal objects, or parts of himself, then the idea that those internal objects or impulses will disappear after being placed outside is a delusion.

Sometimes it is an unbearable phantasy of an internal object that has to be got rid of. Some murderers murder because they think that they have murdered. The wish to murder becomes a phantasy of having murdered and containing a corpse. This they get rid of by externalizing the corpse, by producing one outside.

Such mechanisms can be shown sometimes to underlie neurotic behaviour in borderline cases. For instance, I had a borderline obsessional patient who used to deal with hunger by defecating. The underlying unconscious phantasy was that the perception of hunger was a bad thing inside him that he could get rid of by defecating. He had many conscious rationalizations of this behaviour. He dealt similarly with mental pain. When his mother, to whom he was extremely attached, died, he experienced no mourning, but had numerous dreams about her. He would write them down in a notebook and forget all about them. This was a mental equivalent of defecation. He would evacuate his pain into the notebook, and in that way get rid of it. The pain could be his own sensation – hunger, the psychic pain of mourning an object, or an object – the dead mother felt as dead faeces inside him that he could defecate into the notebook.

The mental mechanisms involved here are not very different from the ones I assume to underlie the behaviour of the child-murderer and of Nielsen.

Murders of prostitutes are common. A murderer of prostitutes, A, claimed that he was driven to kill them because the voice of God commanded it. One could say that he saw in the prostitutes his sexual mother, but failed to recognize their reality as separate, different people, and was deluded in his unconscious belief that they were his sexual mother. Such hatred of a sexual mother is also linked with a delusional picture of the mother herself. All her other characteristics are split off, and she is seen as nothing but a vehicle of obscene sexuality. We know from our clinical practice that in such a situation the child's own sexuality is also projected into the mother. Therefore killing a prostitute would be killing both his sexual mother and his own projected sexuality.

Freud has established that in cases of pathological jealousy, for instance, the patient projects into the woman his own homosexual wishes for intercourse with a man. It is his own hateful sexuality that the murderer attacks in his prostitute victim. And yet killing is also a guilty act, so that projection was not enough for A to justify the killing. His wish to kill was projected on to a god who ordered him to do so. I have no psychoanalytical knowledge of A, but his actions are partly understandable to me through experience with some of my patients. I still remember a rather hairy moment in my practice as a young psychoanalyst when a schizophrenic patient told me, rather sadly, that he did not like killing, but that there was nothing he could do now; all his voices (he used to have eight of them) now combined into one voice to tell him that he must kill me because I was all bad. I knew what the stimulus was in this situation. He saw a man's hat in the hall. The patient was quite unaware either of his sexual desires or of his sexual jealousy in relation to me. The perception of the real situation and of his own desire to kill were replaced by a hallucinatory voice telling him that he must kill me because I was bad.

These, as I said, are very gross examples, but this kind of delusion underlies irrational behaviour of a neurotic type as well. For instance, often compulsions of cleaning, washing, and so on are based on an underlying delusion that the patient has infected the world with his poisonous faeces and that he has to clean the infection away. And the action has to be repeated, endlessly, since the unrecognized impulse to infect remains unacknowledged and therefore active. There are, of course, differences between criminal acts and symptoms in neurosis, two major ones being that in the neurotic and the borderline patient the delusion does not invade the whole personality but is encapsulated in a symptom. Also, the ambivalence is more in evidence. This is clear, for instance, in the Rat Man's manipulations of the stone in the path of his beloved, which Wollheim analyses in detail in *The Thread of Life*.

Often there is also more rationalization of acting out. Criminals and psychotics often have rationalizations for their behaviour too, but neurotics are usually better at it. Rationalization of essentially primitive psychotic processes is easily observed in group thinking – for instance, in the political process. In genocide and racism, in the name of racial purity we wipe out the dirty and dangerous opponent – not very different from the compulsion to kill prostitutes. We also project our responsibility on to higher authorities, like the schizophrenic patient who wished to kill me or A projecting the responsibility into God's voice. But in the group process these delusions are rationalized in a way which makes them appear realistic and sensible. Underlying irrational action are delusions. In the psychotic or psychopathic criminal, they dominate the personality; in the neurotic, they are split off and encapsulated in symptoms. In the group they lead sometimes to guiltless, mad, destructive courses of action.

But if the pleasure–pain principle creates a hallucinatory world which omnipotently satisfies desires, why act as well? Wollheim states that phantasy has a weak link with action. Nevertheless, there is sometimes a strong urge to act out a phantasy, and paradoxically the need to act out is more compulsive than the need to act on the basis of desire. Wollheim raises the question why this should be so. One of the answers he gives is that phantasy aims at perpetuating itself, and acting out perpetuates it.

There are other factors as well. After all, we all want our day-dreams to be realized; but we might abandon them when they turn out to be unrealizable, or when we recognize that if realized they would lead to disaster. Reality always intrudes and an omnipotent phantasy is interfered with, and in the individual who clings to his omnipotence there is a particular compulsion to act on the phantasy in order to maintain the omnipotent world and destroy any reality which threatens it.

There is also a further element. If one's desires are transformed into hallucinated objects, one's thoughts and phantasies are then felt as internal objects that have got to be got rid of if they bring discomfort. And the way to get rid of them is by acting them out. If the wish to murder one's parent becomes a phantasy of a concrete corpse inside oneself, that corpse, the murderer feels, can be got rid of by producing a corpse outside.

Wollheim says that phantasy exerts a lure. It lures one into action. I think that an important element in this lure is projective identification. A person who gets rid of his desires by projecting them into an external or internal object feels enthralled by this object. His motivation is felt not to be in his own desires, but in objects – either external or hallucinated internal objects – whose dictates he has to obey. What in the more normal person is a desire, in the person living on projective identification is the lure of the object.

This kind of functioning leads also to an inbuilt repetition compulsion, because it is a delusion that producing a corpse outside will enable one to rid one's mind of an unwanted part of oneself or a persecuting internal object. Impulses and associated phantasies cannot in fact be got rid of in that way. So acting out brings only temporary relief, and the action has to be repeated again and again.

There is a lure in the objects into which a part of the self is projected; there is a link that cannot be broken or denied if the object is felt to be possessed by a part of oneself and becomes it, because reciprocally the self is then tied and, as it were, pulled by the object in which a part of it is invested.

So far, stimulated by Wollheim's paper on 'Pale Criminality', I have given examples mostly of the kind of projection that may lead to a murderous acting out, having to do with the predominant projection of destructiveness. But a similarly pathological lure can be felt when there is an omnipotent and almost total projection of the libidinal aspect of the self and an idealized object. This kind of lure can be easily observed, for instance, in the syndrome called de Clerambault's. It is a nearly mono-symptomatic form of psychosis most often affecting adolescent girls. The girl forms a delusional idea that a man is in love with her and destroys herself pursuing him against all evidence of his lack of interest. She attempts to destroy his life, and effectively destroys her own. This condition is tragically and beautifully documented in the diaries of Adèle H., the daughter of Victor Hugo (books and a film have been based on the diaries). The other historical case frequently referred to in the literature is male, a Guards officer with a delusion about Queen Victoria. Both ended their lives in mental hospitals as deteriorated schizophrenics.

The psychoanalytic understanding is that such a person has projected into his or her object an early idealized internal object and also all their own libidinal self, so that they see in the object all the good in the world and without it feel empty and useless. In milder forms we can observe this condition in what is known as the erotic transference in psychoanalysis. The patient attributes to the analyst his or her own libidinal desires and is convinced that he or she is in love with the patient, and also projects into the analyst all his or her own faculties, so that he or she feels enslaved by the analyst. Actually, in psychoanalysis this kind of transference seems to affect men and women alike. On the face of it, a projection of good things into the object seems less destructive than projection of destructiveness; but in fact it is equally destructive in that it destroys all perception of reality of the external object and all faculties in the patient himself. Many deteriorate into a psychosis. It is also destructive to the objects of their affection, since such people often keep pursuing their beloved, persecuting and disrupting their lives. In the group situation, similar mechanisms are at play in followers of a charismatic leader, with similarly destructive consequences.

Thus the operation of omnipotent projective identification can explain the paradox that acting on phantasy is acting on the pleasure–pain principle, yet is not acting on desire. The complexities of pathological development in the paranoid-schizoid position lead to dealing with desire by projective identification, and therefore to a method of getting rid of desires. This also throws light on the paradox that a hallucinatory omnipotent phantasy can both have a weak link with action and yet, on the contrary, also compel action.

This is dramatically illustrated, and can be observed in catatonics, who may spend months in total immobility, with no action, yet suddenly be compelled to violent action completely incomprehensible to the observer.

But what is 'acting on desire'? And what is the 'reality principle'? Freud says that the reality principle is the pleasure–pain principle tested in reality. How can it be tested? A principle cannot be tested. A hypothesis can be tested. I think that it is implicit in desire that it gives rise to a phantasy of its fulfilment. It is the phantasy that is like a hypothesis which is being tested.[2] A phantasy is like a wishful hypothesis which is constantly matched with reality. If the phantasy is omnipotent, desire disappears, and phantasy becomes a delusion. But in the more normal infant there is a capacity to perceive a reality different from the phantasy. The phantasy is tested. In a footnote to the 'Two Principles of Mental Functioning' Freud says:

> It will be rightly objected that an organization that was a slave to the pleasure principle and ignored the reality of the external world could not maintain itself alive for the shortest time, so that it could never come into existence at all. The employment of a fiction like this is however justified when one considers that the infant, provided one includes with it the care it receives from its mother does *almost* realize a psychical system of this kind. (xii. 220; my emphasis)

I emphasize 'almost' because an infant that obeyed only the pleasure–pain principle could not survive, whatever the care of the mother. Were he satisfied with the hallucination, he would refuse the food and care of the mother, since the latter never comes up to the ideal expectation. The infant has to tolerate such discrepancies, and its capacities to recognize an object that is not identical with its phantasy and to relate to it is the basis of his maturation. From the beginning of life the infant is faced with the choice of testing his phantasy against reality and letting reality modulate it or attacking reality; that is, primarily attacking and destroying his own capacity for perception. The extent to which the infant can tolerate reality depends both on his inner capacities to tolerate frustration and on the degree of frustration or satisfaction provided by the environment.

Forming a picture of the real object, differentiating it from the hallucinated object, and noting its real characteristics, good and bad, can lead to a search for the action to obtain the most satisfaction from the object. A rational action must be based on recognition of realities.

Freud emphasizes the importance of the recognition of an external reality. This, however, is inextricably linked with the recognition of the internal reality of one's own desires and phantasies. This recognition necessitates toleration of gaps in satisfaction, and therefore of one's own ambivalence towards the desired object.

Again in 'Two Principles of Mental Functioning', Freud speaks of two ways of dealing with this gap. One is the omnipotent hallucinatory phantasy; the other leads to the development of thought. He describes thought as 'experimental action'. I think the original experimental action is the phantasy. Phantasies can be tested by perception; some by action: crying when hungry, biting in anger, attracting attention and love with a smile, and so forth. But there is also an experimental testing of the phantasy without an action. If phantasy is, as I suggest, a set of primitive hypotheses about the nature of the object and the world, one can experiment in phantasy with 'what would happen if . . . '. For instance, 'What if I devoured my mother?' or 'What if I annihilated my mother or my father?' Such a 'What if . . . ?' includes the realization of the consequences of a possible action or its impossibility. It differs from the delusional phantasy which creates an 'as-if' world, and it introduces a consideration of a 'what-if?', a consideration of probabilities of 'what would happen if . . . '. It is the basis of imagination, as distinct from delusion or day-dreams based on a delusion, and a basis of flexible thought and rational action, since rational action takes into consideration the consequences of the action. Rationality necessitates imagination.

I have said that some capacity for this kind of functioning is present from the beginning of development; but it is achieved in small steps by the infant's tolerating discrepancies between his desires and fears on the one hand and reality on the other, and only very slowly does he emerge from his omnipotent world. The real battleground between the two modes of mental functioning described by Freud happens in what Klein described as the depressive position, which she defined as the infant beginning to relate to the mother, and soon after to both parents, as real, whole objects. By 'whole objects' she means that they are seen as real and separate persons. The toleration of experience that the original part-object does not correspond to one's phantasy initiates a withdrawal of projective identifications. As those projections are withdrawn, the object is perceived not as split into its bad and its good parts, but as being a whole which has many different characteristics. At the same time as the splits in the infant diminish, since he is less driven to project unwanted parts of himself and feelings, he feels more whole, and becomes aware of his ambivalence and inner conflicts between contradicting desires. This is a step towards recognizing the real world as perceived and separated from one's self and one's own inner world. And it brings awareness of internal conflict.

The awareness of the consequences of one's phantasies becomes more acute: for instance, 'If I kill the mother I hate, I would lose the mother I love'. 'If I kill my father and destroy my siblings, I shall not regain my mother for myself but shall be landed with a depressed, empty, destroyed, and possibly vengeful, or endlessly possessive, widow,' and so on. And even if the child is aware that he cannot carry out such wishes in external reality, the phantasies are vivid enough to make a change in his internal reality and the kind of objects that inner world is peopled with. Bringing together his good and bad wishes creates guilt and fear of loss of good feelings and good objects in the inner world. Therefore such wishes and phantasies tend to be repressed.

Freud speaks of repression in the passage quoted; he describes the pleasure–pain principle as 'psychical activity [which] draws back from any event which might arouse unpleasure. (Here we have repression.)' At that time Freud saw repression as a general defence mechanism; later he discovered many others. Now we are inclined to think that in the primitive functioning of the pleasure–pain principle, repression plays no part. The state of omnipotently getting rid of pain is achieved by more primitive defences such as splitting, projection, and reintrojection. Repression, as we understand it today, begins to function when the ego is sufficiently aware of the differentiation between external and internal realities to deal with unwanted impulses by repression. Archaic desires, however, are never completely given up. When they are repressed, they find their satisfaction by symbolic expressions. One of Freud's first discoveries was that repressed wishes express themselves symbolically. And symbolism undergoes a significant change in the depressive position.

In the depressive position the phantasy of the object as possessed by projective identification is given up, and is replaced by an object representation in memory and desire which is retained, though it might be repressed.

In his paper 'Success and Failure in Mental Maturation',[3] Money-Kyrle makes the point that in the depressive position there is an integration of various aspects of the original objects so that they become whole and complex, and our attitudes to them are equally complex; but that on the other hand a diversification occurs (Money-Kyrle calls it a 'parallel version'). This is due to the ability to recognize various characteristics of the same original object and find various symbols for the various aspects; and finding appropriate symbols depends on the appreciation of the real qualities of the real object, which is used as a symbol. This leads to enlargement of symbolization.

I think these considerations may also be relevant to the distinction Wollheim makes between dispositional phantasies and occurrent phantasies. According to Wollheim, dispositional phantasies define our personality, character, and modes of behaviour, and are based on archaic introjections. Occurrent phantasies, on the other hand, are mental states; they are stirred by occurrent events. According to Wollheim, the occurrent phantasies may be more or less under the dominance of the dispositional ones.

I think the extent to which the dispositional phantasy dominates the occurrent phantasy may depend on the nature of the dispositional phantasies. If the dispositional phantasies are based predominantly on omnipotent projective identification, the occurrent phantasies would be dominated by them. The event of meeting a prostitute in the case of the prostitute-murderer or a crying little boy in the case of the child-murderer stirs occurrent phantasies which are totally dominated by the compulsion to act out basic dispositional phantasies.

On the other hand, if the basic dispositional phantasies are of the more depressive kind, there is built into them a flexibility and an adaptability to current situations recognized for what they are, so that the occurrent phantasies are more diverse and more appropriate to prevailing circumstances.

In this paper I have tried to address myself to two useful concepts introduced by Wollheim: the distinction between acting on phantasy and acting on desire and that between occurrent and dispositional phantasies. These concepts stimulated me to further thoughts on the functioning of unconscious phantasy. I think his work provides an invaluable bridge between the philosophical and the psychoanalytical understanding of the phenomena of mental life, and exemplifies the cross-fertilization possible between the work of philosophers and that of psychoanalysts.

NOTES

[1] S. Isaacs, 'The Nature and Function of Phantasy', *International Journal of Psycho-Analysis*, 29 (1948); Klein *et al.*, *Developments in Psycho-Analysis* (London, Hogarth, 1970).

[2] H. Segal, 'Phantasy and other Mental Processes', *International Journal of Psycho-Analysis*, 45 (1964); also in *The Work of Hanna Segal* (Free Association Books, London, 1986); and *Introduction to the Work of Melanie Klein* (London, Heinemann, 1964).

[3] R. Money-Kyrle, 'Success and Failure in Mental Maturation', *International Journal of Psycho-Analysis*, 46 (1965), and *The Collected Papers of Roger Money-Kyrle* (Clunie Press, Strath Tay, 1978).

4

Knowing and Valuing: Some Questions of Genealogy

MARCIA CAVELL

'Under what conditions did man construct the value judgments good and evil?'[1] Nietzsche's answer traces a devious path along which desire's natural antithesis between 'good' and 'bad' came to be replaced with a perverse polarity of 'good' and 'evil'.

In the beginning, Nietzsche suggests, the language of value was an invention of those in power. More or less synonymous with 'noble', 'beautiful', and 'strong', 'good' was the Greek aristocracy's description of itself. In this first stage in the history of values, a single ruling class was composed of warriors and priests; but as culture developed, warrior and priest began to diverge; and in the struggle between them, the priests lost. Yet, over time, they were able to effect an inversion in value whereby the powerful whom they admired and envied, so in a way loved, were reviled as sinners. Under the banner of Christian love, weakness sought to mortify strength, and accepted – even glorified – its own humiliation. 'In the earliest phase', Nietzsche writes, 'bad conscience is nothing other than the instinct of freedom forced to become latent, driven underground, and forced to vent its energy upon itself.'[2] The invention of guilt, which the Judaeo-Christian tradition proclaims its greatest spiritual treasure, represents rather the ignoble triumph of resentment and self-disgust.

Freud's debt to Nietzsche is nowhere more apparent than in his views about valuing. In the climactic fifth chapter of *Civilization and its Discontents*, Freud says that the clue to mankind's discontents under the yoke of civilization is supplied by 'one of the ideal demands of civilized society. It runs: "Thou shalt love thy neighbour as thyself" ' (xxi.109). What could the source of such a strange and impossible demand be, Freud asks, other than the need to counter an aggressive instinct so violent that it threatens to destroy both the individual and society? Whereas Nietzsche lays guilt at the door of the Judaeo-Christian tradition, Freud traces it further back to aggression deep in the heart of the human creature and to the species' need to handle aggression in a way that allows communal life to continue. The unhappy solution, he thinks, so far a tenable though costly compromise in the cosmic war between Eros and Thanatos, is that aggression, in the form of guilt, is directed back on to the self.

Like Nietzsche, Freud sees the moral sense as the uneasy resolution in a dialectic between impotence and power, love and hate. In Freud's story the roles of strong and weak are played not by social classes, of course, but by parent and child. The dependent child rages against the powerful adult whom the child hates and resents, but also loves and admires. The child finally resolves the conflict by identifying with the one he would like to replace and whose retaliatory vengeance he fears. But for both Nietzsche and Freud the final outcome is the same: resentment and aggression, flourishing secretly in the dark of the mind behind a mask of love; self-hate fuelled ever more by the inhibition of instinctual energy, repression, and the creation of a mortal enemy within the self.

Like Nietzsche's, furthermore, Freud's genealogical account seems to say that in their attempts to root values in some objective facts about reality, philosophers have been digging in the wrong place. The moral sense does not reflect, as traditional religion would have it, a transcendent moral order; rather, it projects on to the world one's own subjective states.

This last is very generally, and with some interesting turns and distinctions, the lesson about valuing that Wollheim finds in psychoanalysis. In *The Thread of Life* (1984) he distinguishes two broad views about morality. On one, it is primarily a set of propositions which are true. On the other, it is primarily a part of psychology (p.198). It is the second view, he says, which he favours. He then distinguishes between morality in what he calls 'the narrow sense', which is motivated primarily by such negative emotions as the fear of punishment or retaliation, and valuation, which is based primarily on love. These two kinds of morality evolve respectively, the argument continues, from the psychological mechanisms of introjection and projection as described particularly by Melanie Klein. For now it suffices to say that projection is a defence against anxiety whereby one attributes one's own states of mind to objects in the external world. It is a reading of reality that mistakes the subject, oneself or an aspect of oneself, for the object – that is, the external world or an aspect of the external world. What in particular is being projected in the ascription of value, Wollheim claims, is 'archaic bliss . . . love satisfied' (p.215).

Wollheim is almost alone among Anglo-American philosophers in regarding psychoanalytic theory as a serious contribution to moral philosophy, and this is a contribution of his own. But I find an important element in the Freudian legacy that is very different from the ones Wollheim emphasizes. As already suggested, one genealogical line supports something like his view; but there is in Freud a second line that I will call 'the objective view', which describes a continuum of valuing that both begins and ends with the discovery of real objects in the external world.[3] Wollheim reduces ascriptions of value to subjective preferences, albeit distorted by projection, introjection, and other defensive mechanisms. He implicitly accepts the familiar fact/value dichotomy according to which valuing, unlike perception, for example, reflects no properties in the external world, or none that we have not put there. The objective view suggests that this dichotomy is based on a deep mistake; for thinking itself, the view holds, arises out of an interpersonal situation in which love, loss, and valuing play essential roles. The view claims that love of a certain sort is essentially connected not with the imposition of something private on to an object, but with discovering it as a truly valuable object in a real and public world.

The objective view is radical in that it also undercuts the familiar distinctions between the subjective and the objective, knowing and loving, by suggesting that desire plays a necessary or logical role in the concept of the objectively real, that interpersonal interactions of an affective nature are a necessary condition of thought, and that the concept of the intrinsically valuable emerges in the acknowledgement of another person as an *other*, separate from oneself. In the light of this view, even the Oedipal complex looks less like a private affair to be explained in terms of subjective and largely unconscious processes – though Freud surely thought it this as well – than like the child's full entrance into intersubjectivity, which is not to deny that later developments in the history of the individual may lead – perhaps always do – to the kinds of phantasies that 'the Oedipus complex' describes.

At most implicit in Freud, the objective view is more explicit in those of his followers known as 'the object relations' theorists, among whom I shall later discuss only Melanie Klein, since I agree with Wollheim in thinking that Klein, too, has made a distinctive philosophical contribution to moral philosophy – though here, as well, I locate her contribution rather differently.

I should say immediately that the objective view I attribute to Freud and Klein is certainly not worked out in their writings, and that it lives side by side with other views with which it is incompatible. My choice of Freudian texts, furthermore, is tendentious, as, undoubtedly, is my reading of them.

In 'Formulations on the Two Principles of Mental Functioning', Freud imagines an initial infantile condition of psychical rest, from time to time disturbed by the peremptory demands of internal needs, which the infant organism immediately 'satisfies' for itself in the form of hallucinatory wish-fulfilment. Freud describes such a creature as governed by the pleasure principle, a condition which in a pure form is surely as mythical as the one Hobbes refers to as 'the state of nature', which could not in any case last for long. Freud writes:

> It was only the non-occurrence of the expected satisfaction, the disappointment experienced, that led to the abandonment of this attempt at satisfaction by means of hallucination. Instead of it, the psychical apparatus had to decide to form a conception of the real circumstances in the external world and to endeavour to make a real alteration in them. A new principle of mental functioning was thus introduced; what was presented in the mind was no longer what was agreeable but what was real, even if it happened to be disagreeable.

In a footnote Freud remarks:

> It will rightly be objected that an organization which was a slave to the pleasure principle and neglected the reality of the external world could not maintain itself alive for the shortest time, so that it could not have come into existence at all. The employment of a fiction like this is, however, justified when one considers that the infant – provided one includes the care it receives from the mother – does almost realize a psychical system of this kind. (xii. 219, 220)

The usual way of reading these passages is to say that hallucination is how the baby briefly handles the absence of the mother and the gratification that she brings. This reading suggests a view of the infant as solipsist, self-sufficient, and uninterested in the external world. But the provision that 'one include the care it receives from the mother' suggests another reading, according to which the baby is not an isolated, self-enclosed organism but part of an interpersonal field. From a God's-eye point of view, what the baby 'hallucinates' will often be the real object or mother. On either reading, Freud's thought-experiment makes the logical point that for a creature who experienced no gap between desire and fulfilment, for whom gratification appeared as soon as desire arose, there could be no distinction between appearance and reality. Many philosophers have held that just this distinction provides for intentionality, the feature of being about something that is the hallmark of the mental. If this is so, then Freud's view is that the mental has a necessary connection with desire, with the experience of need and lack. (Hallucinatory wish-fulfilment is said to be the activity of another kind of thought or mentality which Freud calls 'primary process' and which presumably exists prior to experience of the external world. This is one of Freud's views that is incompatible with the objective view I attribute to him. My answer is that the incompatibility is to be found in Freud, and that in any case he fudges on the questions of whether or not, and in what sense, 'primary process' is mental.) Freud tells us that the concept of an object as a real thing in the world is dependent on pain and impotence, on frustration and dependency, and, more specifically, on real other persons, who will also be the child's first objects.

Freud vacillates in his writings between a view which takes self-love in some form to be primary and an alternative view which sees love of self and love of another, awareness of self and awareness of an object other than oneself, as emerging from the same matrix. It is the second view I am developing. The view is present as early as *Three Essays on the Theory of Sexuality*, where, in one of his most frequently quoted passages, Freud writes:

> At a time at which the first beginnings of sexual satisfaction are still linked with the taking of nourishment, the sexual instinct has a sexual object outside the infant's own body in the shape of his mother's breast. It is only later that he loses it, just at the time, perhaps, when he is able to form a total idea of the person to whom the organ that is giving him satisfaction belongs. As a rule the sexual drive then becomes autoerotic . . . The finding of an object [later, after the latency stage] is in fact a re-finding of it. (vii. 222)

That is, sexuality comes into its own as an instinct with the loss of the real object, known as such by the child, and with a compensatory turn towards an imaginary object. Self-love in the form of autoerotism arises as a response to object loss, and only when the child is able to conceive of another person as a real object separate from himself.[4]

Again Freud writes:

> An infant at the breast does not as yet distinguish his ego from the external world as the source of the sensations flowing in upon him. He

gradually learns to do so, in response to various promptings. He must be very strongly impressed by the fact that some sources of excitation, which he will later recognize as his own bodily organs, can provide him with sensations at any moment, whereas other sources evade him from time to time – among them what he desires most of all, his mother's breast – and only reappear as a result of his screaming for help. In this way there is for the first time set over against the ego an 'object', in the form of something which exists 'outside' and which is only forced to appear by a special action. (xxi. 67)

The reciprocal concepts of self and other are acquired, Freud suggests, in completion of the following circuit: a condition of felt need, a scream of pain, and in response the appearance of an object, specifically a person, that relieves the pain.

To Ferenczi these passages suggest the idea of 'stages in the development of the sense of reality'.[5] The first, he says, describes the foetus whom we may imagine as having, in its state of plenitude, a sense of omnipotence; the second describes the infant who achieves temporary satisfaction through hallucinatory wish-fulfilment; and the third, the infant who has learned that some of its wants will be met if it makes the right signals.

Ferenczi's story implies, as Freud also sometimes does, that the child knows what it wants prior to making its 'signals', that the infant whose mother 'magically' arrives at the moment of its need believes that it has produced her out of its own omnipotent power. But there is another reading of Freud which says instead that, prior to its communications with others, the infant is neither solipsist nor believer, for the reason that it has no real concepts at all. Until there is frustration there is no way that the child can distinguish itself from the world, and no way for it to have concepts with which to think the world. The crisis that propels it to a new principle of mental functioning is the absence of the mother. This is the view that on independent grounds I think to be right, but I will simply assume it here. It suggests something like the following: the infant is biologically programmed to do things that other people will interpret as meaningful signals for help. Its cries are meaningful to us, but not to it.[6] What is initially a cry without meaning to the crier, not a sign intended to be understood in a particular way, becomes meaningful through the behaviour it produces in another.

As just stated, this theory about the interpersonal nature of thought is in no way peculiar to Freud or to psychoanalysis. Their contribution is to remind us that these communications are emotionally laden; that first speech occurs in the context of demand, gratitude, and anger;

that even the ideas of space and time which are fundamental to our idea of reality are acquired through experiences in which lack, love, and mourning play an essential part.

In a passage from *Beyond the Pleasure Principle* made famous by Lacan, Freud muses on the meaning of his eighteen-month-old grandson's game with a cotton-reel. Over and over again the child casts the spool away from him with a syllable that sounds like '*fort*' (gone) and reels it back with a joyful '*da*' (here). Freud links the game to the child's attempt to master the painful experience of his mother's departure. Playing with the cotton-reel, Freud thinks, allows the child to repeat an experience in which he was painfully passive, the one left, making it tolerable by reversing the active and passive roles.[7] But in light of the importance that Freud gives to the processes of separation and individuation in such works as 'Mourning and Melancholia', we might rather interpret the child's activity as an attempt to take in its discovery of interpersonal reciprocity; if its activity in relation to the mother consists in its ability to summon her to him, her ability to answer him is a function of a principle of activity that is hers. And this implies that as it is by her initiative that she comes, so by that same initiative can she go; therefore the child's power over her is limited. The one who answers my call, the child is discovering, can do so only because she is not part of me; nor is she, like my own limbs, at the end of my will; as she is someone who can leave, so I am someone who can be left. She is not here, but I discover that she is somewhere, there where I am not.

The concept of objective reality, then, has an inescapably interpersonal dimension: it is that which is neither exclusively yours nor exclusively mine, but the common field for our different points of view. The sounds '*fort*', '*da*', mark places in a game which is essentially both spatial and erotic and in which language and thought are together in the making, along with the discovery of other minds. 'Writing', Freud says in *Civilization and its Discontents*, 'was in its origin the voice of the absent person; and the dwelling-house was a substitute for the mother's womb' (xxi. 91). Whether there will one day be machines that can think in the sense that we think is an empirical question. Freud supports a conceptual claim to the effect that 'thinking' in this sense has necessary connections with desire and love.

I am suggesting on Freud's behalf that there comes to be something we can speak of as the child's point of view only as it discovers a point of view which is not its own. If this is so, then the child's discovery of other minds provides a different model for interpersonal understanding than the familiar one that guides many psychoanalysts and philosophers. On this familiar view, I understand your state of mind through some sort of imaginative projection of my own states on to you. On the objective view, the child comes in the first instance to have its own beliefs and desires in the process of discovering some of the beliefs and desires of another, recognized by the child to be separate and different from itself.

Acknowledging the otherness of other minds is one of the organizing principles of psychological development, Freud thinks, and also its principal stumbling block. He examines some vicissitudes of the process of separation in 'Mourning and Melancholia', where he traces a certain form of depression to conditions in which, rather than accepting object loss, the patient attempts, in phantasy, to incorporate the lost object into himself, on the model of the baby at the mother's breast. Mourning is the normal way in which one registers the real loss of a loved object, not only a loss of the object's presence through death or absence but also of the object's esteem or love, or a loss in the form of disappointment in the object as a suitable target for one's esteem and love. A pathological counterpart of mourning, melancholia is caused by the attempt to avoid acknowledging the loss that would normally elicit mourning. Melancholic introjection is to be understood as such an attempt at avoidance, one which distorts the agent's views of both external and internal world, for it causes a split within the subject's own self.

> So we find the key to the clinical picture: we perceive that the [melancholic's] self-reproaches are reproaches against a loved object which have been shifted away from it on to the patient's own ego . . . In this way an object-loss was transformed into an ego-loss and the conflict between the ego and the loved person into a cleavage between the critical activity of the ego and the ego as altered by identification. (xiv. 248, 249)

Melancholia gives us a view, Freud says, of the constitution of the human ego in which one part sets itself over against another part, 'judges it critically, and, as it were, takes it as its object'. This is of course how Freud describes the superego or conscience, of which melancholia, he says, is nothing less than a disease. We are to understand, I believe, that whereas melancholia is mourning forestalled, the healthy conscience evolves from an acknowledgement of loss and a process of mourning undergone. The mourning in question is a response to the recognition that one's loved object is not one's exclusive possession; that one is sometimes an outsider in relation to her and a third object, which in principle – though of course Freud doesn't say so – might be an activity or an abstraction, as well as a person; and that time and death are limits to desire in the ways they are.

Oedipal 'identifications' are of many sorts, on Freud's view. Some are by definition distortions of reality, that is of the child's own perceptions of reality; for example, identifying with the parent who has been idealized or whose aggression has been exaggerated in a denial, perhaps, of one's own hostility. And at the edge of pathology, though an inevitable one, Freud seems to say, Oedipal identifications are less a modelling of oneself after another than a blurring of identities.

But there is another sort of identification distinctive of 'the Oedipal' as naming the child's full arrival into the human community that is not a blurring of identities but a full awareness of individuation. In this sense to 'identify' with someone is simply to imagine the world from the perspective of the beliefs and desires one attributes to her, knowing that some of them are different from one's own. This identification attends the knowledge that one's own point of view is partial, that one may be an outsider in the dialogue of others, that one is but one person among many, each with his or her own beliefs and desires and claims on the world.

Identification of this sort is the ground of dialogue, which presumes awareness of both similarity and difference. If I cannot assume that you and I mean more or less the same things by some of our words and that we share some beliefs in common, there is no way I can begin to understand you. But if at the same time I don't know that I sometimes need to make an effort to understand you, I will simply hear in your words an echo of my own.

In summary, the Oedipal stage – whenever it can be said to occur – is such in virtue of the fact that the child is now in a position to acknowledge certain facts about the human condition and to love another person as separate from itself. But the facts are painful, and therefore subject to distortions that are described again and again in the psychoanalytic literature since Freud. One is asked to acknowledge simultaneously one's dependence on others and the fact that one can lose them, to achieve an ability to fend for oneself while remaining connected to them. There may then be a strong temptation to try to make oneself self-sufficient by denying the need for others or their intrinsic value.

In exploring the constraints on human knowledge, philosophers typically discuss the implications of the fact that every knower's viewpoint is spatially and temporally partial; one sees the front of the apple, but not at the same time its other sides; one is immediately acquainted only with the present, and must recall the past and make inferences from it about the future. The epistemological constraints that psychoanalysis explores are of a different sort: the ways in which desire and anxiety subvert perception and belief. Knowledge of objects of all sorts is vulnerable, but none more so, for the child at least, than of those 'objects' which are other people, since it is they on whom the child must depend, whose love it most needs, whose anger and displeasure it most fears. The introjective phantasies characteristic of melancholia are motivated, Freud tells us, by such desires and anxieties.

Klein's developmental account[8] picks up from Freud the theme of mourning as constitutive of the human self. From the very beginning, Klein thinks, the infant has some rudimentary idea of other persons as psycho-physical entities, or 'objects'. But it does not understand other persons as whole and as separate from itself in ways that adults take for granted. Klein takes the breast as emblematic of objects for the infant. Such objects may be parts of persons, from our point of view; from the infant's, they can be physically incorporated or introjected, also spat out or projected. In the first few months of life the infant occupies a paranoid-schizoid position in which it is subject to rage and extreme anxiety. It experiences these painful emotions along with the frustrations which are to some degree the cause of them, as intrusive quasi-material objects, against which it defends itself by projecting them, in imagination, into other persons. The infant is also subject to splitting (imagining the one object, itself or the other, as two, the all-good and the all-bad, need-gratifying and need-frustrating), idealization (imagining the object as all-good as a denial of the infant's bad rage), projection, and introjection.

But if the object of desire that the child, in phantasy, takes in is in reality truly and sufficiently gratifying – and more or less reliably so – the infant's rage becomes less. The infant's tendency to envy 'the withholding breast' is tamed, and the infant can feel gratitude instead. It enters the depressive position, which Klein thinks occurs in the second quarter of the first year. In the depressive position the infant is capable of recognizing the wholeness both of the object and of itself as subject. That is, the infant realizes that the same object of desire can be both good and bad, both gratifying and frustrating; and that it is itself the same creature whether feeling grateful towards the object or willing its destruction. This realization leads to guilt in relation to the object and to the wish to repair the harm it has done or the harm it has phantasized it has done. Hence the infant's depression, an analogue of normal mourning.

On my view, and that of most psychoanalysts, gratitude and mourning presume a degree of cognitive development that a very young infant simply does not have. But one can leave aside the empirical question of when this development occurs and focus, rather, on Klein's very interesting thesis that gratitude and mourning are emotions which register crucial developmental changes. The thesis is not only psychological, but also philosophical; for in the most general sense, gratitude is a moral attitude, related to such other moral attitudes as indebtedness, obligation, and the recognition of goodness. The philosophical implication, then, is that certain moral emotions play a constitutive role in the human self.

One of the things that makes gratitude and mourning such key developmental moments is that among the conditions for them are certain fundamental, true beliefs about oneself and about the external world. (Klein does not put the point this way: she does not specify that among the conditions for gratitude and mourning are certain beliefs that identify them as these particular emotions.) Gratitude and mourning peculiarly acknowledge value, the existence of an objective world, and one's place in it. The infant who feels gratitude acknowledges that it has been given something real and something that is valuable, of course, to the infant. But this is not a projection of anything on to either the received object or its giver. The infant who mourns has made another move along the continuum of valuing; for it has discovered that the mourned 'object' is itself a source of valuing. The object is valuable not only to the infant but also to itself. And it holds objects valuable; among them, the infant.

I use the word 'acknowledge', as I have throughout, to indicate a recognition of facts – for example that what one wants and thinks one needs is simply not available in a given case – that bear directly on desire and that may therefore prompt phantasizing of various sorts. Because of their bearing on desire, one would expect that acknowledgement of such facts could take place only in an emotional state like sadness, dismay, anxiety, frustration, or mourning. Here is another of the philosophical insights of psychoanalysis: if belief is often subverted by anxiety and desire, nevertheless knowledge of reality begins in such affective states, and some facts can be known (acknowledged) only through feeling. If someone says that he has wilfully and maliciously harmed another and that he believes such harm to be wrong, yet truly (neither consciously nor unconsciously) feels no guilt, we suspect him of insincerity. If someone professes love for another whom he believes he has just lost for ever, yet truly feels no sadness or grief, we think his love rather shallow.

What are the acknowledgements in the case of gratitude? My answer depends on a view of the emotions that I shall simply assume: in the typical case, an emotion is caused by beliefs and desires or pro-attitudes of some sort; these beliefs and desires cause the emotion, provide the reasons why someone has the emotion that he or she does, and identify it as the particular emotion it is – gratitude, say, rather than simply relief or pleasure. An analysis of gratitude will then consist in locating the network of beliefs and desires which have this function.[9]

First of all, I take gratitude to be an essentially interpersonal emotion. If there is such a thing as an impersonal gratitude to no one in particular (say, for being alive, even though one does not believe in God), it is derivative from the more typical interpersonal case in which one feels gratitude to someone with regard to x. Beyond this condition, if Mary can truly be said to feel grateful to Sarah for x, the following must be true: (1) Mary desires x or believes that x is desirable. (I am not sure what to say if Mary does not think x is desirable but believes that Sarah believes Mary will find it so.) (2) Mary is pleased to have x. (3) Mary believes that she has been given x by Sarah (x may be an opportunity or a blessing of some kind, as well as a thing). (4) Mary believes that she could not have procured x by or for herself, or at least not easily. (If she thinks otherwise, then she will not feel grateful, though she may think that what Mary has done is generous or kind.) (5) Mary believes that Sarah intended to give her x. (If Mary stole x from Sarah, or if Sarah accidentally left it at Mary's house, and so on, then Mary may be delighted with x, perhaps grateful to her lucky star, but not to Sarah.) (6) Mary believes that Sarah believed that Mary would find x desirable. (Brer Rabbit is delighted that the fox, falsely thinking that rabbits hate briar patches, threw him into one; but Brer Rabbit is not grateful, or at least not grateful to the fox.) In sum, gratitude towards another person depends on acknowledging the limitations of one's own will in relation to its objects, acknowledging the existence of another person as an agent who has beliefs and intentions, some of which are benevolent towards oneself, and acknowledging a degree of dependence on that person.

Mourning, at least as described by Klein, requires all this and more: a recognition that persons, both the mourned and oneself the mourner, are 'whole' persons in the sense defined earlier (I am the same person whether I am feeling anger or love towards you, as you are the same 'object' of my different passions). This true belief about the nature of persons is then among the conditions for mourning. Another requirement, again on Klein's account, would seem to be the valuing of a person not only as a means to some end of one's own, but for him or herself, perceived as unique and irreplaceable. Winnicott makes this condition more explicit than Klein. He speaks of an essential stage in object love as marked by 'the subject's perception of the object as an external phenomenon, not as a projective entity, in fact recognition of it as an entity in its own right'.[10]

In short, whatever the sorts of projective and incorporative phantasies that may or may not precede mourning, it seems itself to be a valuing distinguished from other valuings precisely by the fact that the view of the object is not distorted by phantasy and that the object is held to be intrinsically, rather than merely instrumentally, valuable. I am not sure what Wollheim means by calling valuing the projection of 'archaic love . . . bliss satisfied'. Presumably he has in mind a phantasy of union. If so, and restricting ourselves simply to the valuing of other persons, then this idea of valuing leaves out the appreciation of the separateness of the other person, together with an ability to discern the other's feelings even though they are different from, perhaps even in conflict with, one's own.

If gratitude and mourning have the importance in the development of valuing – indeed, in the development of the person – that Klein suggests, then the categorical distinction which Wollheim draws in *The Thread of Life* between obligation and valuing would seem to be misguided. He writes:

> Whatever may be the content of obligation, obligation itself is primarily self-directed. It is self-directed, though it may be other-regarding. For it expresses itself in a thought that a person has about what *he* ought to do . . . . It is also true that a person may well have thoughts about what others ought to do, but my conviction is that either these thoughts do not express obligations or they require some circuitous interpretation. For they have no clear root in our psychology. (p. 224)

But if a certain stage in the genealogy of valuing that I have called mourning represents, in part, a sort of Kantian recognition that some 'objects' are valuable not only as means but also as ends and that they are real objects in a real and public world, then it is not a big step to the further idea that these objects are entitled to respect from others as well as from oneself. So I see no justification for saying either that obligation is primarily self-directed or that third-person ascriptions of obligation have no root in our psychology.[11]

Many emotions, I have said, presume a certain characterization of the object. My analysis of gratitude was based on this premise. If you are angry with me, presumably you feel guilty; presumably you believe you have done something shameful or wrong. But love, by contrast, Wollheim claims,

> presumes no special perception or characterization of its object. Love is not deserved. The love of a person for an object is fundamentally a response to a certain relation in which the person stands, and knows that he stands, to that object. In the most archaic situation of all, love is anaclitic: it is a response – a response, not the response, for in these same circumstances envy is another likely response – to the relation of total dependence. In later life, love is the response to whatever relation of mutuality it is with which the person tries to displace that of total dependence. (p. 212)

If this claim is right, it may be because 'love' covers such a range of emotions, states, and relationships that no one thing is presumed for them all. Freud and Klein distinguish love which is primarily a response to a relation of total dependence on the object from love for an object which is perceived to be gracious or gratifying; both are different from love which *truly* perceives its object as gratifying; and both are different again from love which in addition perceives its object more or less as it is. Klein suggests that gratitude, whenever it occurs, is a kind of love that presumes a certain characterization of the object: the grateful person believes that the one towards whom she is grateful is, in respect to her 'gift' at least, 'good'. Mourning does not presume any particular perception of the loved object; but it does presume a perception of it that is relatively undistorted. Love, even 'archaic' love, together with the separation which can be experienced as such only when the lost object is loved in some sense, motivates an understanding of another's point of view; motivates, that is, a relatively accurate characterization of the object. Wollheim's view of valuing as projective rests, like Hume's, on a categorical distinction between fact and value. But if love, gratitude, and mourning have the character I have been arguing, then they call this distinction into question.

What I have said so far seems sufficient to challenge Wollheim's claim that valuing is a result of projection, at least if he means to be basing that claim on Freud and Klein. But let me say more. Wollheim distinguishes between simple and complex projection, and it is the second from which valuing supposedly results. Here is a case of simple projection: Mary feels angry; the anger makes her anxious; so she unconsciously projects her anger on to the environment or on to a part of the environment, say, John. As a result, Mary no longer perceives herself as angry but believes that John is. While John may be angry in fact, to call Mary's belief that he is angry a projection is to say that her belief is caused not by a perceptible state of anger in John, but rather by her own anger, together with her wish not to be angry or not to know that she is.

In both simple and complex projection 'something inner is projected on to the outer world' (p. 214); but there are two differences between these forms of projection. First, whereas in simple projection there need be no correspondence between the agent's state and the object in the world on to which he projects it, in complex projection the outer world has to collude more substantively with the inner world. And second, in simple projection the projected property and the property that the agent, as a result of projection, believes another to have, are the same; whereas in complex projection the properties may be different. Thus in the simple case, 'I am angry' becomes 'He is angry'; in the complex case 'I am angry' may become 'He is critical (of me)'. Nietzsche's account of the ethics of rancour in which 'I envy him and I hate him' are transformed into 'He is evil' is another example of complex projection.

Wollheim's fullest account of complex projection appears in *Painting as an Art* (1987) in his analysis of what he calls 'expressive perception', the perception, for example, of a landscape as melancholy. He says that while simple projection is typically 'haphazard and responsible solely to inner needs and demand', expressive perception seems to be a response to features of the perceived scene. The solution, he thinks, is to say that the capacity for complex projection, of which expressive perception is a species, is something that develops. As time goes on, the 'suitability of some part of the world to support projection . . . becomes apparent only through trial and error'. (p. 83). There is then a slow transition from projection to expressive perception.

But what will the difference be between saying that x is suitable to support a perception of the world as y and that x is suitably perceived as y? And if the latter is true, then might not the perception be caused by x alone? In general, the concept of unconscious, psychological acts, which like projection or introjection are performed as a defence against perceptions that cause anxiety, rests on the assumption that the agent has, or might have, other perceptions which somehow more nearly represent things as they are and which are caused by them in the appropriate way. The function of unconscious mechanisms of defence is to create new perceptions in place of the old, or to sever one set of perceptions from another set. So it is hard to see a role for projection in either veridical or 'suitable' perception, however we are to understand the latter.

Earlier I offered a reading of Freud and Klein according to which valuing is not a projection of something subjective on to an object, but a discovery of aspects of reality. Now I want to say, furthermore, that I think this view of valuing is right. I won't try to argue it here, but merely to suggest the line such an argument might take. Assume that the concept of a real, external, objective world as that which one's 'private', 'subjective' beliefs are about is acquired only through interpersonal experiences that are affectively coloured in the ways Freud and Klein describe, and in which love, itself a valuing, plays an essential role. Assume, further, that being in possession of such a concept is a prerequisite for thought.[12] If these assumptions could be shown to be correct, then I would see no reason for holding truth to be any more objective than value, or value any less objective than truth.[13] The idea that there are true things to be said about the world, no less than the idea that some things in the world are valuable, depends on the understanding that there are different points of view regarding the same one world, as this understanding is necessary for the ideas of truth and value. Truth and value – in principle, one no less decidable than the other – would then together be part of the fabric of thought, though there are ample reasons why disagreement about the good and the bad should be more violent, intractable, and more frequent than disagreement about the size, the place, and the shape of things.

I began by recalling Freud's debt to Nietzsche. Let me conclude with a less obvious pairing of Freud with Plato, whom Freud invokes in his first theoretical treatment of sexual love. I am not suggesting that Freud was influenced by Plato, but that Freud's views ring interesting changes on the Platonic themes that connect knowing, loving, and valuing. In his *Three Essays on the Theory of Sexuality*, Freud alludes to Aristophanes' fable, reported in the *Symposium*, in which love is described as originating in a kind of ludicrous Fall. According to Aristophanes, the original human beings were spherical creatures who were uppity and troublesome; so the gods punished them by cutting each into two. Love is our doomed attempt to achieve a wholeness which once was ours and which can never be ours again.

Freud does not refer to Plato's own view, presented through the figure of Socrates, that while love indeed originates in lack, most lovers misconstrue what they lack. Aristophanes' comic fable illustrates this misconstrual: we think we long for another creature, necessarily as incomplete and insubstantial as ourselves, when what we truly long for transcends particularity, embodiment, and lack. Knowledge begins in desire, which is by definition an unstable state; it will be completed with the absorption of the knower into a realm of Being that is timeless and incorporeal and that is at once the fulfilment of desire, reality, and goodness. Ordinary, sexual, embodied love is the first step towards reunion, but of an order not glimpsed by Aristophanes.

Though he protests that love must be left to the poets, Freud nevertheless has a good deal to say on the subject. He agrees that love originates in an experience of lack, and that we were once a part of what we lack. It is *à propos* this agreement that he alludes to Aristophanes. (For Freud, of course, the longed-for reunion is with the mother, whom one begins to know as 'an object' in the very experience of deprivation.) Freud also holds that there is typically, and always at first, a misconstrual, both of the object of love and of that happiness which possession of the beloved aims to achieve. Child or narcissist, focused as each is on her own needs, seeing the beloved as some kind of reflection of herself, misconstrues both herself and her loved object. Perhaps one remains for ever prey, furthermore, to phantasies that deny the facts of separation, that imagine a lost union more perfect than any one ever knew, as answer to a present pain.

But like Plato, Freud also holds, I have been maintaining, that without desire there can be no knowledge. As love motivates various misperceptions of reality, so it also provides the route, the only route, by which reality in its fully human dimension can be perceived. In the form of communication with others, love is the condition for language and thought. Beyond that, it instructs us in the limits of our power, the nature of ourselves and our relations with other persons, and space and time as dimensions that define loss and separateness. Finally, love yields that knowledge of other minds without which neither dialogue nor the idea of an intersubjective truth would be possible.

Of course Freud's conception of reality is vastly different from Plato's. Whereas Platonic epistemology distinguishes between belief, which is ensnared in the sensible world, and knowledge, which transcends it, Freudian epistemology distinguishes a minimal sort of knowledge – knowledge denied or repressed or shorn of its emotional significance (there is another minimal sort of knowledge which he calls the 'preconscious') – from an acceptance of what is here and now. For Freud, reality is not what we would know if we were free of our human constraints, but what we know if we acknowledge them;

and valuing another embodied person as real and separate from oneself is the very model of such acknowledgement. The Freudian view of knowledge, which asks us to reconsider the relation between knowing and valuing, knowing and feeling, knowing and loving, is as radical as the Freudian view of morality.

NOTES

[1] Nietzsche, *The Genealogy of Morals*, in *The Birth of Tragedy and the Genealogy of Morals*, tr. F. Goffing (Doubleday, Garden City, N.Y., 1956), p. 151.

[2] Ibid., p. 220.

[3] For a fuller discussion of this view in Freudian theory, see M. Cavell, 'Interpretation, Psychoanalysis, and the Philosophy of Mind', *Journal of the American Psychoanalytic Association*, 36/4 (1988), pp. 859–79; *idem*, 'Solipsism and Community: Two Concepts of Mind in Psychoanalysis', *Psychoanalysis and Contemporary Thought*, 11/4 (1988), pp. 587–615.

[4] Cf. J. Laplanche, *Life and Death in Psychoanalysis*, tr. and ed. J. Mehlman (Johns Hopkins University Press, Baltimore, 1976), ch. 2.

[5] S. Ferenczi, 'Stages in the Development of the Sense of Reality', in *Sex in Psycho-Analysis*, tr. C. Newton (Dover, London, 1956).

[6] Since Kleinians attribute very complex phantasies to infants, they would presumably hold that the infant's communications are meaningful to the infant as well as to us. Its cries are expressive of phantasies in which it believes; for example, that it is spitting out its 'badness' into another. Depending on how early Kleinians think such phantasizing occurs, I may part company with them on this issue.

[7] Lacan writes: 'This reel is not the mother reduced to a little ball by some magical game . . . it is a small part of the subject that detaches itself from him while still remaining his . . . The activity as a whole symbolizes repetition, but not at all that of some need that might demand the return of the mother . . . It is the repetition of the mother's departure as cause of a *Spaltung* in the subject – overcome by the alternating game, *fort-da* . . . whose aim, in its alternation, is simply that of being the *fort* of a *da* and the *da* of a *fort*' (J. Lacan, 'The Transference and the Drive', in *Four Fundamental Concepts of Psycho-Analysis* (W. W. Norton, New York, 1981), pp. 62, 63).

I read the passage in Freud as a way of saying that language, thought, desire for the other, and the concept of reality as something external to oneself arise in the same logical moment. Lacan's reading has certainly informed mine. But if I understand Lacan's views in general, he holds that there is some pre-linguistic mental state in which the child is at one with itself and also with its mother. On this view, it is the Oedipal complex which introduces language, the knowledge of separation, and a rupture in the self. Lacan's most famous slogan is that the unconscious is the language of the other. If this means that an unconscious mental state, like the mental in general, is dependent on language and that language is necessarily interpersonal, then I agree with him. But then I'm not sure what we can mean in attributing a psychological sense of oneness to the child prior to language. Furthermore, Lacan holds that 'reality', like language, is a social construct. This is not the place to say why I think both views are wrong. Briefly, however, my view is this: of course the vocabulary which a child learns has existed prior to him, and this vocabulary is arbitrary. But communication, thought, and the content of mental states are dependent both on communication between persons and on the existence of a real, external world with which the communicants interact and which they share.

[8]   See M. Klein, *Envy and Gratitude and Other Works 1946–1963* (Hogarth, London, 1984).

[9]   R. M. Gordon has recently argued such a 'cognitivist' view of the emotions in *The Structure of Emotions* (Cambridge University Press, Cambridge, 1987), though he is by no means the only one.

[10] D. W. Winnicott, *Playing and Reality* (Tavistock, London, 1971), p. 89.

[11] In a personal communication, Richard Wollheim has pointed out that he can account for valuations like this: 'It would be good for you to do *x*.' But on his account, such valuations express no more than subjective beliefs.

[12] See D. Davidson, 'Rational Animals', in Le Pore and McLaughlin (eds), *Actions and Events. Perspectives on the Philosophy of Donald Davidson* (Blackwell, Oxford, 1985).

[13] Some arguments for a position like this are given in S. Lovibond, *Realism and Imagination in Ethics* (Blackwell, Oxford, 1983); S. Hurley 'Objectivity and Disagreement', in *Morality and Objectivity*, ed. T. Honderich (Routledge, London, 1985); and D. Wiggins, 'Truth, Invention and the Meaning of Life', in *Needs, Values, Truth* (Blackwell, Oxford, 1987).

5

Naturalism, Psychoanalysis, and Moral Motivation

SAMUEL SCHEFFLER

One of the great themes of Kant's *Foundations of the Metaphysics of Morals* is the incompatibility of our own pre-philosophical understanding of morality with any purely naturalistic account of moral motivation: that is, with the idea that our reasons for behaving morally stem ultimately from our natural attitudes, sentiments, or inclinations, or from other features of our psychology. Kant believes that, rightly or wrongly, we ascribe to morality a special kind of motivational authority, a kind of authority which could not possibly have a purely naturalistic source.

As Kant sees it, the motivation that we think of as distinctively moral is motivation by a sense of duty. And motivation by a sense of duty is a peculiar kind of motivation, which we sharply distinguish from motivation by sentiment, however other-directed the sentiment may be. Motivation by a sense of duty neither derives from nor depends on the presence of a feeling or sentiment, and it can move us to action even in the absence of any prior inclination to do the right thing. When one is motivated by a sense of duty, one is responsive to the authority of reason rather than to the urgings of one's natural inclinations; one acts as one does because one sees that there are good reasons to do so, whether or not one happens also to feel like it. Although it may often happen that people do the right thing out of sentiment or inclination and although their motives on such occasions may have admirable features, nevertheless, these motives do not count for us as distinctively moral, and they do not exhibit the special form of praiseworthiness which is moral praiseworthiness.

Kant thinks that this is our own implicit pre-philosophical view of the matter, our common understanding, as revealed by our patterns of moral thought and judgement and our practices of moral comment and assessment. For example, Kant says that the commands of morality as we ordinarily think of them are not conditional on the presence in the agent of any particular sentiment or sentiments. We do not regard morality as telling us how to treat people if, say, we happen to like them or feel sympathetically disposed towards them. Rather, we regard it as setting limits to the ways in which we can treat individuals even if we don't like them or sympathize with them or, for that matter, know them. This suggests that, for us, to be motivated *morally* – by morality – is to be motivated by a conception of the treatment one owes to people as people, however one happens to feel about them, rather than by some feeling or sentiment or inclination. And in fact, Kant thinks, this suggestion is confirmed by looking at the cases in which we actually judge someone's motives to display moral worth. On the one hand, he argues, personal warmth and affection, for all their human importance, are not in themselves the kinds of motives that we think of as distinctively moral; so we tend not to assign moral worth to acts when we believe that such sentiments alone are prompting them, and that a sense of duty is playing no motivational role. On the other hand, we are prepared to classify an act we take to be performed out of duty as issuing from a morally worthy motive even if we think that a sense of duty is the agent's sole motive for acting as he does, and that all his natural inclinations and leanings either are silent or militate against the dutiful act. Thus we can imagine a case in which someone refrains from violating a person's right despite the fact that he dislikes that person, that he would benefit from violating the person's right, and that he is not by temperament a warm or sympathetic individual. Kant thinks that we are prepared to consider the agent's motive in such a case to be morally worthy if we are convinced – rightly or wrongly – that he really is acting out of a sense of duty, rather than out of some hidden desire which the act promises to satisfy in some unobvious way. Indeed, Kant thinks that, if we are convinced that the person is acting out of a sense of duty, then we are likely to be all the more impressed with the moral quality of his motivation, given that it is opposed to his own natural inclinations and interests and must therefore overcome them in order to be effective.

Supposing that Kant is right to say that motivation by a sense of duty is ordinarily distinguished from motivation by sentiment or inclination, might not the sense of duty nevertheless be thought of, compatibly with our ordinary understanding of it, as one of our natural attitudes more broadly construed? Kant's conviction that this question must be answered in the negative derives from his understanding of the relations among morality, reason, and freedom and, complementarily, among nature, determinism, and the absence of freedom. And this understanding, too, he takes to be continuous with our ordinary views.

As I have already implied, Kant does not think that we are always correct when we judge that a particular person has on a given occasion acted from a sense of duty. Indeed, he does not think we can be sure that we are ever correct. As is well known, Kant insists that it is easy to make mistakes about people's motives, so much so that we cannot be certain that we have ever actually encountered even a single instance of someone's acting from a sense of duty. Moreover, Kant understands as well as anyone that the very idea of motivation by a sense of duty, if understood as resisting assimilation within a naturalistic account, raises formidable theoretical difficulties. It is not easy to see how there could be such a thing as motivation independent of one's natural attitudes or inclinations. The fact remains, Kant thinks, that we do indeed ascribe to morality a kind of authority over our motives which is not dependent on what our natural attitudes or inclinations happen to be. Hence any naturalistic account of moral motivation really amounts to a denial of the existence of moral motivation as we understand it. That by itself does not imply that naturalism is wrong, only that it is inevitably sceptical or deflationary.

Naturalistic accounts of moral motivation have become more sophisticated since Kant's day. Like other naturalisms, they have thrived as the intellectual prestige of the sciences has continued to grow. Some of these accounts are explicitly deflationary; that is, they accept a more or less Kantian interpretation of our pre-philosophical conception of moral motivation, and take themselves to show that there is nothing in our actual motivations that answers to that pre-philosophical conception. Others purport to be compatible with the correctness of our pre-philosophical ideas as they understand them. For accounts of these two types, Kant's criticism of motivational naturalism presents two different challenges. For the purportedly non-deflationary accounts, the challenge is to explain how the truth of such an account is compatible with the correctness of our pre-philosophical ideas, given Kant's argument about the anti-naturalistic import of those ideas. The most straightforward way to meet this challenge would be to show that Kant is, to one degree or another, mistaken in his interpretation of our common understanding of moral motivation. Perhaps the idea that we are unwilling to count motivation by sentiment or inclination as moral motivation is simply a mistake. Or perhaps, although Kant is correct up to a point, he fails to see that there is some particular sentiment which differs in crucial respects from all others and which we are prepared to recognize as a source of moral motivation. Or perhaps the sense of duty, although not analysable as a sentiment or a feeling, can nevertheless be reckoned, compatibly with our ordinary understanding of it, among our natural attitudes more broadly construed.

For the explicitly deflationary accounts, the challenge is different. Obviously, such accounts are not embarrassed by Kant's claim about the incompatibility of motivational naturalism with our common understanding of morality, for they agree with it. The challenge, however, is to explain how the truth of such an account is reconcilable not with the correctness of our pre-philosophical ideas, but with our acceptance of those ideas. If, for example, moral motivation in fact consists in motivation by some natural attitude or inclination, how are we to explain the fact that people ordinarily conceive the two as distinct? An explicitly deflationary account cannot meet this challenge by denying that people *do* ordinarily conceive of the two as distinct, for then it will cease to be deflationary. Instead, such an account must provide an 'error theory', an explanation of why we think that motivation by a sense of duty is distinct from motivation by sentiment or natural attitude even though it really isn't.

Broadly speaking, then, Kant's criticism of motivational naturalism challenges both deflationary and purportedly non-deflationary naturalistic accounts to demonstrate their compatibility with our pre-philosophical understanding of the motivational authority of morality. However, whereas the purportedly non-deflationary accounts must demonstrate their compatibility with the *truth* of our pre-philosophical understanding, the explicitly deflationary accounts must demonstrate their compatibility with our pre-philosophical *acceptance* of an opposed understanding. Despite the continuing popularity and increased sophistication of naturalistic accounts, such accounts still strike many people as unsatisfying. One reason for this, I believe, is that their responses to the Kantian challenge seem unconvincing to many.

Before explaining why, we must first raise the question of what the specific motivational sources of morality are, according to contemporary naturalistic accounts. Although such accounts vary in the responses they give to this question, two types of accounts are particularly prominent. Accounts of the first type are psychologically agnostic; they claim only that moral conduct is motivated by some 'desire' or other (taking that term in the broad sense that is now standard in analytic philosophy), but do not specify which desire or desires in particular do the job. Accounts of the second type are more psychologically specific; they identify the relevant motivating factor as 'sympathy', thus taking over a bit of eighteenth-century terminology with which Kant was familiar. I will refer to accounts of these two types as 'standard naturalistic accounts', or simply 'standard accounts'.

We may now observe that we have before us two independent distinctions within the class of standard accounts. First, there is the distinction between those accounts that are purportedly non-deflationary (or 'non-revisionist', as I shall sometimes say) and those that are explicitly deflationary. Second, there is the distinction between the psychologically agnostic accounts and what I will call the 'sentimental' accounts, which see sympathy as the source of moral motivation. Since these two distinctions cut across each other, we have four types of standard accounts altogether: agnostic non-revisionist (ANR), sentimental non-revisionist (SNR), agnostic deflationary (AD), and sentimental deflationary (SD).

It is not difficult to understand why standard non-revisionist accounts, whether agnostic or sentimental, do not seem to provide convincing responses to the Kantian challenge. Recall that the task for non-revisionist accounts is to identify some natural attitude(s) which our pre-philosophical understanding can be shown to regard as the source(s) of moral motivation, thereby demonstrating how the truth of such an account is compatible with the correctness of our pre-philosophical ideas. As I have indicated, however, ANR accounts remain schematic in that they hazard no opinion on the question of which specific kinds of desires motivate moral conduct. Instead, they typically concentrate on trying to establish, on general philosophical grounds, the broader thesis that all conduct, and hence moral conduct in particular, is motivated by desire. In so doing, they clearly leave open the formal possibility of an adequate reply to the Kantian criticism, but they do not themselves provide one. Indeed, they tend not to address the criticism directly at all. SNR accounts, meanwhile, appear to be in a still less favourable position relative to the Kantian criticism. For they seem incompatible with one of the strongest elements in Kant's interpretation of our common moral understanding: namely, his ascription to us of a willingness to view an act as morally motivated even if the agent's temperament is not notably warm or sympathetic and even if he must overcome considerable personal antipathy towards the beneficiary of the act in order to do what he does. It might of course be denied that we are willing to count cases like this as examples of moral motivation, but Kant's reading of our ordinary attitudes seems to me more persuasive on this point.

Standard deflationary accounts do not appear to fare much better
in attempting to meet the version of the Kantian challenge that faces
them. The task for deflationary accounts, as I have said, is to provide
an 'error theory' which will explain why it is that we regard the sense
of duty as different from any natural attitude or sentiment even
though, on such an account, it really isn't. AD accounts, however, fail
by virtue of their schematic character to take up this challenge directly
at all. And SD accounts seem forced to maintain something of very
dubious plausibility: namely, that our mistake consists in perceiving
as a distinction between the sense of duty and any sentiment whatsoever, including sympathy, something that is really a distinction
between one form that sympathy can take and all other sentiments,
including other forms of sympathy. This would mean, for example,
that the person who (as we might say) forces himself to do the right
thing, even though he must overcome great personal antipathy to do
so, should be seen as having had his antipathy outweighed by an even
more powerful sympathetic tendency.

The difficulty that standard naturalistic accounts have had in meeting the Kantian challenge is less surprising than two other difficulties
such accounts have faced. For the Kantian challenge, whatever its
ultimate force may be, is in any event a challenge to motivational
naturalism *per se*. By contrast, the other difficulties I have in mind are
generated by the need to explain two phenomena that one might
expect to be grist for the naturalist's mill, since they serve to illustrate
the complex ways in which moral motives and beliefs are implicated
in, and entwined with, important features of human psychology and
social relations.

The first phenomenon is one that I refer to as 'the resonance
of morality'. By this I mean the ramification of moral concerns
throughout our mental and social lives. Consider, for example, the
range of powerful human emotions and attitudes that seem both to
be capable of spurring us to action and, in their central forms at least,
to presuppose moral beliefs, in that they could not be experienced by
someone who had no such beliefs. Guilt, remorse, indignation, resentment, conscientiousness, and a sense of indebtedness, for
example, all seem to fall into this category. Thus, as a number of
philosophers have pointed out, one can feel angry at being ill-treated
without having any moral beliefs; but one cannot resent the ill-treatment unless one believes that it was wrong or unjustified or unfair.[1]
And one can feel kindly disposed towards a benefactor without having
any moral beliefs; but one cannot feel indebted unless one believes
that one owes something to those who have treated one well. These

simple observations, and others like them, testify to the fact that moral concerns, rather than constituting a self-contained element of human personality, are instead woven throughout the fabric of human emotion and motivation. They also testify to the interpersonal significance of moral concerns. For emotions and attitudes like those under discussion are important elements in our repertoire of interpersonal responses. Someone who actually lacked any moral beliefs, and who therefore never experienced such emotions, would be bound to strike us as humanly incomplete. Imagine, for example, a person who never felt guilt or remorse for his actions, no matter what he had done; who never felt moral outrage or indignation at the ill-treatment of another person by someone else; who never felt resentment, no matter how badly or unfairly he himself had been treated, or indebtedness, no matter how well; and so on. Not only would such a person's repertoire of human responses be significantly incomplete, but this incompleteness would tend to inhibit a range of significant attitudes and reactions towards him on the part of others, including attitudes and reactions not themselves having independent moral presuppositions. It would thus raise doubts about the desirability, if not the possibility, of entering into various sorts of human interactions and personal relations with him. If this is right, it appears both that moral concerns are implicated in a wide range of human emotions and attitudes and that a liability to experience these emotions and attitudes is in turn a prerequisite for participation in important human relationships of various kinds.[2] In this sense, moral concerns typically resonate not only throughout the personality of the individual, but throughout the web of human social relations as well.

Standard naturalistic accounts, whether revisionist or non-revisionist, offer no adequate explanation of these facts: no adequate account of how, given the content of our moral motivations, moral concerns come to have this kind of intrapersonal and interpersonal significance. Once again, the psychologically agnostic accounts, because they are schematic, contain nothing that debars them from providing an adequate explanation; but neither do they provide one. And the accounts based on sympathy are again in an even worse position. For, first, the resonance of morality casts quite general doubt on the idea of moral motivation issuing from any one discrete sentiment or self-contained conative unit. And second, it seems particularly incredible psychologically that *sympathy* should be the source of all our resentment, guilt, remorse, conscientiousness, and so on. In saying this, I am not forgetting the considerable efforts that sentimental accounts have traditionally devoted to explaining how it is that the sympathetic motive is capable of being engaged by the very wide and seemingly heterogeneous array of considerations that figure in our moral lives. Such accounts have indeed worked hard to explain how such an apparently diverse collection of considerations – considerations of rights, fairness, justice, honesty, generosity, courage, benevolence, and so forth – could all seem salient to an individual in virtue of his being sympathetic. Hume, for example, argues at great length that, despite their apparent diversity, many such considerations have in common their utility, and that it is this utility that engages the sympathetic motive. However, the problem I am now discussing has to do with the adequacy of sympathy to explain the apparent variety and complexity not of the considerations that strike us as morally salient, but rather of our own moral emotions and attitudes.

The second phenomenon that standard naturalistic accounts have difficulty in explaining is the psychological delicacy of moral motivation, its ready liability to disfigurations and deformities of various kinds, and the psychological subtlety of the features that distinguish it from those disfigurations and deformities. The importance of this phenomenon for moral philosophy, although insufficiently appreciated by many, has often been emphasized by Richard Wollheim. Consider, as two examples of the phenomenon, the kind of behaviour we describe as 'self-righteous' and the kind of attitude we classify as 'excessively moralistic'. In these two cases, each of which would repay closer examination than it has yet received from moral philosophers or than it will receive from me in this essay, our descriptions suggest that we regard morality as implicated, but in a distorted or inappropriate way, in a portion of the agent's motivational repertoire. Another example of the same thing is provided by the condition that Freud referred to, in a phrase borrowed from Nietzsche, as 'pale criminality',[3] a condition about which Richard Wollheim has published an illuminating discussion.[4] 'Pale criminality' is the condition of one who commits a crime *because*, rather than in spite, of its forbidden status and for whom the crime, rather than producing guilt, helps instead to discharge it. Here, too, morality is implicated in a motivational pattern; but everything has gone wrong, it seems, with the way it is implicated.

Other examples of the disfiguration of moral motivation could be cited, but self-righteousness, excessive moralism, and pale criminality will suffice to illustrate my present point, which is that standard naturalistic accounts offer no satisfactory explanations of such phenomena. That is, they do not provide any adequate account of the evident psychological relationships between disfigurations like those I have mentioned and appropriate moral motivation. As usual, the psychologically agnostic accounts simply do not engage the question. And the sentimental accounts leave such disfigurations looking utterly baffling and incomprehensible. For one cannot plausibly represent phenomena like self-righteousness, excessive moralism, and pale criminality as transformations or distortions of the sympathetic motive. None of them can plausibly be diagnosed as a matter of too much sympathy, say, or too little, or selective sympathy, or misplaced sympathy. Rather, the point seems to be that none of them has anything much to do with sympathy. Yet each of them seems clearly to stand in some important psychological relationship to appropriate moral motivation; so their very existence casts doubt on the adequacy of sentimental accounts.

By contrast with the standard accounts, psychoanalytic theory provides a striking example of a naturalistic theory of human motivation that has the resources to offer serious explanations of the phenomena of resonance and disfiguration. Of course, psychoanalytic theory remains extraordinarily controversial despite its profound influence on our culture, and people who reject it outright will also reject its explanations of these phenomena. Even for such people, however, the advantages of these explanations should be evident, and should therefore help both to illuminate the deficiencies of the standard accounts and to indicate some of the characteristics that satisfactory non-psychoanalytic explanations would have to have.

The classical Freudian account of moral motivation, in broad outline, goes something like this.[5] The repository of an individual's moral standards is the superego, a psychic structure that is formed in the young child as part of the process by which the child attempts to resolve its 'Oedipus complex'. During the Oedipal period, the child experiences intense sexual and aggressive wishes with respect to its parents. So intense are these desires and so undeveloped is the child's grasp of the difference between wish and deed that the child becomes greatly alarmed at the consequences that it imagines these desires will bring in their wake. It therefore seeks to withdraw some of the intense emotional energies that are focused on its parents, and is aided in doing this by a process of identification with the parents. This process, which builds on already existing identifications, involves establishing within the self a psychic structure, the superego, which resembles certain aspects of the parents as the child perceives them. These aspects include, *inter alia*, parental prohibitions against the child's fantasied sexual and aggressive behaviour, the very prohibitions responsible for the terror the child experienced in thinking about the consequences of its Oedipal wishes.

The establishment of the superego has several important results. First, the prohibitions that previously issued from external authorities now issue from within the self as well; external commands have been internalized. Second, some of the aggressive and libidinal energies previously directed at the parents are replaced by intrapsychic emotions. For example, some of the love and admiration previously directed at the parents is now directed instead at that portion of the self that has been remade in their image; in Freudian jargon, a narcissistic cathexis replaces abandoned object cathexes. And, just as important, some of the hostility and aggression previously directed at the parents is now directed by the superego against other parts of the self, against the ego in particular, and is experienced by the child as guilt. Third, whereas previously the child's primary incentives to restrain its sexual and aggressive wishes were its desire to please its parents and its fear of displeasing them, now it is motivated, in part at least, by its desire to please its own superego (to please itself) and its fear of displeasing the superego (its fear of self-punishment). With time, as the child matures socially, emotionally and intellectually, the superego is modified by new influences, including, typically, more realistic conceptions of the parents. As this happens, so too the child's moral standards develop and become more mature. The superego never altogether outgrows its origins, however, and the primitive elements that participated in its formative manifestations are always liable to reassert themselves under sufficient psychological pressure. Achieving an optimal balance among the superego and other psychic structures is invariably a difficult and delicate matter; developmental circumstances can all too easily lead either to an excessively strong superego or to a weak and underdeveloped superego, either of which is capable of making for considerable psychological trouble.

This sketchy summary overlooks many significant complexities, changes, and obscurities in Freud's various accounts of the psychology of morals. And it ignores altogether the numerous modifications, variations, and alternatives that other psychoanalytic theorists have proposed. Some of these matters will concern us later. Even this sketchy summary, however, incomplete and oversimplified though it is, suffices to indicate why psychoanalytic theory has the resources to offer more serious explanations than do the standard accounts of phenomena like the resonance of morality and the disfigurations to which moral motivation is susceptible.

Let me mention some of the most obvious of the features that enable the psychoanalytic account to provide such explanations. First, the theory represents the human personality as having a structure of extraordinary complexity, and locates our motivations to be moral in the interplay between central elements of that structure. Second, it insists that the impulse to restrain oneself which moral motivation requires does not exist from birth and does not come easily, but must instead emerge gradually out of a conflict between powerful amoral urges directed at others and an even more powerful wish for self-preservation. Third, by emphasizing the central roles of imagination and internalization in the processes by which this conflict arises and moral motivation emerges from it, the theory reveals the dependence of the end result both on the vagaries of the child's intellectual and appetitive idiosyncrasies and on highly contingent features of the child's environment, including, most dramatically, the personalities of its parents, but including also the make-up of other family members, as well as the family's material, physical, psychological, and social circumstances. Fourth, by representing moral motivation as the product of conflicts among some of the most intense motivations the young child has, and by emphasizing the hazards and complications of the process whereby moral motives are established, it makes it clear both that appropriate moral motivation involves a delicate balance among powerful psychic forces and that where, as often happens, that balance is, to one degree or another, imperfectly achieved, the results can be explosive.

In view of these features of the psychoanalytic account, I hope it is clear why I think that psychoanalytic theory has the resources to explain both the way in which moral concerns resonate throughout human personality and the ready liability of moral motivation to disfigurations and deformities of various kinds. Any other theory hoping to explain these phenomena will need to be comparably resourceful; but the standard accounts, which are either psychologically agnostic or psychologically insipid, display no such resources.[6]

I said earlier that phenomena such as the resonance of morality and the delicacy of moral motivation should be grist for the naturalist's mill, and that the inability of the standard accounts adequately to explain such phenomena was therefore more surprising than the inadequacy of their responses to the Kantian criticism. Given the greater success of psychoanalytic theory in explaining those phenomena that one would expect a naturalistic theory to be able to explain, we may well wonder whether psychoanalysis is also in a better position to respond to Kant's challenge to naturalism. And indeed it is. For, on the psychoanalytic account, the commands of the superego are not guide-lines for the satisfaction of some sentiment we feel towards other people. On the contrary, they have precisely the function of overriding sentiments, sentiments that are among the earliest and most primitive manifestations of the strongest feelings we are capable of directing towards others. Thus psychoanalytic theory has no difficulty in agreeing with Kant that we distinguish motivation by a sense of duty from motivation by sentiment or in agreeing that we ascribe to morality a very special kind of authority over our motives. Moreover, it has no difficulty explaining, in its own terms, why this is so.

It is instructive to note, as Freud did in his discussion of group psychology (xviii. 107) and as defenders of sentimental accounts certainly do, that there are close conceptual connections between sympathy and identification. In view of those connections, the psychoanalytic and sentimental accounts may be thought to have more in common than they initially appear to. We must remember, however, that whereas the psychoanalytic account singles out certain particular identifications which are said to play a vital role in the formation of the emerging personality, seeing them as the source of the mature moral attitudes which regulate our conduct towards other people, the sentimental accounts locate the ultimate source of those attitudes in our generalized capacity for sympathetic identification. And that capacity, whatever its importance, remains on the whole too weak, peripheral, and variable a psychological force to be capable of explaining the extraordinary motivational authority we attribute to morality.

Some contemporary motivational naturalists have found it congenial to express their opposition to Kant by saying that morality consists of hypothetical rather than categorical imperatives. Revealingly, Freud formulated his own view differently. 'Kant's Categorical Imperative', he wrote in 'The Economic Problem of Masochism', is 'the direct heir of the Oedipus Complex' (xix. 167). In *The Ego and the Id* he elaborated on this point as follows:

> The superego owes its special position in the ego, or in relation to the ego, to a factor which must be considered from two sides: on the one hand it was the first identification and one which took place while the ego was still feeble, and on the other hand it is the heir to the Oedipus Complex and has thus introduced the most momentous objects into the ego. . . . As the child was once under a compulsion to obey its parents, so the ego submits to the categorical imperative of its superego. (xix. 48)[7]

In saying that psychoanalysis is in a better position than the standard accounts to respond to Kant's challenge to naturalism, I do not mean to say – though neither do I wish to deny – that that response is ultimately successful. My claim is merely that the psychoanalytic response appears on the face of it to be a stronger response than those offered by the standard naturalistic accounts. How successful one thinks it is, in the end, will depend on a variety of factors, including, most obviously, one's assessment of the overall theoretical plausibility of psychoanalysis, an issue that obviously falls well outside the scope of this essay. A less ambitious question is whether the psychoanalytic account should be understood as deflationary or non-deflationary, as compatible or incompatible with our pre-philosophical understanding of moral motivation. The answer to even this less ambitious question, however, also depends on issues that are too large and too complex to address adequately here: issues about the details of the psychoanalytic account and their interpretation and about the metaphysical content of our commonsense moral attitudes.

Thus in this essay I cannot hope to arrive at a conclusion either about the ultimate success or failure of the psychoanalytic response to the Kantian challenge or about the deflationary or non-deflationary character of that response. With regard to each of these topics I must content myself with venturing a less ambitious opinion. In the first case it is the opinion, which I have already attempted to defend, that the psychoanalytic understanding of moral motivation constitutes a more formidable naturalistic opponent to the Kantian view than do the standard accounts. In the second case it is the opinion, for which I have thus far offered no defence whatsoever, that such an understanding is at least less obviously deflationary than many would suppose.

In forming the first of these opinions, I have been influenced by Richard Wollheim, who, despite occasional protests about a lack of interest in moral philosophy, is one of the few philosophers I know of who has thought seriously about the implications for moral philosophy of psychoanalytic thought. But, although I would expect Wollheim to find the first of my two opinions congenial,[8] the second marks out what I take to be an area of disagreement. Rather than attempt a general defence of my opinion, I will devote the remainder of this essay to a discussion of some specific reservations I have about Wollheim's published views on these matters. I will focus on his account of the psychology of obligation, an account he treats as having significantly deflationary implications for our understanding of that moral category.

In *The Thread of Life* (1984) Wollheim writes:

> I want to record the point, which to my way of thinking is the central contribution that moral psychology has to make to moral philosophy, that morality – that is, morality in the narrow sense, which I take (stipulatively) to be that which has obligation at its core – and value have

fundamentally different sources. One (morality) derives from introjection, the other (value) derives from projection. One is in its origins
largely defensive and largely coercive, the other is neither. One tries to
guard against fear, the other to perpetuate love. These are all exaggerations, but worth making. (p. 216)

Wollheim associates morality in his narrow sense with the superego,
but his account of the establishment of the superego, which is heavily
influenced by the work of Melanie Klein, differs markedly from the account I sketched earlier. First, although Wollheim does not make
the point explicitly, he appears to agree with Klein in conceiving of the
establishment of the superego as occurring much earlier than the
classical Freudian view would have it.[9] Second, his account differs
from the one outlined earlier in virtue of his reliance on two other
elements of Kleinian theory: namely, Klein's account of 'internal objects' and her contrast between depressive and persecutory anxiety.
Third, the processes which result in the establishment of the superego
are not thought of by Wollheim as processes of *identification*. The
superego is not the result of the child's identifying with anyone, and
initially at least it appears to the child as altogether menacing and alien.
Indeed – and this is the final point of contrast that I will mention – the
superego when first established is conceived of by Wollheim as unre-
mittingly hostile and punitive. There is no mention of it as also constituting an object of displaced admiration or as having the capacity to
dispense gratifying forms of approval and reassurance.[10] Instead, the
'two most general truths about the dominion of the superego' are said
to be that 'the dictates . . . [it] imposes on the infant are utterly alien
to him in inception' and that 'the dominant response of the infant to
the superego is terror' (p. 201).

Wollheim says that the harsh and alien character of the superego
means that

> Morality faces a challenge of remarkable gravity, which can be put very
> simply: Morality is from first to last, in its origins and throughout our
> lives, simply a price that we pay, and go on and on paying, for relief
> from external fear. We interiorize the fear by substituting an internal
> for an external object, we placate the internal representative of the fear
> by the sacrifice of instinctual gratification, the gain in tranquility out-
> weighs even the crippling loss in satisfaction, but the sacrifice has
> nothing independently to recommend it. (pp. 204–5)

He adds that this challenge can be met and morality provided with
a 'happier interpretation' (p. 205) if one or both of two things can be

shown to be true. The first is that the establishment of the superego satisfies some significant need other than relief from fear, and the second is that the subsequent development of the superego provides some benefit other than the continued avoidance of fear. He goes on to argue that both these things are in fact true, and in both cases his argument assigns, or is said to assign, an important role to value. Value, according to Wollheim, 'originates in the projection of archaic bliss, of love satisfied' (p. 215). It exerts, or is capable of exerting, a 'softening influence' (p. 218) on obligation. And the integration of value and obligation produces 'morality broadly conceived'. As Wollheim puts it, 'Morality broadly conceived is an amalgam of morality narrowly conceived and the sense of value: it is morality constructed at once upon obligation and upon goodness' (p. 221).

However, even when obligation is integrated with value and thus set within the context of morality in the broad sense, Wollheim does not believe that all our ordinary thinking about obligation can be vindicated. He writes:

> Whatever may be the content of obligation, obligation itself is primarily self-directed. It is self-directed, though it may be other-regarding. For it expresses itself in a thought that a person has about what *he* ought to do: though he may well, and appropriately, think that what he ought to do is something for the benefit of others. It is also true that a person may well have thoughts about what others ought to do, but my conviction is that either these thoughts do not express obligations or they require some circuitous interpretation. For they have no clear root in our psychology. Often they aren't in place, and then they represent the presumptuousness, the arrogance, for which morality is such a traditional medium of expression. (pp. 224–5)

Taken together, Wollheim's account of the psychological origins of obligation, his description of the contrasting psychological characters of value and obligation, his distinction between the narrow and broad conceptions of morality, and his remarks about the inappropriateness of third-person ascriptions of obligation combine to create a highly deflationary picture of obligation and its psychological roots.

However, it seems to me that that picture is not supported by the details of Wollheim's own account of the psychology of obligation. Recall the challenge to morality that Wollheim describes and his understanding of what is required if the challenge is to be met. The challenge is to demonstrate that morality is something more than just a price we pay for relief from fear; and it can be met by showing either that the setting up of the superego satisfies some need in addition to relief from fear or that the subsequent development of the superego provides some benefit beyond continued avoidance of fear, or both. As I have said, Wollheim suggests that both these things can be shown. The need that is met by the establishment of the superego is the child's need to control its aggression once it accomplishes the cognitive feat of recognizing that the person toward whom it has been directing that aggression is the very same person as the person it loves. The benefit that is provided by the development of the superego, under favourable circumstances, is a transition from what Wollheim calls 'mere internalization' to identification; from a state of affairs in which the superego is menacing and alien to one in which it is identified with and comes to constitute a personal ideal. Wollheim, exploiting a famously problematic shift in Freud's use of terminology,[11] suggests that this transition may be described as the evolution of the superego into the ego-ideal. As a result of this evolution, he says, a 'preoccupation with what a person should do gets overlaid by a concern about how he should be' (p. 219).

On the face of it, what is striking about these two claims that Wollheim makes for the superego is that, if accepted, they undermine the view of obligation as exclusively a defence against terror, and they do so without in any obvious way invoking value. In other words, they appear to represent more benign aspects of the psychology of obligation itself, rather than the 'softening influence' of value on obligation. In the first case, obligation serves to perpetuate love, despite the fact that that role is explicitly assigned by Wollheim, in the passage contrasting the origins of obligation and value which I quoted, to value as opposed to obligation. In the second case, the development of the superego into the ego-ideal is a result not of projection, which is the mechanism associated by Wollheim with the psychology of value, but rather of what he calls a shift in the 'grade' of internalization. And internalization, as Wollheim uses the term, is part of introjection, the mechanism he associates with the psychology of obligation.[12] The upshot is that the features of the superego that make it possible to answer the challenge to morality, to the extent that it can be answered, do not represent the influence of value on obligation or the amalgamation of the one with the other. They are, instead, internal to the psychology of obligation as Wollheim has described it.

Why does Wollheim think otherwise? I must confess that I do not know. It is true that his discussion, in connection with the first of the two features, of the need to control aggression so as to preserve love leads him into an elaboration of the idea that love generates, *via* projection, a perception of the beloved as good or valuable. But nothing in the latter idea alters the fact that it is the superego and the obligations associated with it that satisfy the need for control of aggression which love is said to require. In any case, Wollheim himself says that 'value clearly has a bigger role to play' (p. 216) in connection with the second feature of the superego – its transition into the ego-ideal.

The section of his book that deals with that transition (ch. 7, § 10) is framed by two sentences which assert the importance of the connection between value and obligation. In the sentence that immediately precedes the section, Wollheim speaks of 'the literalism, the legalism, that impose themselves on the injunctions and prohibitions that issue from the superego – until they in turn fall under the softening influence of value' (pp. 217–18), and he concludes the sentence by saying that it is to the latter point that he turns next. In the sentence that immediately follows the section, Wollheim gives his definition of morality broadly conceived as an amalgam of value and obligation. Thus the sentence immediately preceding the section indicates that it *will* be concerned with the relation of value and obligation and the sentence immediately following the section indicates that it *was* concerned with that relation. Yet, as I have said, the section itself is devoted to a discussion of the transition from the superego to the ego-ideal, and, as I have also said, Wollheim's account of that transition does not in any obvious way invoke either value or projection. It focuses instead on a change in the 'grade' of internalization: on the shift from 'mere internalization' to identification. It concerns the process by which a previously introjected figure ceases to seem alien and terrifying and comes instead to be identified with. The psychology of value, as Wollheim has characterized it, plays no role. Thus there appears to be a discrepancy between, on the one hand, Wollheim's explicit remarks associating the transition from the superego to the ego-ideal with the beneficial influence of value on obligation and, on the other hand, his more detailed description of that transition itself.

It will naturally be objected at this point that the very notion of an ego-ideal falls under the heading of value, for it depends on the idea of certain forms of personality or ways of living being prized, admired, or valued. In so far as Wollheim suggests that the transition from the superego to the ego-ideal has something to do with value, it will be said, this must surely be what he has in mind. And indeed, this interpretation seems to be confirmed by the passage in which he warns that the ego-ideal, for all the benefits it brings, also makes possible a narcissism in which a person sees himself as 'the source of all value that he needs' (p. 221). (This, incidentally, is the only time that the word 'value' appears in the section discussing the transition from the superego to the ego-ideal.)

Now it may well be that this objection correctly identifies the connection Wollheim sees between value and the ego-ideal. Moreover, the objection may well be correct in asserting that there *is* such a connection. However, the question is what the objection shows. For the fact remains that, on Wollheim's account, the ego-ideal – with whatever connections to value it may have – emerges from a change in the 'grade' of internalization, and that internalization is part of the mechanism associated by him with the psychology of obligation. The ego-ideal does not derive from projection, which is the mechanism associated by Wollheim with the psychology of value. Thus the effect of the objection, if it is correct, is to support Wollheim's claim that there is a connection between the ego-ideal and value, but only at the cost of undermining the sharp distinction he draws between the psychology of value and the psychology of obligation.

This point can be pressed further. Each of the two 'redeeming' features of the superego that Wollheim mentions might be taken as revealing a way in which the psychologies of value and obligation, when functioning effectively, are mutually entwined. In the one case, obligation perpetuates love, the same love that projects value. In the other case, an alteration in the psychological processes by which the sense of obligation is established and sustained makes possible both a new dimension of value and a modification in the sense of obligation itself.

Wollheim's discussion of the transition from superego to ego-ideal is followed by an appreciation of John Stuart Mill. Wollheim sees Mill as having recognized the differing sources of obligation and value and as having gone to great lengths to integrate the claims of those two disparate moral categories. If there is anything at all curious in this, it is the implied suggestion that Mill was unusual in seeking to bring the claims of obligation and value into harmony. Surely attempts to integrate obligation and value – the right and the good – are central to the agenda of moral philosophy as standardly conceived.[13] And although Wollheim may well be correct in suggesting that the task of integration can be illuminated by an attention to the psychological bases of the two categories, it would be surprising if what we discovered at the psychological level were two radically independent structures or processes, one fearful and punitive, concerned exclusively with obligation and what one should (not) do, the other loving and reparative, concerned exclusively with value and what one should be.

After all, a conception of what one should do implies a great deal about the kind of person one should be, and a conception of what one should be implies a great deal about the kinds of things one should do. Thus it would be a considerable surprise if the psychologies of being and doing proved to be anything other than multiply interwoven. And nothing in psychoanalytic thinking on these matters, either as Wollheim reports it or as reflected in the extensive psychoanalytical literature on the relation between the superego and the ego-ideal,[14] seems to me to support such a surprising conclusion.

It remains only to add that I see very little in all of this to encourage the thought that obligation is primarily self-directed or that third-person ascriptions of obligation are generally inappropriate. Wollheim says in *The Thread of Life* that thoughts about the obligations of other people 'have no clear root in our psychology' (p. 225). This claim seems to me implausible on the face of it, since it is hard to see how a pattern of assessment and judgement that is so firmly entrenched in human practice could lack secure roots in our psychology. How, then, would its prevalence and persistence be explained? Wollheim says – and this may be his answer – that often such thoughts 'represent the presumptuousness, the arrogance, for which morality is such a traditional medium of expression' (p. 225). But this remark is not altogether consistent with the claim of rootlessness, since arrogance and presumptuousness themselves typically have clear roots in our psychology. More important, the claim of rootlessness seems inconsistent with the considerations concerning the resonance of morality discussed earlier. In particular, the human importance of resentment and related attitudes testifies to the secure place that thoughts about the obligations of others have in our psychology. Even if it is supposed, however, that thoughts about one's own obligations have roots in individual psychology that are stronger or genetically prior to or simply different from any roots that thoughts about the obligations of others may have, it does not follow from this that thoughts of the latter type are not 'in place' (p. 225). After all, thoughts about one's own happiness, one's own desires, and for that matter one's own mind may, with as much or as little initial plausibility, be said to have psychological roots that are similarly to be distinguished from their third-person counterparts, but that does not – scepticism aside – make the counterpart thoughts inappropriate. If it is said that assignments of obligation involve the ascription of reasons for action and that they differ in this way from thoughts about people's happiness, desires, or minds, it must be asked why this difference is significant and whether the move from the first to the third person is just as problematic in the case of other, non-moral reasons for action or in the case of reasons for belief. And although Wollheim is certainly correct to remind us of the way in which moral judgement is all too often used as a vehicle for the expression of arrogance and presumptuousness, it must be remembered that human arrogance expresses itself in many ways and that, as I'm sure Wollheim would agree, it is not unheard of for it to manifest itself as disparagement of the 'literalism' and 'legalism' of obligation in the name of some allegedly more refined or sublime set of values.

None of this goes to show, by any stretch of the imagination, that the psychoanalytic understanding of moral motivation is fully compatible with our ordinary conception. I hope it helps to indicate, however, why I think that the issues in this area are less clear cut than they may sometimes seem.

NOTES

1 John Rawls writes: 'To deny that self-interested persons are capable of resentment and indignation is not of course to say that they cannot be angry and annoyed with one another. A person without a sense of justice may be enraged at someone who fails to act fairly. But anger and annoyance are distinct from indignation and resentment; they are not, as the latter are, moral emotions' (*A Theory of Justice* (Harvard University Press, Cambridge, Mass., 1971), p. 488). And Bernard Williams says that if an amoralist objects 'to other people treating him as he treats them, this will be perfectly consistent so long as his objecting consists just in such things as his not liking it and fighting back. What he cannot consistently do is *resent* it or disapprove of it, for these are attitudes within the moral system' (*Morality: An Introduction to Ethics* (Harper and Row, New York, 1972), pp. 3–4).

2 Rawls writes: 'The moral feelings are a normal feature of human life. We could not do away with them without at the same time eliminating certain natural attitudes . . . [A] person who lacks a sense of justice, and who would never act as justice requires except as self-interest and expediency prompt, not only is without ties of friendship, affection, and mutual trust, but is incapable of experiencing resentment and indignation. He lacks certain natural attitudes and moral feelings of a particularly elementary kind. Put another way, one who lacks a sense of justice lacks certain fundamental attitudes and capacities included under the notion of humanity' (*Theory of Justice*, pp. 487–8). See also P. F. Strawson, 'Freedom and Resentment', in *Freedom and Resentment and Other Essays* (London, Methuen, 1974).

[3] See Freud, 'Some Character-Types Met with in Psycho-Analytic Work' (xiv. 311-33).

[4] Wollheim, 'Crime, Punishment, and Pale Criminality' (1988).

[5] Many of Freud's writings touch on one or another aspect of the psychology of morals. However, the following works are especially significant: 'On Narcissism: an Introduction' (xiv. 73–102); 'Mourning and Melancholia' (xiv. 243–58); *Group Psychology and the Analysis of the Ego* (xviii. 69–143); *The Ego and the Id* (xix. 12–66); 'The Economic Problem of Masochism' (xix. 159–70); 'The Dissolution of the Oedipus Complex' (xix. 173–9); *Civilization and its Discontents* (xxi. 64–145); *New Introductory Lectures on Psycho-Analysis* (xxii. 5–182). There is a reasonably clear statement of what I am calling the 'classical Freudian account' in C. Brenner, *An Elementary Textbook of Psychoanalysis* (International Universities Press, New York, 1955).

[6] It should be noted, however, that psychoanalysis stands in different relationship to the agnostic and sentimental accounts. It is incompatible with the sentimental accounts, for the psychoanalytic and sentimental answers to the question of what in particular motivates moral conduct are inconsistent. By contrast, there appears to be no fundamental inconsistency between the psychoanalytic and agnostic accounts; for the latter, which are schematic, may be supplemented by some more specific answer to the question of what in particular motivates moral conduct, and the psychoanalytic account, provided that it can appropriately be interpreted as deeming moral conduct to be motivated by 'desire', represents one possible supplement. Still, the fact remains that the agnostic accounts by themselves do not offer serious explanations of the phenomena under discussion.

[7] Freud's reference here to the superego as 'the first identification' may appear to conflict with my earlier remark that, on the Freudian view, the process of identification that forms the superego 'builds on already existing identifications'. However, elsewhere in *The Ego and the Id* (ch. 3), Freud himself suggests that the process of identification that forms the superego often consists in an 'intensification' of an identification that is already present and pre-dates the Oedipus complex. The apparent inconsistency between these two passages from *The Ego and the Id* appears to be resolved by some remarks that Freud makes in the *New Introductory Lectures*. There he says that the formation of the child's superego results from 'a strong intensification of the identifications with his parents which have probably long been present in his ego', but adds that this 'intensification' represents the first time that identifications are produced or strengthened in compensation for object loss, and that it therefore has a special 'emotional importance' (xxii. 64). The passage from *The Ego and the Id* which speaks of the superego as 'the first identification', when placed in the context of the full paragraph from which it has been excerpted, admits of a consistent interpretation along the

same lines, and this was presumably the interpretation that Freud intended.

[8]   In *The Good Self and the Bad Self* (1976), Wollheim says that he is inclined to regard naturalism concerning 'the origin of morals' as 'not only the one form in which naturalism is acceptable but the form in which it is correct' (p. 24).

[9]   It should be noted that in recent years there has been increasing acceptance among non-Kleinian psychoanalytic theorists of the idea of pre-Oedipal superego developments. See on this point J. Arlow, 'Problems of the Superego Concept', *Psychoanalytic Study of the Child*, 37 (1982), pp. 229–44; R. Gillman, 'Pre-œdipal and Early Oedipal Components of the Superego', *Psychoanalytic Study of the Child*, 37 (1982), pp. 273–81; A. Holder, 'Pre-œdipal Contributions to the Formation of the Superego', *Psychoanalytic Study of the Child*, 37 (1982), pp. 245–72.

[10] For a discussion urging the importance of these aspects of the superego, see R. Schafer, 'The Loving and Beloved Superego in Freud's Structural Theory', *Psychoanalytic Study of the Child*, 15 (1960), pp. 163–88.

[11] For discussions of this shift, see J. Sandler, A. Holder, and D. Meers, 'The Ego Ideal and the Ideal Self', *Psychoanalytic Study of the Child*, 18 (1963), pp. 139–58; R. Schafer, 'Ideals, the Ego Ideal, and the Ideal Self', in *Motives and Thought: Psychoanalytic Essays in Honor of David Rapaport* (Psychological Issues, vol. 5, Monograph 18/19), ed. R. Holt (International Universities Press, New York, 1967), pp. 131–74; J. Strachey, Introduction to Freud, *The Ego and the Id* (xix. 3–11).

[12] For Wollheim's use of the terms 'identification', 'incorporation', 'internalization', and 'introjection', see *The Thread of Life* (1984), pp. 120–9. It should be noted that psychoanalytic writers differ considerably in the ways they use these four terms and that this has sometimes created significant confusion. For a systematic discussion of these issues, see R. Schafer, *Aspects of Internalization* (International Universities Press, New York, 1967). See also R. Schafer, 'Internalization: Process or Fantasy?', *Psychoanalytic Study of the Child*, 27 (1972), pp. 411–36.

[13] In *Psychoanalysis and Moral Values* (International Universities Press, New York, 1960), Heinz Hartmann writes: 'This distinction between the ego ideal and other aspects of the superego has been seen and formulated in many philosophies of morals, as the distinction between 'the good' and the 'ought and ought not' – the imperatives. Actually, in all ethical systems both elements are represented though in different degrees' (p. 28).

[14] See Arlow, 'Problems of the Superego Concept'; O. Fenichel, *The Psychoanalytic Theory of Neurosis* (Norton, New York, 1945); Hartmann, *Psychoanalysis and Moral Values*; Hartmann and R. Loewenstein, 'Notes on the Superego', *Psychoanalytic Study of the Child*, 17 (1962), pp. 42–81; E. Jacobson, 'The Self and the Object World: Vicissitudes of their Infantile Cathexes and their Influence on Ideational and Affective Development', *Psychoanalytic Study of the Child*, 9 (1954), pp. 75–127;

J. Lampl-de Groot, 'Ego Ideal and Superego', *Psychoanalytic Study of the Child*, 17 (1962), pp. 94–106; S. Novey, 'The Role of the Superego and Ego-Ideal in Character Formation', *International Journal of Psychoanalysis*, 36 (1955), pp. 254–9; H. Nunberg, *Principles of Psychoanalysis* (International Universities Press, New York, 1955); G. Piers and M. Singer, *Shame and Guilt* (Charles Thomas, Springfield, Ill., 1953); A. Reich, 'Early Identifications as Archaic Elements in the Superego', *Journal of the American Psychoanalytic Association*, 2 (1954), pp. 218–38; *idem*, 'Pathologic Forms of Self-Esteem Regulation', *Psychoanalytic Study of the Child*, 15 (1960), pp. 215–32; J. Sandler, 'On the Concept of Superego', Psychoanalytic Study of the Child, 15 (1960), pp. 128–62; Sandler, Holder, and Meers, 'The Ego Ideal and the Ideal Self'; J. Sandler and B. Rosenblatt, 'The Concept of the Representational World', *Psychoanalytic Study of the Child*, 17 (1962), pp. 128–45; R. Schafer, 'The Loving and Beloved Superego in Freud's Structural Theory'; *idem*, 'Ideals, the Ego Ideal, and the Ideal Self'; R. Spitz, 'On the Genesis of Superego Components', *Psychoanalytic Study of the Child*, 13 (1958), pp. 375–404.

6

Three Types of Projectivism

A. W. PRICE

The beauty of that fair-faced boy, for instance, sitting with his head bowed over his manuscript in a hollow he had chosen between the sand-dunes and the sea – it was there now only because he, Linton, was there, and after he had passed it would be gone. For there was no such thing as beauty apart from a human interpretation of it. The beauty Linton saw in that seated figure was relative to himself. For those seagulls it did not exist; for the next person who went by it might not exist: and it was the feeling it aroused in him which he was no longer able to express.

Forrest Reid, *Brian Westby*

(1) It has become a commonplace that 'realism', not least in the context of values, is a single catchword that, capturing no single position, demands defining or discarding.[1] It will be a contention of this essay that the same is true of one opposed label, 'projectivism'. This term may be, or has been, attached to at least three different, if related, positions, which have been variously championed: what I shall call 'reductive projectivism' has been argued by Simon Blackburn,[2] 'nihilistic projectivism' by J. L. Mackie,[3] and 'genetic projectivism' by Richard Wollheim.[4] The view that I shall come to is that only the second and third merit the title 'projectivism', and that of these only the last is plausible. I shall end by trying out the projectivist project psychoanalytically, along lines that I rather intend to be illustrative than hope to be illuminating. My goal will be the prospect of an understanding that, itself impartial with regard to any plausible forms of 'realism' or 'anti-realism' about values, may take the heat out of that old quarrel; however, all I can hope to deliver, here or

anywhere, is the prospect, and not the understanding itself. I am indebted to Wollheim for pointing the way, with an eye to reality and not to fashion, in pages that are compelling but all too concise; may my stumblings elicit further directions.

(2) Take a particular aesthetic experience: I am looking at a sunset, discriminating the specific colouring that holds for a few minutes and appreciating it aesthetically; that is, I suggest, responding with that specific sentiment which that colouring calls forth. I may thereby count as perceiving in the sunset a specific beauty. How are the sentiment and the beauty related here?[5]

The colouring and the sentiment are related *externally*, by a causal relation: the colouring happens, because I have a certain sensibility, to evoke the sentiment in me.[6] But the beauty and the sentiment are related not externally, but *internally*: they are related not in that the beauty causes the sentiment (only the colouring *cum* the sensibility do that), but in that to perceive that beauty *is* to feel that sentiment (or at least, in a less happy case, where I have a migraine, say, to feel the lack of that sentiment – cf. Coleridge's poignant line 'I see, not feel, how beautiful they are!'); further, that sentiment is precisely – supposing that its physiognomy is precise – the affective aspect of *that* perception. At the tightest, there is no cognitive route to that beauty that does not run by way of that sentiment, and no psychological route to that sentiment that does not run by way of that perception.[7] To the interrelation of beauty and sentiment we may apply this sentence from David Wiggins: 'Surely an adequate account of these matters will have to treat psychological states and their objects as equal and reciprocal partners, and is likely to need to see the identifications of the states and of the properties under which the states subsume their objects as interdependent.'[8] I once called this mutual relationship 'the image of a modern marriage';[9] Blackburn, in a letter to me, called it, less respectfully, a 'mystical marriage'. My phrase earned his, but neither does full justice to the interdependency: each partner lives solely for the other. It is true that the sentiment may be lacking, not just because I fail to feel it, but because no one with my sensibility is looking at the sunset during the crucial minutes. Contrariwise (though less conceivably in a case of precise appreciation), the beauty may be lacking, at least to the sunset, because I am misperceiving its colouring. It remains the case that the beauty is operative, so to speak, only in the sentiment (it cannot show up in any other way); while the sentiment is not only aesthetic, and so perceptual, but perceptive precisely of *this* beauty

(3)   So far, I believe, this is all true; but it can seem mysterious (a 'mystical marriage' indeed). Perhaps the mystery can only be dispelled by denying or qualifying the equality. May not the sentiment come first and the sunset be dressed by the sentiment in borrowed robes? May not, in suggestive jargon, the beauty be created in the mind's eye by 'projecting' the sentiment? Seductive, possibly, is a famous passage in David Hume:

> Thus the distinct boundaries and offices of *reason* and of *taste* are easily ascertained. The former conveys the knowledge of truth and falsehood: the latter gives the sentiment of beauty and deformity, vice and virtue. The one discovers objects as they really stand in nature, without addition or diminution: the other has a productive faculty, and gilding or staining all natural objects with the colours, borrowed from internal sentiment, raises in a manner a new creation.[10]

But before we are seduced, we need to distinguish different possible interpretations of Hume's position. One is *reductive projectivism*. It is implicit in this remark by Blackburn: 'A moral *sensibility* . . . is defined by a function from *input* of belief to *output* of attitude.'[11] To apply this to my aesthetic example, an aesthetic sensibility is defined by a function from input of dispassionate perception to output of sentiment. Implicit here is the view that the notions of belief or perception have no role to play in characterizing the attitude or sentiment, which (at least in principle) is specifiable independently of any mention of a value possibly attaching to its object. Talk of perceiving an aesthetic value in an object is reducible to a description of a sentiment accompanying a perception of, for example, a colouring.

Another interpretation is *nihilistic projectivism*, nihilistic in that it denies that the value really exists. Mackie provides a forthright statement:

> Although the only hard fact of the matter is that the speaker and others have or would have certain sentiments, . . . we tend to project these sentiments onto the actions or characters that arouse them, or read some sort of image of these sentiments into them, so that we think of those actions and characters as possessing, objectively and intrinsically, certain distinctively moral features; but these features are fictitious.[12]

Presumably the ficticity goes with the objectivity, but what is that? One possibility, in application to my aesthetic example, is this: we think of the beauty of the sunset as externally related, as a cause, to the sentiment; but all in the sunset that causes my sentiment is its colouring.

Thirdly, there is *genetic projectivism*. This holds that sentiments, of a kind, come first: there are primitive sentiments which precede any evaluations and whose projection is the genesis of values. But it doubts whether the educated sentiments that develop out of those are specifiable independently of values. In the aesthetic case, it all began, let us suppose at the onset of puberty, when sunsets began to produce feelings in me; but my present sentiments would not be what they are if they were not experiences of *seeing* beauties *in* sunsets.

Do we have to choose between these as alternatives? Genetic projectivism is diachronic in explanation, whereas reductive projectivism is synchronic in analysis; the relation of either of them to nihilistic projectivism demands reflection. I shall now argue that reductive projectivism, as I have just defined it, should not be called 'projectivism' at all; that nihilistic projectivism *is* a form of projectivism but an implausible one, whose nihilism is unnecessary; and that genetic projectivism holds out the best promise of success in de-mystifying aesthetic values, with maximum psychological understanding (though, in any specific form, with a lot of psycho-theoretical baggage) and minimum philosophical *parti pris*.

(4) As we meet it in Blackburn's writings, reductive projectivism purports to be at once projectivist in nature and reductionist in aspiration. (As I stated its second aspect above, it takes talk of perceiving an aesthetic value in an object to be reducible to a description of a sentiment accompanying a perception itself dispassionate.) But I have difficulty in reconciling these two aspects. So, perhaps, does Blackburn himself, as surfaces in a vacillation within his terminology. Projectivism$_1$ interprets the sense of some class of utterances as constituted by their role in expressing attitudes or sentiments which are not descriptive, in that their content is not to be glossed as inviting the ascription of truth or falsity.[13] Projectivism$_2$ makes the claim that we 'project' such an attitude 'when we speak and think as though there were a property of things which our sayings describe, which we can reason about, be wrong about, and so on'.[14] The difference is clear: that we do speak and even think in such ways may tell *prima facie* against projectivism$_1$, while it is explicitly asserted by projectivism$_2$. In either case, it is the task of what Blackburn calls 'quasi-realism' to show that 'even on anti-realist grounds there is nothing improper, nothing "diseased" in projected predicates';[15] but the notion of projection becomes elusive. How does projectivism$_2$ relate to projectivism$_1$, and to quasi-realism? The thesis that we are not merely speaking, but even thinking, 'as though' about properties of things is

ıbly problematic; for we have been told both that the sentiments are not in fact descriptive (in Hume's term, representative), and also that, even given a penurious ontology, there is nothing unapt about how we express them in language or develop them in thought.[16] If the idea is that we really *are* speaking and thinking about 'properties of things', not indeed as a realist might intend that phrase, but in the only sense that it can intelligibly bear,[17] then 'as though' becomes out of place; for it turns out that in one sense (quasi-realist and permissible) our evaluative words and thoughts can be successfully descriptive, while in another (realist and impermissible) they are not even putatively descriptive.[18] 'Projection' becomes in effect a phenomenon of grammar, not a tool of explanation. Blackburn's projectivism reduces to the observation that in evaluations attitudes or sentiments are expressed by nouns and adjectives. I conclude that his account is 'projectivist' only in name.

That might, of course, be a virtue: is anything lacking in an account of values that is rather expressivist than projectivist? Blackburn makes an interesting concession in contrasting aesthetic with moral values:

> Sometimes the beauty of a thing needs perception, and cannot be told. Whereas when it cannot be told how good something was, this is always because some other fact about it resists communication . . . So . . . I incline to find the projective nature of morality much better motivated than the projective theory applied to aesthetic evaluation.[19]

He is supposing an opposition between perceptual and projectivist models of our relation to values, so that values that have to be seen to be appreciated (such as physical beauty) are more recalcitrant for projectivism than values (such as moral goodness) that may be applied at a distance.[20] I suggest that this is true of what is better called 'expressivism', while the opposite holds of projectivism properly so called. It is typical of moral values to be more articulate than aesthetic ones. This derives from two factors, social and psychological: moral values are commonly imparted through the enunciation of moral principles; and these are internalized in the super-ego, which is imagined as addressing to its host prescriptions and prohibitions that are universal as well as particular. As a consequence, the ascription of a moral value to an action invites a degree of disentangling: to call an act 'brave' is to describe its natural features (with whatever vagueness) while expressing an attitude towards acts of that kind which involves the ego's respect for the super-ego's injunctions.[21] Now there are aesthetic judgements that are equally transmissible: take the crude rankings of composers or poets, say, without which the novice would not know where to begin. But it is by a living etymology that aesthetic values show up in perceptual experience and not in imagination or description; physical beauty, for example, must be seen to be recognized (if not to be believed) and, if reported, has always, ultimately, to be taken on trust.[22] Tautologously, physical beauty is perceived in subjacent physical features, but with a complication: beauty suffuses a face, so that all its features seem beautiful, and identifying the beautifying features requires experiment that is not thought-experiment. If, for these reasons, aesthetic valuation resists generalization, it invites not semantic analysis (disentangling from the affective response a dispassionate description that is relevant, restricted, and repeatable), but empirical diagnosis. It is no accident that we speak naturally of moral *attitudes* but aesthetic *sentiments*. Moral attitudes focus on the natural properties that underlie moral values; about what it is like to have the attitudes, there may be nothing distinctive to be said.[23] Aesthetic sentiments focus on the aesthetic values that supervene on natural properties; they possess a distinctive phenomenology germane to the values. Now expressivism replaces talk of values by talk of attitudes and natural properties; but where we have sentiments with a phenomenology answering to values, we must attend to the values to grasp the phenomenology. Here, I believe, is where there is most clearly room, and need, for a genuine projectivism.

(5)   We owe to Wollheim a distinction between *simple* and *complex* projection that is the beginning of understanding. I quote from *Painting as an Art*:

> In its simple form the course of projection runs as follows: A person is, say, sad; his sadness causes him anxiety; as a result of this anxiety, he projects his sadness on to some other figure in the environment; now he no longer believes that he is sad, but he believes that this other figure is sad . . . The course of projection in its complex form runs as follows: A person is (to re-use the example) sad; his sadness causes him anxiety; as a result of this anxiety he projects his sadness on to, more generally, the external world; and now, along with no longer believing that he is sad, perhaps no longer being sad, he begins to experience the external world as of a piece with his sadness (p. 82).[24]

In happier cases, where the feeling is positive, the anxiety will be not because of it, but on behalf of it; and the subject will be not expelling but preserving it, so that it takes on a double life, both in his mind and in the world. Crucial for us is less the function of projecting the emotion than the notion of experiencing the world as 'of a piece with' sadness (or whatever the emotion may be). It remains open that one may *call* the world 'sad', but this usage will be metaphorical.[25] There are limits here; as Wollheim observes, 'When a person is depressed and he projects his depression on to the world, he is not said to experience the world as depressed' (p. 84). He suggests that this reflects 'no principled difference', but 'a mere quirk of usage' (pp. 84–5). Yet one may doubt whether depression invites projection as sadness does: being sad, I enter into the world to the extent that it can be seen as reflecting my sadness; being depressed, I lose interest in entering into the world, so that it strikes me as blank and feature-less, not as reflecting my depression (even though it would not look otherwise if it *were* doing so), but as remaining at a distance. If I am to see the world as sad, I must enter imaginatively into it, and it must have features into which sadness can migrate. (Thus sadness feels imprisoned in sunshine.) Between outer and inner worlds there must be, as Wollheim puts it in *The Thread of Life* (1984), 'a real match or correspondence' (p. 214); metaphor is apt in alerting us to 'the sym-bolic, the emblematic, the awareness of match observed and the elaboration of match invented' (p. 215). Whereas simple projection may be indiscriminate, so that anyone may seem the paranoiac's enemy (p. 214), complex projection is sensitive to, and inventive of, correspondences between feelings and phenomena. Simple projection is like hallucinating, complex like 'seeing-in'. In Aristotelian termino-logy, the object provides the matter and the feeling the form; but not any matter is receptive to any form. Complex projection, unlike simple, thrives on discrimination.

This is also true of a second variety of complex projection, 'where novel predication is brought into play' (p. 215). This variety is our topic: 'This is what the assignment of value is – projection of a complex form, which on the level of judgment is represented by the applica-tion of a new predicate introduced for this very purpose' (ibid.). The internal relation of value to sentiment, definitive at least of aes-thetic value, is thus underpinned by a genetic hypothesis: aesthetic values are perceived in objects (rather than total scenes) that have invited the projection of sentiments by reason of correspondences. We at once face many questions: What is projected? How is it projected? What view of values follows? Until we have answers of a kind, we cannot tell whether we have a theory or just a picture. If projection is not to be a phantasm, we must spell it out as a form of phantasy.

(6) Suppose that there is a call for a projectivism that better fits its name than Blackburn's. What form should it take? I have said nothing explicitly that tells against my second variety, *nihilistic projectivism*; even if the correspondences (which explain *what* gets projected *where*) are real enough, whether they were discovered or elaborated, the values themselves risk showing up as illusions. And a fuller account of projection as a phantasy that presupposes a primitive conception of sentiment may invite a nihilism about values as the only rational corrective. Within a passage in *Painting as an Art* all of which invites attention, Wollheim writes as follows: 'The initiating phantasy represents the emotion as being expelled from the body and then spread or smeared across some part of the world, and the primitive nature of the mental functioning to which projection belongs is revealed in the highly physical or corporeal way in which . . . the expulsive phantasy envisages mental phenomena' (p. 84). In so following Melanie Klein, he rescues projection from the realm of metaphor, and gives it substance.[26] He then remarks that it is an 'enduring effect' of projection as phantasy that it 'dyes the world', thus reminding us of Hume's metaphor of 'gilding or staining' in a context that suggests that the effect is unreal. If the mental functioning is so primitive, its success may be taken to be chimerical, so that unconscious phantasy leaves behind a deposit of falsity to disfigure judgement. However, I am not aware that Wollheim himself ever draws that inference.[27] And part of his account may tell against it: when complex projection is signalled by a predicate (like 'sad') that 'doubles up', the effect is metaphor, not untruth; so we might expect new predicates (like 'beautiful') to take on a sense free of falsehood. After all, phantasy is unconscious, linguistic invention conscious; projective phantasy is the cause of evaluations whose content need not be phantastic. Part of the sense of a predicate may be the perspective within which it can properly be seen as having application. Colours provide a useful analogy: someone who failed to realize that the term 'red', say, is applied to objects by human beings *speaking as human beings* (with the consequence that he felt impelled either to dismiss its application as false, or to reinterpret it relationally, say in terms of how *we* are disposed to see things), would be mistaking its meaning. Analogously, it is plausible to suppose, value-talk is relative (which contrasts with relational):[28] valuers are speaking as human beings about the human world – or, more exactly, about aspects of the human world that fall outside the world that, as scientists, we may reasonably hope to come closer to sharing with intelligent creatures of any species or planet.[29] It is not to be hastily supposed that this talk implicitly has ideas above

its station, say, by purporting to be speaking from a point of view from which no values could ever show up.[30]

Any philosopher who saddles values with insupportable pretensions at least owes us a clear account of what these are. Mackie's pair of terms, 'objective' and 'intrinsic', is hardly clear enough. A more definite pretension would be this: conceivably we speak and think of values as if they were *causes* of valuations; that is, as if they related to sentiments as causes and not as projections. However, this would be an error *a priori*; why suppose that we make it – let alone that it infects the very concept of a value?[31] That we all speak of 'perceiving' values (as easily when engaged in appreciation as when engaged in the philosophy of appreciation) signifies nothing, for two reasons: first, because what we are said to perceive can be an object and not a cause of the perception;[32] and second, because here, as perhaps everywhere in philosophy, 'it is not what you finish by saying, but how you manage to say it, that matters'.[33] Thus the appeal of nihilistic projectivism is to be resisted; I do not believe that it can take on a form at once precise and plausible.

(7) The positive aspirations of *genetic projectivism* are best displayed in illustrative detail (as they will be in § 8); but what it does *not* claim can be set out briefly through contrast, partly now as news, partly in recapitulation.

The reductive projectivist (who, I have argued, would better be described as a 'reductive expressivist') accepts my initial truisms as ways of speaking, but hopes to explicate values through analysing the corresponding sentiments with no reference to values and no talk of perceiving – let alone cognizing – them. I have suggested that this programme is apt more to moral than to aesthetic values. But preliminary optimism or pessimism is cheap; what is worth funding is success or failure in execution. The prudent speculator in philosophical futures will commit himself totally neither to the pessimism of Nietzsche ('Only that which has no history can be defined'[34]) nor to the optimism of those who assume that the only alternative to total analysis is mere mystification. However, any genuine projectivist must resist the parsimonious assumption that explanations and analyses of evaluations will speak only of dispassionate beliefs and associated sentiments: that assumption reduces projection to an accident of grammar. He must rather suppose that, where talk of projection is apt, ascribing values to things (which is a matter of perception and imagination suffused by grammar) makes a difference to the relevant sentiment, lending it an at least quasi-perceptual character that is part of its phenomenology (that is, of what it is like to feel that sentiment); and he may well add that what value-terms express and values correspond to is the whole sentiment, including that aspect of its phenomenology. A more genuine projectivism that was no less analytical would admit three elements: dispassionate belief (in subjacent properties), sentiment or attitude, and complex projection (yielding a perception of values out of sentiments in a way that overlays them – so that the underlying, pre-projective sentiments become postulates, not phenomena).[35] What differentiates genetic projectivism even from this is precisely that it is genetic: the pre-projective sentiments, which remain among the materials of explanation, are supposed rather to *precede* the propositionalized sentiments than to *underlie* them.

Reductive projectivism as I have defined it (after Blackburn) actually excludes nihilistic projectivism; for if ascriptions of values are reduced to expressions of sentiments accompanying dispassionate beliefs, then denying the existence of the values makes no sense – except, in a first-order manner, as a way of rejecting the attitudes. However, a projectivism that imports a different pattern either of analysis or of genesis may invite nihilism; for if ascriptions of values are analysed as involving the projection of sentiments, it may be alleged that the projection produces error. I have argued that this nihilism is gratuitous: we do not have to suppose that projection creates a conception of new properties, conveyed by new predicates, that could never be realized; however 'less than perspicuous' projection itself may have to remain (*Painting as an Art*, p. 85), it is not necessary that the projective properties of which we speak should have false pretensions. This issue affects what can be justified, not what can be explained. Genetic projectivism uses in explanation both primitive sentiments and subsequent perceptions (or quasi-perceptions) of values, but not values themselves; in this way, its ontology is economical. Whether unexplanatory entities can yet be 'real' may be put on the shelf as a question in search of a sense.

(8) Any genetic story deals in three kinds of factor: starting point, motive for departure, and means of advance. A poverty in the first can be compensated by an ingenuity in the last; for purposes of illustration, one need not be too afraid of exaggerating the poverty or of underplaying the ingenuity. I shall keep with a single aesthetic value demanding of a depth analysis: beauty. That fits at once my sources and my admission that projectivism proper is less problematic for

aesthetic than for moral values.[36] Freud and Klein start from different points, neither, indeed, far advanced. Freud starts from the genitals:

> Sexual curiosity . . . seeks to complete the sexual object by revealing its hidden parts. It can, however, be diverted ('sublimated') in the direction of art, if its interest can be shifted away from the genitals on to the shape of the body as a whole . . . There is to my mind no doubt that the concept of 'beautiful' has its roots in sexual excitation and that its original meaning was 'sexually stimulating' (vii. 156; cf. xxi. 83).

Klein ascribes a similar significance to the infant's own genitals;[37] but even behind its desire for the father's penis, she traces a primal desire for the mother's breast.[38] What shakes the infant out of fixation to its original object? Two sufficient misfortunes: in Freud, the ban on incest; in Klein, deprivation and weaning. What enables the infant to diversify its objects? The displaceability or plasticity of libido; that is, 'the degree of facility with which the libido is able to change its object and mode of satisfaction'.[39] By contrast, hunger and thirst have a more obstinate adhesiveness, or viscosity. In consequence libido, unlike them, has a history of development:

> The sexual instinct . . . places extraordinarily large amounts of force at the disposal of civilized activity, and it does this in virtue of its especially marked characteristic of being able to displace its aim without materially diminishing in intensity. This capacity to exchange its originally sexual aim for another one, which is no longer sexual but which is psychically related to the first aim, is called the capacity for *sublimation* (ix. 187).

Where does beauty come in? It comes in, by way of the internal relation of value to sentiment that supervenes on the phantasy of projection, with *love* of beauty. How does this arise from libido? When libido projects itself into new objects. How can it do that while remaining itself? Through sexual symbolism. Most explicit here is Klein: 'Symbolism is the foundation of all sublimation and of every talent, since it is by way of symbolic equation that things, activities and interests become the subject of libidinal phantasies.'[40] The symbolism that serves a sense of beauty is above all visual symbolism: the discarded desire to touch becomes a sublimated desire to look. With looking comes a more sophisticated satisfaction: a desire to look is a desire to look at something answering to that desire, not something that will satiate it (looking is not satiable, though it can become monotonous), but something that correlates, corresponds, with it. If a symbol is to be enjoyed as such, it must rather be contemplated than consumed; and the pleasure of contemplation, to repeat a phrase from *The Thread of Life*, is 'the awareness of match observed' (p. 215).[41] Thus the appropriate object will be at once a visual symbol of the primal object and an emblematic correlate of visual libido. These two roles of the new object are made for each other: it is in a single way that it both symbolizes what libido used to pursue and matches what libido has now become.[42]

By this process of sublimation through symbolization much is achieved. As the lost delights of touch and taste are replaced by the permitted pleasures of sight, gratification that is denied makes way for appreciation that is approved; the child escapes from the biological cycle of need and satiation into the psychological state of admiration, so that sex cedes to love. Climactic drives fuel non-climactic cathexes. Though there is less pleasure, there is more self-satisfaction. Libido, instead of eliminating itself in discharge, comes to recognize itself in its correlates. In these it perceives itself as in a mirror, and sees that it is good; it accepts its objectified self.

In exploring the genesis of a concept, it is important to guard against two opposite prejudices that are usually false: that the upshot owes to its origins only its origin, or that the upshot is really nothing other than its origins. Deep aesthetic values are always erotic (they are watered by no other fountain), but soon not crudely so. The Freudian genealogy does not expose culture as a sham: sublimation evades repression (xiv. 95), and artistic creation is not a symptom formation betraying the return of the repressed. We must distinguish the sublimation of sexuality in an activity from the sexualization of that activity (xi. 79); it is the latter that may well generate inhibition and anxiety. Sublimation supplants the old object and aim by new ones obscurely related to it; to pursue the old goal, in a concealed or inhibited form, is to retain the old anxiety.[43] Yet to exaggerate the distance between starting point and point of arrival is an act of denial: we must not imagine, if I may borrow from Wollheim a warning that he directs against some conceptions of morality, that beauty 'marks the spot where human beings discard their human nature'.[44] Sublimation is never total transformation. Sight becomes sensual, looking becomes quasi-tactual, so that they now in truth register not just colours and shapes, but solid yet yielding bodies. (We may suppose that the very concept of solidity arises especially from a visual perception of the parents that is suffused by the projection of tactile desires.) A modern observation about John Ruskin's *Modern Painters* is true of us all, *qua* aesthetes: '*Look, observe,* and *see* recur with obsessive frequency throughout the book. For Ruskin was eye-driven, even photoerotic, and confessed to a "sensual faculty of pleasure in sight" to which he knew no parallel.[45] Even if just using one's senses can be a simple pleasure in itself (consider how soon infants enjoy watching moving shapes), for the sensing of deep aesthetic values, the eyes must become not a camera, but a repository of human feeling.

To what extent, and up to what point, libido can be civilized varies with the constitution of each individual (ix. 187–8). No doubt there is always loss: the intensity of the new satisfactions is not such as to 'convulse our physical being' (xxi. 79). Yet the loss is also gain: the frustration that initially set sublimation going later keeps it going. As Klein well describes, 'the disparity between man's desire for gratification' and 'the gratification which in reality he obtains' motivates an unending development in which 'we find symbols at work in increasingly complicated inventions and activities'.[46] I have sketched only the prehistory of our concept of beauty. Later on, the process of symbolization can be directed not only by the ruses of the unconscious, but by the evolving mores of a culture (cf. *The Thread of Life*, p. 217). In this way the aesthetic escapes the monotony of the perennial: to an extent, old conceptions of beauty yield to new. The progress of libido is stepwise: newly symbolical targets make possible newly articulated desires, which make possible yet other targets, which make possible yet other desires, and so on with no finite limit. To clarify by example: taking the whole body as its object (and investing it with its projections) libido changes its nature, which enables it to take hills and trees as its object (projectively investing those), which develops it further, and so on. Quite properly, the Freudian narrative has no ending.

(9) The story that I have just told has the crudity of a philosopher's thought-experiment; to borrow some wording from Wiggins, it transforms a bare conception of a symbolism into the conception of a symbolism of great bareness. I shall finish by offering the barest sketch of a richer account.

In the terms of Kleinian theory, I have placed the emergence of a sense of beauty within the paranoid-schizoid position, speaking only of part-objects (genitals or breast) and their symbolization. What we owe to Klein and the Kleinians is its location within the *depressive* position: realizing that the mother whom it hates is the same as the mother whom it loves, so that in attacking the first it may have damaged the second, the child becomes less concerned to evade retaliation than to make reparation. Klein writes, 'The person's sense of guilt and desire to restore the damaged object are a universal and fundamental factor in the development of his sublimations.'[47] New activities, orienting the child towards new objects, appeal as symbolic ways of restoring people whom it has loved and harmed.[48] The experience of beauty becomes the product not just of erotic displacement, but of a sense of wholeness that reconciles love and hate within a single perspective. The work of art, in particular, is perceived as a resolution of their tension. As Adrian Stokes has written, in a passage excerpted by Wollheim:

> Beauty is a sense of wholeness. From the opposing elements that can fuse in the sublime, we may sense at peace the impulse of life and the impulse to death or inertia, so well symbolized by the inanimate nature of the material through which the artist conveys his fantasies and achieves on occasion for outward-thrusting Eros the perfection of arrest.[49]

Hanna Segal has found a similar pattern in tragedy: its achievement is to fix 'the unshrinking expression of the full horror of the depressive phantasy' within an external form ('the formal modes of speech, the unities of time, place and action, the strictness and rigidity of the rules') whose complete contrast with its content becomes 'an unconscious demonstration of the fact that order can emerge out of chaos'.[50] Beauty may then be identified either with the formal aspect (as Segal proposes) or with the totality (as she quotes Rodin as supposing),[51] but to equivalent effect: it is against the confusion of the content that the form stands out as beautiful, instead of blankly marmoreal.

Thus a single tradition offers a multiplicity of ways of redeeming the promise of a genetic account of the profounder values that may do justice at once to our humanity (which is half earthy) and to their transcendence (which is half ethereal). The reductionist and anti-reductionist stances of analytical philosophers threaten an unending war for the possession of an ivory tower; that we need to take over their conceptual acumen within an explanatory programme of sensitive de-mystification is among the lessons to be learnt from the writings of Richard Wollheim.

NOTES

[1] For two different characterizations, contrast Wollheim, *Art and its Objects*, 2nd edn (1980), pp. 231–2, with Crispin Wright, 'Realism, Antirealism,

Irrealism, Quasi-Realism', *Midwest Studies in Philosophy*, 12 (1988), pp. 25–49; for an avoidance of the term, cf. David Wiggins, *Needs, Values, Truth* (Blackwell, Oxford, 1987), pp. 330–1. It will be evident in this essay that I concur with Wiggins.

2 Simon Blackburn, *Spreading the Word* (Oxford University Press, Oxford, 1985), ch. 5–6; *idem*, 'Errors and the Phenomenology of Value', in *Morality and Objectivity*, ed. Ted Honderich (Routledge, London, 1985), pp. 1–22; *idem*, 'How to be an Ethical Antirealist', *Midwest Studies in Philosophy*, 12 (1988), pp. 361–75.

3 J. L. Mackie, *Ethics: Inventing Right and Wrong* (Penguin, Harmondsworth, 1977), ch. 1; *idem*, *Hume's Moral Theory* (Routledge, London, 1980), ch. 5.

4 *Art and its Objects*, ch. 6, esp. pp. 238–40; *The Thread of Life* (1984), ch. 7, esp. pp. 214–15. Fuller on projection, but in relation not to evaluation but to 'expressive perception', is *Painting as an Art* (1987), pp. 82–5.

5 I choose this example because it fits well with what I wish to propose about both the current status and the aetiology of values; I shall later concede that the role of sentiments in morality is more uncertain. Meanwhile, just one complication: to secure that values remain public, we need to add that the appropriate sentiment is a function not merely of the value, but also of the temperament, and indeed of the experience, of its subject; thus, crudely, one man may register hotly what another registers coolly.

6 On some conceptions of secondary properties, it is more exact to say that *seeing* the sunset *as* coloured causes the sentiment; for my purposes, we could leave open what it is in the object that affects me causally.

7 I write 'at the tightest' to cover two classes of qualification: (1) the beauty may be registered by the lack of the sentiment or by an equivalent sentiment (cf. note 5); (2) to the extent that the subject's sensibility is coarse-grained (which it will always be to some extent, and not only for the worse), qualitatively different perceptions may be of the same beauty, registered in the same sentiment.

8 Wiggins, *Needs, Values, Truth*, p. 106. Blackburn seizes upon the words 'equal and reciprocal partners', and more particularly a later phrase 'made for one another' (ibid., pp. 107, 108), to object that, while we may agree that the properties are made for the sensibility, to say that the sensibility is made for the properties 'really startles', asking, 'Who or what makes them like that? God?' ('How to be an Ethical Antirealist', p. 366). In mistaking the metaphorical for the literal, he misconstrues the internal relation as an external relation of mutual adaptation; I think that my text understands Wiggins better (or misunderstands him less).

9 A. W. Price, 'Doubts about Projectivism', *Philosophy*, 61 (1986), p. 219. I owe the divergence between that article and this essay to the influence of *The Thread of Life*.

10 Hume, *Enquiries* ed. Selby-Bigge, (Clarendon Press, Oxford, 1894), p. 294; for a similar suggestion concerning the apparent relation of necessi-

tation, cf. *idem, A Treatise of Human Nature*, ed. Selby-Bigge (Clarendon Press, Oxford, 1896), p. 167, *Enquiries*, pp. 77–8, n. 1.

[11] Blackburn, *Spreading the Word*, p. 192. Cf. ibid., p. 219, n. 21: 'The full explanation of what we do when we moralize cites only the natural properties of things and natural reactions to them.' Blackburn has in mind a different mode of reduction when he opposes projectivism to reductionism (ibid., p. 210).

[12] Mackie, *Hume's Moral Theory*, p. 71.

[13] This conception is dominant in Blackburn's 'How to be an Ethical Antirealist', p. 362, which declares, 'The projectivism is not, of course, new', citing as precursors not only Hume, but also emotivism and prescriptivism.

[14] Blackburn, *Spreading the Word*, pp. 170–1.

[15] Ibid., p. 171.

[16] Blackburn's accounts of conditionalization, the ascription of truth, and the assumption of bivalence (ibid., pp. 189–210) are non-realist, rather than quasi-realist. He shows how we can appraise valuations both evaluatively and logically without any error or even pretence; once he gets into details (often valuably), he never makes out that it is because we are projecting our sentiments and 'gilding or staining' the world that we speak and think as we do.

[17] Cf. a remark in Blackburn, 'Errors and the Phenomenology of Value', p. 11: 'My projectivist . . . affirms *all that could ever properly be meant* by saying that there are real obligations' (my emphasis).

[18] This relates to a difficulty noted by Wright in his review of *Spreading the Word*, that if quasi-realism is too successful, then projectivism becomes inexpressible (*Mind*, 94 (1985), p. 319).

[19] Blackburn is led to say this by finding moral properties more dissimilar than aesthetic ones to secondary properties. I believe that what are worth noting are not *similarities* between values and colours (which would be a two-place relation), but *analogies* between the relations of colours to our visual sensitivity and of values to our affective propensities (which is a four-place relation); this properly leaves open in what manner values can count as 'perceptible' or 'cognizable'.

[20] We may accept the distinction as generally sound: cf. Wollheim on *the acquaintance principle*, 'which insists that judgments of aesthetic value, unlike judgments of moral knowledge, must be based on first-hand experience of their objects and are not, except within very narrow limits, transmissible from one person to another' (*Art and its Objects*, p. 233).

[21] I am not here discarding Wiggins's distinction between valuations and all-in practical judgements (*Needs, Values, Truth*, pp. 95–6): moral valuations and internal commands (in an idiomatic sense of 'command') are related, not identical. Nor am I denying that any interesting moral attitude will emerge out of a complex of feelings, so that the vagueness (which is endemic) comes not of a unitary attitude fuzzy at the edges, but

of innumerable potentialities for affective supremacy, stand-off, compromise, or alliance that are resolved only as the occasion arises.

22   Cf. the ironies in Max Beerbohm's description of Zuleika Dobson, finely
appreciated by William Empson, *Seven Types of Ambiguity*, 3rd edn
(Chatto and Windus, London, 1953), pp. 176–7.

23   Cf. Wright, 'Moral Values, Projection and Secondary Qualities', *Proceedings of the Aristotelian Society*, 62 (1988), p. 11: 'It seems to me very moot
whether there is anyway any distinctive mode of *moral* emotional concern,
identified purely phenomenologically and distinguishable from what we
feel for other kinds of values. Virtue is satisfied when one is concerned
for the right reasons about the right kinds of thing: it is not necessary also
to feel a particular *timbre* of concern.'

24   Cf. also *The Thread of Life*, pp. 214–15.

25   Wollheim writes here of a 'doubling-up of the predicate' (*Painting as an
Art*, p. 84). He warns us against supposing that to call the usage metaphorical is to say the most important thing.

26   Some may prefer a *via media* between Blackburn's grammatical conception of projection and Wollheim's Kleinian one. Possibly my remarks
towards the end of § 4 could be developed into an account of projection
in terms of 'seeing as'. One problem will be to keep projectivism localized;
any concept can colour how we see things, yet not all concepts are
projective. However, it may be specially characteristic of sentiments to
generate concepts (of values) by causing us to see things as being of a
piece with themselves.

27   Indeed, it is striking that he does not do so in *Art and its Objects*, pp. 238–40.

28   For the distinction, cf. Wiggins, *Needs, Values, Truth*, p. 107.

29   Cf. P. F. Strawson, *Skepticism and Naturalism: Some Varieties* (New York,
1985), ch. 2. The passage from Forrest Reid that served as an epigraph
to this essay (from *Brian Westby* (Faber and Faber, London, 1934),
pp. 20–1) is as instructive in insight as in illusion: Linton is wrong to
suppose that beauty passes with the passer-by; he is right to hold that
beauty exists only within the perspective of those susceptible to it. So
long as we relativize, we may safely go to extremes. (Why not?) I would
admit, for example, the existence of essentially amatory values: when in
love, I may ascribe to its object a special value that he indeed possesses
– but only relative to the point of view of a lover resembling myself; if I
wallow in my appreciation, that is because I am implicitly aware that it
is non-contingently an expression of *my love for him*.

30   More subversive, at least of 'the presumptuousness, the arrogance, for
which morality is such a traditional medium of expression' (*The Thread
of Life*, p. 225), is a moral relativity not *to*, but *within*, the human perspective: deserving of demotion are any moral values that claim to be
humanly inescapable, but may properly vary between different human
cultures or ideologies.

31   Cf. my 'Doubts about Projectivism', pp. 222–3.

[32] Cf. Leonardo's advice to his pupils (alluded to in *Painting as an Art*, p. 46) to imagine seeing forces in combat on discoloured walls.

[33] Blackburn, 'How to be an Ethical Antirealist', p. 363 – a point whose salutariness is unexaggerable.

[34] Nietzsche, *Genealogy of Morals*, ii. 13; cited approvingly by Wiggins, *Needs, Values, Truth*, p. 67.

[35] A useful test for distinguishing genuine projectivism from quasi-projectivism surfaces in Blackburn when he raises the good query as to whether, if sentiments open one's eyes to special properties, one might then have a response to these new properties that differs from, and perhaps even conflicts with, one's original response to the subjacent properties: 'Or is it somehow given that what comes back is what went in – that the property perceived impinges on us with the same emotional impact required for perceiving it? How convenient! But how clumsy of nature to go in for such a loop!' ('How to be an Ethical Antirealist', pp. 365–6). Where the quasi-projectivist finds only a single sentiment, genuine projectivism (whether diachronic or synchronic) may well find three: an original sentiment, a transform of that sentiment that is what comes of it through projection, and a second-order sentiment, provoked by the projection (which allows us to perceive our sentiments in the projective properties of their objects), which in some cases will constitute a reaction formation against the first-order sentiment. If this sounds over-elaborated, take an Oedipal example: I unconsciously hate my father; I perceive him as hateful – which involves hating him in a new way; I recoil from the hate that the perception makes apparent.

[36] Obviously many aesthetic values are more superficial (like prettiness), and arise from projection alone, without the symbolization I shall describe. Less obviously, it is not fatal to *genetic* projectivism to concede that it may be impossible to generalize about the phenomenology of our current moral attitudes (cf. note 23): moral values may originate from distinctive sentiments, and then – because of their role in our lives, which is practical rather than phenomenological – become partly independent of sentiment.

[37] Klein, *Love, Guilt and Reparation, and Other Works: 1921–1945* (Hogarth, London, 1975), pp. 85, 104.

[38] Ibid., p. 408; cf. *idem, Envy and Gratitude and Other Works 1946–1963* (Hogarth, London, 1975), p. 83.

[39] J. Laplanche and J.-B. Pontalis, *The Language of Psycho-Analysis* (Hogarth, London, 1973), p. 319.

[40] Klein, *Love, Guilt and Reparation*, p. 220.

[41] However, Andrew Ford put it to me that the symbolic object is unconsciously desired in the same manner as the primal object, namely for a possession that would abolish the distinction between subject and object; the poignancy of the experience of beauty would then be that this desire can never be fulfilled.

[42] Freud finds *his* starting point confirmed by the fact that, as he alleges, the genitals themselves are never found beautiful (vii. 156, n. 2; xxi. 83). This raises a pair of objections: that it is not always true of the genitals (cf. Jean Genet), and that it is always false of the breast. But both are superable. The male genitals become for Genet symbols of masculinity; that is, symbols of symbols of themselves. The breast is given up to escape frustration, not repression; so here libido more readily returns to its primal source, seeing the breast as beautiful. When it does so, it sees the breast not just as 'the prototype of maternal goodness' (Klein, *Envy and Gratitude*, p. 180), but as its symbol; that is, as the symbol of many symbols, for the breast is appreciated in a new way as the symbol of all the services of the mother, themselves symbolic of what she once offered the child, namely, her breast. In either case, the beauty remains a product of symbolization.

[43] Cf. Klein, *Love, Guilt and Reparation*, pp. 89–90.

[44] Wollheim, *The Sheep and the Ceremony* (1979), p. 38.

[45] John D. Rosenberg, *The Darkening Glass: A Portrait of Ruskin's Genius* (Routledge, London, 1963), p. 4.

[46] Klein, *Love, Reparation and Guilt*, p. 104.

[47] Ibid., p. 254, n. 3; for an example, see p. 218.

[48] Klein, *Envy and Gratitude*, pp. 258–9.

[49] Stokes, *The Image in Form: Selected Writings of Adrian Stokes*, ed. R. Wollheim (Harper and Row, New York, 1972), p. 73.

[50] Segal, 'A Psycho-Analytical Approach to Aesthetics', in *New Directions in Psycho-analysis*, ed. M. Klein, P. Heimann, R. E. Money-Kyrle (Hogarth, London, 1955), p. 400.

[51] Ibid., pp. 401–2.

7

Aggression, Love, and Morality: Wollheim on Rousseau

NICHOLAS DENT

In recent years, many philosophers have contended that an adequate account of the nature and claim of moral requirements must involve an adequate account of the motives, interests, and desires of persons – that is, must incorporate or derive from a satisfactory philosophy of mind. For the most part, however, this claim having been made, the commitment it entails is not followed through. Or, where some follow-through is made, the account of motive and mind offered remains heavily dependent on the legacy of Aristotle or Hume. Richard Wollheim stands virtually alone, in this context, in bringing to bear a much denser and more sophisticated account of mind and of psychological processes in an attempt to make sense of 'the moral'.

Although in what follows I take issue with one application Wollheim has made of the form of account he favours, I wish to make clear that I do so in the belief that his form of account is thoroughly powerful and illuminating. My objection will be that, properly understood, Rousseau's work should be found congenial to, not antipathetic to, someone who takes Wollheim's ideas seriously – as I do. I believe, indeed, that with Wollheim's account to hand, it begins to be possible to read Rousseau rightly. The pity is only that, here, Wollheim would appear to have acquiesced in a misreading which his own views provide the very resources for removing.

I

On pages 272–3 of *The Thread of Life*, Wollheim is discussing certain aspects of the phenomenon of projective identification. He writes of a person who projects into an institution or authority 'the superego who has instilled . . . guilt in him' (p. 272). By doing so, that person is deceived into a sense of 'inner liberation' (ibid.). He believes he is 'now unburdened of his superego, that he is a conscienceless agent' (ibid.). Wollheim goes on:

> It is just this phantasy of the criminal law and its enforcement as a projected superego, as conscience expelled into the outer world, that Rousseau attempted to normalize in the central doctrines of the *Social Contract*. (p. 273)

This superego which may be projected into an authority is the resultant of other processes of projection and introjection, which have burdened their bearer with intolerable thoughts and feelings. Wollheim outlines some of these processes (pp. 201ff.). The mere possibility of frustration of the child's sensual desires 'ignites' within it aggressive desires which are projected on to an external figure upon whom the child is dependent. This figure is then perceived as menacing the child because, so to say, vested with the child's own aggression: the figure appears singularly frightening and malign (see also pp. 213–14, 121). The child then, by way of a phantastic attempt to protect itself from the threat this figure poses, incorporates – or introjects – this figure (or group of figures). Through this process, the superego is established, or at least that 'form' of the superego which controls the child's desire and aggression by fear, the fear of retaliation by the introjected figure (pp. 210, 207). The superego appears as

> a figure set over and against the child, remorselessly haranguing it, dictating to it, criticizing it, chastising it: in response the child imagines itself as experiencing terror, and the upshot of such phantasies is that the child is left terrorized. (p. 201)

In addition, the superego is phantasized as privy to the most inward inflections of the child's desire and anger, and it exacts the most intense demands which 'neither derive from nor do they trouble to mould themselves to the child's own needs and feelings' (p. 201).

It is the burden inflicted by this figure (or set of figures) that is found unendurable. A search for relief is set in train, which involves projective identification of the kind referred to at the start. Some let-up in the relentless persecution is procured, however partial and short-lived.

Wollheim contends that it is not in this form only that the control of aggression may be procured by virtue of anxiety generated by an internal figure (p. 210). Through the cognitive advance of recognizing that the same figure who is attacked is also loved, the child may become capable of feeling guilt at having inflicted (in phantasy or reality) harm on a loved figure. The child may come to fear loss of that person's love and to have the desire to mend the hurt to the loved person (p. 211; see also p. 217). These capabilities and dispositions of the child are not primarily rooted in retaliatory fear. They arise from the pain of having hurt what one cherishes. Complex processes of introjection and identification are also involved here, but the outcome of these can be that the child comes to want to be just the sort of person (it imagines) this loved figure is and to possess the same repertoire of feelings, attitudes, and so on as they do (pp. 122ff., 218ff.). In this way, the child takes on attitudes and purposes which serve to regulate its aggression and desire, but does so in this case for the sake of the furtherance and fulfilment of its own love. We may call this the 'growth of the superego into the ego-ideal' (p. 219).

With this framework of account of the evolution of the moral sense to hand, Wollheim makes certain generalizations about morality (which he allows are 'exaggerations'). He distinguishes morality 'in the narrow sense', which has 'obligation as its core', from 'value'. The former derives from introjection, and is 'largely defensive and largely coercive', trying to guard against fear (of persecutory aggression). The latter derives from projection and tries to perpetuate love (p. 216).

If we return now to the 'conscienceless agent', Wollheim has this to say about the toll that the projective identification exacts from someone deceived into this condition. The principal cost is 'depersonalization', the loss of awareness of what his own dispositions and feelings are and the belief that he is surrounded by others who have the most intimate knowledge of him and the most malign designs upon him. Such a person is mad, and incapable of friendship (pp. 270, 275).

Thus, Wollheim's comment on Rousseau has two aspects to it. First, it suggests that – within the phenomena of moral psychology – Rousseau has given primary place to the superego, that implacable, relentless figure haranguing the person, in distinction to the ego-ideal with its objective of perpetuating love. Second, it suggests that Rousseau has attempted to make normal a condition of (delusive) flight from the unendurable burden that such a superego imposes, rather than a condition of restorative and collaborative relationship grounded in love. Rousseau's supposedly ideal civil community comprises, in fact, a construction erected to disguise unowned and unacknowledged aggression on an enormous scale.

My principal purpose here will be to try to show that this assessment of Rousseau's conceptions is ill-founded. But in doing so, I hope also to show something further, which will give greater justification for my picking up on what is, after all, only a passing remark of Wollheim's, not amplified or given substantial support by him. For it will transpire, as the argument proceeds, that the ideas in moral psychology that Rousseau primarily deploys display an extraordinary congruence at many points to those at work in Wollheim's discussion (and in Klein's, from whom, of course, Wollheim takes many thoughts). So far from its being the case that Rousseau's views consist in an attempt to normalize expelled aggression, we shall see that he was peculiarly aware of the significance and deforming power of aggression and looked for ways – both individual and social – by which aggression could be regulated without recourse to fear, terrorization, and the like. I am not suggesting that Rousseau had to hand proto-forms of the notions of introjection, splitting, identification, and so forth. Thus, there can be no argument that his ideas do not have their limits. But for all that, there is a great deal in Rousseau's discussions that both illuminates, and is illuminated by, the structure of ideas which Wollheim is proposing.

I shall be considering *Emile*[1] as the source for my contentions. Wollheim, I know, speaks of the *Social Contract*. It is, of course, always possible that Rousseau should have failed to carry over the central insights of *Emile* to that other work. I think, however, that this is most unlikely, and I shall very briefly indicate how a more sympathetic and valuable reading of the *Social Contract* is possible if we bring to bear on it the perspective generated by the arguments of *Emile*. It is out of the question to attempt to enforce the reading comprehensively here.

II

Emile is a long and complex work. I shall have to be pretty selective and brief in my account, even of those limited parts of it relevant to the present issue.

A very great deal of the first two books of *Emile* is given over to a consideration of the fate that may befall the desire, and desirous self-assertion of an infant or child. Rousseau does not here specifically mention or deploy the idea of infantile sexuality, despite his own experiences of that and of the great centrality he later affords to sexuality.[2] But the significance to the child of the frustration of its desires generally is made decisive in Rousseau's consideration of affective and moral development and characterology.

In order to assess the justice of Wollheim's appraisal, it will be crucial to see whether Rousseau gives major place to the child's own aggression in relation to the frustration of his desire or whether – from the first – Rousseau is apt to characterize the place and role of aggression in human relations and transactions in a way which implies that he perceives its significance only when already projected on to or into another person (or authority or institution). Rousseau's renowned remark(s) to the effect that man is by nature good, but corrupted and depraved by society, may strongly suggest the latter immediately.[3] For this suggests a characterization of man as a spotless innocent, violated and outraged by malign others, the perfect self-image complementing unrecognized aggression. If this is what Rousseau begins with, then it is most likely that the rest will bear the imprint of this original misconstruction.

But is this, in fact, how Rousseau does proceed? (If it is not – as I shall now try to show – then it may be wondered what becomes of his idea of 'natural goodness'. I shall not pursue this point here.[4]) Consider the following passage:

> It is a disposition natural to man to regard everything in his power as his . . . Hence, the child who has only to want in order to get believes himself to be the owner of the universe; he regards all men as his slaves. When one is finally forced to refuse him something, he, believing that at his command everything is possible, takes this refusal for an act of rebellion. All reasons given him . . . are to his mind only pretexts. He sees ill will everywhere. The feeling of an alleged injustice souring his nature, he develops hatred towards everyone; and, without ever being grateful for helpfulness, he is indignant at every opposition.
>
> How could I conceive that a child thus dominated by anger and devoured by the most irascible passions might ever be happy? . . . With their desires exacerbated by the ease of getting, they were obstinate about impossible things and found everywhere only contradiction, obstacles, efforts, pains. Always grumbling, always rebellious, always furious, they spent their days in screaming, in complaining . . . Weakness and domination joined engender only folly and misery. Of two spoiled children, one beats the table and the other has the sea whipped. (*Emile*, ii. 87–8; this passage is typical of many)

Out of this we may note Rousseau's comments that the child takes refusal 'for an act of rebellion' and 'sees ill will everywhere'. It is very plain that Rousseau is arguing that this is the child's own construction of the significance of what is going on, a construction born of, expressive of, the child's own hatred, a hatred which is projected on to others and presents them as being hostile and malign towards him. Rousseau is clearly not saying that the child is the victim of ill will. (Another very clear instance of Rousseau's awareness of projected aggression may be found in *Emile*, iv. 228, in his comparison of 'two young men'.)

However, Rousseau's claim here needs more careful examination. For it may be said that I have misrepresented his position in two ways. First, I attribute to Rousseau the view that the perception of a hostile figure is a projection *native* to frustrated desire. But, in the passage quoted and in several others, it would appear that Rousseau regards this as an acquired propensity, or a propensity dependent upon other acquired traits, and not as – or not wholly as – 'native'. The child has to have been 'spoiled', flattered into delusive expectations and beliefs, by the mishandling of him by others. It is only in view of this that he becomes 'devoured' by irascible passions. This then suggests a failure to recognize the inherent disposition to aggression. Aggression is admitted only in an already projected character.

Second, and directly allied to this former point, Rousseau may seem to suggest that the child's hatred arises in the form of response to the (believed) ill will directed towards him by others, in which hatred the child appears to himself to be vindicated. Here, too, there would seem to be no recognition that (in very many cases at any rate) the supposed ill will suffered is a phenomenon 'devised' by the child's own projected hatred and aggression, operating at a more basic level.

I should maintain that neither of these objections can be sustained. Although there are indeed passages where Rousseau claims that 'we fill up his [the child's] young heart at the outset with the passions which later we impute to nature' (*Emile*, i. 48; see also i. 66, i. 69, ii. 86, for instance), this does not, I think, comprise his deepest and best thought. We can find the latter in such a passage as this:

> I shall never forget having seen one of these difficult cryers . . . struck by his nurse. He immediately kept quiet. I believed he was intimidated . . . I was mistaken. The unfortunate was suffocating with anger; he had lost his breath; I saw him become violet. A moment after came sharp screams; all the signs of the resentment, fury, and despair of this age were in his accents. I feared he would expire in this agitation. If I had doubted that the sentiment of the just and the unjust were innate in the heart of man, this example alone would have convinced me. (i. 65–6)

Consider also:

I have seen imprudent governesses animate the unruliness of a child,
incite him to strike, let themselves be struck, and laugh at his feeble
blows, without thinking that in the intention of the little enraged one
these blows were so many murders. (ii. 97–8-n.; see also surrounding
text)

It may seem quite inappropriate that Rousseau should invoke any
notion of justice here, let alone an 'innate sentiment' of justice. But
what Rousseau is doing is amplifying his idea, expressed at the start
of the passage from ii. 87–8 quoted above, that it is a natural disposition for man to regard 'everything in his power as his' – that is, as
what he has an absolute, peremptory title to the unobstructed enjoy-
ment of. His argument is that this idea, or sentiment, is implicit in a
reactivity of resentment, fury, rage, and so on, for such reactions
include some conception of oneself as abused or ill-served. Resentment at frustration of desire embodies the idea that one should have
had what one desired; and that idea Rousseau says is one of justice
(at least in respect of what is owed to us; see ii. 97). There need be
no question of either of the following possibilities having been in
Rousseau's mind: first, that one, or the child, represents itself originally as an outraged innocent, the victim of an injustice, faced by a
malicious attacker. This would be a *secondary* deployment of the idea
of oneself as violated in one's entitlements. The point rather is that
the original aggressive response incorporates some conception (however inchoate) of being abused in being frustrated. That conception
need not be a further elaboration in a situation already perceived in
terms constructed by projection. Second, the 'sentiment' in question
is not supposed by Rousseau to be sound, or well grounded. On the
contrary, it may be ludicrously disproportionate. The intensity of the
aggression, the magnitude of the projectively constructed 'affront'
believed in, is the measure of the originally assumed title. We well
know that the former can be very great; so, automatically, follows the
inference to the greatness of the latter. This point is evident in these
remarks of Klein's:

Some babies experience strong resentment about any frustration and
show this by being unable to accept gratification when it follows on
deprivation. I would suggest that such children have a stronger innate
aggressiveness and greed than those infants whose occasional outbursts
of rage are soon over.[5]

We might understand Rousseau as making more explicit some of
the notions implicit in appeal to the idea of 'resentment', as here. At

the very least, I should have thought that his discernment of the murderous hate in the blows of 'the little enraged one' was some proof of his willingness to recognize the intensity of aggressiveness in his accounts of human sentiments and behaviour.

The second objection – closely connected to the first – was that Rousseau represents the child's aggression always as a response to what he perceives as the ill will and malice of others. Thus the contribution of the child's aggression to depicting his own circumstances in these terms is denied. The comments made already should remove this complaint. Rousseau clearly enough explains the role of the child's own projections in 'creating' a world in which he is being attacked. Rousseau was furthermore quite clear that figuring oneself as unwarrantedly ill-used, as an outraged innocent, was (often) no more than a further expression of resentment towards others for their failure to be at once compliant to one's will, the imperious demands of which are an aggressive expression. (See for instance i. 67–8, ii. 88, 91.)

Rousseau goes on to make many suggestions as to how the aggressive predispositions of a child may be moderated and moulded, so that not every human encounter takes for him the form of a trial for dominion. He suggests, as is well known, that the child be brought up, to begin with, in artificially contrived seclusion from the possibility of actually encountering the opposing will of another person. In this way, Rousseau hopes, the child's own phantasy of a contending will set against him will not be confirmed and consolidated. Clearly, many of Rousseau's specific pedagogic proposals are of dubious value. But one thing is evident throughout, that his whole educational intent is shaped by an awareness of the depth and pervasiveness of aggression in a child. It would be a pardonable exaggeration to say that Rousseau saw this aggression as the single most central cause of human and social deformation. He did not hope to procure (ineffectual) amelioration of this by devising structures in which aggression could be denied or disowned by projecting it into another. It is perhaps worth remarking, too, that in one passage he sees aggression as originating in the primitive relation of dependence that a child has upon his parents. 'Parents', Rousseau writes, increase a child's weakness 'by exacting from him what nature did not exact. They do so by subjecting to their will the bit of strength which he has for serving his own, by changing into slavery on one side or the other the reciprocal dependence in which his weakness keeps him and their attachment keeps them' (ii. 84; see also ii. 86).

Finally on this theme – and arising directly out of these observations – Rousseau says that 'the words *obey* and *command* will be proscribed from his [the child's] lexicon, and even more so *duty* and *obligation'* (ii. 89). It is wholly proper to make a connection between this and Wollheim's remarks (quoted earlier) about morality 'in the narrow sense' as coercive.

III

Is there anything in Rousseau's thought which suggests that he was looking for a 'happier interpretation of morality', one in which the control of aggression is not procured by persecutory anxiety (Wollheim, *Thread of Life*, p. 207)? Here again I want to suggest that Rousseau articulated rather perceptively the outlines of an account which is strikingly like that which Wollheim favours. Rousseau explores at length and in detail in book iv of *Emile* the nature of compassion (or pity) and how such concern may regulate aggression out of a desire to 'perpetuate love'. In this, he identifies and examines the role of reparative and restorative concerns in relation to real (or imaginary) injuries one has inflicted on others. I shall look at only one or two points from this discussion.

Rousseau writes that

a young man raised in a happy simplicity is sensitive to the shame of displeasing, to the regret of having offended. If the ardour of his inflamed blood makes him too intense, easily carried away, and angered, a moment later all the goodness of his heart is seen in the effusion of his repentance . . . He would want to redeem the blood he has shed with his own. All of his fury is extinguished, all of his pride humiliated before the sentiment of his wrong. (iv. 220–1)

This passage does not appear unprepared for, as a mere assertion. In the immediately preceding pages (see for instance iv. 213), Rousseau has examined the role of pleasure and gratification in the infant's life and how this gives rise to the idea of a generous, giving figure towards whom the child can feel love and gratitude. And this, he says, sows the seeds of benevolence in the child's own disposition, the first germs of humanity, which find their fuller realization in human bonds mediated through compassion and sympathy. Compare this, from Klein:

There is much evidence, gained retrospectively in the psycho-analysis of children and even of adults, that the mother is very early on felt to be an injured object, internalized and external. I would suggest that this complaining injured object is part of the super-ego. The relation to this injured and loved object includes not only guilt but compassion, and is the fundamental source of all sympathy with others and consideration for them.[6]

Rousseau does not make the mistake of supposing that compassionate and aggressive dispositions are, so to say, compartmentalized, so that the loved object is 'split' from the hated one and no restoration is made to one and the very same object for the (supposed) injury. He indeed shows, with considerable subtlety, how ready we can remain to retain hostile attitudes towards the person for whom we yet feel compassion and a desire to mend their condition (or make amends for it, phantasized as our doing). We are only too ready to suppose, he contends, that our sympathy will be taken for weakness or subservience in the face of the other, whom we will perceive as punitively exacting payment from us for their sense of wrong, disclosing both our own (and sometimes also the other person's) continued aggression (see iv. 226, 233–4). But, despite the continuing possibility of the extinction of pity by aggression, Rousseau contends that the restorative concern we have rooted in love and gratitude promises a mode of incorporation of the need and being of others into the economy of our own desires which may procure restraint of aggression without the curb of retaliatory fear. And just as the well-being of others can come to occupy such a position in our desires, so also our own being and well-being can find a like place in the structure of desire and concern of another person.

We can see in this, in outline at any rate, the possibility of a mutually acknowledged footing of equal respect and care obtaining between persons, arising from the concerns and needs native to the psychological characteristics of each of them. The requirement of restraint towards another need not be, nor be perceived as being, an imposed – and resented – persecutory demand. Rather it would comprise, for each person, an expression of their own creative and reparative power and concern. This assessment is plain in Rousseau's own description of his objective:

> I would try to show how the first voices of conscience arise out of the first movements of the heart, and how the first notions of good and bad are born of the sentiments of love and hate. I would show that *justice* and *goodness* are not merely abstract words – pure moral beings formed by the understanding – but are true affections of the soul enlightened by reason, are hence only an ordered development of our primitive affec-

tions; that by reason alone, independent of conscience, no natural law can be established; and that the entire right of nature is only a chimera if it is not founded on a natural need in the human heart. (iv. 235)

Although it is out of the question to examine Rousseau's conception of conscience further here, it should be clear enough from this passage alone that Rousseau does not associate our natural need and concern for goodness with achieving the (delusive) condition of being a 'conscienceless agent'. On the contrary, the suggestion is plain that conscience and a commitment to justice and goodness are both originally rooted in 'movements of the heart', in 'primitive affections', which comprise parts of our own proper need and nature. To divest oneself of conscience would not be a way of procuring intact self-possession in Rousseau's eyes; it would be a form of radical self-estrangement, of depersonalization.

It remains open to someone still to argue that when Rousseau turns his attention to the constitution and regulation of the civil state, to the mode of life of man as a citizen, he puts aside all these insights and proceeds on another basis altogether. I would hope to have suggested, however, that this is unlikely; certainly he thought the progress to civil relation and standing was (or ought to be) crucially continuous with the forms of affective and moral relation and standing just (cursorily) examined. I believe that it would only be in view of a *prior* misconstruction of Rousseau's approaches to the issues of moral restraint and relation that there would be any serious inducement to read his ideas about the civil state in the terms Wollheim suggests. Taking those misconstructions away leaves such a reading looking very strained.

Thus we might conjecture that the terms and conditions of civil association – which are the expression of 'the general will' and comprise that law the common subjection to which constitutes several persons as united in civil community one with another – will principally be those of justice and goodness that Rousseau here adverts to. We might further conjecture that he saw in this case too the relevant forms of justice and goodness arising from that relation of mutual recognition and care which is founded in a love and compassion which is inherent in the psychological need of each person. It is not the case, then, that the criminal law of Rousseau's state has vested in it and carries for each citizen the burden of their aggression. Such law, on the contrary, embodies each person's desire to achieve for themselves and others a footing of common care and regard, a desire derived from the reparative concerns of love. I do not propose to try to enforce these conjectures here. But they do provide, I suggest, a basis for a happier interpretation of Rousseau's account of civil society and law.

The resources in Rousseau's arguments that I have been drawing on come, as I said, mostly from book iv of *Emile*. Within the framework of the whole book, Rousseau claims to be discussing the condition of someone aged around fifteen, someone on the verge of adolescence. This may cause problems, for it may suggest that Rousseau does not, and cannot, locate these reparative and restorative desires in appropriate conjunction with the aggressive impulses attributed to infancy. These problems are largely illusory in fact. For, first, Rousseau makes it quite clear that the aspects of feeling and desire to which he is now centrally attending have their origin in the earliest experiences of the child (see iv. 213 for instance). But also, second, we should not take too seriously Rousseau's chronological mode of presentation of his views. His major interest is in examining the various diverse facets of human affects, desires, and so forth. He uses the framework of a sequential development largely (though not wholly) as a frame for sorting out these various elements into manageably discussable 'lumps', without intending us to believe that these things necessarily occur in a particular time order.

Finally, however, it is very striking that Rousseau does at this point make some very close connections between Emile's enlarged sensibility and involvement with others and the onset of sexuality (see iv. 214–15).[7] One can only speculate as to whether Rousseau might have grasped the possibility of infantile sexuality had he carried his own conclusions to their limit.

IV

If anything of what I have argued is cogent, it now becomes problematic to see how the sort of representation of Rousseau's ideas offered by Wollheim could have gained credence at all. I do not know the answer to this. But Wollheim is not alone. Consider the following:

> To lead men to happiness through *vertu* and to *vertu* by laws founded
> on the unshakeable principles of universal morality, designed to restore
> to human nature all its rights and all its primal dignity; to re-forge the
> immortal chain that must bind man to God and to his fellow-men by
> destroying all the forces of oppression and tyranny which fill the earth
> with fear, suspicion, pride, baseness, egoism, hatred, greed and all the

vices that draw men far from the goals assigned to society by the eternal legislator; this . . . is the glorious enterprise.

Here, perhaps, we hear the accents of 'moral totalitarianism'. And, it is also suggested, we see in this 'the influence of Rousseau'. But the author is, in fact, Robespierre.[8]

NOTES

[1] References are to the translation by Allan Bloom (Basic Books, New York 1979), by book and page number.

[2] See for instance *The Confessions*, tr. J. M. Cohen (Penguin, Harmondsworth, 1953), i. 25–6; *Emile*, iv. 214–15, v. 429–31. See also Bloom's note 2 to *Emile*, iv.

[3] Rousseau expresses this thought on many occasions, in slightly different ways. For instance, in *Emile*, iv. 236–7, in his *Lettre à Christophe de Beaumont*, and in *Rousseau juge de Jean-Jacques*.

[4] I discuss this point at length in Dent, 'The Basic Principle of Emile's Education', *Journal of Philosophy of Education*, 22, 1988.

[5] Klein, 'Our Adult World and its Roots in Infancy', (in *Envy and Gratitude and Other Works* (Hogarth, London, 1975), p. 249.

[6] Klein, 'Some Reflections on *The Oresteia*', ibid., p. 239; see also *idem*, 'On Mental Health', ibid., p. 269.

[7] See note 2 above.

[8] See N. Hampson, *The Life and Opinions of Maximilien Robespierre* (Blackwell, Oxford, 1974), pp. 30–1.

8

The Future of a Disillusion

G. A. COHEN

1. It looks as though the Soviet Union, or the pieces that it may soon become, will embrace capitalism, or fall into a severe authoritarianism, or undergo both of those fates.[1] That is not an original thought. While a certain amount of humane socialist rhetoric survives even now in the Soviet Union, few observers believe that from its present crisis there will emerge a state, or states, characterized by an attractive form of socialism. But it costs me a lot to endorse that unoriginal thought, and I want to explain why.

In 1912 my mother was born, in Kharkov, to secular Jewish parents of ample means, her father being a successful timber merchant. When she was just five years old, the Bolshevik revolution occurred. My grandfather's business continued to provide well for the family during the period of the New Economic Policy,[2] and my mother was consequently quite well-heeled, with plenty to lose, but she nevertheless developed, across the course of the nineteen-twenties, in schools and in youth organizations, a full-hearted commitment to the Bolshevik cause. This she took with her in 1930 when, the NEP having given way to a regime less amenable to bourgeois existence, her parents decided to emigrate to Canada, and she left the Soviet Union, not because she wanted to, but because she did not want to part with her emigrating parents and sister.

In Montreal, my mother, who could not speak English, and without, at eighteen, an advanced education, tumbled down the class ladder to a proletarian position. She took employment as a sewing machine operator in a garment factory. Before long, she met my father, a dress-cutter, who, unlike her, had an impeccably proletarian pedigree (his father was a poor tailor from Lithuania), and no secondary education. Their courtship unrolled in the context of long hours of factory work, struggles to build unionism in the garment trade, and summer weekends at the country camp some forty miles from town that was set up by and for left-wing Jewish workers. My parents married in 1936 and I appeared, their first-born, in 1941.

My mother was proud to be – to have become – working class, and through the thirties and forties, and until 1958, she was an active member of the Canadian Communist Party. My father belonged to the United Jewish People's Order, most of whose members were anti-religious, anti-Zionist, and strongly pro-Soviet. He was not in the Party itself, not because he had ideological reservations, but because his personality was not conducive to Party membership. Members of the Communist Party were expected to express themselves with confidence and with regularity at branch meetings, and my father was an unusually reticent man with little capacity for self-expression.

Because of my parents' convictions, my upbringing was intensely political. My first school, which I entered in 1946, was named after Morris Winchewsky, a Jewish proletarian poet. At Morris Winchewsky we learned standard primary school things in the mornings, from non-Communist Gentile women teachers;[3] but, in the afternoons, we were taught Jewish (and other) history and Yiddish language and literature by left-wing Jews and Jewesses whose first (and in some cases, so it seemed, only) language was Yiddish. The instruction we got from them, even when they narrated Old Testament stories, was suffused with vernacular Marxist seasoning: nothing heavy or pedantic, just good Yiddish revolutionary common sense. Our report cards were folded down the middle, with English subjects on the left-hand side and Yiddish on the right, because of the directions in which the two languages are written. One of the Yiddish subjects was *Geshichte fun Klassen Kamf* (History of Class Struggle), at which, I am pleased to note, I scored a straight *aleph* in 1949.

One Friday in 1952, the Anti-Subversive (or, as it was commonly known, the Red) Squad of the Province of Quebec Provincial Police raided Morris Winchewsky and turned it inside out, in a search for incriminating left-wing literature. We were in school when they came, but, whatever happened in other classes, the raid was not frightening for those of us who were then in *Lehrerin* ('teacheress') Asher's charge, because, having left the room for a moment in response to the knock on the door, she soon returned, clapped her hands with simulated exuberance, and announced, in English: 'Children, the Board of Health is inspecting the school and you can all go home for the rest of the day!' So we scurried down the stairs, and lurking at the entrance were four men, each of them tall and very fat, all of them eyes down, and looking sheepish.

In the event, no compromising materials were found, since the school had been careful to keep itself clean, but a parallel raid on the premises of the United Jewish People's Order, which ran the school, did expose pamphlets and the like. Those premises were consequently padlocked by the police and their owners were denied access to them, within the terms of a Quebec law later struck down by the Supreme Court of Canada. And, although Morris Winchewsky was not forbidden to continue, the raids caused enough parents to withdraw their children from the school to make its further full-time operation impractical.

Accordingly, we were cast forth, as far as our formal schooling was concerned, into the big wide non-Communist world. But some of us, and I, now eleven, was one of them, departed with a rock-firm attachment to the principles it had been a major purpose of Morris Winchewsky to instil in us, and with full and joyous confidence that the Soviet Union was implementing those principles.

The first blow to that confidence fell in June of 1956, when the American State Department published the text of the speech discrediting Stalin that Nikita Khruschev had delivered, four months earlier, at a closed session of the Twentieth Congress of the Communist Party of the Soviet Union. The Party in Quebec was stunned by the 'Khruschev revelations'. Its top six leaders resigned their memberships in September of 1956. They were, like most Party people, dismayed by what Khruschev had said, because it implied that they had conducted their political lives (and, therefore, their lives) under a massive illusion. But they also felt dismayed for the further reason that national (that is, Toronto) Party leaders who were fraternal delegates at the Twentieth Congress had concealed the de-Stalinization speech when reporting back to the Canadian Party. The six Montreal-based Quebec leaders felt betrayed by the national leadership, and, once they had left, the membership of the Party in Montreal felt not only, like its erstwhile local leadership, betrayed, by Toronto, but also abandoned, by six admired and much-loved comrades whose departure was accompanied by no explanatory statement, who called no meeting to share their burden with the membership, who just went without saying goodbye.

In an atmosphere of confusion and distress, high-tension meetings of an unstructured kind and open to all Party members were held in the remaining months of 1956, at the premises of the Beaver Outing Club,[4] which was a recreational society sponsored by the Party. As leader of the younger teenage portion of the Quebec Division of the National Federation of Labour Youth,[5] I sat agog at those meetings, a silent witness of a little piece of history in the making. I watched the Party split into two groups: hard-liners and soft-liners. While willing (just) to repudiate Stalin, the hard-liners were for minimal change in the Party's mode of work, while the soft-liners had an appetite for reconstruction and renovation.[6] The hard-liners called themselves 'Marxists' and their opponents 'revisionists', and the latter called themselves 'the New' and the others 'the Old' (or, sometimes, the 'dogmatists'). My mother was enthusiastically New, as were the other members of the Party branch she chaired: the line of fracture in the Party was running between rather than within branches.

After eighteen further months of factional dispute, a convention was called to elect a new executive of the still leaderless Quebec Party. Two high functionaries came from Toronto, where the Party was far less wracked, to supervise accreditation of delegates to the electoral convention. Their sympathy was with the hard-liners, and they ensured that duly selected representatives of 'New' Party branches were denied their right to vote, on spurious technical grounds. I believe – but here my recollection is somewhat hazy – that this was the trick the Toronto supervisors pulled: they delayed dispatch to New branches of the forms on which delegates' names were to be inscribed, so that, when those forms were filled in and returned, they could be declared invalid for having arrived too late. Through that or some comparable form of manipulation, the convention was made to produce a uniformly Old executive, and, in the aftermath, those of the New persuasion, my mother included, gradually fell away from the Party: they had, in effect, been disfranchised. Six or seven years later, when my mother taxed one of the Toronto emissaries, a personal friend, with the role he had played in the misconstruction of the 1958 convention, I heard him say something like, 'Bella, in politics you sometimes have to do things that are not pleasant.'

A year or so before the 1958 convention, the leader of the Quebec division of the National Federation of Labour Youth resigned in disillusionment (to become an academic anthropologist), and the Quebec NFLY just collapsed, so fast that I would not have been able to leave it had I wanted to. Nor would I have wanted to leave it then: my mother, after all, was at the time still a committed Party member. I felt, morosely, that it was leaving me.

In September of 1957, with the NFLY gone and me too young for a Party that was anyway growing too Old for me, I entered McGill University, a convinced Marxist with no suitable organization to belong to, and I joined the thoroughly tame Socialist Society which was all that McGill then had to offer.

2. Through the rest of the fifties, and into the early sixties, I was what some would have called a 'fellow traveller'. The Party rapidly became too rigid for me to consider submitting myself anew to its authority, but I remained basically pro-Soviet. Seeds of doubt had been sown, and I knew that there was much over there that deserved to be criticized, yet I still believed that the Soviet Union was a socialist country, struggling towards community and equality, and amply meriting every leftist's allegiance.

But in the thirty years and more that separate the disappearance of the National Federation of Labour Youth and the disappearance, now occurring, of both the Sovietness and the Unionhood of the Soviet Union, my views have undergone further evolution, and for a long time – perhaps two decades – they have included a pretty adverse assessment of the Soviet Union's claim to be a socialist society. Some people have therefore found it surprising that I should be saddened by what I perceive to be the impending final abandonment of the Bolshevik experiment. They can understand that I must regret the impact of the experiment's termination on how socialism is assessed, an impact which results from the widespread tendency to identify the Bolshevik and socialist causes. But they notice that my dejection goes beyond such matters of political calculation, and they wonder why.

The answer is that, although I have long since sustained little hope that things in the Soviet Union might get substantially better, in a socialist sense, there is, in certain domains, and people are prone to overlook this, a vast difference between nourishing little hope and giving up all hope. The small hope that I kept was, as it were, an immense thing, since so much was at stake. And now that residual hope has to be forsworn. So a feeling of loss is not surprising.

And there is also another and perhaps less rational motif here, which I would do well to avow. It is true that I was heavily critical of the Soviet Union, but the angry little boy who pummels his father's chest will not be glad if the old man collapses. As long as the Soviet Union seemed safe, it felt safe for me to be anti-Soviet. Now that it begins, disobligingly, to crumble, I feel impotently protective toward it.

3. Since this piece is for a volume dedicated to Richard, he is present to my mind as I write, and his presence causes me to remember how impressed I was by something Sigmund Freud said about the Soviet

Union in his 1927 essay on *The Future of an Illusion*, when I first read it, more than twenty-five years ago.

In chapter 1 of that book, Freud propounds a theory about the structure of society which any leftist would judge reactionary. He begins by remarking – and with this many leftists, I among them, would readily agree – 'that there are present in all men destructive, and therefore anti-social and anti-cultural trends' (xxi. 7).[7] It is his next step which is reactionary, for Freud proceeds to bisect humanity into radically distinct groups. On one side of the divide are the 'lazy and unintelligent masses' in whom the destructive tendency is so strong that it 'determine[s] their behaviour in human society'. What is more dangerous, these people are not isolated from each other in their submission to unruly instinct, for they 'support one another in giving free rein to their indiscipline'. It is, accordingly, 'impossible to do without control of the mass by a minority', and, fortunately, such a minority exists. For there is also another group of people, who possess the capacity for self-control that the masses lack, who have 'master[ed] their own instinctual wishes', and who therefore have the ability to exercise mastery over others. That ability endows them with the right – and the duty – to rule, for

> it is only through the influence of these individuals who can set an example and whom masses recognize as their leaders that they can be induced to perform the work and undergo the renunciations on which the existence of civilization depends' (xxi. 8).

Having read thus far, I was disappointed to see Freud, who was in so many ways above conventional notions, endorsing the old aristocratic fiction that because of their deficient inherent nature, 'for the mass of mankind . . . self-control chiefly means obeying their governors.'[8]

But now, having laid out his own view, Freud acknowledges the counter-argument that 'cultural regulations' superior to those which have prevailed to date might reduce the negative consequences of biology, and, in deference to that argument, he enters a moderately hopeful qualification. The destructive instinctual drives are, he insists, basic biological fact, but the fact that, as things stand, only a minority are able to discipline them without assistance might not be a biological one:

> One may question whether, and in what degree, it would be possible for a different cultural environment to do away with the two charac-

teristics of human masses which make the guidance of human affairs so difficult.[9] The experiment has not yet been made. Probably a certain percentage of mankind (owing to a pathological disposition or an excess of instinctual strength) will always remain asocial; but if it were feasible merely to reduce the majority that is hostile towards civilization today into a minority, a great deal would have been accomplished – perhaps all that can be accomplished. (xxi. 9)

That was somewhat better than what went before, but the whole message was still hard for a committed Marxist to take, so it was with relief, and pleasure, that I read, in the final paragraph of the chapter, that Freud had

> not the least intention of making judgments on the great experiment in civilization that is now in progress in the vast country that stretches between Europe and Asia . . . What is in preparation there is unfinished and therefore eludes an investigation for which our own long-consolidated civilization affords us material. (xxi. 9)

That Freud did not propound the negative prognosis on the Soviet experiment suggested by the general tenor of his chapter was doubly satisfying, for a still pro-Soviet reader with a strong affection for Freud and his writings. First, it showed that Freud was not, so early as 1927, as anti-Soviet as the main course of his chapter had caused me to fear, and I therefore did not have to classify him, with a heavy heart, as a paid-up member of the enemy camp. But second, my pro-Soviet (as opposed to my socialist) convictions being, at the time, already embattled, it was a relief not to have to cope, on top of everything else, with an acid Freudian scepticism, which I would have respected, despite my confidence in the falsehood of the premises on which it would have been based: people are not always consistent, especially in things that matter a lot to them.

4.   That solace means little now, for we can no longer say about the Soviet Union that 'what is in preparation there is unfinished'. It is finished, all washed up, and the question that arises for those of us who think that and who were attached to the Soviet Union is: having sustained this loss, what do we do now?

The loss affects both those who (like me) had once believed, and had not abandoned all hope, that the Soviet Union would realize the socialist ideal, and, *a fortiori*, those who still believed, only yesterday, that it was in fact realizing it. And although the ideal in question presented itself differently to different believers, it included, for all of us, the following elements, and was, consequently, prodigiously demanding: instead of the class exploitation of capitalism, economic equality; instead of the illusory democracy of class-based bourgeois politics, a real and complete democracy; instead of the alienation from one another of economic agents driven by greed and fear, an economy characterized by willing mutual service.

People react in different ways when they conclude that no progress towards the ideal which they once thought the Soviet Union was realizing will occur there in the foreseeable future. Their reactions depend on how they are disposed to account for the Soviet failure, on how they conceive the relationship, in general, between political ideals and political practice, and on aspects of their emotional make-up, such as how robust they are. These variations generate a ramified taxonomy, and, without trying to depict all of it, I proceed to describe some of its salient branches.

First, there are those who both preserve their belief in the ideal and sustain their commitment to pursuing it, with a fresh view about how and/or where and/or when it is to be achieved.

Others repudiate the unachieved ideal, sometimes after careful reconsideration of its claims, and sometimes through a form of self-deception in which they let those claims fade from their minds. In either case, a new ideal is adopted and a new politics elected, but those who pass on to them without reflection and in recoil from their loss are practising what Jon Elster has called Adaptive Preference Formation, a process in which, irrationally, a person comes to prefer A to B just because he believes that A is available and B is not.[10]

Still others form a mixed collection of types who have it in common that they turn away altogether from politics. Some of them still acknowledge the authority of the original ideal, but they are convinced that it is impossible to realize, or virtually impossible, or anyway something they can no longer summon the energy to fight for: perhaps, when they let the baton fall, they hope that someone else will pick it up. Others reject the ideal and are unable to embrace a different one. To all of these nothing now achievable seems worth achieving, or worth the effort of their own depleted power. When they look at the political world, 'Vanity of Vanities' is what they are inclined to say.

In what follows, I shall endorse sustained pursuit of something like the original ideal, but first I want to say a word about the Vanity of Vanities response, because I have been tempted by it myself in moments when the old ideal has appeared to me to be hopelessly over-ambitious; and also about the response of Adaptive Preference

Formation, because, so it seems to me, it is a temptation to which many on the left are currently succumbing.

5. Vanity of Vanities, or, rather, the form of it that has tempted me, says: genuine socialism is impossible, or virtually impossible, to achieve. It is overwhelmingly likely that the best we shall ever get is some kind of capitalism, and it is for others to find the strength to fight for a better capitalism. Here the old ideal remains bright, but the will collapses, and, integral to its collapse, both helping to induce it and feeding on it, is a pessimistic judgement of possibility that spreads its gloom across perception of the whole feasible set, so that the person says: what is really good is not to be had, and there is nothing good enough for me to devote myself to.

A period of withdrawal following disappearance of what one hoped would fulfil one's dream is, of course, entirely natural. Time is needed to work things through. What is more, depression about the failure of the Soviet Union, as it supervenes in those of us who reluctantly rejected its claims decades ago, perforce has a complex structure, one element in which is self-reproach, since what is lost is a long since denied (yet also fiercely clung to) love.[11] Against such a psychological background, it may be unwise to expect to reach full clarity of purpose quickly. It is nevertheless right to oppose the movement from a per- haps necessary depression to a settled Vanity of Vanities attitude.

If Vanity of Vanities sees nothing good when the best appears lost, Adaptive Preference Formation[12] treats the best it can find as the best that could be conceived. In Adaptive Preference the grass looks greener on *this* side of the fence: the agent's assessment ordering bends round to favour what (he thinks) is in the feasible set. In my opinion, this pathology is visible in a movement of thought which is widespread in contemporary European socialism.

6. Let me explain. Nineteenth-century socialists were for the most part opposed to market organization of economic life. The pioneers favoured something which they thought would be far superior, to wit, comprehensive central planning; and their later followers were en- couraged by what they interpreted as victories of planning, such as Stalin's industrialization drive and the early institution of educational and medical provision in the People's Republic of China. More re- cently, however, socialists have decided that central planning is a poor recipe for economic success. And now there is among socialist intel- lectuals an intelligent movement, but also, and alongside it, an un- thinking and fashion-driven rush, in the direction of a non-planning

or minimally planning market socialist society. Market socialism is socialist because it abolishes the distinction between capital and labour: there is no separate class of capitalists facing workers who own no capital. But it is unlike traditionally conceived socialism in that its worker-owned firms relate to one another and to consumers in standard market-contractual fashion. I think it good from a socialist point of view that market socialism is being brought to the fore as an object of advocacy and policy: these socialist intellectuals, even some of the fashion-driven ones, are performing a useful political service. But I also think that market socialism is at best second best, even if it is the best (or more than the best) at which it is now reasonable to aim, and that many socialist intellectuals who think otherwise are indulging in Adaptive Preference.

Now, the Adaptive Preference response sometimes has some good effects. Like the rational policy of Not Crying Over Spilt Milk, it may prevent fruitless lamentation and wasted effort. But Adaptive Preference also has great destructive potential, since it means losing standards that may be needed to guide criticism of the *status quo*; and it dissolves the faith to which a future with ampler possibilities may yet be hospitable. If you cannot bear to remember the goodness of the goal that you sought and which is not now attainable,[13] you may fail to pursue it should it come within reach, and you will not try to bring it within reach. When the fox succeeds in convincing himself that the grapes are sour, he does not build the ladder that might enable him to get at them.

In 1983 there appeared an important book by Alec Nove, called *The Economics of Feasible Socialism*.[14] One point of including the word 'feasible' in its title was or should have been to abjure the claim that the arrangements recommended in the book are the best conceivable. I do not think that Nove would say, for example, that the market socialism he recommends fully satisfies socialist standards of distributive justice, though he would rightly say that it scores better by those standards than market capitalism does. Notwithstanding that relative superiority, market socialism remains deficient from a socialist point of view, if only because, in socialist perception, there is injustice in a system which confers high rewards on people who happen to be unusually talented and who form highly productive co-operatives.

In 1989 there appeared another important book, by David Miller, called *Market, State and Community*,[15] which, like Nove's, advocates market socialism. But in chapter 6 of his book, Miller seems to me to promote Adaptive Preference Formation. It is, in my view, a serious mistake to suppose that any market system (except, perhaps, the very special one – of which I shall say more later – designed by Joseph Carens) could conform to the requirements of distributive justice. Yet in chapter 6 Miller argues that market socialism tends to reward desert and therefore is, substantially, distributively just. I disagree both with the premiss (that market socialism tends to reward desert[16]) and with the inference (that it follows that it is just[17]) of that argument, and I also reject its conclusion (that market socialism is just[18]).

I do not say that we should aim to achieve, in this era of ideologically rejuvenated capitalism, a form of socialism very different from what Nove and Miller describe. As far as immediate political programmes are concerned, market socialism is probably a good idea. But Miller's (and others') claims for it are grander, and they should not be accepted. One reason why they should not be is discussed in the next section.

7.   Karl Marx was no friend of market socialism, but he did describe a second best to full communism, which he called 'the first phase of communist society',[19] and his criticism of that transitional form of society seems to me to bear against market socialism too.

Marx's first phase of communism is a non-market society in which remuneration is supposed to track labour contribution. That is the meaning of its ruling principle: to each according to his work. If, as David Miller thinks, contribution establishes desert and rewarding desert suffices for justice, then Marx's lower phase of communism would possess the virtue that it rewards desert and is therefore just: perhaps, indeed, more just than any market socialism could be.

That last speculation is however, a pretty idle one, since measuring contribution in a non-market society requires questionable assignments of product to heterogenous labours, and to labours of different skill levels;[20] and while a market society assigns salaries to labour in an automatic process free of the application of contestable criteria, it is impossible to treat those salaries as measures of *contribution*, influenced as they are by vagaries of bargaining power and other accidental market circumstances. It is accordingly, difficult to compare the relative merits of the two forms of socialism as devices for rewarding producers according to their contribution.

But let us here set aside the question of whether Marx was right to prefer a non-market socialism to a market one, and also the problem of how labour contributions are to be measured. Of greater present relevance is that Marx's strictures against the principle of reward to contribution expose the anti-socialist (because bourgeois) character of market socialism's reward structure. While pointing out that first-stage communism abolishes capitalist exploitation, since differential access to means of production is gone, and no one consumes more labour value than he produces, Marx criticized the principle of reward for contribution because of the (unjust)[21] inequality that it generates. For Marx, it is indeed a recommendation of low-stage communism that the bourgeois principle of reward for contribution is in this society not just invoked as ideological rationalization but actually instituted, so that 'principle and practice are no longer at logger-heads'. But he did not doubt that reward for contribution is a bourgeois principle, one which treats a person's talent 'as a natural privilege'. Reward for contribution implies recognition of what I have elsewhere called the principle of self-ownership.[22] Nothing is more bourgeois than that, and the Gotha critique lesson for market socialism is that, while market socialism may remove the income injustice caused by differential ownership of capital, it preserves the income injustice caused by differential ownership of endowments of personal capacity.

8.   Before we settle for market socialism, let us recall why socialists in the past rejected the market. Some of their reasons were better than others, and here I shall review what I take to be the four principal criticisms of the market in the socialist tradition, starting with two that I consider misplaced, and ending with two that I consider sound. The market has been judged (1) inefficient, (2) anarchic, (3) unjust in its results, and (4) mean in its motivational presuppositions.

(1) To say that the market is inefficient is to criticize it in its allocative as opposed to its distributive function, where the first concerns the assignment of resources to different productive uses (so much steel to housing and so much to automobiles and so many engineers to each and so on) and the second concerns the assignment of income to owners of productive factors (who are, in a purely socialist market socialism, owners of labour power only). Manifestly, allocation and distribution are in intimate causal relationship, but the bottom line of this first criticism relates to allocation alone: it is that the market is wasteful, variously over-and under-productive, and here the question of who in particular suffers from that waste is set to one side. And the reason for the wastefulness, so the criticism goes, is that in a market economy producer interaction is unplanned.

We now know that the traditional socialist view about the market's lack of planning was misconceived. It failed to acknowledge how remarkably well the unplanned market organizes information, and, indeed, how difficult it is for a planning centre to possess itself of the information about preferences and production possibilities dispersed through the market in a non-planning system. Even if the planner's computer could do wonders with that information, the problem is that there are systematic obstacles to gathering it: to that extent, Von Mises and Hayek were right. And the traditional socialist critique also failed to appreciate the degree to which it would prove possible to correct for market deficiencies through an external regulation which falls far short of comprehensive planning.

(2) There was, however, in the traditional socialist objection to the absence of a plan, a separate emphasis that the market's generation of massive unplanned outcomes, considered just as such, that is, apart from the particular disbenefits and injustices of those outcomes, means that society is not in control of its own destiny. Marx and Engels did not favour planning solely because of the advantageous economic consequences that they thought it would have, but also because of the significance of planning as a realization of the idea, derived no doubt from the Hegelian legacy under which they laboured, of humanity rising to consciousness of and control over itself. The advent of the planned society was seen as 'the ascent of man from the kingdom of necessity to the kingdom of freedom'.[23]

In my view, that idea is entirely misplaced. Individual self-direction, a person's determining the course of his own life, may have value *per se*, but collective self-direction does not.[24] David Miller perceptively claims that five values (conceived not instrumentally but as valuable in themselves) have inspired socialists,[25] and I think (as he does) that we should dump the first one – conscious social purpose – on his list. It is not the same thing as democracy, for a democracy can decide that some things should not be subject to collective purpose. And I think that it should decide what to put within collective purpose on a purely instrumental basis, that is, according to the tendency of collective action to promote or frustrate other values, and notably the other four on Miller's list, which are freedom, equality, community[26] and democracy itself. There is harm to no one in the mere fact that social purpose is lacking, though society-wide decision-making is, of course, required for instrumental reasons, such as, sometimes, to promote individual freedom.

I turn to criticisms of the market which seem to me to be unanswerable. They are (3) that the market distributes in unjustly unequal amounts, about which enough has been said above, and (4) that it motivates contribution not on the basis of commitment to one's fellow human beings and a desire to serve them while being served by them, but on the basis of impersonal cash reward. The immediate motive to productive activity in a market society is usually some mixture of greed and fear, in proportions that vary with the details of a person's market position. In greed, other people are seen as possible sources of enrichment, and in fear they are seen as threats.

The history of the twentieth century encourages the thought that the easiest way to generate productivity in a modern society is by nourishing the motives of greed and fear, in a hierarchy of unequal income. That does not make them attractive motives, and the fact that the first great experiment in running a modern economy without relying on avarice and anxiety has failed, disastrously, is not a good reason for giving up the attempt for ever. Philosophers least of all should join the contemporary choruses of dirge and hosanna whose common refrain is that the socialist project is over. I am sure that it has a long way to go yet, and it is part of the mission of philosophy to explore unanticipated possibilities.

What is true and, as the interest in market socialism shows, widely appreciated is that different ways forward must now be tried. And in the light of the misallocating propensity of comprehensive planning on the one hand and of the injustice of market results and the moral shabbiness of market motivation on the other, it is natural to ask whether it might be possible to preserve the allocative function of the market, to continue to get the benefits it provides of information generation and processing while extinguishing its normal motivational presuppositions and distributive consequences. Such a project of differentiation is the aspiration of Joseph Carens's ground-breaking book called *Equality, Moral Incentives, and the Market*.[27] The book figures forth a system in which what looks like a standard capitalist market organizes economic activity. There are (pre-tax) profit-maximizing capitalists, and workers who own no capital, but people acknowledge an obligation to serve others, and the extent to which they discharge it is measured by how close their pre-tax income is to what it would be in the most remunerative activity available to them, while taxation effects a post-tax distribution of income which meets a demanding standard of equality. Here, then, producers aim, in an immediate sense, at cash results, but they do not keep the money that accrues, and they seek it out of a desire to contribute to society. As Carens has recognized, there are serious problems with the scheme,[28] but it seems to me one amply worth refining, and I hope to address that task in some of my own future work.

9. It can be hard to maintain dedication to that kind of work in a climate where it is regarded as irrelevant. When you are out of joint

with the times, you look for sources of confidence to strengthen your resolve. In closing, I shall mention two of mine.

When I did graduate work at Oxford, it was the prevailing notion that there were in philosophy plainly right and plainly wrong answers, that a hard-headed clear-mindedness would without too much ado generate the right ones, and that the latter were likely to be not surprising but already familiar. In 1963 I left Oxford to lecture in the department where Richard had just become Professor. On Wednesday afternoons he presided over a staff discussion group in which the prevailing notion was different from at Oxford, and one that I experienced as liberating. It was that on any large philosophical question there were bound to be different views (that was the operative word), that it could be hard to tell which one was right, and that there was no reason to suppose that the right one was comfortable or long since known. I remember how Richard would restore a sense of perspective, when one of us had rehearsed some accepted wisdom, by uttering a corrective sentence which began 'Well, there is, of course, the other view, that . . . ' And I also remember the thrill I felt, listening to his beautiful inaugural lecture, *On Drawing an Object* (1965), when he said of his predecessors A. J. Ayer and Stuart Hampshire that they did not encourage 'the desire to agree' (p. 6). In times like these, Richard's generous liberalism is a good thing to have experienced, and to remember.

The other source of strength that I want to mention relates more to politics than to philosophy, but it too implies an admonition against surrender to the pull of conventional thinking. It is the end of the letter which Friedrich Engels wrote to his comrade Friedrich Sorge, the day after Marx died:

> Local lights and lesser minds, if not the humbugs, will now have a free hand. The final victory is certain, but circuitous paths, temporary and local errors – things which even now are so unavoidable – will become more common than ever. Well, we must see it through. What else are we here for?
> And we are not near losing courage yet.[29]

NOTES

[1] I am deeply grateful to Arnold Zuboff, who spent many hours finding and removing faults in drafts of this essay. I also thank Jim Hopkins for support and criticism. The present essay was produced substantially, in

1989, and the above remark, and some further conjectures below, may now read somewhat strangely. But they belong to the mood in which the essay was written, and I cannot alter them without spoiling its integrity.

2   I do not know what the family's condition was in the turbulent post-revolutionary period which preceded the adoption of the NEP in 1921.

3   They were Gentile because discrimination against hiring Jewish teachers in the Quebec school system meant that there were few Jewish aspirants to the profession. And they were non-Communist not only because most people were, but also because the Communist minority consisted mainly of French Canadians (the majority linguistic group), Jews, and not fully assimilated Ukrainians. Most English-speaking Montreal schoolteachers at primary level were genteel women of British Isles extraction: not a category abounding in subversives.

4   Those familiar with Montreal might like to know that this place was on the north side of Mount Royal Avenue, opposite Fletcher's Field, just West of what was then the Young Men's Hebrew Association and what is now a Université de Montréal sports centre, and above a delicatessen called, at different times, Shap's, Dunn's, and Nu-Park.

5   The NFLY (pronounced 'enfli') was, in all but name, the Young Communist League. The Communist Party had been outlawed when, because of the Molotov – Ribbentrop Pact, it refused to support the war against Germany. So it changed its name to the Labour Progressive Party, and the YCL became the NFLY. (The Party reassumed its original name in 1959. In announcing the nomenclatural reclamation, the *Canadian Tribune* (the Party paper) explained that 'Communist Party' was being readopted because it was 'scientifically more correct'.)

6   The line of the soft-liners was not all that soft. Thus, for example, the Soviet action in Hungary in the autumn of October 1956 was regarded, at the time, by virtually everyone in the Party, as an entirely justified suppression of a Fascist rebellion.

7   'Trends' translates *Tendenzen*; 'tendencies' would be better.

8   *The Republic of Plato*, tr. F. M. Cornford (Oxford University Press, Oxford, 1945), p. 78. For an argument against the Plato – Freud view, see my *Karl Marx's Theory of History* (Oxford University Press, Oxford, 1978), pp. 212–13.

9   These are that 'they are not spontaneously fond of work and that arguments arc of no avail against their passions' (xxi. 8). But, given the rest of the chapter, and Freud's ideas about gratification-deferral, the first of these characteristics, the 'spontaneous' aversion to work, is best interpreted as a biological universal, so that it is, for Freud, only the second characteristic, the insensitivity to argument, that distinguishes the masses from their leaders: in other words, the latter, too, have 'no love for instinctual renunciation', but *they* are 'convinced by argument of its inevitability' (xxi. 7). I grant that so interpreting Freud goes awkwardly with his entertaining the possibility that 'a different cultural environment'

might 'do away with' the masses' lack of 'spontaneous fondness' for work, but, as far as I can see, the line between nature and culture cuts at different points in different formulations in this chapter of Freud.

¹⁰ For further discussion of the phenomenon, in general terms, see note 12 below.

¹¹ See Freud's telling remarks in 'Mourning and Melancholia' (xiv. 240).

¹² That is the name applied by Jon Elster to the phenomenon in question: see his brilliant (albeit, as we shall see, verbally flawed) discussion of (what he also calls) "Sour Grapes" (*Sour Grapes*, (Cambridge University Press, 1983, Ch III), to which I am greatly indebted. 'Sour Grapes' is undoubtedly a snappier name than 'Adaptive Preference Formation', but, despite Elster's official, or at least initial, identification of them with one another (see ibid., p. 110), 'Sour Grapes' is not a good name for adaptive preference, because the latter is a general phenomenon and the fox's attitude in the Sour Grapes story is in two ways but a specific form of it.

In all adaptive preference formation, A is preferred to B because A is (readily) available and B is not, but the comparative preference can be the upshot either of judging A better than it would otherwise (that is, but for the unavailability of B) be judged or of judging B worse than it would otherwise be judged (or, of course, of both). The fox is in the second position. He downgrades the grapes he does not have: he does not upgrade the condition of grapelessness. But much adaptive preference formation, including some of the preference for market socialism discussed in the next section, goes the other way: the available thing gets upgraded. (At p. 119 Elster appears to restrict 'Sour Grapes' to downgrading the unavailable, despite his use of it as an alternative name for adaptive preference formation as such at p. 110.)

One may moreover, come to prefer available A to unavailable B either because of a change of criteria caused by knowledge of the feasible set or because of a (similarly caused) change of factual judgement about how A and B stack up against unreformed criteria. 'Sour Grapes' proper, in the story of the fox, illustrates the second thing, an irrational change of factual judgement (and, despite what Elster says at p. 123, in the English version of the story as well as in the French). As for the recent turn towards market socialism, it surely reflects reassessment, to different degrees in different cases, both of facts and of criteria, so 'Sour Grapes' would, once again, be misleading here. (To make matters more tangled as far as Elster's exposition goes, at p. 123 he (not unreasonably) contrasts 'adaptive preferences' and 'adaptive [factual] perception' and in effect treats the 'Sour Grapes' story as a case of the latter, so that 'Sour Grapes' is in the end not even an instance of what he originally identified it with!)

¹³ If you cannot do that, you will be relevantly like those who 'fail to experience mourning. Feeling incapable of saving and securely reinstating their loved objects inside themselves, they must turn away from them more than hitherto and therefore deny their love for them' (Melanie

Klein, 'Mourning: Its Relation to Manic-Depressive States' (1940), in *Contributions to Psychoanalysis* (Hogarth, London, 1973), p. 336.

[14] Alec Nove, *The Economics of Feasible Socialism* (George Allen & Unwin, London, 1983).

[15] David Miller, *Market, State and Community* (Oxford University Press, Oxford, 1989).

[16] For 'desert', supposing that there is such a thing, divides into what Joel Feinberg would call comparative and non-comparative forms, and I am convinced that the two need to be confused with one another for the stated premiss to seem true. There is, moreover, the further difficulty that the market rewards results, which are imperfectly correlated with effort, which is also (if anything is) a source of desert, and to which the market is blind. For these and other points, see my 'David Miller on Market Socialism and Distributive Justice', typescript available on request; and see Feinberg, 'Noncomparative Justice', *Philosophical Review*, Vol. LXXXIII (1974) for the distinction between comparative and non-comparative desert.

[17] For desert is not the only relevant dimension of justice. There is also, for example, need, and Miller's attempt to finesse the latter in the present connection is unsatisfactory. See Miller, *Market, State and Community*, pp. 295–6, and my 'David Miller' § 3.

[18] Since I think it is unjust, for reasons that may already be apparent, and which are amplified in the next section.

[19] Marx, 'The Critique of the Gotha Programme', in *Marx/Engels Selected Works in One Volume* (Lawrence and Wishart, London, 1968), p. 324. What Marx called 'the first phase of communist society' is what later Marxists called 'socialism' (as opposed to 'communism').

[20] Because of the difficulty of finding criteria for assigning product to individuals, Soviet bureaucrats often got away with defending their bloated salaries on the principle of reward to contribution. They sometimes implied that they would be failing in their obligation to help realize the lower stage of communism if they gave up their large dachas.

[21] The adjective has to go in parentheses because Marx disparaged the notion of justice, and, so I have claimed, did not realize that he believed passionately in it (see my review of Allen Wood, *Karl Marx*, *Mind*, (1983), pp. 440–5).

[22] See my 'Self-Ownership, Communism and Equality', *Proceedings of the Aristotelian Society*, Supplementary Volume, 1990, pp. 33–5. (The quotations in this paragraph come from Marx, 'The Critique of the Gotha Programme', p. 324).

[23] Friedrich Engels, *Socialism: Utopian and Scientific* (Allen and Unwin, London, 1892), p. 82.

[24] Except in the here totally irrelevant sense of non-subjection to another collective. Not wanting your society's course to be deliberately determined from without does not imply wanting it to be deliberately determined from within.

[25] Miller, 'Market Socialism', paper delivered to a seminar in Oxford in October 1989.

[26] Endorsement of community as an ultimate value might be thought inconsistent with scepticism about the ultimate value of collective purpose. For if community is valuable, identification with community is valuable, and that might require subscribing to a group goal which community members could not regard as instrumentally justified (by the propensity of pursuit of that goal to sustain community). That represents a complex challenge to what I have said, and I do not want to deal with it here, save by remarking that even if community members could not regard the communal goal as instrumentally justified, how they could regard it and what its true value would be are not the same thing.

[27] Joseph Carens, *Equality, Moral Incentives, and the Market* (University of Chicago Press, Chicago, 1981). The book's significant subtitle is *An Essay in Utopian Politico-Economic Theory*.

[28] See Carens, 'Rights and Duties in an Egalitarian Society', *Political Theory*, 14, no. 1 (February 1986), parts 3 and 4.

[29] Marx and Engels, *Selected Correspondence* (International Publishers, New York, 1934), p. 415.

9

Character, Mind, and Politics: The Socratic Case

AMÉLIE OKSENBERG RORTY

(1) *Intellectualism and psychologism* What role does a person's character have in determining whether she can think, think well and truly, in contrast to being clever the way a sophist might be clever, sometimes saying what is true and even proving it, but without ever understanding its import or using it well? What role can purely intellectual enquiry – the kind that anyone could follow, regardless of character or temperament – play in reforming or improving character and temperament?

For a long time, the Ministry of Education in the People's Republic of China did not give undergraduates access to the main libraries, until the Party cadres were assured that the students had formed the ideological and political character required to have a proper understanding of what they read. It was not solely a matter of their passing an examination on Party history and Party doctrine; it was a matter of the Party cadres' evaluating the applicant's character. The Party held that knowledge does not consist merely of skills or information that can be absorbed, understood, and correctly used by anyone and everyone. The interpretation as well as the use of knowledge is, on this view, at least in part a function of a person's political character, her orientation and commitments; and character is expressed not only by what a person says, but by the whole range of her actions. Let's call this view 'political psychologism'.

There is a profound divide between those who, like the Party cadres in the Ministry of Education, believe that thought and character are directly co-ordinate, and intellectualists, who believe that there is a form of critical and self-corrective rationality whose operations are independent of the psychology of character formation. It is illuminating to classify philosophers as belonging to one or the other party in this divide. Descartes is, in intent at least, an intellectualist. Superficially, Spinoza appears to be an intellectualist; but in truth, he argues that the mind is co-ordinate with, rather than independent of extension. He does not believe that self-reform of an individual can be assured solely by the exercise of pure rationality. Kant dreamt the intellectualist dream, particularly in his theory of the moral force of practical reason. Contemporary latter-day Romanticists – linguistic idealists like Foucault – argue for the creative autonomy of the mind. But unlike Enlightenment intellectualists, they do not look to the autonomy of thought for an independent rational critique of character or politics. For them, the autonomy of mind lies in the power of the unconditioned imagination to construct new modes of 'discourse', rather than that of unconditioned impartial rationality to analyse the preconditions of practical activity. As they see it, the task is that of re-forming psychological and political character by replacing it, rather than correcting it with the aid of reflective understanding. For the most part, neo-Romantics acknowledge that they leave both critique and reconstruction in the hands of power politics. We are brought full circle: it was precisely the fear of leaving matters to power politics that led to intellectualism.

Richard Wollheim has attempted to provide a third way, one that avoids both the apparent naïvety of intellectualism and the resignation that appears to haunt psychologism. In *The Thread of Life* (1984) he develops a position which combines a form of intellectualism with a modified psychologism. He charts the psycho-social development required to develop the capacity for moral and intellectual autonomy. According to this view, only those who have successfully worked through the psychological dramas and traumas of early childhood attachments and identifications can evaluate the appropriateness and rationality of their desires and beliefs. His analysis recounts the psycho-social dynamic biography – the history of the childhood and adolescence – of the *phronimos*. But *The Thread of Life* does not and could not stand alone. Wollheim's early political essays are a necessary supplement: they give an account of the political structures that are required to support the development of moral autonomy. His essays on art – *Painting as an Art* (1987) and *On Art and the Mind* (1973) – also reflect his attempts to reconcile intellectualism with psychologism; he analyses the ways in which perception and aesthetic reactions are affected by our early experience of psychological dependence and power. It is, in part, through perception and aesthetic experience that character affects thought. And it is presumably by working through these effects that a person develops the capacity to see through and beyond her psychological history. Taken together, Wollheim's writings form a coherent whole. So interpreted, they show that the issues surrounding the claims of intellectualism have political ramifications.

Put in political and cultural terms, the question is whether a mal-formed culture bent on realizing harmful ends can carry on a genuine enquiry that would enable it to evaluate, and perhaps correct, its practices. Intellectualists hold that a relatively disinterested enquiry could present a diagnosis and project a correction of social and political ills. Enlightened by an analysis of this kind, a polity could then in principle move towards its own reform. Those who, like Burke and Oakeshott, are sceptical of the possibility of purely intellectual reform, stress the force of tradition in the formation of the character of a ruling class educated in a tradition of public service. The third view – an elaboration of Wollheim's view – would analyse the political conditions that favour the development of a morally sensitive intellectual meritocracy capable of autonomous critical reflection.

(2) *The Socratic case* It was of course Socrates (as depicted by Plato in the early dialogues) who first explored the basic issues concerning the relation of thought, character, and action. His position is, I believe, exasperatingly guarded, ironic, and ambiguous. Its evasiveness is Protean in its disguises. His stress on enquiry, on the centrality of knowledge, marks him as an intellectualist. He seems, further, to be an epistemological egalitarian, ready to talk to anyone and everyone, on the assumption that they are all able to search for the truth. On the other hand, his irony towards eristic combative or erotic seductive interlocutors suggests that he thinks that character and temperament set severe constraints on the possibility of genuine enquiry. To the extent that Socrates is committed to the view that we have innate knowledge of the Forms, he seems to be both an egalitarian and an intellectualist. Yet a Socratic innatist might also hold that the possibility of recollection, the possibility of well-formed enquiry, is constrained by an individual's physical constitution, his character and upbringing, and – as a central factor affecting upbringing – the political structures of his polity.

Socrates was evasive in answering the question 'Can virtue be taught?' and he had good reasons for being evasive. Put so baldly, the question is equivocal. Socrates had to face the problems of those who think that common conceptions about such matters might be ill-formed. The terminology is tainted: Socrates is painfully aware of the fact that in speaking of *aretē* and of *didaskein*, he is evoking the very conceptions he thinks need to be critically examined and perhaps redefined. As Socrates was the first to say, we cannot determine whether virtue can be taught until we have determined what virtue is. But we also need to discover in what teaching consists, who qualifies as a teacher, and what conditions must be satisfied for someone to be capable of learning virtue.

Let us suppose that Socrates' attack on the Sophists has shown that virtue essentially embeds or requires knowledge of what is good and bad. Without such knowledge a person might, even with the best of intentions, bring harm to those he wishes to benefit. Socrates' views on whether virtue can be taught depend on whether that kind of knowledge – the knowledge that is essential to living well – can be taught. The centrality of knowledge to virtue justifies identifying it with knowledge only if knowledge of what is good assures whatever other conditions – say conditions of temperament and character – might be required for living well.[1]

Socrates might be a *moral intellectualist*, identifying virtue with knowledge of what is good and bad, without being an *epistemological intellectualist*. He might hold that virtue is identical with, or is essentially analysed as, knowledge, without holding that knowledge consists solely or essentially in a cognitive attitude. Knowledge of the good might itself require a set of conditions that go beyond having and properly defending true beliefs; it might, for instance, require the active disposition to apply those beliefs appropriately, in any and all contexts where their import is relevant. Whether these extra conditions on knowledge undermine Socratic intellectualism depends on Socrates' account of how knowledge affects acting well and living well.

Certainly the knowledge that is at the core of virtue consists, at the very least, in knowing what is good. But that knowledge goes significantly beyond having justified true beliefs: it involves knowing how to act well. Does this make virtue a craft, a species of *technē* ? The crafts are specialized, and their skills are rarely transferable. A cook is not a shoemaker, and it is rare that even a master rhetorician is a reliable cook. To be sure, the crafts require knowledge that goes beyond technical skills. To make good shoes, the shoemaker must know what kinds of shoes are good, and he can't know that unless he knows why we wear shoes. But it is not, as we say, by virtue of his special craft that the shoemaker knows that we wear shoes to protect our feet rather than to make our legs look seductively lanky.

If virtue were a craft, it would not be among the specialized crafts, since it involves knowing in general – and in particular – what to do, what to avoid, and what to ignore in all sorts of situations. The virtuous know the ends and the relative importance of each of the several crafts; whether, for instance, it is in general the householder or the cook who should determine how sumptuous a meal should be. And the virtuous also know what to do in particular situations, when to wear shoes and when to go barefoot, and not just in childish imitation of Socrates. The virtuous know how to specify and realize the desire for the good that is at the heart of all desire. They act well because they have thought well; and – to the embarrassment of philosophical analysis – they think well because they know what is good.

But how is the ability – and the active disposition – to act well connected with the disposition to enquire, to articulate and defend true beliefs about what is good? Is that ability – the ability to enquire – just one among the specialized skills or crafts? Or is it, like virtue, not a specialized craft but the most general of crafts? If excellence in enquiry is the active ability to search for and discover truth, it seems to stand in a special relation to virtue.

Fusing intellectual skills with skills of action breaks down the distinction between *epistēmē* and *technē*: it does not reduce the one to the other in either direction. But this is the question before us: whether true, well-justified belief about what is good suffices for virtue or whether virtue also requires a certain sort of character, one that cannot just be formed by, or from, well-justified beliefs about what is good.

Socratic knowledge is, at the very least, centrally propositional, in that what a person knows – the content of his knowledge – must be articulable in an unambiguous, testable proposition. But there is more to a person's knowing P than his believing P for the reasons that in fact demonstrate the truth of P. He must also make the distinctions and discriminations appropriate to the truth of that proposition. It is a central feature of knowledge (and for that matter, belief) that the belief and its supporting reasons stand in an appropriate formative relation to the rest of a person's psychology, to what he perceives, to how he classifies things, to what he desires.

To know what water is, it is not enough to understand and demonstrate its chemical formula. It is also necessary to be able to distinguish a glass of water from a glass of ethyl alcohol and to know which of them to drink when one is thirsty. The condition for knowledge – indeed the condition for belief – is a condition for psychological ramification and behavioural permeation. To know P is to accept all its consequences, including those that, by affecting desire, affect action. There are then two independent conditions that must be satisfied: a person knows P just when he can formulate and demonstrate P, *and* when P functions appropriately in the formation of the rest of his beliefs and desires, in such a way that his inferences are informed by P and his actions are formed by desires that have been specified by P and its ramified logical and behavioural consequences.

Virtue not only requires appropriately justified true beliefs about the good; it also requires holding those beliefs in such a way that they permeate a person's psychology, affecting his perceptual and practical discriminations, opinions, desires, and actions. One way of ensuring the second condition is to make it a consequence of Socrates' theory of motivation: if all desire is directed to the good, then beliefs about what is good will naturally permeate psychology and behaviour. That desire – the desire for what is genuinely good – carries a second-order desire, the desire to have well-formed – that is, well-informed – desires. Because we all desire what is good, we attempt to make the intellectual realization of true beliefs permeate psychologically, forming appropriate discriminations, desires, and actions. The ramification of the first condition of knowledge – that the person has and can justify true beliefs, making the appropriate inferences from them – depends on the addition of this premiss: that our desire for the good influences our enquiry and our beliefs; it must be epistemologically effective.

It should by now be clear that Socratic intellectualism requires the support of a theory of desire as well as a theory of knowledge. Indeed the two are the interlocked linchpins of Socrates' position and practice. The view that virtue is knowledge and the view that all men desire the good are required for one another's support. Intellectual knowledge of the good ensures acting well only if we all desire the good and act from that desire. But the view that we do desire the good and act from that desire is defensible only if we do automatically correct our desires when we correct our beliefs about what is good – that is, only if intellectual knowledge of the good ramifies psychologically.

Socrates' warning to Hippocrates in the *Protagoras* – a warning that, in studying with the Sophists, he risks acquiring and being transformed by false beliefs – provides some evidence that Socrates thought that even false beliefs automatically permeate psychology (*Protagoras* 311–314C). The warning suggests that Socrates thought *either* that believing just consists in such psychological permeation or ramification *or* that we are so constituted that beliefs just do naturally permeate psychologically, perhaps because in desiring what *is* good, we desire that our beliefs affect our psychology. In either case, believing is not intellectually contained or constrained.

If Hippocrates courts danger by studying with Protagoras, could he be transformed for the better by discussions with Socrates? Can Socrates transform a casual interlocutor into a serious enquirer? He seems to be willing to enter into discussion with anyone who presents himself, even when it is painfully clear that nothing can transform an obdurate Thrasymachus into an enchantingly brilliant Theaetetus. Are the flaws of temperament that set constraints on the benefits of genuine enquiry the result of intellectual errors? Do these flaws represent false beliefs about what is good, just those sorts of false beliefs that enquiry might correct? An enquiry of that kind need not necessarily start with desire for the truth. An eristic or erotic impulse might prompt someone to join Socrates in an investigation. The optimistic reading of Socrates' view is that no matter how or why someone is drawn into enquiry, his investigation could in principle correct his character flaws by correcting the false beliefs that stand at their heart.

The correction of belief and character might require moving through a number of stages: someone might just happen to fall into an extended discussion with Socrates without being initially psychologically well qualified to engage in serious truth-bound enquiry into the good. It is possible to participate in an investigation, disputatiously tracing the presuppositions and consequences of a variety of beliefs, just for the fun of it, without committing oneself to basing one's beliefs, let alone one's psychology or behaviour, on the outcome of that investigation. Such enquiry is psychologically and practically bracketed. But Socratic enquiry requires that the participants commit themselves to the psychological and practical consequences of their investigation, that they assert only what they genuinely believe – that is, only those beliefs upon which they are prepared to act. Since everyone desires what is good, they ought not affirm beliefs solely for the pleasure of wooing Socrates or for the power of constructing an ingenious argument; instead, they will commit themselves to diligently and fairly testing all candidates for truth.

But there are severe limits to Socrates' egalitarian practice of engaging anyone, even Meno's slave, in an apparently successful dialectical enquiry. When a flawed character such as Alcibiades is erotically led to enquiry, the knowledge of how to argue that he might acquire will not be sufficient to ensure that he acquire true beliefs, still less their appropriate psychological permeation. Temperament seems to affect even the possibility of genuine enquiry, not just the successful permeation of its results. *Socrates* may indeed have intended to have serious conversations with Alcibiades and with Meno's slave, but *Plato* presents these conversations as farcical. Alcibiades remains impish and the slave slavish in all their discussions with Socrates.

The question remains open. Initially, participating in discussion with Socrates might require no more intelligence or character than Meno's slave had. But to qualify as a pupil or as a companion in substantive enquiries into what is good, a person must have the qualities attributed to Theaetetus. He must himself be persistent and vigorous, but not defensive, with a good sense of what is relevant, a retentive memory, and above all a love of the truth. On the interpretation that makes Socrates an epistemological egalitarian, everyone does, in some sense, know or have all the intellectual equipment necessary for the first stage of enquiry, to participate in philosophical conversation with Socrates. At any rate, everyone does, in some sense, know or have what it takes to test his beliefs. Socrates is as ready to talk with the manifestly dense as with the clever. And indeed the clever seem not to fare much better than the dense in discussion with him. But Plato dramatically suggests something else: Socrates' intellectual egalitarianism does not entail egalitarian attitudes towards temperament and character, as they affect an interlocutor's ability to learn from discussion, as well as his ability to learn how to discuss.

Exactly what traits are required? Might there be some non-intellectualist trait that would serve as a pole-vault to bring a person to the right place, so that he moves from Meno's slave's slavishness to Theaetetus's virtues? If there is a candidate for that psychological trait, it is surely *eros*, and in this case an erotic attachment to Socrates. Again, Platonic drama, this time evoking history, undermines Socratic hopes. In the *Symposium* Socrates presents the view that *eros* will, when it is properly understood, effect its own transformation. Reflective lovers acting to realize the true object of their desires to possess what they love must move to the good. But even in the *Symposium* love is not enough; only truth-oriented reflective *eros* can realize its true but opaque object. And if that were not enough to make the point, the example of Alcibiades, surely the most brilliant and persistent among the lovers of Socrates, dashes the hope that the combination of intelligence and love could ensure the proper imitation of the best model of virtue.

Is imitating a virtuous model an alternative way of learning or acquiring virtue, one that might be more effective than engaging in dialectical enquiry? Perhaps instead of focusing on the qualities required for learning virtue, we should investigate those required for serving as a sound model for imitation. If Socrates was the wisest and best and most virtuous man of his time, he seems the natural candidate for being the best available model of virtue. But there are both theoretical and practical problems in the way of learning virtue by imitating a virtuous model. For one thing, the learner must already be set to imitate the model; for another, he needs to be able to identify an appropriate model, Socrates rather than the impressive and formidable Protagoras.

These problems are not as devastating as they first seem. Socrates' concerns about the educative dangers of the arts, about music and drama, suggest that he believed that we just naturally do imitate what is presented to us, without needing any special motivation to do so. And while the problem of identifying the sound model of virtue remains a genuine practical problem, it is not always unsolvable, particularly if the capacity for truth-oriented enquiry is a condition of virtue. We don't have to be expert shoemakers to identify the expert shoemaker who makes sturdy, comfortable shoes; we don't have to be physicians to identify a healer. If identifying the good man is identifying the good enquirer, we are in luck. The good enquirer is the person who successfully tests the claims that are proposed to him, and does so again and again and again. This mode of identifying the moral expert may bring Socrates dangerously close to the Sophists for his own comfort. Still, he shows us how we can in principle distinguish the star sophist from the virtuous enquirer. The model enquirer makes truth the aim of his enterprise, without taking himself to have won the argument just because he has thrown his opponent into confusion. He persists in enquiry until he has satisfied every comer on every question, and he is committed to accepting only those conclusions that he is prepared to apply in practice. In a sense, Socrates did model this virtue; and in a sense, he did not. A perpetual motion machine of enquiry he certainly is. He never ceased to pursue the good by pursuing the argument; and he followed his conclusions wherever they led, in action as well as in thought. But he certainly did not satisfy every comer on every question; he does not satisfy thoughtful critical readers, and he did not satisfy himself. Yet he was the very model of an enquirer, a model of the difference between sophistical and philosophic enquiry.

There are, however, yet further difficulties with learning virtue by imitation. Even if the learner has identified his Socratic model, he still must face the problem of determining just what in that model to imitate. Acquiring virtue by imitation seems to presuppose the very knowledge and virtue to be acquired. Just what is it that the learner imitates – what is it that he does – in imitating the virtuous? After all, Socrates does a lot of things. What does it mean to act like him? Go barefoot when he goes barefoot? Drink deep and remain sober? Surely these are not the virtues of Socrates, though he may have brought his virtues to those actions. Imitators can identify the traits appropriate for imitation only if the model himself can somehow guide them in that very process. Just as *eros* is not enough, excellent models are not enough. Socrates himself attempts to provide the missing link, by trying to guide those who might imitate him. In every imaginable way, he tries to get his interlocutors to argue well: he shows them how to do it; he woos, incites, teases, bullies them into doing it; and he actively engages them in the doing of it. Ideally, the quandary of imitators might be solved by the qualities of the best of models. One of the ways in which Socrates is an exemplary enquirer is that he persists in luring his imitators in the right direction, to imitate him in enquiry rather than in soldiering or giving speeches or banqueting or braving the cold.

The eulogy of Socrates as the wisest, best, and most just man of his time might carry a bitter, ironic undertone. Whether the model of virtue succeeded in making anyone more virtuous remains an open question. On the one hand, Socrates might have taught some virtue even if none of his interlocutors became moral paragons. Acquiring some capacities for critical enquiry – recognizing that a list of examples does not constitute a definition, for example – might, by Socrates' lights, constitute some moral improvement. If following Socrates' example of pressing for precision and disambiguation successfully permeates a person's psychology and practice – if, for example, he becomes more careful about whom he praises and whom he blames – then Socrates would have succeeded in teaching some virtue.[2]

That's on the one hand. On the other hand, many of the interlocutors resist the conclusions that Socrates is trying to elicit from them; sometimes they even resist enquiring with Socrates. Their temperaments and characters were and remain eristic or impulsive or stubborn. But if all men desire the good and if truth-bound enquiry is essential to the good life, then all men, regardless of their temperaments, should in principle move to the good by engaging in such enquiry. Yet Plato's dramatic presentations seem to undermine that claim. It's not just because they have false beliefs that the eristic or impetuous refuse the benefits of enquiry. Indeed, it is more likely that they hold to their false beliefs precisely because they are eristic or impetuous.

Where, then, do we stand on the question of whether Socrates believed that virtue could be taught, either by example or by engaging the young in intellectual enquiry? Socrates seems to have advanced, and practised, an intellectualist position about virtue. To be sure, he never claimed to have taught – or to be able to teach – anyone anything. In a way Socrates' answer to the question of whether virtue can be taught is relatively straightforward. 'If knowledge can be taught, then virtue can be taught. But don't count on it. Though in a sense anyone who has a mind is in principle capable of discovering and recovering knowledge, individual constitutions, temperaments and education often impede genuine inquiry.' Nevertheless Socrates is more evasive on the problem of whether flaws of temperament and education can be remedied by engaging in philosophical enquiry with a virtuous enquirer. Whatever Socrates' position on that issue might have been, the Platonic dialogues do not represent Socrates as succeeding in improving malformed temperaments. Plato's dramatic presentations of Socrates' discussions subtly undermine the direction of some of those discussions. They suggest that even the most brilliant and devoted of Socrates' interlocutors did not learn very much from their discussions with him, about virtue or anything else for that matter.

Did the historical Socrates (in contrast to the Socrates depicted by Plato) teach virtue? Did Socrates the person present the best evidence against Socratic doctrine? Or did Socrates the master dialectician, following the argument wherever it leads, in action as well as in thought, present the best model for his view that enquiry into virtue 'is the greatest human good' (*Apology* 38a1–8)? Socrates did of course manage to teach at least one star pupil how to argue well. That Plato disagreed with his teacher, even about what is presupposed in truth-bound enquiry, is not itself a sign of Socrates' failure. Socrates might have taught Plato a mode of enquiry that enabled Plato to carry the Socratic enterprise further than Socrates himself could or did. And indeed, not only Plato, but all philosophers after him have learned at least one lesson of Socratic virtue, that of a certain kind of philosophic enquiry. Isn't this Nietzsche's charge against Socrates and Plato, that they endangered our more fundamental virtues by making people into dialectical enquirers? Dialectical enquirers who share Nietzsche's critique of traditional morality without sharing his views about the fundamental virtues find themselves coming come full circle. Is philosophical acumen sufficient to qualify someone to pursue a serious enquiry into virtue? Must one have a well-formed character to engage in genuine truth-oriented enquiry?

(3) *Thought, character and politics*   In addressing the issue of whether eristic or impetuous character could be enlightened and reformed by engaging in dialectical discussion, Plato went beyond the terms of Socrates' enquiry to investigate yet another mode of teaching virtue. He turned to an analysis of political practices and institutions to explore the conditions that might ensure the appropriate development of character. By Plato's lights, both the formation of sound character and the development of self-critical rationality, require special political structures, the development of a special political culture. It is not enough for a teacher of virtue to be an exemplary model of virtue. He must also create the objective political and social conditions that direct imitation towards civic virtue.

The differences between Plato and Socrates on these issues are, at least in part, a function of their respective audiences, the beliefs and practices of the interlocutors whom they wished to persuade. Socratic practice is directed to two audiences: the guardians of unexamined tradition on the one hand and the merely ingenious sophistical dialecticians on the other. The former needed to be persuaded that enquiry into what is good is necessary for virtue, the latter that the most ingenious argument is not necessarily the best or the most truthful. But the middle Platonic dialogues are, among other things, meant to defend Socrates and to convince a particular audience that the outrages of the likes of Alcibiades are the expression of character flaws, rather than consequences of philosophic discussions with Socrates.

The *Euthyphro* presents a striking example of Plato's care to present a Socrates who, at least on the surface, scrupulously avoids raising subversive questions that might corrupt the young. Socrates does not directly question the conventional wisdom that filial piety requires protecting an unjust father. With singular tact, he does not ask the Socratic question: Does piety require following justice, regardless of family ties? Similarly, the *Apology* represents Socrates as defending the obligation to respect the law, by drawing an analogy with the obligation to filial obedience and respect. A persistent Socratic enquirer might have asked, 'Who or what should be the true objects of obedience and respect?' Surely only what is good or right, rather than the accidents of birth, should determine the direction of respect. Perhaps Socrates might in the end have defended obeying the law; but it seems unlikely that he would have rested his case on an unquestioned pious analogy. But if Plato is interested in defending Socrates against his accusers, he has good reason to represent Socrates non-Socratically, as not questioning or undermining filial piety.

To defend the virtues of Socrates, Plato represents him as confronted by the limits of intellectualism. Plato had constructive, as well as defensive, aims. He wanted to show that, even at its best, intellectualism requires the support of an educative, political structure, one that forms the character traits of those who could qualify as Socrates' companions in enquiry.

Because Wollheim is committed to analysing the psychological conditions for the possibility of the Enlightenment intellectualist experiment, he must answer Plato's challenge to Socrates. Since he attempts to analyse the psychogenesis of independent, critical rationality, Wollheim needs to address Plato's contention that an intellectualist programme depends on the support of political conditions and social structures. The development of the capacities for rational, moral reflection depends on a principled control of education and the arts, of the structure and even the affections of the family, of popular culture and popular belief, of the economy and the definition of trades and occupations. But although Plato charted an account of the progressive degeneration from an enlightened meritocratic rule to democratic and eventually to tyrannical rule, he did not give an account of the transition from malformed to well-formed polities. It was Rousseau who most systematically and self-consciously attempted to tell the reformer's story, to give an account of the transformation of a malformed society into a polity capable of forming the psychology of moral, autonomous citizens. Not surprisingly, Wollheim – who is clearly not a political Platonist – turned to Rousseau for a democratically oriented analysis of political structures. But Wollheim is keenly aware of the ironic ambiguity of Rousseau's thought-experiments in political therapy. The success of each of these experiments depends on an ideal uncorrupted figure: the education of Émile depends on an idealized tutor; the formation of the Social Contract presupposes an ideal legislator; and maintaining the world of *La Nouvelle Héloïse* requires the guidance of a benevolent patriarch. Despite his sympathies for Rousseau, Wollheim cannot turn to Rousseau for an account of the political structures necessary to support the psychogenesis of autonomy.

Marxist-Leninist Maoists also experimented with a form of political psychologism, attempting to create the institutions they thought necessary for the development of the psychology required for 'correct' political thought. Like Plato and Rousseau, they thought that this requires the state to ensure the ideological correctness of nearly every aspect of public and private life: of education and the occupations, of the size of the family and its child-rearing practices, of every aspect of culture, even of manners and public demeanour. The issue between Plato, Rousseau, and Marxist-Leninist Maoists is not about *what* should be controlled, but about how decisions should be reached, and by whom. Those of us who, like Wollheim, are committed to the Enlightenment intellectualist experiment but who are not convinced of the viability, let alone the desirability, of Plato's and Rousseau's solutions, and who have no sympathy for neo-Marxist political psychologism must accept the task of analysing the political structures that are necessary to support that experiment. Having given us an account of the psychological stages in the formation of critical rationality, Wollheim now owes us an account of the stages in political reform.[3]

NOTES

[1] There are, of course, disputes about what the thesis of the unity of the virtues in knowledge entails. On one interpretation the emphasis is on the epistemic force of virtue: each of the several virtues just *is* knowledge. The various virtues are individuated by the kind of knowledge they manifest (courage is knowledge about what is worth fearing; *sophrosynē* is knowledge about what is genuinely pleasant; justice is knowledge about proper proportions). On another interpretation, the emphasis is on the interdependence of the virtues: the various individual virtues encompass and entail one another. A person is not just unless she is also courageous, temperate, and so on, through all possible permutations, to form one complex virtue. The two positions are of course compatible: the knowledge which constitutes courage might presuppose and entail the knowledge which constitutes justice, etc. But however it is interpreted, the Socratic theory of the unity of the virtues is independent of whether Socrates' moral intellectualism entails epistemological intellectualism, whether the thesis that virtue is knowledge entails the thesis that knowledge has no extra-intellectual conditions.

[2] There is still the problem of whether the doctrine of the unity of the virtues allows regionalized moral improvement to qualify as learning virtue. But this is not a problem limited to virtue. Can someone learn – or for that matter know – some mathematics without being a first-class mathematician?

[3] The germ of this essay was presented at a meeting of the Boston Colloquium on Ancient Philosophy; another version was delivered at the University of Chicago. I am grateful to Claude Evans, Don Morrison, Alexander Nehamas, and Gregory Vlastos for discussion and comments. Anthony Savile gave me constructive suggestions for revising an earlier draft.

10

Utopia and Fantasy: The Practicability of Plato's Ideally Just City

M. F. BURNYEAT

This essay is offered to Richard Wollheim in affectionate memory of our Monday excursions from the Philosophy Department at University College, London, to the Architectural Association School of Architecture, where together we ran a course on the history of ideas. Each year a theme, some lectures by ourselves – the present essay stems from the lectures I gave when the theme was Utopia – and then the educative pleasure of listening to a succession of distinguished speakers from as many disciplines as might contribute to the subject. No one thought to call this 'interdisciplinary'. It was just philosophy as Wollheim encouraged us to live it, unconstrained by departmental boundaries, querying both the questions and the answers of current fashion.

Among the many writings which this generous conception of philosophy has given to a wider public is *Socialism and Culture* (1961), in which Wollheim tried to express socialism as an ideal by tackling the question 'What should be the culture of a socialist society?' Such optimism was not Utopian at the time. It was a philosopher's contribution to a serious and practically minded debate about improving the life of the community.

For an Englishman of my age to re-read that essay now is to enter a world of thought which feels at once familiar and as far away as Plato's *Republic*. Perhaps Plato's *Republic* can help us to hold on to a sense that even when prospects for attaining justice are dimmed, it is important to be thinking about what life and culture might be like in a just society.

M. F. Burnyeat

The Graces, seeking a precinct that would not fail,
found the soul of Aristophanes.

(Epigram attributed to Plato)

(1)   Utopia, according to Sir Thomas More, is a 'no place' (ou-topia) which is also a 'good place' (eu-topia). It is by definition an imaginary ideal.

The city described in Plato's *Republic* is a Utopia in More's sense: a 'good place', called Kallipolis (527c), because it embodies every excellence a city can have (427e, 434e), and a 'no place' because it does not exist anywhere on earth (498d–e, 592b). It exists where it is constructed, in the discourse between Socrates and his interlocutors; that is, in their imagination, and in ours when we read the *Republic*. This is clear not only from the way in which Socrates frequently refers to the ideal city as the city built in discourse or speech or arguments,[1] but also from his use of the verb *muthologein*, to tell a story, to characterize the narrative of the coming to be of the ideal city and the education of the guardians within it (376d–e, 501e).[2]

From this I draw my first conclusion, that the non-existence of the ideal city is a fact of history, not of metaphysics. If the description of the ideal city is an exercise in imaginative story-telling, it must be wrong to think, with Cornford and Popper, that the ideal city belongs to the ideal world in the sense of the world of Forms.[3] Forms are not fictions, and they have no history to be told. In any case there is no such Form as the Form of the ideal city.[4] The Forms relevant to the ideal city are the Forms of justice and the other virtues, excellences common to both city and man (368e, 434d–436a, 441c–442d), and the reason why justice is not exemplified in any actual city (whereas it is, perhaps, exemplified in an actual man: Socrates) is that there has not yet been a philosopher-king with both the power and the understanding to organize society in the right way. It has nothing to do with the metaphysical difference between Forms and their exemplifications.

I do not mean to deny that were a Platonically just city ever to come into being, it would exhibit the imperfection of all earthly things. Not only would it be mortal, fated to be destroyed eventually through internal dissension (545d–546a), but it could not be perfectly or unqualifiedly just in the sense of exactly matching the definition of justice, with no admixture of its opposite (472e–473a, 479a–e). But what this shows is that justice is a Form, not that the just city built in the discussion is a Form. When Socrates calls the city built in words a *paradeigma*, a model or pattern of a good city (472d–e), some readers assume that the word *paradeigma* signifies a Form.[5] Not so. The *paradeigma* made in words is compared to a painting of the most beautiful possible human being. Since the *paradeigma* the painter paints is clearly not the Form of beauty, but an imaginary human exemplification of it, I conclude once again that Kallipolis is a perfect but imaginary particular exemplification of justice.[6] Only so does it make sense for Socrates in the later *Timaeus* (19b–c) to express a wish to see his painted people in motion and actively engaged in some suitable contest. Only so does it make sense for the Athenian in the *Laws* (739d–e) to put the *Republic*'s *paradeigma* on a scale of merit with a second-and a third-best city. Only so (to clinch the point within the *Republic*) could the ideal city turn into a timocracy at the beginning of book viii (545c ff.).

Let no one object that in a famous, highly wrought passage at the end of book ix (592b) Socrates says that perhaps – a hesitation not to be ignored – the city built in words, although it exists nowhere on earth, is set up as a *paradeigma en ouranōi*, a pattern in the heavens. This is no objection because Forms do not exist in the heavens (*Symposium* 211a). Their 'place' is beyond the heavens (the 'supra-heavenly place' of *Phaedrus* 247c); that is, nowhere in the physical universe. (It is clear that the phrase *en ouranōi* is geographical here, not the metaphor 'in Heaven' which it has been turned into by centuries of admiring quotation, because it contrasts with 'nowhere on earth' which itself picks up the pointedly geographical reference to 'the city of his birth' at 592a). What Socrates is hesitantly sugges-ting is that perhaps the starry heavens above provide a visible particu-lar manifestation of the order which the philosopher will seek to establish in his own soul (cf. *Timaeus* 90d with 47a–c and *Republic* 530d; *Laws* 967d–e). Up there in the sky you may find *paradeigmata* (529d) that are *not* imaginary.[7]

I can now be more precise about my claim that the non-existence of the ideal city is a fact of history, not of metaphysics. There are indeed metaphysical obstacles to the realization on earth of perfect justice. These are conceded by Socrates when he says that nothing can be realized in deed as it is spoken in word (473a). But they are conceded only to be set aside. Socrates and his interlocutors would be content if it could be shown that it was possible to establish a reasonable approximation to the ideal city built in words. They agree that the question whether the ideal city is a practicable possibility should be understood as the question whether a reasonable approxi-mation to it is a practicable possibility (473a–b). They are not look-ing, absurdly, for a way to overcome the human (social and political) obstacles which have hitherto prevented the establishment of a city approximating the ideal. They agree, further, as we shall shortly see, that unless some way around these obstacles can be found – unless, that is, the ideal city is shown to be a practicable possibility in the sense just specified – the imaginative effort that has gone into its construction will have been idle day-dreaming, mere wish-fulfilment. It is this distinction between an idle and a serious use of the imagination that I chiefly want to explore here.

(2) One of the most arresting features of Plato's *Republic*, one of the reasons why it has continued through the ages to command the attention of serious thinkers, is its claim to present a Utopia that is humanly practicable. More puts his narrative into the mouth of a character called Raphael Hythloday, whose name derives from the Greek for 'nonsense', 'drivel', and leaves his readers wondering whether the gap between imagination and practice could ever be closed. Plato's selection of Socrates as his story-teller has quite different implications; so too does the insistence with which he makes Socrates argue, as the narrative takes us further and further away from any social arrangements that we or his interlocutors are familiar with, that all this is indeed a practicable possibility. The proposals get more and more extravagant – first the equality of women, then the abolition of the family, finally the philosopher-kings – and Glaucon and Adeimantus become more and more concerned about their practicability. But Socrates accepts the burden of proof, and claims in each case to be able to show that his imaginative construct is possible as well as desirable. As of now, his 'good place' is a 'no place', but we could actually make the journey from here to there.

This claim has been widely disbelieved; Guthrie, for example, cites many others who accord with his view that the *Republic* is 'a purely theoretical exercise'.[8] It is disbelieved in a different way by Leo Strauss, who contrives to argue that the *Republic* means the opposite of what it says, for it is actually a proof of the impossibility of the ideal city.[9] On the other side, the claim has been misunderstood (as I believe and will try to show) by those like Cornford and Popper and many others who have read the work as a blueprint for immediate action in Athens or Syracuse.[10] In the main, however, the repeated claim to practicability[11] has not been examined with the care that is due to it. Plato is called a hopeless idealist, a dangerous idealist, a profound idealist (according to the predilection of the writer), but his own denunciation of impractical idealism is left out of account. I should like to bring it back into account and to suggest that it can tell us something important about the overall project of the *Republic*. Here is the text I have in mind:

> Permit me to take a holiday, just as men of lazy minds are wont to feast
> themselves on their own thoughts when they walk alone. Such persons,

without waiting to discover how their desires may be realized, dismiss that topic to save themselves the labour of deliberating about possibilities and impossibilities, assume their wish fulfilled, and proceed to work out the details in imagination, and take pleasure in portraying what they will do when it is realized, thus making still more idle a mind that is idle without that. (458a)[12]

This is Socrates asking to be allowed to postpone proving the practicability of his proposal to abolish the family. It is a splendid description of day-dreaming and a very clear denunciation of Utopian theorizing which is not constrained by considerations of practicability. At the same time, Socrates implies that it is alright to let one's imagination go in this way, provided the question of feasibility is faced in the end. He promises (458b) that he will examine it later. The distinction, then, between serious and idle uses of the imagination does not lie in the imaginative processes themselves, but depends on the intention to submit your ideas to the test of practicability.

Now this is not the first time that the distinction has been mentioned in the *Republic*. Already at 450d Socrates voiced a worry that the proposal to abolish the family may seem to be just a 'wish-thought', to borrow Shorey's translation of *euchē*, which literally means a prayer. Later, at 456c, when he has proved that it is not contrary to nature to educate women in music and gymnastics, he concludes that it is therefore practicable and that the laws prescribing equality for women are not *euchais homoia*, like prayers or wish-thoughts. The same phrase is used at 499c of the proposal for philosopher-kings: only if it were quite impossible for philosophy and power to be united would it be just for people to laugh at us for vainly uttering wish-thoughts (*euchais homoia*). Finally, at 540d, when the finishing touch has been put to the portrait of the rulers of the ideal city, both men and women, Socrates demands that his interlocutors accept that the account of the city and its polity is not just wish-thoughts (*euchai*); it would be difficult to put into practice, but not impossible provided power is in the hands of true philosophers who will make justice their first and chief concern.

Thus the distinction between day-dreaming wish-fulfilment and practical idealism is a recurring theme in Plato's presentation of his political programme. He is not merely insisting in plain terms that the programme must be practicable as well as desirable. He is deliberately likening the proposals to day-dreams and wish-thoughts. For recall that the difference between day-dreaming and what Socrates is up to lies not in the imaginative processes themselves but in the test at the end. Plato is acknowledging that the institutions of his ideal city look just like the products of fantasy, save for the fact that they are intended to pass the test of practicability.

(3) I want to suggest – it can be no more than a suggestion – that this emphasis on fantasy has an ulterior motive. It is the business of holding women and children in common that starts the theme. The idea of women and children in common having been slipped into Socrates' narrative at 423e–424a, he is called upon to account for it at the beginning of book v. He expresses his concern at its appearing to be a wish-thought (450d), and he embarks on what he calls 'the female drama' at 451c, starting not, as we might expect, with the communality of women and children, but with another topic, that of training up the women to take an equal share in the responsibilities of government. Here he dwells on the jokes and derisive laughter that will greet the proposal (452a–e, 457b; cf. 451a), so much so that many readers have thought that Plato must be writing with Aristophanes' hilarious comedy *Ecclesiazousae* (Women of the Assembly) in mind. I believe that this is right, precisely because it is not until 458e that Socrates explains what he means by the communality of women and children. That is to say, for almost thirty Stephanus pages we are allowed to think that Socrates favours sexual freedom of the kind that Aristophanes portrays. For Plato must know very well what talk of 'women and children in common' will suggest to his audience (e.g. *Ecclesiazousae* 614–15). He is contriving a comic reversal of his own by postponing for so long the news that the ideal city is to enjoy the most austere sexual regime that imagination could devise. The reversal is made all the more pointed by the fact that it is immediately preceded by the day-dreaming passage I quoted earlier. Socrates goes for a walk to indulge his fancies about the communality of women and children, and what he comes up with is compulsory mating festivals where one's partner is determined by a lottery that has been fixed behind the scenes by the state specialist in eugenics. For me at least, the nature and timing of this reversal of expectation establishes a significant connection between the *Republic* and the *Ecclesiazousae*. The question I want to raise, therefore, is whether the intertextual relation is connected with the theme of fantasy.

Scholars in the nineteenth century were so impressed with the resemblances between Plato's *Republic* and Aristophanes' *Ecclesiazousae*, which features both female rulers and the communality of women and children, not to mention communal property, that there was great controversy about whether Plato had cribbed from Aristophanes or Aristophanes from Plato. On the whole it seemed best to have Aristophanes satirize Plato – being a mere playwright, after all, not an original thinker, he would need to take the target for his satire from someone else, someone who had seriously proposed the institution he wanted to make fun of. The chronological difficulty that the *Ecclesiazousae* was produced way back in 393 BC[13] was easily disposed of: there must have been an early, short edition of the *Republic* for Aristophanes to satirize; the larger *Republic* we now have is Plato's counter-attack, and that is why it is full of references to people treating the proposals about women as material for comedy. This hypothesis was confirmed by the authority of Aristotle, who twice says firmly and plainly that no one but Plato had proposed communality of women and children or the abolition of private property (*Politics* 1266a34–5, 1274b9–11). Since both these things are prominent in the *Ecclesiazousae*, Aristophanes must have borrowed them from Plato; for if it was Plato who borrowed from Aristophanes, Aristotle could not have reported as he did – unless it be that Aristotle knew the difference between comedy and serious political philosophy.[14]

I mention this outmoded controversy because it brings out so clearly the pedantic absurdity of the assumption that the only kind of relation there can be between two texts which share certain ideas in common is a relation of thematic indebtedness such that the one question to ask is 'Who cribbed from whom?' In point of fact, the argument for Plato's priority fails even on its own terms, because Aristophanes, like any other literate Greek, could read in Herodotus (iv. 104) of a tribe called the Agathyrsoi who hold their women and children in common for much the same reason as guides the ideal city of the *Republic*, so that everyone may be kin to everyone else and family harmony prevail throughout society (cf. *Republic* 463c–464a). But if this old controversy about the relation between Plato and Aristophanes has faded away, it seems to me that the assumption which inspired it has not. For if the relations between the two texts are not exhausted by the issue of priority, the general agreement nowadays that the *Republic* could not possibly have been written before the *Ecclesiazousae* ought to have led to a renewal of discussion, rather than its cessation. If we know that Plato wrote after Aristophanes, it becomes a question what relation he means to establish between his proposals and the play, not to mention the story in Herodotus. When Plato sat down to write the *Republic*, he knew that what Socrates calls 'the female drama' would evoke thoughts of other texts. He had to ask himself how he was going to cope with these associations in the mind of his readers. My suggestion is that the fantasy theme is Plato's solution to the problem.

On the one hand, he encourages us to think of Aristophanes, by concealing for so long the true meaning of 'women and children in common', by the phrase 'the female drama', by emphasizing the comic potential of his proposals, by repeatedly pointing out that they are just like the products of fantasy. On the other hand, he keeps turning round to insist that these fantasies are indeed humanly practicable – and, by the way, 'women and children in common' means sex for the common good, not sex for fun. He subverts his audience's expectations by saying in effect, 'You are right, this is fantasy; let us take it seriously.' Socrates actually says at one point (452c) that we must ask the joke-makers not to do their own thing but to be serious (*spoudazein*), and what shows that several layers of meaning are involved here is that the request to be serious is itself a joke; since 'doing one's own' or keeping to one's proper task is a crucial element in the *Republic*'s account of justice, a request to the comedians not to do their own thing is a request for injustice.

(4)   I would now like to suggest – again it can be no more than a suggestion – that there is more to the *rapprochement* with Aristophanes than the solving of a literary problem. It is not just a matter of how to write the *Republic* for an audience that knows the *Ecclesiazousae*. More subtly, it is a matter of how to use the *Ecclesiazousae* in the service of the *Republic*'s central philosophical concerns.[15] I would suggest that what Plato admires in the comic fantasy of Aristophanes is its ability to break free of the conventional perspectives of ordinary everyday life. This is important to Plato because the central aim of the *Republic*, dramatized in the parable of the Cave, is (i) to establish by argument the superiority of the absolute, timeless viewpoint of philosophy over the shifting perspectives of ordinary, earthbound existence, and (ii) to plead on the strength of this argument that we must allow the absolute viewpoint to take charge of our souls and of human society. In the ideal city itself, the absolute viewpoint is fostered by ten years' training in mathematics. But we, the readers of Plato's *Republic*, or Glaucon and Adeimantus talking to Socrates in the dialogue, are not prospective guardians who have grown up in an ideal environment, and most of us have not got a spare ten years at our disposal. Yet we need to be brought, somehow, to the absolute viewpoint before we can properly appreciate its superiority and legislate for it to rule in human society. To deal with us, therefore, Plato needs to free our imaginations from the conventional assumptions that hold us back from seeing that we could and should take his proposals seriously. In short, he needs the comic fantasy that will be

banned in the ideal city itself, just as he needs and uses, but at the level of dialectic will finally discard, the powerful resources of imaginative rhetoric that go into recommending the absolute viewpoint in the parables of Sun, Line, and Cave.

My suggestion, then, is this: not merely are we to take comic fantasy seriously, but in Plato's view we must indulge in fantasy *in order* to take it seriously and see its practicability. At any rate, it is no longer mere suggestion, but demonstrable from the text of the *Republic*, that the claim of practicability is itself made from the absolute viewpoint.

(5)   Consider first a passage I have already referred to:

> Our legislation [about women getting the same training for the same jobs as men], then, was not prescribing things impossible or like wish-thoughts, *since* the law we proposed accorded with nature. Rather, the other way of doing things, prevalent to-day, proves, as it seems, unnatural. (456c)[16]

The argument is: these arrangements are in accordance with the nature of women, *therefore* they are practicable.[17] As the speed of the inference shows, Socrates is not arguing that this is something we can do with any woman of our acquaintance. We are not to think of Athenian or Spartan women as we know them. We are to abstract from all the environmental conditions that shape the women of our everyday experience and consider the female of the species as such, the nature of womankind. What is practicable, in the sense that concerns Socrates, is what is consistent with that nature, regardless of whether we could embark on such arrangements in Athens tomorrow. We could not do that, unless it be in Aristophanes' way by having the women pack the Assembly in male disguise so as to vote power to themselves; which is to say that we could not do it in real-life Athens. But that is nothing to the point for Socrates' argument, which adopts a deliberately impersonal species-level view, resuming the analogy drawn earlier between the guardians and watch-dogs and asking whether we would not expect female dogs to have the same training and functions as the male (451c–d).

Plato is a master of what one might call the alienating description: a description which presents some aspect of human life in terms which make it alien to us, as if it were the life of another species or one of the distant tribes in Herodotus.[18] The watch-dog analogy is a typical use of this rhetorical device, as is the stock-breeding terminology in which Socrates later describes the periodic mating festivals of his imaginary city (459a–e). It would be quite wrong, I think, to regard the talk of breeding future generations as metaphor. It is a deliberate attempt to get us to adopt a non-human, impersonal perspective on the human. For the argument for the desirability and the practicability of the new arrangements is grounded in that perspective, and will only appeal to someone whose imagination is capable of distancing itself from the ordinary everyday meanings of sexuality and parenthood.[19]

That this is the standpoint from which the practicability claim is made becomes wholly explicit at 499c–d. Comic laughter at our expense, on the grounds that we are vainly uttering wish-thoughts, would only be just, says Socrates, if all of the following are out of the question: that philosophy and political power were joined together some time in the infinity of time past, that they are joined now in some barbarian region far beyond our ken, that they will be joined some time in the future. Any of these is enough to vindicate the practicability claim. That claim is made, therefore, not with a view to what could be done in Athens or Syracuse, tomorrow or the day after, but from a standpoint of both temporal and geographical neutrality. It is a claim about human nature as such, not about the men and women we know, and especially not – this Socrates makes clear at length (495b–496a, 500b, 535c, 536b–c) – about the philosophers we know.

Nor should we be disturbed by 470e, where we learn that the city which Glaucon is constructing in his imagination is Greek and situated in Greece. The practicability claim requires only that the ideas which convince Socrates and his interlocutors could convince others too (502b). And here the fact that Glaucon and Adeimantus are Greek is much less important than the fact that they are aristocrats, as are many of the readers their brother is writing for. If we, if Glaucon and Adeimantus are persuaded – which they are – that is sufficient proof that somewhere sometime the persuasion could work. Each of them, moreover, is willing to carry out a task of persuasion should the day of Utopia actually come: Glaucon will address the men of culture (the 'lovers of sights and sounds'), and will show them that they do not possess knowledge (480a); Adeimantus will overcome the resistance of those who are sceptical about the nature of philosophers (489a–b), and will endeavour to give the multitude a favourable 'image' of their future rulers (499e–500e; cf. 501c–502a). The whole *Republic* is an exercise in the art of persuasion, designed to lead us from here to there. The ideal city is built in our imagination by persuasive argument, in such a way that successful persuasion in the world of imagination guarantees the possibility of success in the actual world. *Heis hikanos genomenos*: one case in the whole of time will do (502a–b).

Now this standpoint of temporal and geographical neutrality is pre-cisely the standpoint of the true philosopher as described at 486a: because he (or she) is a contemplator of all time and all being, he cannot think that human life is a thing of great importance; therefore, he is not going to be a lover of money or power or liable to the perspectival partialities of the rulers we are familiar with. In a sense, therefore, it takes a philosopher to appreciate the desirability and the possibility of philosophic rule (just as, in book ix, it takes a philosopher to appreciate the greater pleasurableness of the philosophic life). Since, however, neither we the readers, nor Glaucon and Adeimantus the interlocutors, have undergone the education that will make such gran-deur of outlook (*megaloprepeia*, 486a) a settled disposition of the guard-ians' minds, we have to enter into it imaginatively. We need fantasy, comedy, rhetorical persuasion, in order to appreciate how much better life would be under a regime that allowed little or no role to these things. But this is not the paradox it may seem to be if the *Republic* is right and it is the partial, parochial perspectives of everyday existence which make it hard for us to accept that the *Republic* is right.[20]

NOTES

[1] *Logōi* 472d–e; *lexeōs* 473a; *en logois* 592a; cf. 369a–c, 371b, 374a, 379a, 394d, 422e, 428c, 433a, 434e, 450a–b, 451c, 452a, 456d, 458c, 473e, 497c, 530e, 534d, 546b, 557d, 558b, 595a.

[2] The first of these references is all the more emphatic in that it announces the critique of the *muthoi* by which the poets educate people in the ordinary world.

[3] F. M. Cornford, *The Republic of Plato*, translated with introduction and notes (Clarendon Press, Oxford, 1941), p. 171; K. R. Popper, *The Open Society and its Enemies*. vol. 1: *The Spell of Plato*, 4th edn, rev. (Routledge and Kegan Paul, London, 1962), pp. 55, 82, 103, 145, 149. Popper's antagonistic diagnosis of Plato's political aims rests heavily on the belief that there is a Form of city.

[4] This may sound dogmatic, but the onus of proof is on those who think otherwise. For the well-known sentence at *Republic* 596a, which is so often invoked as evidence of a Form for every plurality of things we call by the same name, can equally well be construed, with J. A. Smith ('General Relative Clauses in Greek', *Classical Review*, 31 (1917), pp. 69–71) as positing just one Form for every plurality of things we call by the same name as the Form. I believe that Smith's construal fits the context much better; but the fact that the sentence is ambiguous is

already sufficient to disqualify the argument 'There must be a Form of city because there is a Form for every general term.'

[5] B. Jowett and Lewis Campbell, *Plato's Republic*, the Greek text edited, with notes and essays (3 vols. Clarendon Press, Oxford, 1894), vol. 3, p. 250; Cornford, *Republic*, p. 171. *Contra*, Leo Strauss, *The City and Man* (University of Chicago Press, Chicago and London, 1964), p. 121.

[6] It is true that the context is one in which Socrates has referred to justice and injustice (472c 5, 6); but the masculine *ekeinous* (c7), *ekeinois* (c9), show that the *paradeigma* sought at c4 is the perfectly just man of c5, followed by the most unjust man of c6–7. That these two imaginary (*ei genoito*, c5–6, with James Adam, *The Republic of Plato*, edited with critical notes, commentary, and appendices [Cambridge University Press, Cambridge, 1963] *ad loc*). particulars are the product of an enquiry into justice and injustice suggests an interesting analogy with the objects of mathematical *dianoia*; see M. F. Burnyeat, 'Platonism and Mathematics: A Prelude to Discussion', in *Mathematics and Metaphysics in Aristotle* (Proceedings of the Tenth Symposium Aristotelicum), ed. Andreas Graeser (Verlag Paul Haupt, Bern and Stuttgart, 1987), pp. 213–40, at pp. 227–32, and compare the divine *paradeigma* of 500e with the divine reflections of 532c.

[7] Isnardi Parente protests that I am here reading back into the *Republic* a mathematical model of the heavens which does not appear until the *Timaeus* and is foreign to the astronomy of the earlier work. See Isnardi Parente, 'Motivi utopistici – ma non utopia – in Platone', in Atti del Convegno Nazionale di Studi su *La Citta Ideale nella Tradizione Classica e Biblico-Cristiana*: ed. Renato Uglione (Regione Piemonte, Turin, 1985), p. 139. I reply that, whatever the date of the *Timaeus*, its astronomy is the carrying out of a mathematical project already formulated in the *Republic* (529a ff.). My view of 592b is in agreement with the sober tradition of Cornford, *Republic*, p. 312; W. K. C. Guthrie, *A History of Greek Philosophy*. vol. 4: *Plato – The Man and his Dialogues: Earlier Period* (Cambridge University Press, Cambridge, 1975), pp. 543–4; J. B. Skemp, 'The Spirituality of Socrates and Plato', in *Classical Mediterranean Spirituality*, ed. A. H. Armstrong (Routledge and Kegan Paul, London, 1986), p. 116.

[8] Guthrie, *History of Greek Philosophy*, vol. 4, pp. 483–6 with p. 457, n. 1, pp. 464–5, 469–70.

[9] Strauss, *City and Man*, ch. 2, followed by Allan Bloom, *The Republic of Plato*, translated with notes and an interpretive essay (Basic Books, New York and London, 1968). For a critique of Strauss's approach to the *Republic*, to Plato, and to philosophy, see M. F. Burnyeat, Review of Leo Strauss, *Studies in Platonic Political Philosophy*, *New York Review of Books*, 30 May, 1985, with further discussion 10 Oct. 1985, 24 Oct. 1985, 24 Apr. 1986.

[10] Cornford, *Republic*, p. xxiii, Popper, *Open Society*, vol. 1, pp. 153–6, 195.

[11] Cf. *Republic* 375c–e, 415c–d, 423d–424a, 425d–e, 450d, 452e–453c, 456c, 457a, c, d–e, 458a, b, 466d, 471c–e, 472b–473b, 473c–e, 485a, 499c–500e, 502a–c, 520e–521a, 540d, 592a.

[12] Paul Shorey, *Plato, The Republic*, with an English translation (Loeb Classical Library, London and New York, 1930).

[13] Or at the latest a year or two afterwards. For the evidence, see R. G. Ussher, *Aristophanes: Ecclesiazusae*, edited with introduction and commentary (Oxford, 1973), pp. xx–xxv.

[14] A detailed account, with references, of the nineteenth-century discussions here summarized may be found in Adam, *Republic*, vol. i, pp. 345–55 (Appendix i to book v). The discussions continued a good while into the twentieth century: reports and references in Ussher, *Aristophanes: Ecclesiazousae*, pp. xiv–xx, whose own conclusion is in some ways the strangest of all: namely, that the hypothesis that Plato alludes to Aristophanes is even less likely than the hypothesis that Aristophanes alludes to Plato.

[15] Here I am in complete agreement with Allan Bloom, 'Response to Hall', *Political Theory*, 5 (1977), pp. 323ff. The difference between us is that, following Strauss, *City and Man*, p. 61, n. 15, he supposes that Plato's concern is to make an even better job than Aristophanes of the critique of communality which he [Bloom] finds in the *Ecclesiazousae*. (One of the curiosities of Bloom's essay is that, while insisting that we should read the *Republic* as a drama, he reads the *Ecclesiazousae* as an affair of premises, hypotheses, and the 'must' of demonstrative proof.) Connoisseurs of Straussian exegesis will appreciate the way Bloom, when pointing out at a crucial stage of his argument (p. 327) that the phrase 'Diomedean necessity' at *Republic* 493d is an echo of *Ecclesiazousae* 1029, quietly writes 'philosopher' into a context where Socrates is speaking of sophists. For more of the same, see Bloom, *Republic*, pp. 380ff., beginning 'Book V is preposterous . . .'.

[16] After Shorey.

[17] A parallel move from nature to possibility is envisaged at 485a in connection with the philosopher's qualifications for ruling.

[18] Distance is a great help to the imagination. Even Aristotle did not doubt that the communality of women and children is possible (*Politics* 1261a4–6), probably because he knew of reports that if you travelled far enough, you would find that it was actual (*Politics* 1262a18–20; cf. Adam, *Republic, ad* 463c and the now entertaining excursus in Franz Susemihl and R. D. Hicks, *The Politics of Aristotle*, a revised text with introduction, analysis and commentary, books i–v (Macmillan and Co., London and New York, 1894), pp. 326–31). See further Simon Pembroke, 'Women in Charge: The Function of Alternatives in Early Greek Tradition and the Ancient Idea of Matriarchy', *Journal of the Warburg and Courtauld Institutes*, 30 (1967), pp. 1–35.

[19] I do not mean, of course, that without a special perspective Socrates' proposals are not *intelligible*. Derisive laughter presupposes that they are. What a change of perspective makes possible is persuasion (489a).

[20] In preparing this essay I have been helped by discussion of previous drafts at meetings in London, Rome, and Athens (one such draft appeared in K. Boudouris (ed.), *On Justice* (Greek Philosophical Society, Athens, 1989)) and by the judicious criticism of André Laks, who kindly showed me his own highly nuanced treatment of these questions in a forthcoming publication.

Part II
Bradley and Green

11

Bradley and Moral Philosophy

PATRICK GARDINER

T. S. Eliot once described Bradley's *Ethical Studies* as constituting 'not merely a demolition of the Utilitarian theory of conduct but an attack upon the whole Utilitarian mind'. Whatever Eliot himself may have meant by this, there can be no question that Bradley's critique of current utilitarian doctrines was undertaken on a very broad front. Bradley was not concerned simply to challenge particular arguments which philosophers like Bentham and J. S. Mill had variously offered in support of their ethical positions. Nor, again, was he content with seeking to expose the inadequacies of the criteria they had proposed for resolving problems of moral evaluation or choice. He also set out to undermine the accounts they were wont to provide of the actual sources of human motivation and response, such accounts being in his opinion presupposed by their claims regarding the rationale and ultimate justification of moral action. Thus an important part of his book was devoted to an extended and often highly polemical criticism of hedonist psychology, with its stress upon the pursuit of pleasure as intrinsic to all human desire and its associated tendency to treat pleasurable states of mind as the basic ingredients of happiness, whether individually or collectively viewed.

This psychology Bradley believed to be totally misguided, both in its detailed application and in its underlying assumptions. The particular interpretations it put upon the springs of human behaviour could be shown either to be palpably false to experience or else to evaporate under analysis into a set of uninformative tautologies. At the same time, and more fundamentally, it was prone to misrepresent a notion that lay at the very heart of a proper understanding of moral life and conduct. That was the notion of a self. A self, Bradley argued, could not be regarded as if it were no more than a succession or discontinuous series of conscious states 'swept together' by vaguely specified 'laws of association'. Such a conception, which he ascribed to a number of prominent contemporary writers, manifestly failed to accord with what was involved in being a person, the latter concept being taken to comprehend something unitary and self-determining, capable of acting in response to certain desires and of inhibiting others and of expressing itself in deeds that embodied the will of a concrete individual. It was a self in this 'solid' sense, perceived as possessing a formed and relatively abiding character, that any realistic account of intentional action must accommodate, and its true nature could be grasped only in terms of a perspective wholly freed from the artificial simplicities of the hedonist theory. Among other things, it was necessary to trace the processes whereby complex propensities or concerns of the type essential to moral thought and agency developed, demonstrating how they might intelligibly be seen to have evolved out of what Bradley called 'the crude material of the natural disposition'.

In discussing Bradley's attempt to follow this path within the framework of his own moral psychology, Richard Wollheim has explored with much subtlety and insight some of its implications. Moreover, when assessing its possible merits, he has made suggestive references to ideas drawn from recent psychoanalytical literature on child development, these being held to echo, and in certain respects supplement, significant elements of the Bradleian account. As he would be the first to allow, however, what Bradley had to say on specifically psychological topics constituted only one aspect – albeit an important one – of his overall approach to moral experience. It formed part of a far wider picture, a picture in which sociological, historical, and even (at times) metaphysical considerations also found a place and which was remarkable both for the breadth of its scope and for the richness of its content. Furthermore, and for all its range, the picture in question was at the same time noteworthy as reflecting a distinctive position regarding the proper ambitions of moral philosophy itself and the limits of what it could legitimately achieve. It is arguable that this position was not always consistently adhered to by Bradley himself; none the less, I think that it is clearly implicit in much of *Ethical Studies* and that it underlay a comprehensive dissatisfaction he felt with previous moral theories which certainly included utilitarianism but was by no means confined to it. In any case, it seems to me to represent an outlook that is of more than antiquarian interest, and in what follows I shall sketch what I take to be its general tenor.

Let me begin by taking note of a point to which Bradley frequently adverts at various stages of his book. It concerns the importance of what he sometimes describes as 'vulgar' belief or opinion, but more typically refers to as 'the ordinary moral consciousness'. Its significance is in fact emphasized in the very first pages of *Ethical Studies*,[1] where he embarks on a discussion of the time-honoured controversy between libertarians and determinists on the subject of human freedom. Positions characteristically adopted by writers ranged on opposite sides of this dispute are here largely considered in the light of how far they conform with commonly accepted notions of moral responsibility and, more specifically, with those of desert, guilt and punishment. Both the opposed schools of thought are found wanting on this score, and Bradley puts forward an alternative view of what is involved which is held to do greater justice to our ordinary ideas about the matter. The line taken by his argument anticipates a theme to which he subsequently returns in different contexts and in connection with other philosophical theses. The moral consciousness, he insists in one place, is 'the touchstone of moral theories', and as such demands scrupulous attention to what it affirms.

At first sight this contention might strike us as a fairly familiar one. At the time at which he was writing Bradley was hardly alone in expressing respect for the assumptions of 'ordinary morality'; indeed, he himself said as much, granting in the case of the free will debate mentioned above that neither of the parties to it was disposed to concede that their contrasting positions conflicted with common convictions. It was one thing to pay lip-service to such a criterion, however; it was another to conform to it in practice. Bradley believed that the actual procedures followed by many philosophers tended to be at odds with their professions and that – more often than not – the accounts they gave of everyday thinking in the moral sphere were heavily imbued with theoretical preconceptions of their own; the 'ready-made doctrines' they brought to the facts coloured the interpretations they put upon them. Nor was it surprising that this should be so. For, whatever they might assert to the contrary, theorists of the kind he had in mind were in reality less concerned with comprehending the claims of ordinary thought than with bringing them into line with principles deriving from a supposedly superior standpoint that transcended the outlook of common or 'unenlightened' opinion. Revision, rather than understanding, was here the primary objective, and it was accompanied by an underlying if not always overtly acknowledged suspicion of the prejudices, inconsistencies, and confusions that were believed to infect the affirmations of 'the vulgar'. And the moral tacitly drawn from this was liable to be the complacent one that as philosophers 'we should not be at pains to agree with their superstitions, but . . . rather should esteem ourselves, according as our creed is different from and higher than theirs' (p. 41).

To the elitist spirit informing such attitudes Bradley was strongly opposed, not merely by temperament but in principle. Despite some of his own explicit disclaimers, his philosophical position has often been treated as essentially Hegelian in inspiration, and it has been the salutary aim of discriminating modern commentators to expose the distortions and exaggerations involved in this widespread view. None the less, so far as moral philosophy was concerned there was certainly one crucial respect in which the conception of the subject to which he subscribed corresponded closely to that of his German predecessor. Hegel had been insistent that it was in no sense the business of philosophy to provide 'instruction as to what the world ought to be'; in his opinion the proper role of philosophical ethics was wholly theoretical, which meant among other things that the philosopher should restrict himself to eliciting and rendering intelligible the existing structure and presuppositions of morality as a concretely ongoing form of life and experience. It was not the philosopher's task to offer practical advice; nor was he called upon to afford an external justification of the phenomena he sought to analyse and explain. Bradley's own approach, as presented in *Ethical Studies*, is entirely consonant with these contentions. The philosopher, here as elsewhere, has only one function, namely, 'to understand what is'. Moral philosophy, he declares, 'has to understand morals which exist, not to make them or give directions for making them' (p. 193). Ethical theory, so conceived, was thus essentially interpretive and not prescriptive or normative: it had 'not to make the world moral' but to comprehend 'the morality current in the world'. It followed that there could be no question of the philosopher's constructing an 'ideal' code or 'new morality', or of his invoking some inappropriate model of pure rationality in the hope of endowing such a code with an intellectually unassailable foundation. Nor, again, should we suppose the philosopher to be professionally qualified to give guidance on particular matters relating to moral decision and conduct. Theory was one thing, practice another; and appeals to theory were out of place if we wished to determine in specific cases what was morally right or wrong, what we should or should not do. To imagine otherwise, Bradley maintained, was to 'confuse science with art'; it was to those whose perceptions were rooted in a ground-level experience of life and the world that we should turn for moral advice or illumination, not to persons whose heads were 'full of reflections' and who set themselves above the world in the name of abstract principles or systems of their own contrivance.

To appreciate Bradley's position and to grasp its rationale, it is worth contrasting it with that of a contemporary writer whom he certainly respected but whose cardinal doctrines he himself singled out for concentrated attack. This was Henry Sidgwick. In his closely argued book, *The Methods of Ethics*,[2] Sidgwick had presented a sophisticated version of utilitarianism which was expressly designed to meet the standard objections that had been brought against it and at the same time to show how what he called 'the morality of Common Sense' should be viewed within a utilitarian framework. Sidgwick did not contest the need for moral philosophy to accord careful consideration to everyday thought, much of his essay being in fact taken up with a thoroughgoing and frequently acute analysis of 'our common moral reasoning'. The account of this he provided, however, was critical and not merely descriptive in intent. As against some of its traditional British defenders, who had spoken as if its various precepts could be shown to be both independently self-evident and collectively consistent, he argued that such claims failed to withstand serious examination. Familiar rules and values appeared clear and determinate in their scope only so long as we refused to investigate in detail the range and variety of their actual uses and applications; once this was done, the neat and tidy maps drawn by these philosophers took on a very different aspect. Thus Sidgwick suggested that, when contemplated in a realistic light, the terrain of commonsense morality was apt to look more like a maze of loosely defined maxims and crisscrossing requirements than a tightly organized network of interlocking principles. In some places boundaries were indistinct and landmarks obscured, so that it was hard to know for certain which way one was supposed to go, while elsewhere signposts apparently pointed in opposite directions with no indication given as to which should be taken. There was therefore good reason for regarding it as 'defective', 'incomplete', lacking in what was needed for 'perfection of practice'. And Sidgwick left little room for doubt concerning his own reaction to this unsatisfactory situation. It was not enough for the moral philosopher to come up with a comprehensive analysis of the commonly accepted ideas of mankind; it was also necessary to recognize that he had a further function, namely, 'to tell men what they ought to think, rather than what they do think'. In other words, he should act not merely as the interpreter of ordinary moral thought but as its critic and corrector, Sidgwick referring here to the manner in which in other areas of technical or scientific advance the relatively crude rules and empirical methods of daily life had been superseded by precisely formulated laws which were systematically ordered and deductively related to our practical purposes. If that meant diverging from common sense in some of the positions reached, then so much the worse for common sense. And the same was true of morals. There again it was surely understandable if the judgement of 'trained experts' should at times be preferred to the intimations of unexamined belief or 'instinctive' sentiment.

In Bradley's eyes Sidgwick's book at least had the merit of making explicit the revisionary aspirations that had motivated earlier utilitarians but whose possible implications they had not invariably confronted so openly. There was, moreover, a further respect in which he implied that it had been valuable. For Sidgwick's detailed examination of popular morality helped to dispel certain misconceptions purveyed by theorists of a different ideological persuasion as to what this actually involved; in particular, it had been shown not to possess the clear-cut underlying structure they had been prone to ascribe to it, the components of moral thought that gleamed so immaculately in their display-cases assuming quite another appearance when seen in operation and put to use. What Bradley found basically unacceptable, by contrast, was the spirit that informed the criticisms that Sidgwick had presented and the conclusions drawn from them. His specific strictures on that score were set out in an independent essay entitled 'Mr Sidgwick's Hedonism',[3] but in overall import they were essentially continuous with themes developed in *Ethical Studies*.

One point on which Bradley lays especial stress is the suggestion, implicit in Sidgwick's account, that moral judgement and decision are fundamentally 'jural' in character, a matter of subsuming particular cases under general precepts or rules. Sidgwick spoke as if this were so even at the level of much everyday thinking: the trouble there was that the precepts appealed to lacked the determinacy and certainty desirable from the point of view of a hypothetical 'ethical science' – they were inherently open to exceptions and were also liable to collide with one another at crucial junctures in our practical reasoning. Hence the assumption appeared to be that commonsense morality was at best no more than an approximation to what was ideally required, the latter involving the formulation of more 'complex and delicate' rules which would accommodate individual differences and which in turn would be finally validated by reference to a minimal set of intrinsically indubitable 'axioms', or ultimate principles. Strictly carried through, such a programme would presumably issue in a suitably refined system capable of covering every contingency with perfect exactitude, and Sidgwick was prepared in one place to conjure up a picture of an 'ideal community of enlightened Utilitarians' in which something of the sort would be actualized. Bradley contemptuously consigned this calculative model to the realm of 'apocalyptic literature', but he admitted that it was doubtful whether it was intended to represent a serious possibility. Indeed, Sidgwick himself allowed that many of the *prima facie* non-utilitarian norms embodied in ordinary morality were none the less susceptible, broadly speaking, to a justification in utilitarian terms; he wrote too as if, considered from the latter viewpoint alone, it might often be preferable to leave them as they stood rather than try to replace them. All the same, and notwithstanding these concessions to realism, it appeared that any value he attributed to the various precepts in question remained *au fond* an instrumental one, dependent in the last analysis upon the ways in which their general observance contributed to an overarching and hedonistically conceived end. Furthermore, he argued that it might at times be right for enlightened utilitarians to adopt and quietly recommend rules at variance with those 'popularly taught', provided this was done in carefully chosen circumstances which precluded their setting a public example that would be harmful if universally followed. Thus it seemed to be assumed that an 'esoteric' morality, directly geared to the demands of the utilitarian ideal but strictly reserved for the private use and judgement of certain privileged individuals, might subsist alongside the one that was suited to the dispositions and limitations of 'the vulgar'.

So far as the last of the above contentions was concerned, Bradley left it to the reader to imagine what would be likely to happen if persons 'with no sense nor hold on real life, but gifted with a logical faculty' started systematically making deductions from basic principles of the kind proposed. And the disturbing implications of that consideration were connected in his mind with a more general criticism of the whole conception of the relation of commonsense morality to theory which Sidgwick's approach was not alone in exemplifying. This was the notion that the philosopher, standing back from the multifarious concerns and diverse values which normally engage us as moral agents in the world, should excogitate a unitary scheme of rules and procedures whereby what was defensible in our customary modes of thought could be separated from allegedly irrational or dispensable elements and reduced to a perspicuous order. Sidgwick (as has been seen) wrote as if such a system would ideally conform to a pattern inviting comparison with achievements in the applied sciences; other theorists, less wedded to the model of scientific respectability, had embraced different, though equally austere, paradigms of practical reason. According to Bradley, however, there was something problematic in the very idea of adopting a detached perspective in the manner envisaged, which he saw as often lending an appearance of spurious objectivity to what in fact amounted to no more than subjective opinion or arbitrary preference. Nor did appeals to that idea, accompanied as they frequently were by assumptions drawn from an absurdly simplistic psychology, in any way justify the abstract frameworks within which philosophers sought to confine the diversified field of ethical considerations encountered at the level of actual experience. To criticize ordinary morality for operating with a plurality of precepts and categories that resisted precise formulation or application was to impose an inappropriate standard, misconstruing the role these played in evaluative and deliberative contexts and overlooking their intimate connections with other departments of social life. The situations that typically confronted us in the practical sphere, in all their variety and concrete particularity, were not amenable to determinate and hierarchically arranged principles of the sort hankered after by theorists of a predominantly rationalistic persuasion. By and large they answered to a different style of thinking, one that did not derive its authority from the artificially insulated standpoints postulated by such writers, but had its home instead in the 'living world' of human relations, to which each of us as a social being inescapably belonged.

The doctrine that 'the mere individual is a delusion of theory' and that a person's development as a morally self-conscious subject necessarily occurs within a setting of common practices and inherited traditions is, of course, central to Bradley's well-known chapter in *Ethical Studies*, 'My Station and its Duties'. And it certainly underlay the account of moral judgement which he outlined there, in express opposition to conceptions attributable to other thinkers. Thus he held that our basic forms of thought and conduct were inevitably permeated by internalized norms and attitudes that had been absorbed, through imitation and education, from the social environment in which we grew up. The moral judgements we ordinarily make naturally reflect these; it does not, however, follow that they do so in the fashion which theoretically minded analysts tend to take as their model. On the contrary, and as he himself puts it, they are 'intuitive' rather than 'discursive' in character. The normal situation, in other words, is not one of our having an explicit or prepared general principle 'before the mind' and of our then going on to apply it. Rather, 'we say we "see" and we "feel" in these cases, not we "conclude" ': the particular matter or issue before us strikes us in a certain way, or under a certain aspect, thereby giving rise directly to the judgement in question – 'all that is seen is seen in the form of *this* case, *this* point, *this* instance' (pp. 194–7). Moreover, when considering such judgements, it is a mistake to imagine that those making them must be ready, or even able, to support them in terms of statable rules or discursive reasoning. Far from this being so, Bradley claims that we are in fact apt to 'prize the advice of persons who can give us no reasons for what they say', the 'fineness of their moral perceptions' often being independent of any corresponding 'discursive ability'.

Bradley confesses that the subject is difficult and his remarks on it much briefer than a proper treatment would require. It is true that they are somewhat impressionistic – one may wonder, for instance, whether he always sufficiently distinguishes psychological issues from those of a conceptual character. Yet it is not hard to catch their main drift, which here is more pointedly reminiscent of Aristotelian than Hegelian ideas on ethics. As he himself notes, his references to 'feeling' and 'perception' when characterizing moral judgements are not meant to exclude intellectual grasp or understanding; it is not a matter of their being 'mere isolated impressions'. His contention is rather that the understanding they embody is of a specific kind; the capacity to pick out from a host of circumstances the morally salient features of a particular case or situation is more realistically seen as the unmediated exercise of a practical aptitude acquired through experience than as involving some reflective process of analysis or explicit inference.

Nor is he to be taken as suggesting that moral judgements are essentially emotive or subjective in origin, irrational in the sense of being ungrounded. They have an objective basis in as much as they stand in 'an intimate and vital relation' to the institutions and intertwined beliefs that are constitutive of a community's life, the latter finding expression in the behaviour of participants who identify with their 'general spirit'. Bradley does not deny that, with such practices and beliefs in mind, we may be able to elicit from the judgement someone makes on a given occasion a principle or rule of duty which it can be said to exemplify. Thus we might set out to explain a person's approval of an action by pointing to an aspect, say, of justice or gratitude that intuitively led him to treat it as being of a certain kind. But this does not mean that he consciously referred it to a determinate precept prescribing conduct of that type, going on to read off the appropriate conclusion. In any event, and whatever validity such expository accounts may possess in certain connections, their proper use needs circumspect handling. It is radically misconceived to suppose that they offer a generally plausible or comprehensive representation of the condensed, inexplicit, and highly particularized thinking which is characteristic of the ordinary moral consciousness and which is, moreover, pre-eminently adapted to the complex contingencies and many-sided possibilities of choice presented by life in the everyday world. Although precepts we have 'imbibed' from early on may afford guidance here, Bradley insists that 'example is better'. He implies, too, that it is a merit rather than a defect of our ethical thought that it does not operate with a set of impersonal rules carefully tailored to encompass every eventuality, but depends instead upon capacities for individual response which have been developed in a communal milieu and sharpened through intimate acquaintance with a wide variety of differing cases. Such features of the 'morality of common sense' are to be cherished, not deplored.

It was along these general lines that Bradley sought to interpret moral judgement as it normally and naturally occurs, protecting it from both the misunderstandings and the criticisms which he believed it had suffered at the hands of misguided philosophical theory. None the less, there remained an important consideration to be added to what he said, a consideration of especial significance in the light of the limitations he subsequently went on to ascribe to the doctrine of 'my station and its duties'. Despite the emphasis he laid there upon the typically non-discursive and immediate character of most moral appraisal and deliberation, it was at the same time necessary to recognize that occasions certainly arose – in that context and elsewhere – which presented difficulties and were the source of genuine doubts. This happened in situations of moral conflict, where the agent was confronted by practical dilemmas that involved 'collisions of duties'.

The problem of moral conflict is one to which Bradley recurrently alludes; nor is it surprising that he should have done so. For, as he himself points out, it was a question that had exercised previous theorists and had given rise to varying attempts to resolve the issues it raised. We have already noticed how Sidgwick, disturbed by the apparent presence of such conflicts at the level of common opinion, contemplated their removal through the elaboration of a fully articulated and systematic ethical science. Thus Bradley quotes him as maintaining that in a 'complete theory' of this kind 'no collision of precepts may remain possible'; and that indeed was an aspiration shared – in spirit at least – by numerous utilitarian thinkers wedded to the monistic conception of a single dimension or ultimate standard to the monistic conception of a single dimension or ultimate standard of ethical value. There was, though, another influential approach to be mentioned. For there were philosophers who occupied a quite distinct general standpoint but who also wished to reject the possibility of moral conflict, albeit on different grounds. In the latter connection Bradley referred specifically to a position he associated with followers of Kant. Here the claim was that, since all particular moral laws were 'inviolable' and necessarily incapable of being legitimately breached or overruled, a genuine conflict of duties was inconceivable; we could not, on pain of incoherence, be said to be subject to two such 'absolute' injunctions, compliance with one of which precluded compliance with the other. According to Bradley, however, each of the above approaches was unacceptable, both – albeit in dissimilar ways – once again lying open to the charge of allowing considerations of abstract theory to override those related to the realities of experience. 'Life', he writes, 'is not so simple that we never have to consider more than one duty at a time' (p. 156), and the Kantian contention must be set against the plain fact that in actual practice we seldom, if ever, treat our values and precepts as possessing the strict inviolability or rigidity it attributed to them. Collisions between them can and do occur, and when this happens, we customarily accept that one must give way to the other, suffering 'uneasiness only in proportion to the rarity of the necessity, and the consequent jar to the feelings' (p. 157). But neither, on the other hand, was it justifiable to adopt the alternative view according to which the appearance of conflict could in principle always be eliminated by appealing to a unitary criterion or decision procedure covering all cases. The dilemmas posed are unavoidably apprehended as real, not as merely apparent or imaginary, and it runs counter to our experience as moral agents to suppose that they can be glossed over or removed in the manner suggested. On the contrary, they are liable to confront us as predicaments in which each of the competing moral claims is perceived to be 'serious' or legitimate; and when that is so, we have to deliberate in deciding which should take precedence. Yet Bradley is at the same time anxious to insist that reaching such a decision is still essentially a 'practical', not a 'scientific', matter; it requires 'moral art' rather than 'theoretical deduction' from general rules. The questions presented, he says, 'arise from the complexity of individual cases, and this can be dealt with solely by practical insight, not by abstract conceptions and discursive reasoning' (p. 225).

Thus, although situations involving collisions of duties are distinguishable from the normally unproblematic ones in that they are apt to prompt conscious reflection, it remains true none the less that their resolution finally depends once more on the exercise of intuitive understanding or perception, not on discursive thought. To that extent, then, Bradley's treatment of them can be said to accord with the theme that dominates his discussion of moral judgement in the chapter of his book on 'my station and its duties'; nor does he wish to deny there that such conflicts can certainly arise within the sphere of 'our common social morality'. However, he also sees them as having wider implications. As he was concerned to stress in the following chapter, he considered that the sphere in question, though undoubtedly constituting the necessary basis, or 'cradle', of morality, did not comprise the whole of it: there were further claims which in a broader sense the latter could be held to encompass, these being recognized by the moral consciousness and ones that his own subsequent account of what he called 'ideal morality' was intended to do justice to. While 'man is not man at all unless social', it is also the case that he is 'more than social'; and what this means, among other things, is that occasions may present themselves when we have to choose between duties deriving from our membership of a society and others that strike us as morally compelling, whether from the standpoint of our personal integrity or in the light of certain activities, like artistic work or the pursuit of truth, which are viewed as valuable in themselves and irrespective of their possible 'social bearing'. Bradley concedes that dilemmas of this nature are often the source of great inner mental perplexity. Even so, they unquestionably arise; and when they do, they can be resolved – if at all – only through an imaginative insight that is attuned to the individual case and resists explicit or generalizable formulation. Here, as in other areas of ethical life, it is useless (or worse) to seek enlightenment from a theorist forearmed with a system of impersonal principles and criteria. For true guidance we should go instead to someone who can 'transport himself' into another's position and who 'knows the heart and sees through moral illusion'. And that – Bradley reiterates – can only be a person of tried and various experience, never 'the man of mere theory' (p. 226).

In reading the above remarks, together with others in a similar vein, we should remind ourselves that Bradley was by no means concerned to deny the possibility of theory as such; his objections on this score were confined to what he took to be certain widespread misconceptions regarding the role of moral philosophy and its proper objectives. As was observed at the outset, he held that the function of philosophical ethics was not to rectify or try to reconstruct ordinary morality, but solely to understand it and elucidate its place in human life. A theoretical treatment directed to the latter end was thus in his view perfectly legitimate; and his own account, according to which personal fulfilment essentially involved leading a life wherein the intimations of the moral consciousness were affirmed and given expression, conformed more closely to what he had in mind. The psychological insights embodied in Bradley's particular doctrine of 'self-realization', as well as the problems and obscurities it may also be felt to present, are intricate matters which cannot be broached here. Nevertheless, and without going into these, I think it is possible to appreciate the force of some of his general claims concerning the nature of moral thinking and the limits of ethical theory. Two points seem to me to be of especial significance, and I shall conclude by saying a little about each of them.

In the first place, it is surely a merit of Bradley's approach that he insists upon the need for realism about, and sensitivity to, the social and cultural provenance of our moral ideas. This inevitably colours and shapes our thinking in the practical sphere, and it is something without which we cannot ultimately make sense of ourselves and our status as moral agents. A theorist who attempts to occupy a perspective detached from that background risks dissociating himself from practices and concepts which have played a major part in forming our actual dispositions and which are inseparably bound up with many of our most pervasive concerns and interests. Though often irreducibly diverse and complex, the 'laws, institutions, social usages, moral opinions and feelings' of the world we belong to are subtly interrelated and hang together, composing a shared form of life wherein we can normally be said to 'find ourselves' and that impresses us as being natural and worthy of respect. It is true that Bradley has frequently been accused of undue conservatism in the latter regard, and there may be some justice in the charge. Yet those making it are apt to overlook qualifications he himself introduced, and in the present instance he certainly allowed that there were times when members of a community might consider it to be in a 'confused or rotten condition' and to require reform. His own attitude to this situation is not easy to interpret; but it would be consistent with much that he says to maintain that, to be acceptable, such social criticisms can never be derived from some hypothetical external standpoint. Rather, they must proceed 'from within', revitalizing or extending the range of values which, even if they have become distorted or obscured, remain in a sense implicit in the existing moral ethos. Bradley is prone to stress that, so far as moral decisions and considerations are concerned, we have always to begin from where we are and from what we inwardly grasp and identify with. 'Moral perception must rest on moral experience' (p. 298).

The second point, connected with what has just been said, relates to his account of moral judgement. He makes it clear that his use of the term 'intuition' there should in no way be confused with its employment by moral philosophers who treat it as the name of an *a priori* faculty, the supposed objects of which are self-evident general truths or ethical 'axioms'. That position represented, if anything, the reverse of the one he himself subscribed to, in that it tacitly assimilated moral judgement to thinking of a purely theoretical character. And it was, of course, Bradley's specific contention that the ability to form and apply judgements of the kind in question was essentially a practical ability, rooted in experience and comparable to a skill or art in its capacity to adjust to the particularity of the situations encountered in the moral sphere. In common with a number of his Victorian contemporaries, he displayed a confidence about what 'the ordinary moral consciousness' declares that is liable to strike a little oddly on modern ears. But however this may be, I think it was to his credit that, while emphasizing the natural spontaneity typical of most moral responses, he at the same time showed himself to be acutely appreciative of the elements of quandary and recalcitrance which are a feature of certain practical predicaments. Considerations of the latter type have tended – both in his day and in our own – to be either blurred or by-passed by ethical theorists intent upon treating moral problems as if they should ideally be open to clear-cut solutions provided by an ordered set of principles and procedures. In opposing such tendencies, Bradley seems to me to have exhibited a welcome sensitivity to the importance of flexibility and imaginative resource in a domain in which these qualities have not always received the philosophical recognition they deserve. The picture of the moral agent as a navigator of generally untroubled calm but on occasion hazardous waters may appear a more inviting one than images sometimes suggestive of a rail-bound traveller ploughing his way along routes determined and charted in advance.

NOTES

[1] F. H. Bradley, *Ethical Studies* (Clarendon Press, Oxford, 1927).
[2] H. Sidgwick, *The Methods of Ethics* (Macmillan, London, 1907).
[3] F. H. Bradley, 'Mr Sidgwick's Hedonism', in *Collected Essays* (Clarendon Press, Oxford, 1935), vol. 1.

12
Inscrutability of Reference, Monism, and Individuals

HIDÉ ISHIGURO

Prologue The fact that Richard Wollheim's first book (1959) was on Bradley has always intrigued me. Not that I ever knew much about Bradley. For me Bradley was the philosopher whom Moore and Russell had taken to task for denying the reality of relations, and who had claimed that we are deluded in thinking that there are individual things or particular facts. Such a denial of pluralism seemed on the surface very contrary to Richard Wollheim's whole way of thinking. As someone who had been for many years, a member of the department of which he was chairman I felt that the independence of individuals and a commitment to J. S. Mill's principle of non-interference by the State or by any other body, including university departments, in self-regarding matters seemed to lie at the very heart of his way of thinking. His attraction to Freud and Melanie Klein, and even his interpretations of works of art, seemed also to betray his strong interest in the individual self and its history, not only his own of course, but that of each person. What drew him to an advocate of monism?

Over the years I often thought that I should study the arguments that led Bradley to his monism and examine in greater detail what Richard Wollheim had argued about them. I might not be able to allay my ignorance about British Hegelians very much, but I might understand a bit better the murky questions surrounding modal problems concerning relational facts about individuals, and I might understand better how the many diverse and interesting parts of Richard Wollheim's philosophy related to each other.

Preparing a contribution to this volume provided me with an excellent opportunity to carry out this long-standing homework. This, then, is an attempt to think seriously, with Richard Wollheim of many years ago, about certain problems that Bradley raised, by someone who knows very little about Bradley and the school he represents. What I learned from Bradley and from Richard Wollheim's discussion of him is more about the problem of reference than about relations. I came to realize how seriously they had both tackled this problem and how one can find in Bradley certain forms of argument similar to those which have recently led some important philosophers to give up analysing the notion of 'reference'.

(1) *Denial of particular facts* It is ordinarily assumed that Bradley was a monist who denied the existence of individuals and of particular facts. I have come to realize, however, that it is not at all clear that Bradley denied the existence of individuals. What does it mean to deny the existence of individuals? One can, like Spinoza, be quite clear that there are individual people like Paul and Peter and that there are individual trees and mountains, but deny that they have the metaphysical status of individual substances. This comes from the definition given to the notion of substance more than from anything else. Whatever is causally affected by other things and can be adequately explained only by invoking other things is not, for Spinoza, an individual substance. Bradley's arguments, however, are of quite a different kind. They concern the failure of singular designation and what is now called the 'inscrutability of reference'. And it seems to me that one can, without contradiction, both assume that there are individuals and deny that one can successfully refer to them individually and thus think and talk about them as unique individuals. In order to clarify what either Bradley or Wollheim thought about the matter, let us begin by examining the arguments that Bradley uses in *Problems of Logic*[1] and in *Essays on Truth and Reality*[2] when he attempts to demonstrate that there can be no particular facts by proving that we are doomed to fail in our attempt to make singular judgements. People have assumed that, in this argument, Bradley denies the existence of individuals, presumably because it is in singular judgements that people think that thought and reality meet face to face. It is important to notice, however, that Bradley denies the existence of particular facts by showing the impossibility not of individual things but of reference to individual things.

Bradley uses two main sets of arguments to get to his conclusion. One set concerns the inevitable failure, or so he says, of singular designation, and hence the inevitability that all judgements will turn out to be universal. The second set involves his view that all universal judgements are actually general hypothetical judgements which do not presuppose the existence of anything designated. Combining these two arguments, he attempts to show that we never prove the existence of particular facts. Now the structure of Bradley's inference interested me because Leibniz, who also asserted the second point (namely that all universal judgements can be treated as general hypothetical judgements which carry no existential import) was nevertheless passionately committed to individuals and to particular facts about them. The difference between Leibniz and Bradley lies in their attitude toward the first set of arguments. For although Leibniz discussed the difficulty of referring to one unique possible individual in a different possible world either by a definite description or by a proper name (and showed that a seemingly singular proposition about a possible object will turn out to be a general proposition about a set of objects, each of which is in a different possible world), he nevertheless thought that we can refer to actual individuals. In the case of Leibniz, the fact that he thought that any reference to a possible individual would inevitably refer to indefinitely many possible individuals, each in a different possible world, did not make him deny that if a different possible world were to exist, it would have in it individual people and things and particular facts about them.

What about Bradley?

I will try to show that Bradley's first set of arguments does not really indicate that Bradley denied the existence of individuals or particular facts. Bradley's arguments in this first set, which Wollheim has very clearly analysed and exposed, seem, on the contrary, to presuppose a belief in the existence of individuals. I will suggest that in Bradley's case the move to monism could come only with his second set of arguments – that is, with his claim that all universal categorical judgements are hypothetical – and by also adopting a nominalism of a strong kind. If all universal categorical judgements are hypotheticals carrying no existential import, then in making universal judgements, we would only be talking about what would follow from there being things of certain kinds. As we would not be assuming that there are such entities, we would at most be talking about the nature of the kind of entities that *could* be instantiated in the world. This can quite legitimately be called talk about the world as a whole, rather than about individuals in it, if we also believe that the world is not at the outset divided up in one way into individuals waiting to be discovered. I have come to believe that Bradley may have a stronger case on this issue than Richard Wollheim and Moore seem to have allowed. But let us begin with some arguments pertaining to Bradley's first set and to Wollheim's response to them.

(2) *Designating individuals* Bradley divides singular judgements
into three kinds: the first, which he calls 'analytic judgements of sense'
(using, as he warns us, the expression 'analytic' quite differently from
Kant), are those that describe only something given in the present;
the second, which he calls 'synthetic judgements of sense' (again
using the expression in a way quite unlike Kant), are those that go
beyond the given and describe portions of space and time not directly
perceived; finally, the third are those that are not about events in time
and space at all. An example of an analytic judgement in Bradley's
sense would be that the wall before me is white; an example of the
second, that the road leads to Tokyo; an example of the third, that
the number 3 is prime. Let us follow Wollheim in thinking that, for
the problem in hand, only the first two kinds of judgement are relevant, and, moreover, that since Bradley believed (rightly or wrongly)
that his synthetic judgements depend on his analytic judgements, we
can concentrate on analytic singular judgements of sense. (I myself
believe that the dependence between these two kinds of judgements
must be mutual.)

How do we pick out an object given to us in the present to which
we attribute a property? Bradley discusses three ways in turn: the first
is by descriptions using general terms; the second by demonstratives;
and the last by the use of proper names. Let us follow him in his
attempt to show how each fails to designate a unique object.

When we use a descriptive expression, the description we choose
may apply to other objects besides the object of our attention. Thus
we have no warrant, Bradley asserts, that the description succeeds in
uniquely designating the object. It is Wollheim's opinion that Bradley's claim should not be taken to be about a failure that comes from
our carelessness in describing the object with sufficient precision in a
particular case. That would be about a *de facto* inadequacy which
could be rectified. The claim should be taken, rather, as a fundamental criticism of principle, namely that, whatever description we use to
pick out a single object, it is always possible that there are other
objects that also satisfy it. But is this true?

We may wonder what Bradley thought of descriptions that can
designate at most one single thing or person in this world or in my
present environment: for example, 'the first man to climb the tallest
mountain on earth', 'the most recent explosion of a nuclear bomb'.
Is Bradley suggesting that, even if such a description would pick out
a single person or event in this world, it would pick out different
people and events in different possible worlds? No. I think he is
suggesting rather that, unless we know that there is only one world,

we cannot assume that a kind of thing that is unique in this world may not still have multiple instantiations, since the world may come in duplicates or in any number of multiples. As Wollheim quotes, Bradley writes that any judgement made with a general description 'will be true [or false] of any case whatsoever of a certain sort'.[3] Moreover, instead of continuing, as one might expect, to say that since the fact in reality is one of that sort, the judgement will be true [or false] accordingly, Bradley goes on to infer that 'if so it cannot be true [or false] of reality: for that is unique, and is a fact and not a sort'. Bradley is then saying, it seems, that if one attempts to make a singular judgement by using a general description to refer to a particular thing, even when there is only one thing in this actual world that falls under it, there may always be other things of the same sort that satisfy the description. We will then not succeed in making a judgement that can concern only the thing in reality. The thought itself does not have, as content, this particular fact about this object. If this is Bradley's argument, then surely, I suggest, it presupposes a belief in the existence of multiple individual objects. No monist – that is, no one who denies the existence of individuals – could accuse his opponent of failing to distinguish between an actual individual and other different individuals. We will return to this point later on.

Wollheim follows Bradley in then considering whether the use of additional demonstratives might not enable us to designate a unique thing. There may be many possible presidents of France, but if I point to François Mitterrand while I assert 'This President of France loves Montaigne', surely I am making a judgement about a unique actual individual. Bradley would deny this, because, as Wollheim says, in so far as his theory is one of word meaning and not what is now called 'speaker's meaning', demonstratives are given general descriptive content (by which he means something close to Kaplan's 'character'), in order to have a use. The words 'this' and 'that' must then have a universal content, Bradley holds, if they are to be used for the same purpose on different occasions; and, hence, they are subject to the same difficulty as singular designation using general descriptive words.

Wollheim, like Strawson, defends a view of reference as something that is done by people by the use of words rather than something that words achieve by their meaning alone, and criticizes Bradley's general approach to demonstratives. I completely agree with him that even if one believes that the sense of demonstratives has a universal content and, moreover, that each content is inadequate to pick out a unique individual on its own, this should not lead us to hold that demonstratives fail to designate single individuals in the context of their use. But what seems to me more important at this juncture is to notice that both Bradley's argument and Wollheim's appear to presuppose the existence of individuals which one either fails to or succeeds in picking out singly by the use of demonstratives. Bradley's view seems no more derived from monism than Wollheim's.

Bradley then considers proper names, which, predictably, he believes to have descriptive content, corresponding to the properties of the individual. Arguing against J. S. Mill's view that proper names have denotation but no connotation, Bradley asserts that although there is no prior rule of meaning that makes us attach a particular name to a particular object, once a name is thus attached, if it is to remain to be used as the name of this object, it must come to mean the possession of certain properties that the object has which distinguish it from other objects. Even if the meaning – that is, the connotation – is 'not always fixed', a name must have a connotation in order to denote. And if this is so, Bradley contends, proper names face the same difficulty in securing uniqueness that is faced by general descriptive expressions. Wollheim rightly criticizes Bradley for his shifting use of the word 'meaning'. If a name is to continue to function as a name of someone, it must mean that person; that is, we must be able to point to whom we mean. This does not imply, Wollheim says, that we know what we mean in the sense of connotation, although we may easily be led to think that the connotation is the set of properties possessed by the person whom we mean. We are familiar with the critique of the descriptive theory of names which was put forward by Saul Kripke in his rightly famous *Naming and Necessity* in 1972.[4] Although Kripke's version is less epistemically formulated, what Wollheim says here over ten years before is basically the same and right.

What I would like to point out again, though, is that even if Bradley, like Frege and some contemporary thinkers such as Searle, were to maintain that names have sense in virtue of which they refer to an object and even if Bradley is also sceptical about the success we have in picking out unique individual objects, this does not seem to lead to the denial of individuals. It seems, on the contrary, to presuppose the existence of a plurality of individuals and to point to our failure to pick out a particular one, rather than a set of them.

We should also notice that many recent arguments supporting Quine's 'inscrutability of reference' do not lead to the denial of individuals or particular facts either. For example, in an article with the same title written in 1979, Donald Davidson wrote that 'the simplest, least questionable way of showing that reference is inscrutable depends on the idea of a permutation of the universe, some one-to-one mapping of every object onto another'.[5] In this thought-experiment, whenever a name in the first scheme is said to refer to an object x, in the second scheme it refers to another object that we obtain as a function of the first object, $\phi(x)$, and there is a similar regular shift in what a predicate ascribes to an object in the first scheme and in the second. The very notion of the inscrutability of reference depends on the existence of different objects that are referred to by the same name in each of the languages. The fact that we cannot be sure to which object an expression refers does not lead to monism.

(3) *The nature of hypothetical judgements*   Let us now move to the second set of arguments; these relate to Bradley's contention that all universal categorical judgements are hypothetical judgements. For example, the judgement that human beings are mortal would be the judgement that if something is a human being, it will be mortal. As Wollheim summarizes, 'they say nothing about what is the case, only about what would be the case if a certain condition were satisfied'. Since Bradley has already taken the view that all singular judgements are in reality general judgements, all seemingly singular judgements are hypothetical judgements. As I have said earlier, I believe that this does suggest that the proper subject of such judgements is reality as a whole, and this becomes more convincing as we follow the details of Bradley's argument.

According to him, whenever we want to secure uniqueness of reference for the subject expression, we put into it more and more descriptive elements, but inevitably some facts about the object which are assumed in the given context are left out. The truth of the subject–predicate judgement becomes conditional on the left-out facts also being true of the subject. This means that not only are subject–predicate judgements to be taken as hypothetical judgements; they are doubly hypothetical. By this I mean that the truth of the hypothetical judgement is in turn dependent on further hypotheses. For example, the judgement that 'Caesar crossed the Rubicon' would be of the form 'If x is Caesar, x crossed the Rubicon', which is then spelled out as being of the form of a universal judgement: 'If x is the Emperor of Rome, who conquered Gaul, . . . etc., then x crossed the Rubicon'. This, Bradley says, is not precise enough, and we have to add further conditions which were assumed to hold in the context about which we make this hypothetical judgement. For example, given that p and q were happening in Rome when x was in Gaul, given that x was not too badly injured or gravely ill, if x is the Emperor of Rome . . . etc., then x crossed the Rubicon. If x is a variable, obviously the judgement would not be of any particular designated individual. It is about whatever object there is in the world which would fall under the description given in the antecedent of the hypothetical judgement. In addition, if many of the relevant facts p, q, and so forth are related to other things, then the judgement could indeed be said to be about the world as a whole. And if we do not take the world to be a single complete object, a judgement about the world is not a singular judgement.

We seem to have arrived at a version of monism, or the belief that every judgement we make about things is really a judgement about the world as a whole (although not at the belief that there are no individual things). I believe that to be the reason why Bradley says in the *Logic* that the only hope for the singular judgement lies in complete renunciation.[6] I do not, therefore, agree with Wollheim when he says that 'the exact connexion between this conclusion and the discussion that precedes it is far from lucid' (*Bradley*, p. 62). If we make more and more general hypothetical judgements about unspecified entities in the world, then we will make more and more correct judgements about many individual things in the world. Whereas if we attempt to make singular judgements that are true only of a particular individual, and fail to designate the individual successfully, we may fail to make any correct judgement.

It might be objected that whatever the variable x ranges over in the hypothetical judgements must be the same kind of individuals whose existence is shown not to be threatened, by the first set of arguments on the inscrutability of reference. Why, then, would showing that singular judgements are universal judgements, which in turn are shown to be hypothetical judgements, lead us anywhere nearer to monism? The answer, I believe, is the following. The first set of arguments was shown to presuppose the existence of entities which were already individuated, even if we could neither refer successfully to one of them nor could tell to which one among many we were referring. Arguments based on showing that seemingly singular judgements are hypotheticals are quite different. Over what kind of entity the variable x ranges over depends entirely on the sortal introduced or presupposed by the predicate of the antecedent. We may well be a nominalist of a Lockean kind and believe that the way the world divides itself into kinds depends entirely on the criterion we choose for the application of general words; that is, on a Lockean nominal essence. We may hold that the universe is not divided into basic sortals of any kind; and yet we may agree to the reduction of singular judgements to hypotheticals. We would then be committing ourselves only to the existence of an undivided reality which could be structured in different ways into individuals. This is surely consistent with monism, even if not identical with it. To be, a nominalist and a realist at the same time in the way that Michel Foucault was, for example, is compatible with monism. We will come back to it later. What I want to suggest is that if we are nominalist enough, the view that all singular judgements are ultimately hypotheticals seems to lead to monism.

(4) *'Is' of identity and 'is' of predication.* There is another aspect to this question which we must discuss. This is what Russell, and Wollheim have criticized as Bradley's failure to distinguish between the 'is' of identity and the 'is' of predication. Bradley claimed that all subject–predicate propositions are false, by what appears to be a very strange argument, which I do not completely understand. I will therefore not attempt to explain or defend all of it, but summarize it and raise a couple of points which I believe are intriguing and related to the problem we are discussing. But before we begin our argument, I should perhaps confess that I cannot believe that Bradley held that judgements of the subject–predicate form were really identity statements, as Russell's and Wollheim's criticisms suggest. Russell, who criticized Hegel's assertion that the one is the many, and the many one, had claimed that this comes from Hegel and the Hegelians' failure to distinguish the 'is' of predication from the 'is' of identity. Wollheim similarly ascribes a straightforward confusion to Bradley, and writes in his book that for Bradley 'All subject–predicate statements are really identity statements' (*Bradley*, p. 72).

However, in the *Principles of Logic*, Bradley states unequivocally that 'Judgement is not the assertion that subject and predicate are identical or equal'.[7] He also says that 'the object of judgement is, despite their difference in meaning to assert the synthesis of different attributes'.[8] I think this claim is understandable if we recall his view that subject–predicate judgements are hypothetical judgements of the form: 'if anything is S, then it is P.' S and P are different attributes, but we are saying that for some value of the variable x, x has both S and P.

What, then, does Bradley mean when he writes that in a subject–predicate judgement the intensions are distinct but the extension is identical? Bradley claims that in predication we assert that A is B. (Let us continue to keep in mind that for him this is actually of the form of a hypothetical, 'If anything is A, it is B.'). He then argues that

if we understand a subject–predicate judgement in what he thinks is
the mistaken traditional manner, we can produce a *reductio ad absurdum*: 'If you predicate what is different you ascribe to the subject what
it is *not* and if you predicate what is not different, you say nothing at
all.' The second half seems to mean that if you say 'If anything is A,
then it is A' you say nothing (something Wittgenstein was also to say
in the *Tractatus*). I am not sure whether saying something tautologous
should be described as saying nothing, but we can agree that it does
not say anything factually informative. But the first half is much more
mysterious. Bradley can't be saying the obvious, that if one lies about
the subject or makes a mistake about it, one ascribes a feature that
the subject does not have. What then could he possibly be saying? We
normally think that general terms A and B can be quite different (let
A be 'Confucian' and B be 'Asian'), yet that it could be quite true
that the thing that is A is B. Aren't we talking about the referent of
A and saying that he or she falls under the concept of being an Asian?
And surely this would not be to ascribe to the subject A what he or
she is not. Isn't Bradley's intended *reductio ad absurdum* argument
based on a simple confusion which could be cleared up if he had made
the Fregean distinction between 'sense' (*Sinn*) and 'reference' (*Bedeu-
tung*) as Wollheim suggests?

I think not. And to see why not, let us first recall here that, for
Frege, as a matter of fact, an object's falling under a concept is a
relation between the reference of a proper name and the reference of
a predicate. The sense/reference distinction does not play any role
here. Next we should remind ourselves that though Bradley does not
talk of sense and reference, he does talk of intension and extension.
Bradley asserts that when we try to analyse the logical form of judgements by the grammatical form of subject and predicate ('A Confucian is an Asian'), we should not mix extensions and intensions. We
should not, for example, give an extensional reading of the subject
and an intensional reading of the predicate. According to him, every
judgement has an aspect of intension and an aspect of extension. The
intensions are the universal features expressed by the subject concept
and the predicate concept. And according to him, if the judgement is
informative at all, the subject and predicate would concern some
different universal features. The extension on the other hand is one
and the same. We would express it by a variable which refers to an
element in reality which falls under both the subject concept and the
predicate concept. Using two different universal features, we are referring to reality, he says, and judging that anything that has the first
feature has the other. The point Bradley is making, then, is that

subject–predicate judgements are hypothetical judgements. They are not identities. He is not saying that the 'is' in 'S is P' is actually an 'is' of identity. It is actually a judgement of the 'if, then' form, but a judgement that uses one variable that ranges over both antecedent and consequent. This means that, of one and the same possible object, we are making a judgement that if it is S, then it is also P. As the situation stands, such judgements make no existential claims, and therefore they do not assert the existence of individuals. But neither do they deny the existence of individuals.

(5) *Scrutability and identification dependence* It seems to me that, in defending or attacking inscrutability of reference, two separate problems become confused. One is the claim that agreeing systematically to the truth-value of a whole set of sentences is compatible with a different interpretation of the terms in the sentences, and thus that we cannot get to the reference of terms from the acknowledgement of the truths of the sentences in which they occur.

The facility with which some philosophers have found instances of this is, however, misleading. For example, I find the example used by Donald Davidson, in his 'The Inscrutability of Reference', unconvincing. The example is the sentence 'Wilt is tall'. In one interpretation 'Wilt' is assumed to refer to the person Wilt and the predicate 'is tall' to refer to tall things. In the other interpretation, 'Wilt' is assumed to refer to Wilt's shadow and 'is tall' to refer to the shadows of tall things. (Here we see that Davidson, like Putnam, understands by reference of a predicate not a concept as Frege did, but a set, which for Frege was the extension of a concept and not the concept itself. But this is not the source of my difficulty with Davidson's example.) My difficulty is a very simple one: the truth-condition of the sentences under the second interpretation is parasitic on grasping the truth-condition under the first interpretation. The property of being a shadow of a tall thing is not a measurable property. We all know how our shadows get shorter and shorter as noon approaches. Even if we allow that the situation is, as Davidson imagines it to be, very artificial, so that everything always has a shadow and only one shadow, we have no direct way of establishing that a shadow satisfies the predicate 'is tall' under the second interpretation. It is simply a question of establishing that something is tall under the first interpretation and then of establishing that it is a shadow of that person. The same goes for the name 'Wilt' under the second interpretation. Wilt-likeness of shadows or any observable feature of shadows does not always make them shadows of Wilt. We would have to be able to identify Wilt under the first interpretation and then establish that something is a shadow of him. In other words, a person cannot have the criterion for applying the second interpretation without having the mastery of the first interpretation. This would be observable if we were to investigate the speakers. Certainly it is not as if there were one set of objective situations or events which inscrutably 'causes' two different sets of attitudes and responses. It is not as if there were two independent interpretations of the sentences with identical truth-conditions. The same applies to Quine's rabbits, undetached rabbit parts, and rabbit stages. The identification of the latter types of entity is entirely parasitic on the identification of the first type of entity.

Let us suppose that what we have here is merely an unhappy example and that there can indeed be two or more interpretations of sentences differing in the references of the constituent terms, where the sentences nevertheless share all the truth-values whenever they are taken in either interpretation. This would not provide a counter-example to Bradley's thesis of uncertainty of singular designation which we discussed earlier. Bradley was talking not of sentences but of judgements; that is, of what is thought in interpreted sentences. The question was not whether establishing the truth-value of a sentence may be compatible with taking different interpretations of its constituent singular terms, hence of taking it as expressing the contents of different judgements. The interpretations of the terms were quite clear. There was no doubt as to what the intended judgement was. The problem was rather that there was no guarantee that we had succeeded in picking out one and only one object, although we intended to do so.

The discussion of both these different problems is, however, related to the question of identity dependence of entities mentioned earlier. Identity dependence of individuals of certain kinds on others made us cast doubt on some examples of Quinean inscrutability of reference. Identity dependence of individuals will reduce the kind of singular judgements that are crucial for Bradley's problem. If there are basic individuals upon which the individuation of all other kinds of entities depend, we will only have to see whether we have criteria to single out these basic individuals.

(6) *Space-time and individuation* Kant, Strawson, and Tugendhat all believed that there is one system of identification of objects which is successful in securing the individuation of objects: namely, that of physical objects in space-time. There may be many fat, bald, pimpled men, but *this* fat, bald, pimpled man in the spatial position I am now pointing to is unique. For any sort of physical object, the space-time

system secures for me at most only an object of that kind at a given point. Other objects in the empirical world, whether they be micro, macro, institutional, mental, or even abstract, are supposed to be identified in a way parasitic on the individuation of these basic entities. (That is why indexical words play such an important role in our thoughts about individuals for Strawson and Tugendhat.) What would be Bradley's objection to this? After all, he knew Kant very well.

I think that Bradley's position on this matter is very interesting. Very roughly, he believes that no notion of a determined position in a system, whether it be in a space-time system or in a numerical sequence, provides a criterion of individuation. How does one know that there aren't multiple space-time systems that are qualitatively indistinguishable, or sequences that recur and repeat themselves? Only if we assume there to be a single reality to which we are related, could anything given in a position in space-time be taken to be individuated, i.e. uniquely identified. Let me quote at some length from Bradley's *Problems of Logic*, where he argues for this. After considering the view that it is the idea of 'thisness' which gives us the notion of particulars, Bradley writes:

> We must get rid of the erroneous notion that space and time are 'principles of individuation' in the sense that temporal or spatial exclusion will confer uniqueness upon any content. It is an illusion to suppose that, by speaking of 'events' we get down to real and solid particulars, and leave the airy region of universal adjectives. For the question arises what space and time do we really mean and how can we express it so as not to express what is as much something else? It is true that, in the idea of a series of time or complex of space, uniqueness is in one sense involved; for the parts exclude one another reciprocally. But they do not exclude, unless the series is taken as one continuous whole – and the relations between its members are thus fixed by the unity of the series.

But, he continues:

> There is nothing whatever in the idea of a series to hint that there may not be any number of series, internally all indistinguishable from the first (i.e., there may be many indistinguishable space-times) . . . The mere quality of appearance in space and time cannot give singularity. (*Problems of Logic*, p. 63)

What, then, does Bradley think gives objects singularity? According to him, everything that is given – every sensible phenomenon that is present – both is 'this' and has 'thisness'. But the stamp of uniqueness and singularity comes, he says, from its being 'this' rather than from its having 'thisness'. I interpret him as saying that everything present can be an object designated by a demonstrative 'this', or pointed to. It is a this; that is, it is an object that we are related to. 'Thisness', on the other hand, is some feature of particularity that the object has of which we are supposed to be aware. It is the relation we have to an object that guarantees its singularity, not any feature or quality (Book i, ch. 2, §23). All features are general or universal. Therefore the only way we reach beyond universals that characterize the content of any thought is by reference to the real that appears in perception. It is not the space-time system that is inherently unique; it is rather that we think that a unique reality is given in space-time. Bradley says: 'It is one thing to seek the reality in that series, quite another thing to try to find it as that series.'

This, then, is the basis of Bradley's monism, if it can be so called. His monism is not a denial of the existence of individuals. It claims, rather, that reality has to be accepted as a single unique thing, in order to make sense of any notion of individuation of particulars. No content of judgement, no content of thought, succeeds in being singular. It is of necessity general. Even spatio-temporal thoughts are *per se* general. To be given as 'this', i.e. indexicality, is not a feature of an object, but our relation to a given in reality. And only when the whole of reality is accepted as unique can we say that this relation gives us a unique singular object. This seems to me to be a sound position to take.

I have not discussed Bradley's famous denial of external relations which is put forward in *Appearance and Reality* and which, as Richard Wollheim rightly says, also plays an important role in Bradley's so-called monism. This is because I find difficulties in several of Bradley's arguments there, and do not think that he has established his conclusion. It is important to realize, however, that the doctrine of internal relations does not play any role in Bradley's denial of successful designation of particulars. My point was to show how *this* denial of Bradley's makes more sense than is generally conceded and how the necessity of accepting a single unique reality follows from this argument of Bradley's alone, without leading to the denial of individuals whose existence lies at the core of Richard Wollheim's philosophy.[9]

NOTES

[1]   Bradley, *Problems of Logic* (Oxford University Press, Oxford, 1922).

2   Bradley, *Essays on Truth and Reality* (Clarendon Press, Oxford, 1914).

3   Bradley, *Principles of Logic* (Oxford University Press, Oxford, 1922), pp. 49–50.

4   Kripke, *Naming and Necessity* (Blackwell, Oxford, 1972).

5   Donald Davidson, 'The Inscrutability of Reference', in *Inquiries into Truth and Interpretation* (Clarendon Press, Oxford, 1984), p. 229.

6   Bradley, *Principles of Logic*, p. 104.

7   Ibid., p. 22.

8   Ibid., p. 27.

9   I profited from discussion with the members of the Graduate Center of City University of New York, when I read an earlier version of this paper there in February 1990. I am very grateful to Leigh Cauman and Nick Wadley for improving my style and for making my English clearer.

13

Motions of the Mind

W. D. HART

In his Preface to *The Thread of Life* (1984) Richard Wollheim writes that throughout his thirty-four years in the Department of Philosophy at University College, London, the department 'always exemplified to a high degree the values that happen to please me most: audacity, toleration, a concern for tradition, and a disregard for authority'. He is a champion of those values. Where they are not championed, fear ensues. Fear is sometimes said to tend towards fight or flight, the suggestion being that these are exclusive alternatives. But fight can fuse with flight as a sort of jitters. The jitters are not a fit state for serious thought, and they can become a hard habit to break. By exemplifying to a high degree the values that please him most, Wollheim made his department a desert for jitters and a commonwealth of serious thought. It took me a while to recognize the commonwealth I joined in 1974.

Poets know, and critics say, that a poet must find his subject. It seems to me that this is probably true of everyone who writes seriously, and so of philosophers too. Wollheim says that it was an advantage for him of London, as contrasted with, say, Oxbridge, that London allowed him the time and the liberty to find his subject. One might think that he has at least two subjects: art and the mind. His philosophical range is truly astonishing. But he also has that precious power, essential for depth in philosophy, of making connections. So his work is animated by and exhibits a unity of intellectual insight that makes it idle to count his subjects; one will not appreciate his work on art properly if one ignores his work on the mind, or vice versa.

Wollheim is about twenty years my senior. When I try to imagine getting a hearing for Bradley or psychoanalysis or aesthetics rooted in intimate acquaintance with paintings during the heyday of ordinary language philosophy in England, I am, shall we say, a bit daunted. That experiment shows that he is his own man. Some powerful and independent people seem indifferent to their juniors, or even to enjoy making the way no less stony for their juniors than it was for them. Wollheim, by contrast, is a perceptive and generous man. It took a while for it to dawn on me through my jitters that he did not just tolerate one's trying one's hand at whatever turns one on; he encouraged it with his own interest because it delighted him. His description of friendship in *The Thread of Life* is taken from life. He would never use anyone merely as a means, but he also knew that his junior colleagues needed time, liberty, and respect to find their subjects and grow into them.

Life comes in generations, and it is an iron law of the generations that no generation can repay what it owes to the one before. (When you have children, one thing you learn is that being paid back is not something the generation before ever wanted; one pays that debt to the next generation.) Even so, one wants to offer Richard Wollheim one's best. My working title for this essay was at first 'T. H. Green and the Phenomenology of Choice'. When, over the years, we had talked about and around belief–desire models of action, Wollheim had time and again used the phrase 'identifies himself with one of his desires' to describe deliberation, choice, and the formation of intentions. This phrase struck me. I did not know its provenance, and I never thought to ask him whether it had one; perhaps I took it as his, which in a way it is. Then, independently of Richard Wollheim, Peter Hylton and John Rawls separately prompted me to have a look at T. H. Green's work. (What was this British idealism against which Moore and Russell revolted? What happened to contract theory in political philosophy between Kant and Rawls?) I came to admire Green, and I am angry that he is now so ignored. Book II of his *Prolegomena to Ethics* is called 'The Will', and it is shot through with that striking phrase for choice. When I mentioned this to Wollheim, I am not sure whether he recognized the phrase as his (which shook my confidence), but he did recall, as though calling up an old memory not recently consulted, that when he came to London in the late 1940s, he lectured on Green's *Prolegomena* (which went out of print in 1949). Here there seemed a chance to join two heroes, and chatting with a couple of colleagues confirmed me in my working title.

But titles should denote. Re-reading, to prepare for this essay, as much of Wollheim's work as deadlines allowed I could not find a single reference to Green. Bradley is there, and not just in his first book (1959). Towards the end of *The Good Self and the Bad Self*, his Dawes Hicks Lecture to the British Academy in 1975, in which he draws together the moral psychologies of Bradley and Melanie Klein, he writes that rationalizing moral action must involve reference to how the agent stands relative to his desires, 'to whether (to recycle that phrase) he does or does not identify with them'. In re-reading his work, one thing I was looking for was that phrase of his and Green's that had struck me. I did not find it, and this phrase from his lecture on Bradley and Klein is the closest thing to it I found.

The phrase from *The Good Self and the Bad Self* is not quite Green's; it omits the reflexive pronoun 'himself' as object of the verb 'identify'. But having re-read Wollheim's work with an eye out for Green's phrase (and, I still think, Wollheim's in conversation), the parenthetical 'to recycle that phrase' is striking, for this seems to be the only place where Wollheim approximates Green's phrase in print. Identification as a psychological activity is certainly one of his great recurrent themes; but Leonardo, for example, identifies himself with his mother, and that might seem rather different from identifying with one of one's desires. What phrase was Wollheim recycling in 1975? Could returning to Bradley have reminded him of his lectures on Green in the late 1940s?

My confidence in my subject was shaken, or, at any rate, my confidence that there is much public evidence that Green influenced Richard Wollheim. But even the absence of influence need not deny us a basis for comparison. My re-reading of *The Thread of Life* was delightfully enriched by succeeding immediately upon my re-reading of Book ii of Green's *Prolegomena*. Let us try to think through some of the affinities between these two masterpieces.

Green, with T. H. Grose, edited the first collected edition of the works of David Hume. For this edition, Green wrote a Preface that consumes 371 pages of the first of Nettleship's three volumes of Green's collected works (which does not include the *Prolegomera*). The Preface is not a good read; it is repetitious and quarrelsome, and Green constantly shifts his focus within his sentences, let alone his paragraphs. But the Preface is also wonderful. It is probably the deepest critical examination in English of Hume to have seen, for a time, the dark of print. When Norman Kemp-Smith wrote the next major examination of Hume in English, he made it plain that he was responding to Green. In his first book, Wollheim describes Bradley as backing into his metaphysical position by rejecting the native philosophical school of empiricism. Green broke such a path in his Preface, and it is natural to wonder whether Bradley followed Green down this path. Despite their tone and their criticism, both Green and Bradley honour Hume and British empiricism with their attention. With characteristic grace and tact, Wollheim writes in the Preface to *The Thread of Life* that the philosopher of the tradition to whom his intellectual debt is deepest is David Hume, and that he hopes this is obvious.

Green's central target seems to have been what we might call the atomism of empiricism. At least earlier on, Hume had wanted to do for the mind what Newton had done for matter. In Hume's project, association was to play the part that gravity had played in Newton's. But Hume had no laws of association remotely like Newton's law of gravity; Hume's associations were all *ad hoc*. Newton inherited from Euclid a single general scheme, space, in which any two bodies (or, strictly, points) have a unique, well-defined distance between them, and this quantity was crucial for his inverse square law of gravity. But Hume had nothing remotely like a geometry of the mind. To each body, Newton assigned an intrinsic quantity, its inertial mass. This quantity was founded in a general equivalence relation: two bodies are equally massive when they have to be pushed equally for their speeds or directions to change equally. Newton's second law of motion thus connects force, mass, and acceleration in a universal, systematic, and quantitative way. But Hume had for his putative quantity, vivacity, nothing remotely like Newton's equivalence relation for mass or his second law of motion; vivacity is a fake quantity. Distance and mass are the independent quantities in terms of which Newton stated his law of gravity. Since Hume had no quantities remotely like Newton's, Hume had no way to state any law of association. (To be fair, it should be added that Hume seems later to have given up his Newtonian ambitions.)

This contrast between Newton and Hume is not Green's. He put the criticism more abstractly in terms of unity. We might illustrate Green's point by saying that while in *Principia* the law of gravity describes the unification of the solar system as a system, Hume had no systematic – let alone quantitative – terms in which to describe the unity of the mind, self, or person. In the small, where Kant later distinguished judgements from concepts, Hume does not seem to have apparatus in terms of which to distinguish ideas that are complete thoughts from ideas that are less than thoughts. For example, in the *Treatise* of Human Nature at I. ii. 6, he identifies the idea of a thing with the idea of its existence, which he has no way of distinguishing from the idea that it exists, thus rendering problematic the idea that it does not exist. Here the root of the difficulty is requiring distinct impressions to distinguish distinct ideas; but also Hume has no account of the synthesis, or analysis, of anything so propositional as thought. Yet the most egregious example of this vacuity in Hume is his bundle theory of the self. For the absolute idealists in Germany (Fichte, Schelling, and Hegel) and Britain (Green, Bradley, and McTaggart), the unity of the self seems to have been the paradigm of unity. This, perhaps, was their reworking of the basic function of the transcendental unity of apperception in Kant's transcendental idealism (and Kant remains the supreme commentator on Hume). For the absolute idealists, as for the later, mature Kant, the problem of how system and unity are possible is central; this, rather than problems about universals, platonic Forms, abstract entities or sets, is what they meant by the problem of the one and the many. The unity of the self sets their standard for solutions to the problem of the one and the many, and that standard, contrasted with the role played by justification from sense experience in Berkeley's subjective idealism, may account for what is distinctively idealistic in absolute idealism. They sought to model the unity of nature, its satisfying an explanatory system, on the unity of the, or a, mind.

Richard Wollheim is no absolute idealist, but he is certainly committed to the integrity of the mind. Confronted with Hume's bundle theory of the self, it is natural to object by asking how anything so passive as a mere bundle could act, as plainly we do when we visualize or decide or exhort ourselves. How could a mere stream of consciousness propel any of its currents? Hume might perhaps reply that the illusion that the self (the mind, the person) acts is a misconception of causal relations between items within a bundle that is a self; when I seem to exhort myself, it is really an item in me, like a decision, that causes my exhortation. So if causation is just temporal priority, spatial contiguity, and constant conjunction (whether larded over with the subjunctive mood or not), then perhaps it is only spatial separation that keeps it from seeming as if I perform your exhortations to yourself and only spatial separation that keeps us from merging into a single mind. One suspects that for Green the unity of the self was substantial and axiomatic enough for such results to count as *reductiones ad absurdum* of the bundle theory of the self.

Wollheim has returned to the problem of personal identity time and again. The first chapter of *The Thread of Life* makes it utterly clear that he accepts no bundle theory of the self, no reduction of the mind to the collection of one's mental states. Life, he says, is a process. A person engages in this process; he lives his life. During that process, he undergoes mental states. But the passivity suggested by 'undergo' is misleading, for in engaging in this process, a person carries out many mental activities. Remember how fundamental the activity of imagining (in, for example, projection, introjection, and identification) is in Wollheim's account of living a life. He, like Green, rejects Hume's bundle theory of the self.

But how much like Green? How crisply can we state a thesis here on which they might agree? Perhaps they would agree that there are to be no reductive explanations of the self. But 'reductive' is too much a jargon word for this statement to be forthcoming enough. Perhaps we could state a shared principle of theirs as that explanations of facts about a self (mind, person) will always include other facts about that self (mind, person). As it were, there is no explanatory exit from, or introduction of, the self.

Green states such a principle more or less explicitly; article 114 of the *Prolegomena* is a passage in point. There he writes: 'Should the question be asked, If this self-consciousness is not derived from nature, what then is its origin? the answer is that it has no origin. It never began, because it never was not. It is the condition of there being such a thing as beginning or end. Whatever begins or ends does so for it or in relation to it.' The last two sentences here include an allusion to Kant. Time is a pure *a priori* form of intuition. Green seems to take it for granted that what has such intuition is not in time, rather as if one could not be in a box one built. At any rate, if the mind is not in time, then it does not begin, so there is no question as to how it began. In some ways, then, Green is closer to Kant than most other absolute idealists. In ethics, for example, Bradley followed Hegel's ethics of *Sittlichkeit*, and when he rejected duty for duty's sake, it was both Kant and Green with whom he disagreed. But for the absolute idealists, unlike Kant, it seems to have been theology, rather than a natural science like physics, that was their exemplar of an intellectual enquiry worth taking seriously; perhaps theology presupposed a unity that physics did not. Green seems to try to reduce the presence of theology in philosophy to a minimum; as a writer who had to teach incessantly to support his family, he seems to have had an acute sense of his audience. But that minimum is positive. In the passage cited above, he seems to allude to the eternal and uncreated Creator even of time. If each of us is a fragment or aspect of God briefly embodied, then perhaps it is part of our being made in the image of God that we no more had a beginning than he did. While Green is more allusive than this, he is also firmer and less compromising or apologetic.

In the century between the publication of the *Prolegomena* and *The Thread of Life*, intellectuals have ceased to be able to take theology even this seriously. University College, London, the first college in England without a religious qualification, is known as the godless institution of Gower Street. It is natural that it should not even occur to a philosopher who has spent the bulk of his career there to lean on theology for intellectual support. So the question of what it is for a mind, self, or person to come about might seem even more pressing for Wollheim than for Green. Yet it seems to be an issue on which, while Green is allusive, Wollheim is silent. The question of the origin of minds (in the form of compatibility between dualism and the evolution of people) was put more than a decade ago by Wollheim's good friend Bernard Williams in a series of magnificent lectures on Descartes given at University College, London, at Wollheim's invitation. Of course Wollheim attended those lectures; but while he reflects powerfully on death, and the end of the self, in order to undermine reductive thought-experiments about the self in the first chapter of *The Thread of Life*, he is silent on the origin of minds. In this respect, he may be following the practice of psychoanalytic theory. It is a fact worthy of being remarked that Freud, who was hostile to religion, has no account of the origin of minds. Freud emphasized the psychology of childhood, and Klein included even earlier phases of life. But both seem always to take a mind, self, or person as given at the outset of the accounts and explanations they construct. Those of us who have known two-year-old children know that they have memories. So we should believe that we had memories then. Yet probably none of us remember being two; adult amnesia of earlier childhood is a striking fact, which Freud was the first to try to explain seriously. Part of the phenomenology of that fact seems to be, as it were, that as far back as we can recall, we knew that we were before then too. Psychoanalytic theory does not seem to claim to get behind this phenomenology to the very origin of the mind itself. It thus accords with the principle Wollheim shares with Green. Indeed, psychoanalysis seems more likely than Green so to have informed Wollheim's practice.

Freud himself may have been a materialist; that is, he may have expected that one day neurophysiology would establish that the mind is a physical, perhaps electrochemical, process in the central nervous system; some such view is suggested by the 'Project for a Scientific Psychology', which, though he never published it, retained an influence on his thought that Wollheim describes in *Freud* (1971). If Freud was a materialist, he was much less presumptuous about it than is now orthodox among specialists in the philosophy of mind; however, he may have expected an account of the origin of mind from neurophysiology rather than from within psychology. We are still waiting. It is plainer that Freud held views on another great philosophical problem, that of the freedom of the will, than that he did on the mind–body problem. One could not detach determinism from Freudian psychoanalysis without doing immense, perhaps irreparable, damage to it; but psychoanalytic theory seems at least largely independent of whether materialism is true or false. That liberty (from the glorious future of neurophysiology) is at least in part due to psychoanalytic explanations being given in psychological terms, a gift in accord with the principle Wollheim shares with Green (and which keeps psychology honest instead of fobbing its responsibilities off on the future of some other enterprise, like neurophysiology or computer science).

In conversation (another of his great strengths), Richard Wollheim once described with approval a position on the mind–body problem that he called 'mentalism'. This is a position one might back into by denial. First deny Cartesian dualism: no one can exist unless his body does; no one can be disembodied. Next deny materialism: no one just is his brain ticking over; no one is even the ticking over of his brain. So a mentalist would assert that one's mind and one's body are distinct existences, but the former can exist only if the latter does too. It is as well to recognize that Cartesian dualism often seems bizarre to common sense (as represented by beginners in philosophy), and that materialism often seems equally bizarre to as much of that same common sense as remains unconverted to scientism. So backing into mentalism by denial has something going for it. Even so, the position seems to me besieged by the worst of both worlds. In denying materialism, the mentalist seems to be confronted with the problem of explaining how causal interaction between minds and matter is possible; that is, with the major problem that has always confronted dualists. To deny dualism is to assert that minds are necessarily embodied. A materialist might be able to account for this necessity by the necessity of identity. But a mentalist denies materialism as well as dualism, so he owes us an explanation for the necessity of embodiment. To deny dualism adequately, the necessity the mentalist must explain is not a consequence of the causal interaction for which he must account in order to deny materialism adequately; it is no more necessary that a punch hurt than that a match ignite when struck. One's right hand remains when one destroys one's right fist by opening it, so the fist is not identical with the hand. The fist, however, is the hand clenched; so, since the fist is identical with the hand in a certain state, it cannot exist unless the hand does; what the first causes is caused by the hand clenched, and what happens to the fist happens to the hand clenched. But the mentalist denies that the mind is a state of the body, yet asserts that the mind is necessarily embodied, so he confronts not only the dualist's problem of interaction, but also the separate problem of accounting for the necessity of embodiment. Some problems can be solved, so problems are not refutations; but these seem formidable. If we have backed our way into a *cul-de-sac*, perhaps we have done so as a result of how we set out from the phenomenology of mental activity. For we set out from the difficulty of understanding how anything so apparently passive as the bundle of one's mental states could act, as it seems clearly we do act when we imagine or deliberate. Green, whose problem is unity, and especially the unity of the self, identifies the will with the self; the will is not a special function of the self, but the self in action. In that way Green may have seen agency as what an understanding of the unity of the self should grasp. Mental activity seems to require that the mind be more of a substance (to use the old word) than, for example, Hume's epistemology allows him to admit, and it seems just to describe this requirement as an intimation from the phenomenology (what it is like) of mental activity. Let us then go back to basics (which usually seems to be where the philosophical treasure, if any, lies).

Richard Wollheim writes insightfully about both mental activity and phenomenology in *The Thread of Life*. In general, he approves a belief–desire model of action. A person's action is typically explained by citing beliefs and desires (at least) that are reasonable for the person to have and that make his action a reasonable thing to have done. For example, John is walking towards the refectory at noon because he wants to eat lunch and thinks that the refectory is the best place to get lunch, all things considered. Part of the appeal of this model for Wollheim is that it does not always require that the agent be conscious of the beliefs or desires that explain his action; generalizing the model beyond consciousness is a route into the unconscious, and it is one of Wollheim's important achievements to have made this discovery of Freud's clear to philosophers. As we shall see, Green thinks that the phenomenology of choice is final, a thesis with which Wollheim, after Freud, disagrees. It may still be worth adding that for beliefs and desires to make a person's action reasonable is not incompatible with their figuring in a causal explanation of that person acting as he or she did. On the other hand, the principle Wollheim shares with Green requires that the agent not disappear (by, say, fragmentation, as in Hume) in such a causal explanation. Casting about for an analogy, an absolute idealist might be excited by the question of whether the universe as a whole could disappear from a causal explanation of the evolution of the universe as a whole, and whether in this respect only the universe as a whole is analogous with the self.

Wollheim distinguishes action in general from mental activity. John's desire to eat lunch will not by itself make sense of his walking towards the refectory. To make sense, we expect John to believe that he can get what he wants by his action; that is, that he can get lunch in the refectory. Our expectation seems legitimate for actions John performs by doing something else, as we say; for getting lunch by going to the refectory. But we also seem convinced that there is never an infinite regress or circle of actions such that an agent performs each by performing its immediate predecessor. So, we suppose, there must be things an agent just does; that is, does, but not by doing anything else. So, in so far as the model of action requires of the agent belief about how to satisfy his or her desire, it seems reasonable to waive that requirement for what the agent just does. Things like supposing seem to be things we often just do. Wollheim distinguishes mental activities like supposing from action in general by exempting mental activities from the requirement of those sorts of beliefs that the general model of action demands. On the other hand, many simple bodily movements, like wiggling one's left index finger, seem to be things that most of us can usually just do; asked how we do it, we are lost for words. If this appearance is not deceptive and if we have reconstructed Wollheim's distinction in accord with his intentions, then we might wonder whether all activities are distinctively mental. A philosopher who, like Wollheim, emphasizes the importance of embodiment in understanding our lives, and especially our mental lives, might well welcome ranging many simple bodily movements with mental activities. But perhaps he meant to leave room for the idea that all bodily movements worthy to be classed with actions have mental precursors, like decisions, and that wiggling a finger is a full-blooded action explained by a desire to do so and a belief that, say, a decision to do so is all it takes. This idea at least escapes the incredible regress that looms large in the notion that every decision be explained in part by a belief that a decision to decide is all it takes.

It cannot be overemphasized how *theoretical* the reflections in the preceding paragraph are; it is remarkable how little the mind reads off itself by introspection. It was not just introspection, but more the incredibility of an infinite regress of actions in, as St Thomas would say, essential subordination, that led us to the idea of things we just do, and *thus* for which we lack beliefs about how to do them. Yet it

also stands to reason and coheres with itself that this result be theoretical, not introspective. For if we are right and we lack beliefs about
how we perform mental activities, then it stands to reason and is part
of this lack that in some way mental activities be deficient in phenomenology. The passage in the *Treatise of Human Nature* (I. iv. 6) in
which Hume denies that there is anything remotely resembling an
impression of oneself is justly famous and utterly convincing. (It is
less well known that Hume's account of sympathy in book iii of the
Treatise requires that we have what he calls 'the idea, or rather impression of ourselves always intimately present with us'. This impression goes the way of laws of the association of ideas in Hume's later
philosophical works. Hume deserves the credit Wollheim pays him.)
Understanding the significance of Hume's utterly convincing denial
for the nature of the self and our knowledge, such as it is, of ourselves
has been an abiding agendum for philosophy since Hume. No one
wrestles with it more theoretically than Kant, and it is plain good
sense for Wollheim to try to fit it coherently with the best psychological theory going. If from his conception of mental activity we can
move a jot towards making it stand to reason that mental activities be
in some way deficient in phenomenology, then this is a contribution
from him to understanding the import of Hume's denial.

   But all we have so far is the statement that mental activity be in
some way deficient in phenomenology, and the qualifier 'in some way'
is intolerably slack. It is phenomenology that we seem to perform our
mental activities like supposing and deciding. It is phenomenology
that, asked how we do them or, by doing what, do we accomplish
them, we are often nonplussed. Of course, sometimes we decide
between two alternatives by imagining how each would unfold. But
sometimes we just decide between the two alternatives, and when we
decide by imagining, we typically just decide to imagine. But is it
phenomenology that we perform activities without doing them by
doing something else and without beliefs about how to perform those
activities? In *The Thread of Life* Wollheim explains more carefully than
most what he takes phenomenology to be. Except perhaps for sensations like pains and itches, mental states seem typically to be intentional, which means that they represent, or are of, something other
than themselves; a thought is always a thought that such and such or
of something. An acute analyst takes it that if an emotion like depression seems objectless to its victim, still, it is intentional, but its object
is unconscious. When a mental state is conscious, our most individuating knowledge of it is of its intentional object; we distinguish
among our thoughts by the sentences stating their content, that is, by

what comes after 'that' in phrases beginning 'The thought that'. (The fabulous little old lady who, when told not to talk without thinking, asked how she was to know what she thought until she heard what she said, knew what she was talking about.) Mental states, or at least conscious ones, also seem to have subjectivity. Wollheim follows Thomas Nagel in explaining subjectivity; the subjectivity of a mental state is what it is like to be in that state. (Such likeness seems inevitably experiential or epistemic. But it does not seem crystal clear exactly which or why. Perhaps the subjectivity of conscious mental states is not itself subjective, but instead theoretical. But then one should ask for the theory in which subjectivity figures, and none seems forthcoming.) Wollheim takes the phenomenology of mental states to be the sum of their intentionality and their subjectivity. A complete theory of the mind should explain why these two belong together. Suppose a mental state typically includes, by virtue of its intentionality, a perhaps faulty 'grasp' of the world (which includes the rest of the person in that state) and typically informs, by virtue of its subjectivity, an attitude towards what is thus grasped; then intentionality and subjectivity might emerge in the beliefs and desires explaining subsequent action. To touch the older vocabulary, intentionality belongs to reason, and subjectivity to passion. Reason and passion always come together because, we might say, a creature with only one would not be able to act (except perhaps in rudimentary activity), and thus would be at a radical disadvantage in the struggle for survival.

This unification of reason and passion by natural selection may be less conceptual than the sum of intentionality and passion that Wollheim intended by phenomenology, and it is certainly less conceptual than the unity of intellect and desire that Green claimed in a person. It is a deep question whether one and the same phenomenon can have two or more radically different explanations. Be that as it may, Green is especially interesting on the penetration of desire by intellect. (Surely one of his motives here is to see the master, passion, set beside the slave, reason.) Green distinguishes rather sharply between hunger and the desire to eat. Hunger he classes with the sensations. It has, he suggests, bodily location (say, in the belly), and he seems to deny it intentionality; in the way an image is always an image of something or other, but a pain is not a pain of anything, so neither is hunger a hunger of anything. In Wollheim's terms, hunger has subjectivity but lacks intentionality. The sensation of hunger may lend some of its subjectivity to the desire to eat. But the desire to eat has intentionality. For it is the desire that one eat food, and so represents oneself, eating, and food, and combines them as oneself eating food. In the implicit *a priori* chemistry of thought, the desire to eat has fragments: concepts of oneself, of eating, and of food. In the idealist version, these are more abstractions from the desire than isolable, more primitive elements bound together in the desire by some propositional or intellectual bond; the unity of the desire is prior to its particles. But to have the desire, one must have the concepts, whereas to have the concepts, it does not suffice to have only the desire. Possession of the concepts requires having many propositional attitudes, as we would say, of which those concepts are particles. This does not mean that some range of attitudes is uniformly necessary for having a given concept, but rather that having a concept requires having a large range of attitudes of which it is a particle; Green's was, in logicians' jargon, probably an AE rather than an EA thesis. The skein burgeons: concepts are abstracted from attitudes in which other concepts figure; these concepts in turn figure in yet further attitudes in which yet further concepts figure; and so on, indefinitely. Concepts and attitudes are knit into a whole. Our description of that whole is too abstract to reveal penetration of boundaries between kinds of attitudes. But even Hume was clear that a fear of ghosts is open to criticism on the ground that a belief in ghosts is mistaken. Hume would be hard pressed to explain such connections. But for Green the unity of the mind seems basic; perhaps, as concepts are abstractions from attitudes, so distinctions among attitudes are abstractions from the mind. As it were, the mind is an artefact of its understanding of itself. That gnomic little formula is another attempt to articulate the principle Wollheim shares with Green. Thus Green particularly emphasizes the idea of oneself implicit in the desire to eat. In our formula there is more than a hint of creation of the self by the self, a romantic notion which the absolute idealists admired in Spinoza's concept of substance and one reminiscent of Baron von Münchhausen pulling himself out of the bog by his hair. But Green, as we have seen, concludes that the self does not begin; in so far as it has a history, it has always been developing.

Green, like Wollheim, emphasizes phenomenology. Both take character as a moral notion rather than an explanatory psychological primitive notion. In article 100 of the *Prolegomena*, responding to the apprehension of character as an alien force, Green writes:

> A character is only formed through a man's conscious presentation to himself of objects as his good, as that in which his self-satisfaction is to be found. Just so far as an action is determined by character, it is determined by an object which the agent has thus consciously made his

own, and has come to make his own in consequence of actions similarly determined. He is thus conscious of being the author of the act; he imputes it to himself. The very excuses that he makes for it – not less when they take the form of an appeal to some fatalistic or 'necessitarian' doctrine than in a more vulgar guise – are evidence that he does so. And in such a case the evidence of consciousness, fairly interpreted, is final. The suggestion that consciousness may not correspond with reality is, here at least, unmeaning. The whole question is one of consciousness, a question of the relation in which a man consciously stands to objects (those of desire) which exist only in and for consciousness. If a man is consciously determined by himself in being determined by those objects, he is so really: or rather this statement is a mere pleonasm, for the only reality in question is consciousness.

Here we may have a hint of the idealism in Green's absolute idealism. His basic problem is to explain, or at least describe, unity or system. His paradigm of unity is the unity of the self. It would contravene this unity to derive or construct it from elements, so the self is basic. This fundamentality he seems to construe as requiring that doctrine about the self consist in the deliverances of the self, which need conform to no other constraint. The self he seems to identify with consciousness. The upshot seems to be a finality of phenomenology. After Freud, we, like Wollheim, no longer identify the self with consciousness. Then too, somewhere along the way, perhaps in the origins of analytic philosophy, we lost track of the problems of unity, system, and the one and the many in its nineteenth-century form. So we have no paradigm of unity, and taking the self as basic can seem quaint or superstitious or unscientific to us. For us, phenomenology is no longer final in the way it was for Green. The problem of system is intriguing enough to shake an unreflective confidence that Green is quaint. For example, the later Wittgenstein may have taken the unity of (a) language as his paradigm of unity, and there is more than a hint of a kind of linguistic idealism in his later work.

So we are less sure than Green that we are as we seem to ourselves to be. But this understates the case. For we are not, or should not be, sure even how much of ourselves seems, or appears, to us at all. What we just do seems deficient in subjectivity. Consider, for example, explicit conscious reasoning. As late as Green's day, one could still get away with calling logic 'the laws of thought'. Let us explore one track along which that designation has been withdrawn. When *modus ponens*, for example, is nowadays described, one is presented with a conditional, its antecedent and its consequent (or schematic dummies for these). In an example it will be sentences that one is shown to illustrate the three. It is a virtue of these sentences that inscriptions or utterances (even in silent speech) of the last two are literally and saliently parts or phases of the first; this repetition is relevant to *modus ponens*. Those three sentences may also complete the phrases 'The statement that . . . ', 'The proposition that . . . ', and 'The thought that . . . ' to yield definite descriptions, which may perhaps denote. Someone teaching truth-function theory in a limited time might refuse to argue in detail that truth-values attach primarily to sentences perhaps in context, rather than acts, like statements, or abstracta, like propositions, or mental states, like thoughts. One of the issues he or she would then be skirting is whether the dissection of a thought into ideas is an unfounded projection of the segmentation into words of the sentence completing 'The thought that . . . ' in the singular term purporting to denote that thought; thus there is a real question of the anatomy of thought independent of the segmentation of the sentences used to express that thought. (Note that the introspection of silent speech is no help on this issue, for silent speech is silent utterance of sentences.) Still, let us concede briefly, without argument or explanation, that there are such thoughts and that they stand to each other as do the three sentences in the teacher's example. This second concession is just that the third follows from the first two, and a basic version of following is that the third is true when the first two are. It thus begins to emerge that these thoughts are well called mental states, for we have here at best frames of a film of mental statics. We have no motion picture of how a thinker might have moved, as it were, from being in the first two to being in the third, or have one come to that from denying the third to denying one of the first two; we have no account of the process, the dynamics, of reasoning. Much the same could be said of transformational grammar and the psychological dynamics of speech production.

Aristotle's basic question about the motion of bodies may have arisen in something like the following conjectural way. Suppose one throws a stone. So long as one is still in the process of heaving the stone, it is one's hand that is pushing the stone. But what, he may have asked, explains the stone's continuing to move (for a while, at least) after it has left one's hand? This question never got an answer that was generally accepted. It has never been proved to be a question with, for example, a false presupposition, like whether a bachelor has stopped beating his wife; rather, the question has just never been answered in a way to satisfy others generally. By the seventeenth century, it was just, and pretty much silently, dropped. Instead, certain motions by bodies (those of constant speed and direction) were taken to be natural. Part of taking them as natural was refusing to ask for an explanation of them. Explanations were instead expected for deviations from these natural motions. Newton's first law of motion said that such explanations were to be expected in terms of forces. We have reached the brink of Newtonian dynamics; it is remarkable that nature has answered so long and so well to the inquisition that Newton began.

We do not know whether there is any reasonable chance of doing for the mind what Newton did for matter in motion. It might occur to one to emulate Newton here: perhaps we could take certain motions of the mind as natural and explain deviations from these in terms of a system of psychological forces. It might be fun to go back and ask whether Freud can be read as having attempted some such emulation. But it is as well to admit that 'motion of the mind' is a metaphor. Literal motion is change of place over time. Green, we saw, argued that Hume could not emulate Newton, in part because Hume had no geometry of the mind, no single general scheme, like space, in which (perhaps) mental states (but who knows) stand in favoured, well-defined quantitative relations, like distance. Green would not, I think, deny that there is something like a geometry of the mind. His objection to Hume is that Hume cannot make sense of any such thing, much as he needs it. But for a post-Kantian idealist, the unity of nature is at least its spatio-temporal structure, so if that unity is to be understood on the model of the unity of the mind (that being idealism), then there should be something like a geometry of the mind. Freud too had a structural description of the mind, and Wollheim has shown us how much this description is generated by a through working out of the belief–desire model. Green, who took the phenomenology of choice as final, would probably have balked here. But while the id–ego–superego structural description is not a geometry of the mind, it is doubtless a description to measure against any such geometry, were we ever to articulate one; and that description is generated from thinking about action, which in Green is a mark of the irreducible unity of the self. Perhaps we must emulate Euclid before we can emulate Newton.

No such project seems likely to catch on these days. But it says something about Wollheim that one expects that an admittedly sketchy idea for such a project might please him. In part Wollheim is so generous because of the generosity of his own interests; first-rate analytic philosophers expert in Bradley and Freud (to mention but two interests) are not thick on the ground. Green, like Horace, shows on the page that those who knew him were fortunate, and we who know Wollheim know first hand that such evidence is to be trusted. I doubt I shall ever see his like again.

NOTE

I am indebted to my former colleagues Malcolm Budd and Jonathan Wolff for their audacity, tolerance, concern for tradition, disregard for authority, and helpful comments on an earlier draft of this essay.

Part III
Art and Vision

14
Painting as an Art: Persons, Artists, Spectators, and Roles

ALEXANDER NEHAMAS

Of Richard Wollheim's many contributions to our understanding of art and the mind, four of his ideas are particularly exhilarating. The reason that they are exhilarating, to put the point a bit paradoxically, is that in fact they are only two. More accurately, these four ideas form two pairs. Wollheim has developed one pair in connection with his philosophy of mind and the other in connection with his philosophy of art. The members of each pair are related to one another closely enough to span these two fields and to show that, as Wollheim has consistently urged throughout his career, art and the mind are much more closely dependent on one another than it has recently been fashionable to believe. In short, his views are exhilarating because they are systematic, and the discovery that a philosopher is systematic, like the discovery that an artist has a style, is a cause of rejoicing: it does credit both to the subject studied and to its student. Of course, as Wollheim's own philosophical values suggest and as it is appropriate to point out on this occasion of celebrating them, by far the greatest part of the credit belongs to the subject – to the philosopher who thinks systematically, the author who writes with style.

I

The Thread of Life (1984) begins with the idea that in order to understand what it is to be a person, we must first distinguish between the person, the person's life, and the living of that life – a thing, a product, and a process that culminates in the product. The work's guiding idea is that the basic notion, in terms of which the first two are to be understood, is the third; that is, the process of living a life.

Through a brilliant reading of Ovid's *Metamorphoses*, which concerns the putative transformations of individual human beings into animals or objects, Wollheim shows that the notion of such particular transformations is incoherent. When Cadmus is turned into a serpent, he truly becomes a serpent, and ceases to be the person he was (p. 5). When Actaeon is turned into a stag, he remains Actaeon, a person (or, as Wollheim puts it, barely a person) because he is still the same human being that he was before, trapped now within the body of an animal (pp. 5–7). A living organism cannot be a person *despite*, but only *because* of, the animal that it is.

This implies that if a particular animal is a person, so is (in normal circumstances, as we often say) every other animal that belongs to the same species. To what species do persons, actually or potentially, belong? 'Species are selected as person-species', Wollheim replies, 'either in reality or in fiction, on the basis of how their members live, of how they live in virtue of being members of that species'. This, in turn, leads him to the conclusion that 'whether personhood attaches to certain species, or to members of that species, depends on whether characteristic members of the species are thereby enabled to live in some appropriate way' (pp. 9–10). That appropriate way, of course, is the living of the life of a person, which it is the purpose of *The Thread of Life* to investigate.

Having disposed of the person, the thing, as the primary notion in the philosophy of mind, Wollheim turns to the life of the person, the product, and asks if what a person is can be understood solely in its terms. His argument here is complex and controversial (pp. 10–21), but it is not my purpose to examine its details. Wollheim claims that in order to understand what a person's life is, we must appeal both to a 'unity relation' which establishes the appropriate sort of interrelatedness between the events of which that life consists and to an 'identity relation' which ensures that the same person be involved in the events that constitute a particular life.

Wollheim now points out that these two relations may conceivably diverge, but that even in the event that they do not, we need an account of how they fit together, 'what separate weight [they] pull, or how they conjointly contribute to the picture of a person's life'. He claims that if, once again, we turn to the process of living the life of a person, we shall see that the appropriate connection between the events of a given life is the result 'that comes about through the way persons lead their lives' (p. 20). In addition, we shall see that the identity of the person becomes more important because, since the process of leading the life of a person must be embodied, questions about the identity of the body in question will bear more directly on the nature of that process than the interrelatedness of that life's events: this relation now turns out to be an effect, not a ground, of the way a particular life is led.

The primacy of the process of leading a life over both lives and persons is the first member of the first pair of Wollheim's ideas to which I want to call attention. The second member is connected with the fact that 'a person leads his life at a cross-roads: at the point where a past that has affected him and a future that lies open meet in the present'. For persons in particular, 'the influence of the past is carried by mental dispositions that are set up and persist. . . . Standardly the influence passes through present mental states in which the dispositions manifest themselves' (p. 31).

So the influence of the past on the present, and therefore on the future, is established through mental states. Among mental states, Wollheim pays particular attention to those he calls 'iconic'. These, he writes, are 'crucial to the way in which the past exercises an influence over the present, and we draw upon them when in the present we try to predict, or anticipate, or control, the future'; iconic mental states are all connected with the imagination (p. 62). They allow us to reconstruct our past (in at least two senses of the term 'reconstruct'), understand our present, and anticipate various ways in which our future may unfold. Essential to our ability to have and understand these states and to use them in order to perform these operations is the fact that we assume different roles within them, roles which include, in Wollheim's theatrical analogy, an 'internal dramatist', an 'internal actor', and an 'internal audience' (pp. 65–83). We construct mental narratives in which there are characters, among whom we often include ourselves, and we are affected in particular ways by what these characters undergo. This emphasis on the roles on which an important part of the process of leading the life of a person depends is the second member of the first pair of Wollheim's ideas to which I want to call attention. The construction and interpretation of roles, as we shall see, introduces an element of convention in Wollheim's understanding of both art and the mind.

II

In his recent philosophy of art, Wollheim has made a forceful case to the effect that it is imperative to distinguish between the painter, the painting, and the creative process of which the painting is the product. In parallel to his approach to the philosophy of mind, he has argued that of these three, the fundamental object of understanding, at which criticism is and should be directed, is the process of painting. Wollheim opened his 1984 Mellon Lectures, of which *Painting as an Art* (1987) is the text, with an argument to the conclusion that the traditional question of aesthetics, 'What makes a painting a work of art?', inevitably leads to the prior question, 'What makes painting an art?' (p. 13). And he claims that a good answer to the former question is given only by an answer to the latter which 'holds in effect that a painting is a work of art in virtue of the activity from which it issues – more precisely, in virtue of the way in which this activity is practised' (p. 17).

Just as not every living organism is a person, so, Wollheim argues, not every painting is a work of art. Just as only those living organisms are persons who lead the sort of life appropriate to persons, so only those paintings created in the way appropriate to the production of works of art are themselves works of art. Recalling Wollheim's earlier insistence that living organisms are persons on the basis of the species to which they belong and not in virtue of the individuals they are raises an interesting possibility. This is the possibility that paintings that are works of art are always the products of a process which has resulted in the creation of more than one such work. In other words, it is highly unlikely that painters produce one and only one work of art in their lifetime. This is not an implication that Wollheim points out, and I am not sure that it can be shown to hold on the basis of a general argument. But it is historically plausible, and it therefore offers additional support for Wollheim's view.

A related thesis does follow, however, from some general views that Wollheim holds; and though it is weaker than the idea we have just discussed, it also supports his parallel treatment of art and the mind. This is a thesis to the effect that, even if it cannot be shown that no painter can ever paint only a single work of art, it still is a fact that no painter of any significance can. The thesis follows from Wollheim's criticism of Ernst Gombrich's views on expression and communication in painting and from his own alternative account, which is based on his notion of style.

Gombrich has argued against the traditional idea that there is a simple natural connection between shapes and colours on the one hand and feelings and emotions on the other, by claiming that what particular painters communicate in each one of their works depends essentially on their 'repertoire', the overall set of works they have produced and the range of alternatives within which they work.[1] So, Mondrian's *Broadway Boogie-Woogie*, which looks austere next to Severini's *Dynamic Hieroglyphic of the Bal Tabarin*, appears almost abandoned when placed side by side with most of the rest of Mondrian's truly austere works.[2]

In *Art and its Objects* (1980) Wollheim produced a number of criticisms of Gombrich's position. His central idea is that the notion of the repertoire, which specifies the range of works actually produced by a painter, does not actually support the ascription of alternative choices to the painter in question. Since all we know is what a painter did produce, 'How are we to decide', Wollheim asks,

> whether this is the work of an artist who within a narrow repertoire expressed a wide range of inner states, or of one who within a much broader repertoire expressed a narrow range of states? (p. 62)

To establish a range of alternatives, Wollheim argues, we need to know not only what works painters actually produce but also what paintings, in a sense, they *could* produce. But the notion of the repertoire is too weak for this purpose. What is needed instead, he claims, is reference to the notion of style, 'which cannot be unreservedly equated with that of the repertoire', since it 'has a kind of inner coherence that a mere repertoire lacks' (p. 64). This is the kind of style which Wollheim, following Wölfflin, calls 'individual' and contrasts with 'general' style.[3] Individual style, for Wollheim, has psychological reality and has a genuine explanatory function, unlike general style ('baroque', 'Norwich School'), which is primarily a tool of classification (pp. 26–7). I am not exactly sure how Wollheim thinks we come to form a conception of a particular painter's style, but I am convinced that the process involves the study of that painter's repertoire (the works actually painted) and a serious speculation, based on both psychological and art-historical factors, about works that could have been painted by the artist in question. That is, the attribution of a style begins with a repertoire, and projects a set of possible works on its basis. For Wollheim, therefore, the notion of style is stronger than and includes that of repertoire. This, at least, is what I want to argue, since Wollheim at times (if very tentatively) attributes to style a particularity which contrasts with the essentially plural nature of the repertoire:

> A style may have such an intimate connexion or correspondence with the states that are typically expressed within it, that we do not have to

go outside the work itself and examine related cases in order to gauge its expressive significance. A style may be self-explanatory. (pp. 64–5)

And yet, when he discusses stylistic features in *Painting as an Art*, he consistently invokes a plurality of works by particular painters in order to make his point (pp. 27–36). In addition, the analogy between having a style and knowing a language, on some aspects of which Wollheim insists (p. 27), also suggests that the possession of a style presupposes the execution of a significant number of works.[4]

It is important to note that there is no definite number of paintings which painters must produce before we can attribute a style to them. This, in turn, may suggest that the attribution of individual style is less a psychological discovery, as Wollheim believes, than the result of a value-judgement to the effect that some painters are important enough for us to construct narratives of their development which have internal coherence. Wollheim may reply that what allows such narratives to have internal coherence is precisely the psychological fact that some painters develop style in his sense, that their coherence reflects the psychological dispositions and abilities manifested in style. But I am not sure that this reply is convincing: the history of art offers a number of cases in which merely a change in evaluation – and not a psychological discovery – has demoted a style to 'a manner'.[5]

Whether Wollheim's psychological account of style is or is not ultimately correct, the point remains that no painter who develops a style (and that includes all painters of artistic significance) could have painted only one work of art. And this gives Wollheim's approach at least some initial plausibility, for part of what makes a painting a work of art for him is precisely, as we shall presently see, its creation through a process animated by the intention to communicate content or meaning. And the preceding argument has shown that at least part of content (whether this content, in turn, is or is not given a strong psychological construal) can only be communicated by a painter with a style, a creator of at least a number of works.

In so far as the process which leads to the creation of paintings that are works of art is an activity on the part of a person, Wollheim argues that understanding it necessarily involves a reference to the intentions of the agent engaged in it. And these intentions, if painting is to be practised as an art, must have a certain nature and exhibit certain relationships to one another. To illustrate these relationships, Wollheim introduces the notion of 'thematization' (pp. 19–25), which is, very roughly, equivalent to the idea that one element on the painted surface is used so as to make another element salient: 'Thematization is always for an end' (p. 22). And the most general end to which thematization is devoted is

> the acquisition of *content* or *meaning*. Thematization is by and large pursued so as to endow the resultant surface with meaning. And meaning may in turn be glossed as that which we grasp when we understand a painting: when we understand, not some fact about the painting, but the painting itself. (p. 22)

In addition, painting practised as an art also aims at visual pleasure or delight, both at giving and getting it (pp. 22, 98–100).

I believe that there may be a problem here, created by Wollheim's extremely broad notion of meaning on the one hand and his great austerity in considering painters as artists on the other. From chimpanzees to children and psychotics, from politicians and businessmen who distract themselves to the decorators of old-fashioned restaurants and of banks and other corporate monuments who 'once, probably, were artists, but who now paint exclusively for money and the pleasure of others', we are given an immense continuum of painters who, 'though they fall short of being so in varying degrees', all fail to be artists (p. 13). Yet, it seems to me, nothing prevents 'world-politicians who paint for distraction' (a description of their motives) or 'madmen who set down their visions' (a description which fits the victims of 'art therapy' and, perhaps, Van Gogh as well) from intending to communicate meaning, if meaning is construed simply as whatever we grasp when we understand a painting. What of the painters of military recruitment paintings and of propaganda works more generally? What of purely religious works? It seems possible that though more paintings than Wollheim admits communicate meaning, not all pictorial meaning is artistic. If so, then we need an independent account of the latter if we are finally to understand the process that results in those paintings which Wollheim is willing to consider really, and not merely apparently, as works of art.

It is not my purpose, however, to pursue this sort of difficulty here, for I believe that Wollheim's views raise considerably more interesting issues. To see what those are, we must realize that Wollheim is very concerned to characterize his account of pictorial meaning as a *psychological* one. 'What a painting means', he writes, 'rests upon the experience induced in an adequately sensitive, adequately informed, spectator by looking at the surface of the painting as the intentions of the artist led him to mark it' (p. 22). And this, he insists, implies that 'if we are to understand when and why painting is an art, we must consider it in the perspective of the artist' (p. 36).

This view sounds aggressively old-fashioned, but it is given a new twist, and is connected with Wollheim's philosophy of mind in the exhilarating manner that systematic connections entail, by his going on to claim that

> it is crucial to recognize that, though adopting the perspective of the artist requires us to give pride of place to what the agent does, it does not require us to stop there. Above all, it does not require us to ignore or reject the point of view of the spectator. It requires us only to rethink it. And, if we start to rethink it, the first thing to strike us will be that the distinction between agent and spectator is primarily a distinction not between persons but between roles. And the second thing to strike us is that not merely can these different roles be adopted by the same person, but there is one person, one kind of agent, who must do so. That is the artist. The artist is essentially a spectator of his work. (p. 39)

The systematic parallel should now be clear. In the philosophy of mind, Wollheim considers the process of leading the life of a person primary, and, in turn, considers the ability to take on different roles and thus affect that life essential to the process. Similarly, in his philosophy of art, he emphasizes the primacy of the process of painting, and argues that it is essential to this process that a person engaged in it assume both the role of the artist and that of the spectator.

III

Why must painters assume the role of spectator in relation to their own works? Wollheim's answer is complicated and original. Its first step consists in his view that the basic feature which distinguishes a surface which merely has paint on it from a painting is the latter's 'twofoldness'. Most paintings are for Wollheim representational. Representation is for him a very general notion: all it 'requires is that we see in the marked surface things three-dimensionally related'. What we usually consider representation Wollheim calls 'figuration', the species of representation 'in which we identify the thing we see in front of something else as, say, a man, a horse, a bowl of fruit, the sky, the death of an animal' (p. 21). Now in all representational paintings, spectators can see *in* the painted surfaces other things while at the same time being aware of the fact that what they are looking at are painted surfaces and not duplicates or surrogates, in any sense, of the things seen in them.[6]

It might be objected to Wollheim that his establishing of such a close connection between twofoldness and representation has two counter-intuitive consequences. First, it implies, as he openly acknowledges, that 'the correct perception' of truly abstract works, like Barnett Newman's *Vir Heroicus Sublimis*, 'perception that coheres with the fulfilled intention of the artist, is not characterized by twofoldness' (p. 62). Yet Wollheim seems to think that twofoldness, the seeing of one thing in another with which it is not confused, is essentially connected with the communication of content, and that this latter feature, in turn, constitutes the central feature of painting when it is practised as an art. Accordingly, the connection between abstract works, the communication of content, and art remains obscure.

I am not sure what Wollheim's attitude toward this issue would be. Perhaps, as his characterization of Newman's works as 'vast machines' might suggest, he does not think that truly abstract paintings are in fact works of art; but, in view of the fact that his broad characterization of representation results in a radical reduction in the number of abstract works, he might not find this consequence troubling – though I remain uneasy about it. Alternatively, one might claim that it *is* a real question whether abstract paintings really do communicate any content at all: the issue has long been the object of debate. Therefore, the problematic status assigned to them by Wollheim's view is actually a consideration in its favour. On the other hand, one might also begin to doubt whether the notion of 'the communication of meaning or content', on the hypothesis that at least some truly abstract paintings are works of art, can function as the explanation of what it is that turns painting into an art after all. Or finally, we might argue, along the lines long made familiar by Clement Greenberg, that abstract painting communicates content precisely by turning attention to its surface, by calling attention to the fact that it is a surface that is merely painted, in contrast to the pre-modernist painting to which it consciously opposes itself.[7]

A second counter-intuitive consequence of Wollheim's view is that *trompe l'œil* works, which for most people are the most realistic works there are, but for Wollheim 'do not invoke, indeed [they] repel, attention to the marked surface', also turn out not to involve twofoldness, and are for this reason non-representational. My own response to this problem is that Wollheim is here taking his own view too literally. *Trompe l'œil* works are in fact 'designed to baffle our attention to the marks upon the surface'; but the point remains that one knows that they are paintings and that what one is seeing in them (though not, of course, in Wollheim's sense, *in* them) is a set of marks cleverly disguised. *Trompe l'œil* works startle only momentarily, even if they can do so repeatedly.

The idea that painting is twofold is one of Wollheim's most important (if controversial) contributions to our understanding of representation in general. It constitutes, as we have said, the first stage of his answer to the question concerning the artist's posture. The second stage of that answer consists in the view that twofoldness, the ability to see a marked surface as representing something else with which it is not confused, is in turn the product of a much more general, perhaps innate, ability on the part of human beings. This is the ability to *project*, to see in various objects, many of them neither representations nor paintings nor even artefacts at all, other things, some of which are figures and some of which are simply three-dimensional arrays (pp. 46–59). It is, of course, in its simplest forms one of the most primitive abilities which we have. But the tendency to ground some of our most sophisticated practices on what are ultimately simple and basic needs and activities is characteristic of Wollheim's way of doing philosophy and one more indication of the systematic nature of his thought.[8]

Because of its elementary nature, however, the ability to project can be engaged in by anyone who is so minded, and almost anyone, if we speak in general terms, can see almost anything *in* almost anything. It is precisely for this reason – and this now provides the complete answer to the question about the artist's posture with which this section began – that it is crucial for painters to be spectators of their works. They must assume the spectator's role so as to exercise as much control as they possibly can over what other spectators of their works will see *in* them. They want to ensure that spectators of their work will see what the painters want them to see in their works, and not anything they please. By assuming the role of spectator, painters *become* spectators, and thus come to know what spectators can see in their works.

This is why, as Wollheim forcefully and controversially insists, we can speak in terms of standards for a spectator's seeing what is *in* the painting correctly or incorrectly. Painting as an art involves the intentional manipulation on the part of artists of their tools and materials as media for the production of a meaning which is to remain under their control. And it is just for this reason that, as we have seen, Wollheim is so concerned to insist that we must always, when we approach a painting, adopt 'the perspective of the artist' (p. 36).

It might be tempting to identify Wollheim's view with what he calls

> the Contagion theory [which] holds that, in each and every case, for
> the spectator to grasp what the artist meant, there must be re-created
> in his mind when he looks at the painting precisely the mental condition
> out of which the artist painted it. This view was embraced by Tolstoy
> in old age, but it has little else to recommend it. (p. 44)

The identification would be unjustified because Wollheim does not
require such a strict correspondence between the mental states of
artists and spectators. Even so, his approach is old-fashioned to the
extent that it remains resolutely psychological. As he writes, his

> general account of pictorial meaning . . . locates meaning in a triad of
> factors: the mental state of the artist, the way this causes him to paint,
> and the experience that a suitably informed and sensitive spectator can
> be expected to have on looking at the artist's picture. (Ibid.)

As such, it is an account which, as Wollheim clearly insists, sets him

> against all those schools of contemporary thinking which propose to
> explain pictorial meaning in terms like rule, convention, symbol system,
> or which in effect assimilate pictorial meaning to . . . linguistic
> meaning. These . . . include structuralism, iconography, hermeneutics,
> and semiotics. (Ibid.)

Wollheim's scant attention to all such recent developments in art
criticism and theory has provoked some harsh criticism.[9] It may also
have prevented him from finding a few intriguing, if far from definite,
connections between his own views and those he deplores. What
conclusions one is to draw from those connections, if I am right in
claiming that they exist, is not, however, something about which I am
willing to speculate.

IV

In order to establish the connections I have in mind between Wollheim's psychological account of pictorial meaning and the more conventionalist approaches with which he contrasts it, I need to put
together two of his views in particular. The first is his insistence, with
which I am in profound agreement, that artists and spectators are not

persons but roles persons assume, or as Hobbes would have put it 'persons artificial'.[10] The second is the importance Wollheim attributes, as we have seen, to the fact that artists have always been spectators of their works, that they have always adopted the particular posture of facing their works as they have been working on them. I will try to suggest that the proper interpretation of these two views in turn suggests a number of parallels between Wollheim's psychological realism and its more 'up-to-date' alternatives. Another way of putting this point would be to say that Wollheim's view is less psychological, or at least less realistic, than he says it is; conversely, conventionalist accounts may be more deeply implicated in psychology than their adherents tend to admit.[11]

We have seen that Wollheim attaches great importance to the seemingly banal and insignificant fact that painters have always positioned themselves in front of their paintings, eyes open, while they are working on them. The explanation for this, he claims, is not the obvious one: painters do not assume this posture in order to see what they have done, which would imply that they might in principle come to a point where they no longer need to do this. Rather, like a driver, who cannot ever drive with closed eyes, 'the artist does what he does *with* the eyes'. But unlike the driver, who always proceeds along a predetermined path, the artist creates the path in the very process of painting, and therefore also does what he does '*for* the eyes' (pp. 43–4). Painters assume their usual posture, if I may put it this way, not to see what they have done, but to see what they are doing.

Assuming this posture puts painters in the position, in the role, of spectators of their work. And though Wollheim does not make this point himself, it follows from this that, as spectators, painters address not the painting itself, since that is not yet completed, but instead the process of its creation. This, indeed, may be another consideration in favour of Wollheim's view that the creative process is the primary object of interpretation and criticism.

In the Preface to *Painting as an Art*, Wollheim describes his having developed

> a way of looking at pictures which was massively time-consuming and deeply rewarding . . . it often took the first hour or so in front of a painting for stray associations or motivated misperceptions to settle down, and it was only then, with the same amount of time or more to spend looking at it, that the picture could be relied upon to disclose itself as it was. (p. 8)

In fact, much of the substantive criticism in *Painting as an Art* reveals itself to be the result of such a procedure and of such an aim: the interaction of an incredibly discriminating and attentive spectator devoted to the detailed scrutiny of an individual work of art.

Yet, in an earlier work, Wollheim gave a characterization of criticism according to which what we just saw him write may commit him to what he there calls 'an unduly atomistic' conception of criticism. 'Certainly', he continues,

> in seeking to understand a particular work of art, we try to grasp it in its particularity, and so we concentrate on it as hard as we can: but at the same time we are trying to build up an overall picture of art, and so we relate the work to other works and to art itself. Nearly everything that we learn about a work that is of critical value contributes to both projects.[12]

The issue, I believe, is one of emphasis, not inconsistency. But the emphasis makes a difference.

To see that this is so, and how the difference is related to the connections between Wollheim's view and its competitors, I now want to turn to a consideration of Marcel Duchamp's last work, *Given: 1. The Waterfall, 2. The Illuminating Gas (Étant donnés: 1° La chute d'eau, 2° le gaz d'éclairage)* (1946–66). It is not clear where this work begins. Towards the very end of the substantial Duchamp collection in the Philadelphia Museum of Art, there is a doorway leading into a darkened room in which little if anything is at first visible, despite the fact that a traditional label for a work is placed near the doorway (but inside the room, so that it can easily be missed). The room is often not noticed by visitors.[13] It is sometimes described in terms like the following:

> At the end of a narrow, underlit room, little more than a corridor, stands an ancient weather-beaten door of wood, arched and encased in a surround of bricks. One senses at once that the door cannot be opened but one is drawn towards it as if by a magnet, and as one comes closer one becomes aware of two small holes, at eye level, drilled through the wood. Beyond the door lies an extraordinary sight.[14]

But even if one does not miss the room, one is still, in most cases, at a loss as to what to do next. Especially after having been baffled by Duchamp throughout the collection that one has just gone through, it is very easy to suppose that the door is all there is to the work, to take a quick look at it, and be on one's way; the door exerts nothing like 'magnetic' attraction. In addition, the peep-holes do not immediately come into focus, for the placement of what is behind the door is such that no light comes through them unless one has already taken a number of steps toward them – at which point they become brilliantly illuminated.

It is only if one already knows about the work or sees others looking through the peep-holes or is relatively self-confident that one actually goes up to the door. And it is only then that one realizes that there is more in this room (or is it *in* the room?) to be seen.

Still tentatively, one looks through the peep-holes, and is immediately attacked – there is no other word for it – by a scene of violent ambiguity. Beyond the door there is a brick wall with an irregular oval opening. And beyond the wall, bathed in extremely strong and stark light, there is an unexpected three-dimensional arrangement against a background of a brightly retouched photograph of autumn foliage which includes a mechanical waterfall pouring its waters into a pond, and the naked body of a woman on her back on a bed of twigs, holding a gas lamp in her left hand somewhat in the manner of a lying Statue of Liberty. She is spread-eagled, her shaved pubis directly in front of the spectator, 'with no false prudence or sense of shame' in Golding's words.

These words, however, which appear so natural on a first, casual look conceal a vast number of problems. The woman's body initially appears very realistic, but a careful look dispels that impression. The body, first, is in three-quarter relief. Second, the material of which it consists has a visible crack which helps to undermine the easy original illusion. Third, the anatomy of the body is impossible: for example, it has no pelvis. The body gradually comes to seem more like the representation of a mannequin, a lifeless figure, to which notions of prudence and shame are inapplicable.

In addition, the woman's head, with the exception of a wisp of blond hair, cannot possibly be seen, and the same is true of the right side of her torso as well as of both her feet. The peep-holes are positioned in such a way that no amount of effort will enlarge the field of vision Duchamp has created for his viewers. It is easy to feel that the invisible parts are indeed there, but there is actually no way of verifying that on inspection. Given the fact that only part of the woman's body is visible and, in particular, that her face is not, the question whether, supposing that perhaps she is not a mannequin, she represents someone alive or dead, someone tortured or transported, can receive no answer: 'This *tableau vivant* . . . travesties itself as a *nature morte*.'[15] Once again, the moral vocabulary of prudence and shame is shown to be inappropriate.

It is likely that most spectators strain to see a little more of the scene than is visually available to them: the arrangement is designed to tantalize them in that direction. But this takes time, and inevitably produces embarrassment, which is especially profound if others are waiting their turn. The room is darkened, but not dark enough to hide one's face. People tend to slink away from the door, sometimes expressionless but often shaking their heads shyly and also a bit conspiratorially if perhaps with a certain air of superiority: they have gone through it already; those behind them don't know yet what awaits them behind the door.

What awaits all spectators of *Étant donnés*, is, as with everything Duchamp did, not only an exercise in bad taste in the name of belittling art, but also a commentary on the art of the past, out of which, in a number of that word's senses, he himself came. This is not only because of the stunning thematic similarities of the work to Courbet's *L'origine du monde* (1866) and *La femme au perroquet* (1866). The connections between *Étant donnés* and the art of the past are vastly more complicated. The peep-holes through which the scene must be observed are of crucial importance. Their effect is to immobilize the work's viewers in a strictly physical sense, to place them in fact in the very position which has been assumed to be the ideally correct viewpoint in much of the theory behind modern Western painting. Nothing could be more traditional, more classical, than this physical embodiment of a theoretical principle. Further, the peep-holes, together with the work's ambiguously prurient subject-matter, have a further important effect. They force the work's spectators to spy at, and derive some sort of erotic pleasure from a figure that represents something inanimate, or perhaps dead. Having placed them literally in the position of the classical beholder, *Étant donnés* turns its spectators into explicit voyeurs. This is not only a change in the etymological root from which the terms are derived. *Étant donnés* profoundly affects the activity of looking at works of art, and part of the embarrassment that is palpable in the semi-dark room – whose partial illumination is now revealed to have a purpose and significance of its own – proceeds precisely from this fact.

I doubt that Duchamp aimed to produce what Wollheim calls 'visual delight' in his viewers, if by this we understand a pleasure produced by the perception of beauty. But what he may have succeeded in doing is to suggest, first, that spectators have always been voyeurs in at least some circumstances, and, second, that some of the visual pleasure, in the sense of pleasure produced by the perception of beauty, which undoubtedly some of the great works of the past and the present continuously give us, may itself be the product of voyeur-ism. This is anything but a flattering description of average museum-goers, art critics and historians, or aestheticians – but then flattery was never among Duchamp's aims.

The point I have been trying to make by bringing all these disparate factors together is the following. If Duchamp is successful in *Étant donnés* (and note that here I am following Wollheim in speaking of the individual achievement of an individual artist), then he confronts us with a new interpretation of the relation between the spectator and the painting which has ramifications for the history of art in general. This interpretation of the spectator's role, I claim, was not available to earlier artists, whose works we may now begin to look at with slightly different eyes. In this manner, Duchamp's *Étant Donnés* es-tablishes a new convention for looking at paintings. I use the word 'establish' on purpose, because it is ambiguous between discovery and invention. I also use the word 'convention' on purpose, because though painting may spring from a fundamental human need, the *roles* of painter and spectator, filtered as they are through countless cultural layers, cannot be conceived simply in natural or universal terms.

Duchamp's achievement, if such it is, enables us, among other things, to look at Caravaggio's pictures of young boys in a new and different way, quite distinct from anything that preceded it. Arthur Danto once remarked that he could see *that* Caravaggio's paintings were exciting pictures without being excited by them. But the pleasure we get out of these paintings may actually be, it seems to me, the pleasure of the voyeur – the pleasure of observing and intercepting, as it were, the pleasure that someone else is feeling through the perception of a beautiful object of desire. And since at least part of the pleasure involved in Caravaggio's paintings is already visual, we may find ourselves, if this interpretation is correct, in the position of second-order voyeurs.

In addition, *Étant Donnés*, by violently cutting its visual space in unnatural (or, at least, unconventional) ways, reminds us of the fact that very often there are things we want to see in pictures but cannot. Duchamp accomplishes this, as I just pointed out, by his unusual spatial arrangement. But by doing so, he brings to the foreground and makes explicit a principle to which, Wollheim claims, 'no painting can be expected to subscribe'. This is the principle of always telling 'the whole truth' about one's subject. Wollheim offers this principle a cogent logical justification: no painting can represent its object as belonging to every kind of which it is in fact a member (*Painting as an Art*, p. 70). Duchamp gives this principle a physical embodiment as well; the borders of paintings are, after all, natural obstacles, and where a scene ends in space is also a reason why not everything about a subject can be shown. In *The Adoration of the Mystic Lamb*, van Eyck successfully represented 'an angel blowing the bellows of an organ, even though, since the angel is behind the organ [and between it and the panel's border], everything except a tress of the angel's hair and a sliver of drapery is not visible' (p. 65). But he also, by the same token, failed to represent the whole angel and much more besides. Paintings necessarily exclude, and they exclude not only because of the logical fact that any subject belongs to innumerable classes, but also because of the much more brute fact that pictures are limited, physical objects.

If this interpretation is correct, Duchamp establishes a convention which allows us, as spectators, to do things with paintings which couldn't have been done before. It also, to the same extent, allows us to construe painters as agents in ways which were not possible before and in ways in which they might never have been able to understand their own work. Correct understanding of a painting need not involve seeing it as its maker saw it, because makers – that is, painters – are, like spectators, roles – and how such roles are conceived can change radically and affect not only the art of the future but also that of the past. What Stanley Cavell has written in regard to style can be applied equally well to this conception of roles:

> A new style not merely replaces an older one, it may change the significance of any earlier style; I do not think this is merely a matter of changing taste but a matter also of changing the *look*, as it were, of past art, changing the ways it can be described, outmoding some, bringing some to new light – one may even want to say, it can change what the past *is*, however against the grain that sounds.[16]

The importance of the fact that such conventions can be established and that they can govern, retrospectively, the understanding and appreciation of works of visual art does not in any way show that visual meaning, as Wollheim correctly denies, is like *linguistic* meaning (pp. 22, 44). But it does suggest that visual meaning may be more like *literary* meaning, in the case of which changes which cannot possibly be anticipated at a time retroactively involve a different understanding of earlier texts.

What I would now like to conclude by suggesting is that in so far as both artist and spectator are roles on Wollheim's own account, their nature is more variable and more subject to revision than *Paint-*

ing as an Art allows. As roles, both artists and spectators are constructed. The elements that enter into their construction are in great part supplied by art and its history and by the changes to which these are subject. The constructs that these elements in turn constitute cannot be automatically or even easily identified with the real persons who play the roles of artist and spectator on each occasion. Once Wollheim allows that the artist is a role, as he does, then he has to face the fact that roles are constructed according to conventions, even if persons, on his view, are not. Conversely, if role-playing is in fact as important to our own self-understanding as *The Thread of Life* suggests, then understanding persons may involve more elements of convention than we have been tempted to suppose so far. And even if there is such a thing as 'a common human nature' (*Painting as an Art*, p. 8), it is far from clear that it is the only determinant of the meaning of our visual works of art. What originates in a natural need can well develop into a cultural convention, and its components may no longer be distinguishable from one another.[17] Understanding an artist, in short, is understanding a role. But understanding a role – that is, giving it an interpretation – is not obviously the same as understanding a person, at least on Wollheim's official view of what a person is and how persons are to be understood. That there are connections between them, however, seems to me undeniable: what those connections are is a subject which we are only now beginning to address. Wollheim, who has helped us so much in our efforts to understand persons and roles, as well as artists, may now also be thanked for challenging us to try to understand, in addition, the relations between them.

NOTES

[1] Ernst Gombrich, *Art and Illusion* (Princeton University Press, Princeton, 1961), ch. 11; *idem*, 'Expression and Communication', in *Meditations on a Hobby Horse* (Phaidon, London, 1971), pp. 56–69.

[2] Gombrich, *Art and Illusion*, pp. 366–70.

[3] See *Art and its Objects*, p. 65; *Painting as an Art*, pp. 26–36, and 'Pictorial Style: Two Views', in *The Concept of Style*, ed. Berel Lang (University of Pennsylvania Press, Philadelphia, 1979), pp. 129–41, where the contrast is drawn also by appealing to the terms 'taxonomic' and 'generative'.

[4] The process through which style is established by an artist and understood by a critic may be likened to the process whereby a grammarian tries to construct a theory of meaning – by observing, that is, the occurrences of actual linguistic expressions and projecting their possible uses

– according to W. V. Quine in his 'Meaning in Linguistics', in *From a Logical Point of View* (Harper and Row, New York, 1961), pp. 47–64. Needless to say, Quine's conclusions about meaning are considerably more negative than Wollheim's views concerning style and the communication it makes possible.

5   There is an asymmetry between painting and literature in this case; for a single novel may in fact establish an author as an artist. But I am not sure what this shows. David Carrier was kind enough to discuss the general issue of the psychological nature of style with me, and to raise a number of acute and pertinent points.

6   Wollheim discusses 'seeing *in*' in detail in *Painting as an Art*, ch. 2. He introduced the notion in 'Seeing-As, Seeing-In, and Pictorial Representation', included in the second edition of *Art and its Objects*, pp. 205–26.

7   This final argument, to gain plausibility, has to be supplemented by the considerations given by Arthur C. Danto in 'The Artworld', in *Art and its Significance*, ed. Stephen David Ross (State University of New York Press, Albany, 1984), pp. 470–82, regarding the manner in which pairs of opposite predicates become artistically relevant together. Thus, when the property of being representational became itself a concern of modernist painters (at least of those whom Wollheim would consider truly abstract), its absence also became relevant and acquired the ability to communicate content. The same, of course, could be said, *mutatis mutandis*, for the contrast between figural and non-figural works also characteristic of modernism. The implication of this approach, however, is that the 'flatness' of modernist painting does become at least part of the content communicated by abstract works. Wollheim discusses and rejects a Greenberg-inspired account of visual meaning in *Painting as an Art*, pp. 23–5.

8   See for example *Art and its Objects*, p. 112.

9   See for example Rosalind Krauss, 'Only Project', *The New Republic*, 12 and 19 September 1988, pp. 33–8.

10   I have argued a similar claim in regard to literary authors in my essay, 'Writer, Text, Work, Author', in *Literature and the Question of Philosophy*, ed. A. J. Cascardi (Johns Hopkins University Press, Baltimore, 1987), pp. 267–91.

11   Again, this is the main burden of the argument in relation to literature in the essay cited in note 10.

12   Wollheim, 'Criticism as Retrieval', in *Art and its Objects*, pp. 189–99.

13   Interestingly, after an earlier version of this paper was delivered at the meeting of the Eastern Division of the American Society for Aesthetics in the Spring of 1989, a number of people who went to the museum to see the work confessed that they had not been able to find it. Duchamp would have liked that.

14   John Golding, *Marcel Duchamp: The Bride Stripped Bare by her Bachelors, Even* (Allen Lane Penguin Press, London, 1973), p. 95; quoted by Dalia

Judovitz, 'Rendezvous with Marcel Duchamp: *Given*', in *Marcel Duchamp: Artist of the Century*, ed. Rudolf E. Kuenzli and Francis M. Naumann (MIT Press, Cambridge, Mass., 1989), pp. 184–202. See also the classic description by Anne d'Harnoncourt and Walter Hopps, '*Étant Donnés*: 1° *1a chute d'eau*, 2° *le gaz d'éclairage*: Reflections on a New Work by Marcel Duchamp', *Philadelphia Museum of Art Bulletin*, 64 (1969), pp. 6–58.

15 Judovitz, 'Rendezvous with Marcel Duchamp: *Given*', p. 189.

16 Stanley Cavell, 'Music Discomposed', in *Must We Mean What We Say?* (Scribner's, New York, 1969), p. 184. I offer a general argument regarding the past's 'malleability' in my book *Nietzsche: Life as Literature* (Harvard University Press, Cambridge, Mass., 1985), ch. 5 and 6.

17 On the interpenetration of the concepts of 'nature' and 'culture', see Clifford Geertz, 'The Growth of Culture and the Evolution of Mind', in *The Interpretation of Cultures* (Basic Books, New York, 1973), pp. 55–83.

15

On Looking at a Picture

MALCOLM BUDD

(1) When you look at Monet's *The Seine in Thaw*,[1] you are looking at a marked surface. But if you see it as Monet intended it to be seen, as a depiction of a river with melting ice drifting along it, you do not see it merely as a surface marked in a specific way, as you might see a puzzle picture or a Chinese character as a mere configuration of lines which means nothing to you. Yet neither do you see it as you would see the Seine if you were actually to see the Seine in thaw and were to recognize what you saw as a thawing river: your experience in front of the picture is not an experience of the same intrinsic nature as one of seeing and recognizing a thawing river. Nevertheless, your experience of the picture as a depiction of a river in thaw does appear to involve both an awareness of the marked surface and an awareness of what a thawing river looks like. For if it did not involve any awareness of the marked surface, you would not take yourself to be seeing a *depiction*, and if you were unaware of what a thawing river looks like, you would not see Monet's picture as a depiction *of a river in thaw*. The problem is to explain in what way your experience of Monet's picture involves a visual awareness of a marked surface and also a visual awareness of a river in thaw; and unless this problem can be resolved, the distinctive artistic values of depiction and the value of the experience of seeing a depiction of reality rather than that reality itself must remain uncertain.

But the idea of a visual awareness of a river is ambiguous. It covers both experiential and dispositional forms of visual awareness – experiential, as when you see a river or visualize one in the mind's eye; dispositional, as when you possess the capacity to recognize a river if you see one or recall in your mind's eye how a river looks. Accordingly, a visual awareness of a river can be introduced into the experience of seeing Monet's picture either in an experiential or in a dispositional form, and in whichever form the visual awareness is recruited to the experience, this can take place in more than one way. If it is introduced in a dispositional form, the general idea is likely to be that the intrinsic nature of the experience of seeing Monet's picture as depicting a thawing river consists in the visual awareness of its surface, which is interpreted as a depiction of a thawing river on the basis of the spectator's awareness of how a river in thaw can look. But if it is introduced in an experiential form and it is also recognized that the experience of seeing Monet's picture involves an awareness of the picture's surface, then the experience will be credited with a complex intrinsic nature, containing an experiential awareness, presumably of different kinds, both of the marked surface and also of a river.

The outstanding advocate of the view that the experience of depiction should be understood in the second of these two ways is Richard Wollheim. He has argued persuasively against alternative conceptions of the nature of pictorial experience, and in his book *Painting as an Art* (1987) he has constructed an exceptionally rich and illuminating account of the art of painting which is founded upon his own conception of the experience of seeing what a picture depicts. His principal claim is that the experience of depiction is grounded in, and can be defined in terms of, a particular kind of visual experience, one which has a distinctive phenomenology involving a visual awareness not only of the marked surface, but also of what is depicted. What exactly is this special kind of seeing, and does it form a secure basis for the impressive structure erected upon it?

(2)   It will be helpful first to take a step backwards and reconsider the question of whether the experience of seeing Monet's depiction of a thawing river can be assimilated to the experience as of really seeing a thawing river. For there is a persistent tendency to construe pictures, especially those that are to some degree or in a particular respect realistic, as being in some way illusionistic. Can such an equation be so lightly dismissed? The natural place to look for an answer to this question is the work of E. H. Gombrich, the most powerful advocate of the view that pictorial experience involves illusion; moreover, a consideration of his claims will be doubly useful, for Gombrich's position is one of the most important against which Wollheim has defined his own.

One of Gombrich's principal contributions to the understanding of pictorial representation is the emphasis he has placed upon the fact that any artist works in a medium and so is restricted in his representational ambitions by the limitations of his material, the ways in which the material (tapestry, lace, mosaic, pencil, oil paint) can be used artistically. But used to what purpose, if the purpose is to represent the world? Not, of course, to reproduce the subject; that is to say, to produce a replica or facsimile of it. Nor to reproduce the exact appearance of the subject. For – apart from certain exceptional cases in which the nature of the subject fits the medium perfectly – it is not possible to create a picture which looks exactly like what it depicts, except from a point of view that denies the spectator the normal visual access to the picture. It is because an artist's medium precludes the matching of his picture with its subject that, in Gombrich's words, 'no artist can copy what he sees'.[2] What, then, can the representational artist achieve? Gombrich's answer is that he can render his subject in terms of his medium; which is to say that he can transpose some of the relationships in his subject into the terms of the medium.

Now it might be thought to follow from the fact that there is in general no possibility of match between picture and subject that a picture must deliver to the spectator a different visual experience from one of the kind he would have if he were actually seeing what is depicted. But Gombrich is right to resist this conclusion, and he goes further when, in one of the accounts of realism, naturalisms, in *Art and Illusion*, naturalism, he elucidates realism in terms of illusion. According to this account, in front of a realistic picture the spectator experiences the illusion that what is depicted is before his eyes, in the sense in which he might experience the illusion of seeing someone when looking into a good mirror. Gombrich has repeatedly emphasized that he rejects the equation of illusion with false belief, and also the weaker view that someone who experiences an illusion thereby has a false belief about his environment.[3] By an illusion he means a perceptual experience that is caused by a seen object but that represents the world differently from the way the object is. A visual illusion of a river is a visual experience as of seeing a river – a visual experience whose representational content[4] is that there is a river before the subject – but one which is not actually the perception of a river. Making use of the convenient ambiguity of the notion of representational content, Gombrich's claim is therefore that the spectator of a naturalistic picture undergoes a visual experience whose representational content is identical with the representational content of the picture: if the picture depicts a certain state of affairs, the spectator's experience represents that state of affairs as really obtaining.

It is his theory of perception that allows Gombrich to combine the two claims that, first, no artist can copy what he sees and, second, realistic pictures induce illusions of what they represent. He concedes that if the spectator attends to the marked surface of the picture, he will be able to detect any number of differences between the picture and what it represents, so that his experience of the picture will not be an illusion of what it depicts. But there is another way in which the spectator can look at the picture, and he is required to adopt this different approach if he is to experience the picture as being a realistic depiction. Rather than attending to the nature of the marked surface of the picture, he must project on to it an image of what is absent, the subject it depicts. He is encouraged to do this by the picture in so far as it is realistic; and it is possible for him to do this because perception is not the passive receipt of information about the environment, but is grounded in the mechanism of projection. Since what image will be projected is underdetermined by the nature of the perceptual stimulus and is dependent upon the character of the subject's visual system, his mental set, and various other factors, disparities between the nature of the marked surface of the picture and the nature of what it depicts, which affect the light reflected to the eye, do not preclude the possibility that the picture will create the illusion of seeing what it depicts. When the spectator's attention is not directed to the marked surface of the picture, differences are overlooked, gaps are completed, and the mechanism of projection operates to produce the intended illusion: the depicted scene apparently lies before the spectator, who 'sees' what is not there.

It is unnecessary to examine this theory of perception, for Gombrich's position, although consistent, is inadequate, as can most easily be seen by considering the qualifications he is forced to introduce. For in normal perception of a picture, information will be presented to the spectator's eyes which will affect his visual experience in such a manner that its representational content will not be just what it would be if the spectator were actually seeing the state of affairs depicted. Accordingly, Gombrich recognizes that the illusions he believes realistic pictures to be capable of inducing will rarely be complete, and in fact they will be complete only for a stationary eye whose field of vision is within the boundaries of the picture surface.[5] And this is sufficient to undermine the force of his claim that a picture is realistic to the degree that it is effective in inducing an illusion of what it depicts. For if it is only under highly artificial conditions that a realistic picture will induce an illusion of its subject-matter, a spectator who looks at such a picture in a normal manner will not experience the illusion it is capable of producing. And if, as will be the case, a spectator experiences a picture as being realistic when he looks at it in a normal fashion, his finding it realistic is not the same as his being induced by it to undergo an illusion of seeing what it depicts.[6]

It would be fruitless to insist that illusion is a matter of degree[7] and to retreat to the thesis that the experience a spectator has in front of a realistic picture is *similar* to an illusion of seeing what is depicted. For the issue is not whether the spectator's experience is more or less like an experience of seeing the item depicted, but in what ways it is like or unlike such an experience. If it had been shown that the only way in which the visual experience of looking at the surface of Monet's picture differs from an experience of seeing a river is of the same kind as that in which the experiences of seeing similar shades of colour differ, Gombrich's position would be viable. But if one of the experiences contains a visual awareness of the presence and character of a marked surface and the other does not, the concept of illusion is misplaced in a description of the first experience.[8]

If a spectator of Monet's picture were to experience an illusion of seeing what is depicted, it would not be possible for him to be concurrently visually aware of the marked surface as a marked surface. For it is not possible for his visual experience to possess incompatible representational contents of the kind that such concurrent awareness would require: the world in front of his eyes cannot be represented to him as being an opaque marked surface and also as being a river in thaw. Now Gombrich's account of seeing a realistic depiction is buttressed by a more general claim about pictorial experience, which applies to all pictures, not just those that are experienced as being realistic. This maintains that it is *impossible* for a spectator to attend to the character of the marked surface of a picture and simultaneously see what is depicted. If this claim were correct, Gombrich's thesis about the experience of a realistic picture would gain plausibility, although it would not thereby be established. For one explanation of the alleged impossibility would be that the visual awareness of a marked surface as a marked surface has a representational content incompatible with the representational content of seeing what is depicted, and one way in which this could be so in the case of a realistic picture would be for the second experience to be an illusion. But Gombrich's argument for the alleged impossibility of a dual awareness of the presence and character of a marked surface and the nature of what the surface depicts has been shown to rest on a false analogy;[9] accordingly, his illusionistic account of realistic pictures can derive no support from this source.

It is impossible to resist the conclusion that Gombrich has failed to provide a good reason for the view that the experience of a depiction, even a depiction experienced as being realistic, essentially involves an illusion of seeing what is depicted. He has therefore given no reason for the assimilation of the experience of seeing a thawing river depicted in Monet's picture to the experience as of seeing a thawing river. Neither has he shown that it is not possible to see the character of the marked surface of the picture and at the same time see what is depicted therein. The possibility of a dual awareness – a dual visual awareness – of a marked surface and what is depicted forms the foundation of Wollheim's technical notion of 'seeing-in', in terms of which he elucidates the idea of pictorial representation. It is now time to return to the question, What is it to see one thing in another?

(3) Wollheim's explanation of the concept of seeing-in exists in two forms, early and late, the first of which construes the dual visual awareness as a duality of experiences, the second of which replaces this with a duality of aspects of a single experience. I begin with the early account, certain features of which carry over into the more recent theory.

This original explanation of the notion of seeing one thing in another consists of two parts.[10] The first assigns to the experience of seeing-in three basic characteristics, which endow the experience with a distinctive phenomenology. The second specifies the perceptual project associated with seeing-in, and uses this association to explain the possession by seeing-in of all three of the features from which its distinctive phenomenology arises.

The first property assigned to seeing-in concerns the range of items that can be seen in something, and this range is said to cover both particulars and states of affairs. Now if seeing-in is to be used to elucidate pictorial representation, this must indeed be its range, for both particulars and states of affairs can be depicted, and, accordingly, a spectator of a picture can see depicted either a particular or a state of affairs. Looking at Monet's picture, you can see a river depicted, and you can see that depicted ice is depicted as drifting down the depicted river. But this characteristic of seeing-in is not especially helpful, for it does not distinguish seeing-in from certain other species of seeing, and in particular from seeing face to face (to use Wollheim's favoured locution).

The second characteristic assigned to seeing-in is that it does not need to meet the so-called requirement of localization. The requirement of localization demands that there must be an answer to the question of whereabouts in something another thing is seen. Hence the stipulation that seeing-in does not need to meet this requirement means that there need not be any answer to the question of whereabouts in one thing another is seen, so that the reason why a spectator may be unable to specify where in the first item he can see the second is that there is no such place. But the assignment to seeing-in of this characteristic is, I believe, problematic, as is clear from a consideration of the cases Wollheim introduces in support of the view that seeing a picture as a depiction of something does not require localization.

These cases fall into two classes: depictions of particulars and depictions of states of affairs. Now the instances of the first kind are unpersuasive. Wollheim cites two depictions of a crowd in which only some members of the crowd are depicted: in the first, the other members are hidden by a fold in the ground; in the second, they are cut off by the frame. The claim that seeing what is depicted in these pictures does not meet the requirement of localization exploits the fact that someone can be said truly to see a collection of items or a discontinuous aggregate, even though there are members of the set that he does not, perhaps cannot, see. This runs parallel to the fact that a picture can be said truly to contain a depiction of a set of items even though not all the members of the set are depicted. It is unsurprising that if a picture depicts a collection, but not every member of the collection, the whereabouts of the collection in the picture cannot be precisely specified and, accordingly, a spectator cannot identify exactly the location of the collection he sees depicted. What the spectator can do is to specify the location in the picture of each depicted member of the collection. It would be specious to maintain that seeing a depiction of a continuous item (a person, say) need not meet the requirement of localization on the ground that parts of the item might not be depicted; and there is no relevant difference concerning localization between the depiction of such a discontinuous aggregate as a crowd and the depiction of a continuous item, part of which might be obscured by another depicted item or cut off by the frame. The requirement of localization must be met by each depicted part of a depicted particular.

If we now turn to the instances of the second kind – depictions of states of affairs – there is a simple explanation of the fact that they do not satisfy the requirement of localization, but this explanation undermines the significance of that fact. The reason why a spectator is under no obligation to specify whereabouts in a picture he can see the state of affairs depicted by that picture – the gathering of the storm, that the stag is about to die, the degradation of the young rake – is that a state of affairs, unlike a particular, lacks a location (or at least a circumscribed location that would allow the satisfaction of the requirement of localization). And since it is an immediate consequence of the inclusion of states of affairs in the range of seeing-in that seeing-in does not need to meet the requirement of localization when what is seen in something is a state of affairs, nothing is added to the characterization of such cases of seeing-in by the stipulation that they do not need to meet the requirement.

So the requirement of localization has an unproblematic application to the perception of a depiction of a particular, but it must be applied at the level of depicted parts; and its failure to apply to the perception of a depiction of a state of affairs is a direct consequence of the nature of a state of affairs. The characterization of seeing-in by reference to the fact that it does not need to meet the requirement of localization therefore does not align it perfectly with the seeing that takes place when a spectator sees a depiction as a depiction of its subject. But in any case it is unilluminating to characterize seeing-in by reference to this requirement, for, as in the case of the assignment to seeing-in of its proper range, it does not enable seeing-in to be distinguished from face-to-face seeing: a spectator can see, not only depicted but also in reality, a crowd some members of which are out of view, that a stag is about to die, the gathering of a storm, or the degradation of a young rake. And hence only the third feature assigned to seeing-in can define a distinct species of seeing.

This third feature is that seeing-in permits simultaneous visual awareness of the surface in which something is seen and that which is seen in it.

Wollheim argues that there is a thesis, 'the twofold thesis', which is true of pictorial representations and which ensures that seeing a marked surface as a depiction of something allows simultaneous visual awareness of the marked surface and what is depicted in it. This twofold thesis maintains that the visual attention of a spectator who sees what is depicted in a picture *must* be distributed between the marked surface and the item depicted; and Wollheim advances three considerations in support of the twofold thesis.

The first is that the twofold thesis provides an account of the distinctive phenomenology of seeing something as a depiction. But even if we concede that the experience of seeing something as a depiction has a distinctive phenomenology, this is an inconclusive reason, as Wollheim admits, since it does not follow that the experience has the phenomenology assigned to it by the twofold thesis.

The second maintains that the explanation of the fact that perspectival distortion of what is depicted is not necessarily brought about by changes in the spectator's viewing point that would cause perspectival distortion if what were seen were the object itself is that the spectator is, and remains, visually aware not only of what is depicted, but also of the marked surface of the picture. This is unconvincing, however, for there is a much better explanation of the fact that a depicted object maintains a relatively constant appearance when the spectator changes his position in front of the picture: the object itself is not being seen, and changes in the viewing point do not reveal hitherto unseen parts of the object, but only the same disposition of marks on the surface. The argument will appear plausible, I believe, only if it is tacitly assumed that the spectator sees the actual object, not a depiction of it.

The third consideration claims that a spectator's admiration for the way in which an artist has created a depiction by marking the surface of his picture in a particular manner would not be possible if the spectator had to alternate his visual attention between the marked surface and what is depicted in it. If this claim were correct, however, it would not establish the twofold thesis, because the possibility of twofold visual attention would not imply that it is an essential feature of the experience of depiction. But in fact the claim is unfounded, for no reason has been given for accepting the conclusion that the only way in which artistry in marking a picture's surface to create representational effects could have received recognition is through simultaneous twofold visual awareness. An alternation in the spectator's visual attention would seem to be sufficient for the recognition of and consequent admiration for the artist's artistry.

These considerations fail, therefore, to establish the twofold thesis about pictorial representation, and, without its support, the definition of seeing-in in terms of a dual visual awareness does not place seeing-in securely within the domain of the perception of depictions as representations of their subjects. Seeing-in permits simultaneous visual awareness of a surface and what is seen in it, but seeing what a picture depicts has not been shown to require, and so to allow, simultaneous visual awareness of the surface and what is depicted therein.

It should be noted that seeing-in is characterized as permitting simultaneous *visual* awareness of the surface in which something is seen and that which is seen in it. It is essential to Wollheim's claim that seeing-in is a distinct species of perception with its own phenomenology that it should receive such a characterization. Hence, the appropriateness of seeing-in as a candidate for the experience of seeing what is depicted is not secured by the plausible thesis, which is weaker than the twofold thesis, that it is possible (perhaps mandatory) for the spectator to be simultaneously aware of the nature of the marked surface and what is depicted. For such a dual awareness might be not a twofold visual experiential awareness, but a single visual awareness (of the marked surface) combined with a non-experiential awareness (of what is depicted), as in the case of reading with understanding a handwritten sentence, which allows the reader's attention to be distributed between the handwriting and the meaning of the sentence. The comparison that Wollheim seeks to exploit between the appreciation of pictorial representation and the appreciation of poetry, which is grounded in a simultaneous awareness of the sound and the meaning of words, is therefore not to the point.

(4)   As yet, we have seen no reason to accept seeing-in as the seeing that takes place when a spectator sees what is depicted in a picture. But perhaps this is because we do not fully understand the concept of seeing one thing in another, and especially the idea that seeing-in involves a visual awareness not only of the surface before the eyes, but also of the item seen in it, which is not before the eyes; and if we were to understand the concept of seeing-in better, it might recommend itself as the seeing involved in seeing a depiction as a depiction. To achieve this deeper understanding, we must turn to the second part of Wollheim's account, which seeks to fill out the notion of seeing-in by specifying the perceptual project that underlies it and that explains the possession by seeing-in of all three of the characteristics assigned to it in the first part of the account. This further elucidation underscores Wollheim's commitment to a double visual awareness in the analysis of pictorial experience.

We are told that seeing-in derives from a special perceptual capacity. This special perceptual capacity presupposes the normal capacity to see things present to the eyes, but it also includes the capacity to undergo visual experiences of things that are not present to the eyes – things absent or non-existent. When this special perceptual capacity operates, Wollheim writes, 'visions of things not present . . . come about through looking at things present' (*Art and its Objects*, p. 218). And these visions or visual experiences of what is not present to the eyes are not merely caused by the visual awareness of what is present, which dies at the moment it gives birth to its progeny, but are sustained in existence and derive their character at least in part from a continued visual awareness of what is before the eyes, so that the subject undergoes two visual experiences, one of seeing what is present and one of seeing what is not. Seeing-in, Wollheim writes, 'is the cultivation of a special kind of visual experience, which fastens upon certain objects in the environment for its furtherance' (ibid., p. 223); what seeing-in consists in is the union of the cultivated experience with the visual awareness of what supports this experience.

Now, as I have indicated, Wollheim uses this elaboration of the idea of seeing-in to account for the fact that seeing-in has precisely the set of characteristics he has already assigned to it. But if what I have said about these characteristics is correct, it is not to be expected that his explanation will be entirely successful, and I am going to pass over it in silence. For there is a fundamental weakness in the elucidation of seeing-in, and this weakens whatever force his explanation might be thought to possess. The general idea is clear: seeing-in consists of two experiences, one of which – the visual awareness of the features of the item before the eyes – generates and sustains the other – the vision of something not present to the eyes. But there is an obvious lacuna: the nature of this second, cultivated experience has been left blank, and it is difficult to see how it could possibly be filled in. It is certain that this experience is not intended to be one indistinguishable by the subject from a corresponding instance of face-to-face seeing, for this would have the consequence that when seeing-in is appropriately exercised upon a depiction, it yields an illusion of seeing the item depicted. This interpretation would be inconsistent with Wollheim's long-standing opposition to illusionistic accounts of seeing what a picture depicts, and it would render his conception of seeing-in a mere substitution for Gombrich's oscillating illusion account – the view that the spectator's experience is an alternation of an illusion of seeing the item depicted and a visual awareness of the qualities of the picture surface – a mere substitution for this of the simultaneous occurrence of the same two experiences. Moreover, this suggestion would be absurd, for it would involve the ascription of incompatible qualities to a spectator's visual field, as we have already seen. But if the cultivated experience contained within seeing-in is not intended to be an illusion of seeing what is not present to the eyes, what kind of visual experience is it supposed to be? It seems impossible to answer this question in a plausible way; but without an answer, it is not possible to understand the idea of seeing-in, for it has been incompletely characterized.

(5)   Perhaps it will be thought that the weakness in this first account of seeing-in stems from the conception of seeing-in as consisting of two visual experiences, and that this weakness has been repaired in Wollheim's later account.[11] For in this more recent account the idea that seeing-in involves two experiences is replaced by the idea that it is a single experience, but one that possesses two aspects. I shall argue, however, that this merely conceals, and does not remove, the weakness, and that this second conception of seeing-in not only inherits the weakness of the first, but develops weaknesses of its own.

In this new account, seeing-in is credited with a distinctive phenomenology, 'twofoldness', which now refers to the possession by a single experience of two aspects, a 'recognitional aspect' and a 'configurational aspect'. So in this later conception seeing-in not only permits, but demands, a dual visual awareness, and this duality is one of aspects, not experiences. The configurational aspect is a visual awareness of the marked surface facing the spectator, and the recognitional aspect is an awareness of depth in which one thing is seen in front of another – a boy in front of a darker ground, for example. And neither of these aspects can have a separate existence: an instance of the one can occur only in combination with an instance of the other. For although each aspect of a seeing-in experience can be described as though it were a case of face-to-face seeing – a simple visual awareness of a marked surface or an experience of seeing a boy – this is not what it is. Moreover, it is illegitimate to enquire about the experiential resemblance between either aspect of the complex experience and the simple face-to-face experience after which it is described; for 'the particular complexity' of the seeing-in experience makes its phenomenology incommensurate with the phenomenologies of the two simple experiences.

Now the reason given for deeming it illegitimate to raise a question about the experiential resemblance between the recognitional aspect (for example) of a seeing-in experience and the face-to-face experience after which it is described is unconvincing. For whatever the particular complexity of the twofold experience is supposed to be, why should it render the phenomenology *of its recognitional aspect* incommensurate with that of the face-to-face experience? If we accept the thesis, however, it is clear how this new conception of seeing-in protects it against the objection brought against the original conception – the objection that seeing-in is undercharacterized, because the nature of the cultivated component experience is left blank and there is no indication as to how it should or could be filled. For if it is illegitimate to ask how experientially like or unlike the recognitional aspect of a seeing-in experience is to the corresponding or analogous face-to-face experience, and yet it is this face-to-face experience which provides the model for the description of the recognitional aspect, then the nature of the recognitional aspect cannot be elucidated in any way, and it is therefore inappropriate to press for an elucidation. But I believe that this apparent strength of the new conception is nothing but a veil drawn over the original weakness, which cannot be repaired by fusing the two experiences of the first account. For the blankness of the original cultivated experience is passed on to the recognitional aspect of seeing-in, with the result that the twofoldness of the single seeing-in experience is rendered incomprehensible. The insistence that the recognitional aspect and the corresponding face-to-face experience are experientially incomparable undermines the force of the idea that for any recognitional aspect there is an analogous face-to-face experience after which it can be described. The recognitional aspect cannot properly derive the only description it can be given from an experience with an incomparable phenomenology: the alleged experiential incommensurability prevents the description of the one from being modelled on the description of the other – or, if it is so modelled, makes it inappropriate, indeed mistaken. Hence, the so-called recognitional aspect of seeing-in merely masquerades as an analogue of a face-to-face experience; and when the description it has wrongly borrowed is stripped from it, it not only has no other description to clothe itself in, but is revealed as having no nature of its own.[12]

The problematic nature of the double aspect account of seeing-in is exacerbated by Wollheim's thesis concerning the relative prominence of the two aspects of the experience. He claims that either aspect can be more prominent than the other, and that when one aspect becomes overwhelmingly prominent, the recessive aspect evaporates and seeing-in is replaced by an experience of a different kind. At one extreme, the configurational aspect evaporates, and seeing-in is succeeded by an experience of visualizing the object of the preceding recognitional aspect; at the other, the recognitional aspect evaporates, and seeing-in is replaced by an experience of seeing face to face the object of the preceding configurational aspect. But there are two problems with this idea. The first and less serious is this: if the evaporation of the configurational aspect leads to an experience of visualizing the object of the former recognitional aspect, why should this recognitional aspect be described as though it were a case of face-to-face seeing, rather than visualizing? The second is this: if the gradual recession of one aspect does not transform the other aspect into something of a different kind – and what could this be? – the two aspects must be two experiences, the configurational aspect an experience of seeing face to face and the recognitional aspect one of visualizing. For at the moment when one aspect drops right away, on one side there is the other (untransformed) aspect and on the other side an experience which is either an instance of face-to-face seeing or an instance of visualizing. Why should the recognitional aspect, say, be thought to vanish at the very moment when it has become so prominent that the configurational aspect slips away?

The foundation of Wollheim's thought about pictorial representation is the belief that the awareness or recognition of what is depicted is both experiential and specifically visual; it involves the awareness of depth in the sense that something is seen as being in front of something else;[13] and yet it is neither an illusory experience of seeing face to face nor an experience of visualizing in the mind's eye. My claim is that this has finally led him to the construction of an elusive amalgam of two will-o'-the-wisps. For it is not only the recognitional aspect of seeing-in whose nature is problematic; an equal difficulty arises for the configurational aspect. Wollheim's thesis is that the phenomenology of the configurational aspect of an experience of seeing-in is likewise incommensurate with that of the analogous face-to-face experience. But if we now consider the nature of this face-to-face experience, it is apparent that the thesis of incommensurability deprives the configurational aspect of a nature of its own. The face-to-face experience is one of seeing a flat[14] differentiated surface without seeing anything in it (in Wollheim's sense). This face-to-face experience therefore does not involve a visual awareness of depth in what is seen; it must consist in the visual awareness of a two-dimensional coloured expanse, either at a definite or indefinite distance from the subject. If the phenomenology of the configurational aspect of a seeing-in experience is incommensurate with the phenomenology of such a face-to-face experience, the configurational aspect cannot be the visual awareness of a two-dimensional coloured expanse. But it cannot involve an awareness of depth, which is confined to the recognitional aspect of the seeing-in experience. Hence it consists of nothing at all.

Perhaps it will be thought that this is too easy a dismissal of the double aspect conception of seeing-in. But the problem created by the thesis of incommensurability cannot be evaded, and it arises in a stark form in the application of seeing-in to the perception of a class of pictures that Wollheim countenances, pictures which are *abstract* representations.[15] An abstract pictorial representation is a picture that represents a non-figurative or abstract item, and the recognitional aspect of an appropriate seeing-in experience directed at such a picture might involve just the awareness of planes of colour being in front of other planes. If the configurational aspect of this experience is restricted to the visual awareness of a two-dimensional coloured expanse, the two aspects of the experience would appear to be incompatible with each other. But if it is not restricted in this fashion, then there will be two awarenesses of the relative distances of (the same) coloured planes, one in the configurational, the other in the recognitional aspect; and the only way in which this could be accommodated is by the specification of different senses of the expression 'visual awareness of depth', which would need to be definable independently of the concept of depiction.

(6) The collapse of seeing-in should, I believe, lead to the rejection of the assumption upon which it is based, that the awareness of what is depicted in a picture is both experiential and specifically visual, its heart consisting in a visual awareness of something lying in front of something else. It is unclear what Wollheim supposes this visual awareness of depth to be, and in the absence of any explanation, the suspicion must arise that it is nothing other than the experience of seeing something *as if it were a depiction* of one thing lying in front of another, the idea of which presupposes, and so could not be used to analyse, the concept of depiction.

But if this assumption is rejected, what should take its place? The answer arises from a consideration I introduced at the beginning of the paper. The consideration is that you would not see Monet's *The Seine in Thaw* as a depiction of a river in thaw if you were unaware of what a thawing river looks like. This condition can be generalized: whatever a picture depicts, you would not see it as a depiction of that thing if you were unaware of what that thing looks like. And since, first, depiction is always from a point of view and, second, the appearance of something changes in accordance with the point of view from which it is seen, the condition can be expressed more precisely in this way: whatever a picture depicts, you would not see it as a depiction of that thing if you were unaware of what that thing looks like from the point of view from which it has been depicted. It is a short step to the conclusion that it is in virtue of your knowledge of how something looks that you are able to see a picture as a depiction of that thing.

I believe this conclusion is correct if it is interpreted in the right manner. It must not be interpreted in such a way as to rule out the possibility of learning what a certain kind of thing looks like from a depiction of something of that kind. If you have no idea what an aardvark looks like, you can acquire knowledge of its appearance from a depiction of one, and thereby gain the capacity to recognize an aardvark if you see one. But this is possible only if you are in some way informed that the animal you see depicted is an aardvark or you somehow work out that this is what it must be. Unless this is so, although you may be able to see an aardvark depicted, you cannot see that one is depicted. Furthermore, if you have no idea of what an animal, a tongue, an ear, a tail, or a leg looks like, then, although you may be able to see one depicted, again you cannot see that one is depicted. Interpreted in this manner, therefore, it is true that you are not in a position to see a picture as a depiction of its subject unless you are aware of the visual appearance of what it depicts. Moreover, if you possess the capacity to see pictures as depictions, your awareness of something's appearance enables you to see what is depicted by a picture of that thing. Hence a constraint on a viable theory of pictorial experience is that it should respect, and be such that it can explain, the fact that a spectator who is unaware of how a certain kind of thing looks is not able to experience a depiction of that kind of thing as such a depiction, whereas in general someone familiar with its appearance suffers from no such disability.

It is clear that an account of depiction in terms of seeing-in fails to satisfy this constraint. For it is stipulated that the phenomenology of the recognitional aspect of a seeing-in experience directed at Monet's picture cannot legitimately be compared with that of a face-to-face experience of seeing a river. Accordingly, there is no reason why a spectator should be familiar with, or possess an awareness of, the phenomenology of such a face-to-face experience in order to undergo a seeing-in experience the recognitional aspect of which is supposed to deliver to the spectator what is depicted in Monet's picture.

There are many approaches to the topic of depiction that are not based on the assumption that underlies Wollheim's. I shall consider just three. First, it might be suggested that the awareness of what a picture depicts, unlike the visual awareness of the picture surface, is not itself experiential, but instead a matter of understanding or interpreting the marks on the surface in the right manner. This suggestion can assume two significantly different forms. One of these does not build into the manner of interpretation any reference to the spectator's awareness of the visual appearance of what is depicted – as in Nelson Goodman's theory[16] – and it is thereby disqualified in virtue of violating the constraint that a spectator sees that a river is depicted in Monet's picture only if he is aware of the visual appearance of a river. The other does build in such a reference and is therefore compatible with the acknowledgement of this constraint – as in Flint Schier's theory, according to which a depiction is interpreted by engaging with the spectator's capacity to recognize with his eyes something of the kind depicted.[17] In my view, however, such an account is misconceived, because the awareness of what a picture depicts is experiential, as can perhaps be seen most economically in the switching of awareness that can take place in the perception of ambiguous figures.

The second kind of approach is based on the imagination. What it seeks to do is to add the imagination to the visual awareness of the picture surface in such a manner that it generates the experience of seeing what is depicted. This addition can take place in a number of ways. In its simplest form, the suggestion is that the spectator imagines of his visual awareness of a picture that it is an instance of seeing what is depicted, so that the surface of the picture is imagined to be a transparent plane through which what is depicted is seen. But this primitive form of the proposal is certainly inadequate, for it ties the spectator's awareness of what is depicted too loosely to the character of the picture surface, and – a related point – it does not capture the experiential nature of the awareness of what is depicted, reflected in the characteristic inability of the spectator to see a picture in any other way than the one which imposes itself on him and which the artist intended. The most sophisticated version of this approach is Kendall Walton's, which overcomes the weakness of the simple form, but only at the cost of requiring that if there is to be such a thing as seeing a depiction as a depiction, there must be rules of make-believe in accordance with which the imagination is exercised upon the awareness of the picture surface.[18] It is important to recognize that a spectator's engagement with a depiction will usually involve much more than what is barely constitutive of the experience of seeing the picture as a depiction of its subject; but while the imagination plays an essential role in the richer experience, it is mistaken, I believe, to attempt to build it into the unadorned experience. Hence the fact that this kind of theory satisfies the constraint that I have identified as governing a viable account of pictorial experience is insufficient reason to recommend the theory.

The third approach to the topic of depiction has its roots in Wittgenstein's consideration of the heterogeneous collection of experiences that he grouped under the heading 'noticing an aspect'.[19] This includes contemplating the face of someone whom you have not seen for a number of years and suddenly seeing his former face in his new one, contemplating the expression on someone's face and suddenly seeing it as a malicious smile, and seeing the duck–rabbit figure first as a picture of a duck's head and then as a picture of a rabbit's head. In each case, a certain concept is integral to the specification of the intrinsic nature of the perception. This concept is the concept of that which is seen in the item in question, or what the item is seen as – the concept of how the person's face formerly looked, the concept of a malicious smile, the concept of a picture of a duck's (or rabbit's) head, and so, derivatively, the concept of a duck's (or rabbit's) head. It is for this reason that Wittgenstein asserts that what you see in the dawning of an aspect is an internal relation between the seen object and others. Now you cannot see this internal relation unless you are familiar with the look of whatever you experience the seen object as being related to, so that this account, applied to the perception of pictures, perfectly satisfies the requirement of an acceptable theory of pictorial experience. Regrettably, Wittgenstein does not characterize the nature of the internal relation that is perceived to hold between a depiction and what it depicts.

The finest attempt to specify the required relation is Christopher Peacocke's, which represents it as an experienced resemblance between the shape of the appearance of the depiction in the spectator's two-dimensional visual field and the shape that would be presented in the spectator's visual field by the depicted item if it were to be seen from a certain point of view.[20] Although this is not the place to evaluate Peacocke's proposal, it is instructive to place it correctly in relation to Wollheim's, especially since this relationship has been doubly misrepresented, first by Peacocke, subsequently by Wollheim. Peacocke suggests that his account can be seen as an attempt to remove any obscurity from Wollheim's idea of seeing one thing in another. But his proposal cannot properly be thought of as an elucidation of Wollheim's original double experience conception of seeing-in (which Peacocke is referring to), since his proposal does not analyse the seeing appropriate to depictions in terms of two visual experiences. Wollheim acquiesces in the description of Peacocke's proposal as an attempt to analyse further the notion of seeing-in, although he is sceptical of its success (*Painting as an Art*, p. 360). But it could not be thought to elucidate Wollheim's later double aspect conception of seeing-in (which Wollheim has in mind), for it conflicts with this conception in at least two significant ways. First, Peacocke's conception, unlike Wollheim's, does not credit a spectator's visual awareness of the picture surface when he sees a picture as a depiction with a nature that is experientially incommensurate with that of the relevant face-to-face experience and which disallows its separate existence. Second, the experience of visual field shape similarity is not a visual awareness of depth, but an awareness of a resemblance between the intrinsic properties of two two-dimensional visual fields, one actual, the other hypothetical.

(7) I have argued that Wollheim's account of pictorial representation in terms of seeing-in is an unsure basis for his theory of painting as an art. But my essay would present a misleading picture if it were to close on this note. In the first place, it is necessary to stress that much of the theory of painting developed in *Painting as an Art* – the account of the practice of painting as an art, the analysis of expression in painting, the elucidation of the idea of the unrepresented spectator in the picture, the discrimination of the various kinds of meaning paintings can possess, and the attributions of particular meanings to the works of certain artists – survives the collapse of one of its foundation stones, and I am not alone in thinking of the book as one of the outstanding contributions to the subject. Secondly, my essay is unrevealing in one important respect, and it is time for me to revoke the self-denying ordinance I have passed upon myself and which has constrained what I have written.

Wollheim's writings have enriched many fields, especially those of philosophy, psychoanalysis, and art, and anyone concerned with these areas has reason to be grateful for the nourishment his work offers. But my own debt to him greatly exceeds all I have learnt from studying his writings, considerable though this is. For it was my exceptional good fortune to be a member of the philosophy department at University College London during the greater part of his tenure of the Grote Chair of the Philosophy of Mind and Logic. The environment he created was distinguished by its friendly and tolerant atmosphere, which encouraged individuality to flourish, enabling the development of unusual talents, interests, and projects, and it was deservedly admired for the amount and variety of serious philosophical thought that flowed from it. However, it was not merely the congenial and intellectually exciting nature of this environment, but his central presence within it that played a crucial role in my own development. For when I entered his department fresh from Cambridge, I brought with me an extraordinarily narrow conception of philosophy – narrow both in its restricted philosophical method and in its understanding of where the centre of the subject, and accordingly the most significant problems, are located. This conception did not long withstand the daily impact of his personality and the gentle scepticism with which he met my youthful certainties. Moreover, the progressive liberalization of my requirements of philosophy as a serious discipline went hand in hand with a redirection of my interests within the subject. For the eagerness with which he engaged in philosophical discussion, the particular bias of his interests, the breadth of his vision, and his wide culture encouraged me to see the philosophy of art, when informed by an adequate philosophy of mind, as a subject deserving of as much respect and careful consideration as any other field of philosophy. Furthermore, it was his own concern for and thoughts about pictorial representation that heightened my awareness of the importance and difficulty of explaining the idea of depiction and the kinds of visual experience involved in understanding pictures and that provoked me to attempt to clarify and develop my rudimentary ideas on the topic.

This essay is a reasoned rejection of one of his leading ideas, and is certainly poor recompense for what I have gained from him – from his writings, his lectures and seminars, his example, and his company. But I believe that it is a product of a value dear to him, the quality he christened 'systematic irreverence' (*On Art and the Mind*, pp. 6–7), and which helped to give to the department he directed its distinctive character. In this respect, if no other, I hope that what I have written pleases him.

NOTES

[1]   I was fortunate to have the opportunity of looking at this picture with Richard Wollheim when we attended a colloquium at Ann Arbor in March 1988. The painting is in the University of Michigan Museum of Art, Ann Arbor, and it is one of the two pictures reproduced in Wollheim's *Painting as an Art* (Thames and Hudson, London, 1987), that he had not seen when the book was published. In my paper I use Monet's picture only as an example of a river-picture (in Goodman's sense), and ignore the fact that it is a picture of a particular river, the Seine. I believe that the concept of an F-picture is more fundamental in the theory of pictorial representation than the concept of a depiction of a particular thing, and I am concerned only with the first concept.

[2]   Gombrich makes this claim a number of times in *Art and Illusion* (Phaidon Press, London, 1962); see p. xi.

[3]   See for example Gombrich, 'Illusion and Art', in *Illusion in Nature and Art*, ed. R. L. Gregory and E. H. Gombrich (Gerald Duckworth, London, 1973).

[4]   I follow Christopher Peacocke's use of this term in his *Sense and Content* (Clarendon Press, Oxford, 1983), ch. 1. The 'representational content' of

a visual experience is the way the experience represents the world as being.

5   James J. Gibson, *The Ecological Approach to Visual Perception* (Lawrence Erlbaum Associates, Hillsdale, N. J., 1986), p. 281.

6   For other criticisms, see Wollheim, 'Reflections on *Art and Illusion*', in *On Art and the Mind* (1973).

7   Gombrich, 'Illusion and Art', p. 196.

8   Gombrich is prepared to concede that a spectator's visual experience characteristically reveals to him that he is face to face with a picture. But he appears not to recognize the difficulty this creates for his emphasis on the idea of visual illusions in the experience of pictures. See his 'The Sky is the Limit: The Vault of Heaven and Pictorial Vision', in *Perception: Essays in Honor of James J. Gibson*, ed. Robert B. MacLeod and Herbert L. Pick, Jr. (Cornell University Press, London, 1974).

9   See Wollheim, 'Reflections on *Art and Illusion*' (1963); 'Seeing-As, Seeing-In, and Pictorial Representation', in *Art and its Objects*, 2nd edn (1980), pp. 213–4; and *Painting as an Art*, (1987), p. 360; also Michael Podro, 'Fiction and Reality in Painting', *Poetik und Hermeneutik*, 10 (1983).

10   Wollheim, 'Seeing-As, Seeing-In, and Pictorial Representation'. Wollheim develops his account by drawing a contrast between seeing-in and seeing-as (his original candidate for the experience involved in seeing a depiction as the depiction it is). Here I ignore the contrast with seeing-as and extract the analysis of seeing-in. I am sure that Wollheim is right to reject any analysis of pictorial representation in terms of the particular concept of 'seeing-as' that he articulates. For what would a picture be seen as? There are two possibilities: either as the item it depicts or as a depiction of that item. But to see Monet's painting as a picture of a river is not to see it as a river. And although Monet's painting should be seen as a picture of a river, this concept of seeing presupposes the concept of depiction, and cannot be used to elucidate it.

11   Wollheim, *Painting as an Art*, ch. 2, B 1–11; 'Imagination and Pictorial Understanding', *Proceedings of the Aristotelian Society*, Supplementary volume 60 (1986), §§ 2–3.

12   An unwelcome consequence of the denial that the phenomenology of the recognitional aspect of a seeing-in experience can be compared with the phenomenology of an experience of seeing something face to face is that it becomes impossible to make sense of the application to pictures of the property of realism, naturalism, lifelikeness, or truth to nature. Wollheim puts forward (*Painting as an Art*, ch. 2, B 10) the unusual view that this property must be elucidated in terms of a particular kind of reciprocity which obtains between the recognitional and the configurational aspects of a seeing-in experience when this experience prompts the spectator to regard a picture as realistic. But in whatever manner realism is best understood and whatever kind of reciprocity this is supposed to be, there

can be no question of a depiction capturing well or badly an appearance of reality unless the recognitional aspect is allowed to possess a content comparable to that of a face-to-face experience. And this is denied to the recognitional aspect by the insistence that its phenomenology is incommensurate with that of a face-to-face experience.

[13] This feature is present as early as 'On Drawing an Object' (§§ 24–6), reprinted in *On Art and the Mind*. See also *Art and its Objects* (1980), § 13.

[14] It is certainly unnecessary that the surface should be flat, but the stipulation rules out irrelevancies. It is not essential to the recognition of the subject of a picture that its surface should look uneven.

[15] Wollheim, *Painting as an Art*, ch. 2, B 7; 'On Drawing an Object', § 25.

[16] Nelson Goodman, *Languages of Art* (Hackett Publishing Co., Indianapolis, 1968).

[17] Flint Schier, *Deeper into Pictures* (Cambridge University Press, Cambridge, 1986).

[18] Kendall Walton, 'Pictures and Make-Believe', *Philosophical Review*, 82 (1973), pp. 283–319.

[19] Wittgenstein, *Philosophical Investigations* (Basil Blackwell, Oxford, 1953), II. xi.

[20] Christopher Peacocke, 'Depiction', *Philosophical Review*, 96 (1987), pp. 383–410.

16

Seeing-In and Seeing Fictionally

KENDALL L. WALTON

Richard Wollheim's writings on pictorial representation combine philosophical enquiry into the nature of the medium – enquiry involving issues of philosophy of mind and language, as well as aesthetics – with examination of the place that painting and other visual arts have in our lives and critical observations about individual works and particular artistic styles. He brings to this multifaceted enterprise a rare combination of philosophical sophistication and aesthetic perceptiveness. The philosophical side of Wollheim's work is dominant in *Art and its Objects* (1980); aesthetic and critical considerations come to the fore in *Painting as an Art* (1987). But both are evident in both books, and all his work on the visual arts is sensitive in both directions.

It is not surprising that an aesthetically sensitive theory of pictorial representation, of what it is for something to be a picture, should emphasize the phenomenology of the experience of looking at and appreciating pictures. At the heart of Wollheim's theory is a special kind of visual experience that he calls 'seeing-in'.[1] One sees a woman in a drawing of a woman, and Henry VIII in Holbein's portrait. By according a central place to this visual experience, Wollheim accounts for the special visual nature of the medium, and accommodates the intuitively evident contrast between pictorial representations and verbal symbols, between depiction and description. In emphasizing this contrast, Wollheim follows in the spirit of Peirce's distinction between 'icons' and 'symbols', signs that are linked to their objects by virtue of, respectively, resemblances and conventions. Wollheim explains depiction in terms of seeing-in, rather than resemblance (although some resemblance theorists might utilize the notion of seeing-in in specifying a special kind of resemblance relevant to depiction); but his account of depiction shares the intuitive plausibility of resemblance theories, while avoiding their most glaring difficulties.

I heartily endorse the basic motivation of Wollheim's project. A primary objective of my own account of depiction, which treats pictures as props in visual games of make-believe, is to clarify and give proper weight to the idea that pictorial representation is a genuinely visual medium. Although my theory and Wollheim's are very different, their central tenets are more complementary than conflicting, and they are better regarded as allies than as rivals. The make-believe theory can be understood to provide a way of explaining Wollheim's fundamental notion of seeing-in, which, to my mind, he leaves seriously underexplained. I shall not argue for the make-believe theory here or spell it out in any detail.[2] But I shall examine several features of Wollheim's discussion and suggest how the two theories can be made to mesh.

What is seeing-in? Wollheim describes it as an experience characterized by the 'distinctive phenomenology' of twofoldness: an experience with two aspects, a 'recognitional' aspect and a 'configurational' one. The viewer attends simultaneously to what is seen and to features of the medium. 'When I look at the representation of a woman, . . . on the one hand, I recognize or identify a woman, and, on the other hand, I am aware of the marked surface.'[3]

Wollheim insists that these are not two distinct experiences occurring simultaneously, but rather, two aspects of a single experience.[4] It is not entirely clear how in general experiences are to be individuated, or what the difference is between two experiences and two aspects of a single experience. Wollheim describes the two aspects as 'distinguishable but inseparable' (*Painting as an Art*, p. 46). But the point cannot be that neither can occur without the other. The configurational aspect, at least, can occur without the recognitional one; a viewer might be aware of the lines of a drawing of a woman without recognizing the woman. Whether the kind of recognizing involved in seeing-in can occur without the configurational aspect is harder to decide, pending clarification of what kind of recognizing it is. (One certainly need not pay attention to the configuration of lines and shapes in a picture in order to recognize a woman, any more than one must pay attention to a friend's facial features in order to recognize him in the flesh.) The important point may be that, when one looks at the picture in the expected manner, in addition to recognizing the woman and also observing the painted surface, one experiences relations between the features of the painting and what is seen in it. 'In Titian, in Vermeer, in Manet we are led to marvel endlessly at the way in which line or brushstroke or expanse of colour is exploited to render effects or establish analogies that can only be identified representationally' (*Art and its Objects*, p. 216).[5] I would urge that the viewer does not merely come to realize, as a result of perceiving both the marks on the surface and the image of a woman, how the marks work to produce the image (indeed, one may not be explicitly aware of this); rather, the viewer sees how they do. And seeing this involves both seeing the marks and recognizing the woman.

Twofoldness is important. I am sure that it has a lot to do with the interest that visual representations have for us. But the experience of seeing-in is hardly explained by pointing out that it involves the phenomenology of twofoldness. An explanation in terms of the two aspects of twofoldness is only as good as our understanding of the aspects, and the recognitional one is mysterious. In what sense does a spectator, on viewing a painting of a woman, recognize or identify a woman? One does not literally do so, of course, there being no actual woman there to recognize or identify. Neither does there appear to be a woman there; it does not seem to the viewer that he is recognizing an actual woman. Wollheim rightly denies that in viewing pictures we experience illusions, and he emphasizes the discontinuity between recognizing a boy in a picture and recognizing one in the flesh (*Painting as an Art*, pp. 46–7). Until we understand better what the recognitional aspect of seeing-in amounts to, we will not have explained what pictures are.

In *Painting as an Art*, Wollheim associates the recognitional aspect of seeing-in with the experience of seeing depth in a flat surface. 'When seeing-in occurs, two things happen: I am visually aware of the surface I look at, and I discern something standing out in front of, or (in certain cases) receding behind, something else' (ibid.).[6] The experience of seeing depth in a flat surface is familiar enough, as is that of seeing a woman in a design; but being familiar with a phenomenon is not the same as understanding it. Again, it is not that one actually observes one thing to be in front of another; nor does it seem to one that one does. Except in unusual cases, the surface is and appears to be flat.

Wollheim's purpose in connecting seeing-in with seeing depth in flat surfaces is not so much to clarify seeing-in as to indicate the range of cases in which it occurs. In viewing many paintings often regarded as non-representational, one sees one plane or shape or line in front of another. Many of the works of such artists as Hans Hoffmann, Piet Mondrian, and Mark Rothko demand seeing-in, Wollheim claims, and qualify as representational along with portraits and landscapes, although the former are not 'figurative' as the latter are. I think

Wollheim is right about this.[7] My worries concern the idea that seeing depth is *necessary* for seeing-in. If seeing-in is limited to cases in which one sees depth in a flat surface, our perception of sculptures, of theatrical performances, and of the flag and target paintings of Jasper Johns (which portray flat things on flat surfaces) would appear not to qualify.[8] Wollheim seems willing to exclude sculpture, theatre, and Jasper Johns's paintings from the class of representations in his sense (*Art and its Objects*, pp. 225–6). It is his right to use 'representation' in a narrower sense than others might, of course. But surely what he calls representations are instances also of a larger genus which includes many sculptures, most theatre, and Jasper Johns's works, and in addition such non-visual but perceptual representations as musical portrayals of the sounds of galloping horses and bird-songs. Whatever one's terminological preferences, we need a theory that will clarify what representational pictures have in common with depictions (as I prefer to call them) of these other sorts, as well as the ways in which they differ.

In all these cases appreciators participate in what I call perceptual games of make-believe: visual games in the case of paintings, sculptures, and Jasper Johns's canvases, auditory ones in the case of representational music,[9] and games that are both visual and auditory in the case of theatre. It is fictional, in one's game, that one sees a woman or one plane in front of another or a target or flag or that one hears galloping horses or the singing of birds or that one watches Lear pacing the floor and listens to his ragings. Depictions are (to put it very briefly) things whose function in a given social setting is to serve as props in sufficiently rich and vivid perceptual games of make-believe.

Participation in these games involves (actually) perceiving the work in a special way, a way imbued with certain imaginings. It is crucial that we understand clearly the nature of the imaginings. The idea that one simply imagines a horse upon seeing a picture of a horse is a non-starter. As Anthony Savile notes, 'there is a world of difference between being brought to imagine something by seeing this mark or that [on the canvas] and being brought to see something in a picture by seeing this mark or that'.[10] A vivid description of a horse may induce a reader to imagine a horse, without her seeing a horse in the letters on the page. Seeing-in is a perceptual experience, one that goes beyond perceiving the marks on the canvas. Imagining a horse is not itself a perceptual experience, even if it is a result of perceiving the marks, and perceiving the marks is just that, even if it causes one to imagine a horse.

Is it that, rather than merely imagining a horse, one imagines the brown mass of colour that one perceives on the canvas to be a horse?

Savile says that the viewer does not do this, and surely he is right again.[11] But the viewer does, in addition to imagining a horse, imagine seeing a horse. And she imagines her actual perceiving of the canvas to be an act of perceiving a horse. (She does not imagine her perceiving to be both a perceiving of the canvas and also a perceiving of a horse, of course; she imagines of the perceiving which is in fact a perceiving of the canvas that it is a perceiving not of the canvas but of a horse.) Imagining seeing a horse is imagining in a 'first person manner' (not just imagining that one sees a horse). In addition, the perceiver imagines this 'from the inside'.[12]

Engaging even in this special kind of imagining is not sufficient for seeing a horse in the picture, however. One could look at the picture and then, in a separate (non-perceptual) act, imagine in the manner I have just described. This would not be seeing a horse in the picture. We should note, in the first place, that there is no good reason to insist that imaginative acts must be deliberate or under the subject's control.[13] Dreams are obvious counter-examples, and so are many of the imaginings that make up day-dreams. The imagining of a viewer who sees a horse in a picture is not deliberate, but a spontaneous response to the marks on the canvas; she just finds herself imagining in a certain manner as she looks at the picture. And she is best regarded not as seeing the picture and *also* engaging in this spontaneous imagining, but as enjoying a *single* experience that is both perceptual and imaginative, her perception of the picture is coloured by the imagining. (Probably she enjoys a succession of experiences, each of which is both perceptual and imaginative.) The experience of recognizing an (actual) tree as a tree is not a *combination* of a pure perception and a judgement that what one perceives is a tree. It is rather a perceptual experience that is also a cognitive one, one coloured by the belief that what one is experiencing is a tree. Likewise, to see a horse in a design is to have a perceptual experience coloured by imagining one's perception to be of a horse, a perceptual experience that is also an imaginative one.

If we call this experience of imaginative perception one of seeing a horse in the picture, it is seeing-in of a kind that occurs also when one sees busts of emperors, theatrical productions, Jasper Johns's paintings, and Hoffmann's *Pompeii*. In an analogous sense one *hears* Lear's ravings in the voice of the actor portraying him and bird-songs in the notes of Beethoven's 'Pastoral' Symphony. This gives us a broad notion of *perceiving-in*, on which one might base the inclusive notion of depiction or (perceptual) representation that we want. One can then proceed to investigate differences among the many varieties of depic-

tions. For instance, in some cases – sculptures and works
like Hoffmann's *Pompeii* – it is plausible that the representational work
itself or part of it is an object of one's imagining. Perhaps we imagine
one portion of Hoffmann's canvas to be in front of another or a
block of marble to be an emperor's head, whereas we do not imagine
a stretch of painted canvas to be a woman or a horse. Our perceptual
games of make-believe and the imaginative perceptual experiences that
participation in them involves vary in many other ways as well.

Thinking of seeing-in in the way I have sketched is the key to
understanding the twofoldness that Wollheim rightly stresses. The
recognitional aspect of seeing a woman in a picture consists, roughly,
in the viewer's perception of the picture being bound up with his
imagining, in the manner I described, seeing a woman. The configurational aspect comes into play not just because perceiving the marks
on the surface induces this imagining, but because the imagining is
about that perceiving; one imagines of one's perceiving of the marks
that it is a perceiving of a woman. Thus the two aspects of the
experience are intertwined: the imagining partially constitutive of the
recognitional aspect has as an object the perception that constitutes
the configurational aspect. Of course, the viewer imagines also of his
perceptions of *particular features* of the design (particular lines, patches of colour) that they are perceptions of particular features of a
woman (tousled hair, penetrating eyes). Thus one observes connections between the marks and the 'image' of a woman.

In 'Imagination and Pictorial Understanding' Wollheim claims that
(leaving aside a certain 'vapid' sense of imagination) 'imagination has
no necessary part to play in the perception of what is represented'
(p. 46). His 'principle reason for holding this . . . is that we have a
perfectly good explanation of how we perceive representations without invoking imagination', an explanation in terms of 'a very specific
visual capacity', namely, seeing-in (ibid.). It is true that one can give
an explanation, of a sort, of depiction without saying anything about
imagining. One can *point* to the familiar phenomenon of seeing-in,
and then characterize depiction in terms of it. But that ignores the
question of what seeing-in is. We have no right to assume that seeing-
in does not involve imagining; that in order to explain it, rather than
merely point it out, and hence to give a full account of the perception
of pictures, one would not have to bring in imagining. That, I argue,
is indeed the case. Even some of Wollheim's own observations seem
to point in this direction. He associates an experience in which the
recognitional aspect of seeing a boy in a stained wall is emphasized
to the extent that the configurational aspect – and hence twofoldness

– is lost with the experience of 'visualizing the boy in the mind's eye' (*Painting as an Art*, p. 47). Isn't visualizing a boy engaging in a certain kind of imagining? Wollheim considers it 'plausible' that 'the most primitive instances of the perceptual capacity with which seeing-in is connected . . . are to be found in dreams, daydreams, and hallucinations' (*Art and its Objects*, p. 217). Surely dreams and day-dreams, in any case, are exercises of the imagination.

Wollheim points out that although dreams and day-dreams may anticipate seeing-in or be continuous with it, they lack a crucial element. Actual seeing-in occurs when 'the relevant visual experiences cease to arise simply in the mind's eye: visions of things not present now come about through looking at things present' (ibid., pp. 217–18), as when one follows Leonardo's advice 'to look at damp-stained walls . . . and discern there scenes of battle or violent action and mysterious landscapes' (ibid., p. 218). To do this is to engage in the kind of visual game of make-believe that I described, one in which actual things serve as props; and this involves imagining one's perceptions of various features of the stained wall to be perceivings of, for instance, various parts of a battlefield.

Wollheim's idea seems to be that seeing-in is a *sui generis* kind of experience which does not admit of explanation in other terms (beyond pointing out the phenomenology of twofoldness). That this is so cannot be assumed without argument, and it is in any case an unsatisfying conclusion. We would like to be able to understand seeing-in by relating it to other phenomena if we can. My proposal not only links the kind of seeing-in that Wollheim recognizes, that which occurs in the perception of pictures, to our experiences of sculpture and theatre and to the 'hearing-in' that listeners of music occasionally engage in; it also links seeing-in, in explicitly specified ways, to other imaginative experiences: to visualizing, dreaming, daydreaming, and children's games of make-believe. This does not involve denying that seeing-in is an experience of a very special kind. Seeing-in differs significantly from other exercises of the imagination, as well as from other perceptual experiences. But it need not remain mysterious. We can say what is special about it; we can specify how it differs from, as well as how it is similar to, other imaginative experiences and other perceptual ones.

'One consequence of holding to [a psychological account of pictorial representation]', Wollheim observes, 'is that it sets me against all those schools of contemporary thinking which propose to explain pictorial meaning in terms like rule, convention, symbol system, or which in effect assimilate pictorial meaning to something very different, which is linguistic meaning' (*Painting as an Art*, p. 44). 'Pictorial meaning' and linguistic meaning are indeed very different. Depiction is not just another language like English or Hungarian or Tagalog. Nor is it merely a language (or symbol system) with conventions satisfying certain special conditions like Goodman's density and repleteness requirements. No such conditions will themselves account for the perceptual nature of depiction. On this Wollheim and I are in full agreement.

But Wollheim apparently holds that the perceptualness of depiction is incompatible with pictorial meaning being conventional or involving conventions or rules (ibid., p. 361, n. 21). This is highly questionable. A lot depends on what is meant by 'conventions' or 'rules', of course. If the conventionalists' idea is supposed to be that one first observes the picture and then, in a separate act, figures out what it depicts by applying a rule or convention, then there is no special visual experience involved beyond merely ascertaining the relevant features of the canvas; one does not see something in the picture,[14] nor does one participate appropriately in a visual game of make-believe. But this is not even how *linguistic* conventions normally work. We automatically recognize a word in a familiar language as meaning what it does; we do not first ascertain the shapes of the letters and then apply the relevant convention to figure out what it means. One's *visual* experience of a swastika may be conditioned by the conventional associations determining its meaning. It *looks* terrifying, ominous, horrible. Yet there is clearly an important sense in which its meaning is 'conventional'.

This, of course, does not constitute the special kind of perceptualness peculiar to depictions. Swastikas are not pictures. My point is merely that if it is true that one's responses to pictures are conditioned by conventions, this fact is not incompatible with one's responses being thoroughly perceptual experiences. In 'Imagination and Pictorial Understanding' Wollheim holds that the visual experience of seeing-in is 'conditioned by the cognitive stock that the spectator holds', and speaks of perception being 'permeated' by cognition (p. 48). One's internalized awareness of rules or conventions may be among the cognitions that permeate one's perception of a symbol. This does not make the experience, coloured by this cognition, any less a perceptual one.

Do people have to learn to perceive pictures, or are we born with the capacity to do so? If this nature/nurture question is what the issue of the conventionality or naturalness of pictures comes down to, its answer is irrelevant to the issue at hand. Wollheim emphasizes nature; Goodman nurture. Surely the truth lies somewhere in the middle. I have no doubt that our ability to 'read' pictures depends in part on natural, inborn propensities, and in part on abilities acquired as a result of experience, but I have little idea how much is nurture and how much nature. Picture perception is a visual experience in any case – one involving participation, of the kind I have described, in visual games of make-believe – regardless of how much learning went into our capacity to enjoy that experience. The imaginings that infect our perception of the picture are no less intimately a part of it if we had to acquire through experience the ability to perceive in a way coloured by those imaginings.

Much of my argument has amounted to applications of the familiar idea that there is no such thing as an 'innocent eye', pure perception unsullied by other cognitions. If we were to understand 'visual experience' in so narrow a sense that participating in games of make-believe in the ways I claim viewers of pictures do will not count as such, we might as well declare ourselves blind, for it is likely that on such a narrow conception nothing would count as visual experience. On a more reasonable construal of 'visual experience', the fact that our experience of pictures is bound up with imaginings and possibly conditioned by internalized conventions will not count against their qualifying as fully visual. Painting is a visual art, and depiction is a visual medium. The make-believe theory explains how this is so.

There are analogies between the issues I have been discussing regarding the perception of pictures and questions about appreciators' emotional responses to fiction. I have argued elsewhere that when Charles, a typical film-goer, watches a horror film in which a ferocious green slime attacks the camera (the spectator), he is not genuinely afraid of the slime, but rather is participating in a game of make-believe in which it is fictional that he is afraid.[15] Some commentators (not Wollheim) have attributed to me the astonishing thesis that Charles's reaction to the film is not a genuinely emotional one, or even that, in general, appreciators are not genuinely moved by fiction.[16] That Charles does not experience genuine emotion follows only if fear of the slime is the only emotion he could be experiencing, and it obviously is not. Perhaps some think that the fact that Charles is engaging in an imaginative activity or that he is doing so because of certain conventions would be somehow inconsistent with his feeling genuine emotion.[17] But there is no need to saddle ourselves with such exotic assumptions. (It is helpful to remember that appreciators' imaginings are likely not to be deliberate, even if they imagine in accordance with internalized conventions, just as the experiencing of emotions is not, straightforwardly, something that one deliberately does.) I see no reason why we should not count the experience I describe of fictionally fearing the slime – or the experience of fictionally grieving for Anna Karenina, for instance – as an emotional as well as an imaginative one; it may be intensely emotional. The heart is no more innocent than the eye, and there is no more justification for thinking that imagination or the functioning of internalized conventions is incompatible with or dilutes emotional experiences than that it is incompatible with or dilutes perceptual ones.

The appreciator's response to fiction may involve other genuine emotions as well. Charles may be genuinely disgusted by the film, or even fear it, while and possibly as a result of undergoing the experience of fictionally fearing the slime. And the work may induce or revive genuine emotions in the appreciator directed toward other things: fear of dangers the appreciator thinks might exist in the real world, pity for real people in situations perceived as analogous to Anna Karenina's.

The make-believe theory is designed to explain the experience of being caught up emotionally in a story and the special visual nature of pictorial representation; it certainly does not deny that there is such an experience or that depiction is especially visual. In claiming it to be fictional but not true that Charles fears the slime, I open the way to understanding his experience to be a genuinely emotional one, notwithstanding his full realization that there is no slime and no danger, and I explain why it is so natural to describe him as being 'afraid of the slime'. In arguing that, on viewing a picture of a woman, it is fictional that one sees a woman, I make it possible for us to understand the viewer's experience as being a genuinely perceptual one which is richer than merely perceiving the marks on the canvas. And I explain why it is so natural to speak of the spectator's 'seeing' or 'recognizing' or 'identifying' a woman, despite the fact that there neither is a woman there nor does there appear to be one.

NOTES

[1] Wollheim also makes use of a notion of a 'standard of correctness' in his account of depiction, though I will not discuss it here. In place of this, my own account employs the idea of a work's possessing a certain function in a given social context. The artist's intentions have a less essential role in my theory than they do in Wollheim's. See my *Mimesis as Make-Believe: On the Foundations of the Representational Arts* (Harvard University Press, Cambridge, Mass., 1990), p. 52.

2 I develop my account of depiction most fully in *Mimesis as Make-Believe*, esp. ch. 8.

3 Wollheim, 'Imagination and Pictorial Understanding', *Proceedings of the Aristotelian Society*, Supplementary Volume 60 (1986), p. 46. See also *idem, Painting as an Art* (1987), p. 73.

4 Wollheim, 'Imagination and Pictorial Understanding', pp. 46–7; *idem, Painting as an Art*, p. 46.

5 Wollheim speaks of a particular kind of 'reciprocity' between the two aspects, to account for 'naturalistic' representation (*Painting as an Art*, p. 73).

6 See also *Painting as an Art*, pp. 60, 62.

7 But I propose a more substantial way of distinguishing among representational paintings those that are 'figurative' from those that are not than he does. See *Mimesis as Make-Believe*, pp. 54–7.

8 At least it would appear that one does not see flags and targets in Jasper Johns's paintings.

9 More narrowly, in the case of what I call depictive music. See *Mimesis as Make-Believe*, pp. 333–7.

10 Anthony Savile, 'Imagination and Pictorial Understanding', *Proceedings of the Aristotelian Society*, Supplementary Volume 60 (1986), p. 21. In attempting to show that imagining is not an essential ingredient of normal picture perception, Savile argues that we fully understand *trompe l'œil* works and see in them what they are pictures of, even in the rare cases in which we are deceived by them. But since 'imagining something to be thus and so is incompatible with my experiencing it to be thus and so and also with my taking myself so to experience it', imagining can't be involved in these cases (ibid., pp. 21–2). I find the assumption that the perceiver who is fooled by a *trompe l'œil* painting sees in it what it portrays and the assumption that imagining is incompatible with being fooled or experiencing a hallucination both highly questionable.

11 Ibid., p. 21.

12 I discuss what it is to imagine in a first person manner and from the inside in *Mimesis as Make-Believe*, §1.4.

13 See Savile, 'Imagination and Pictorial Understanding', p. 23.

14 Wollheim made essentially this point in 'On Drawing an Object', in *On Art and the Mind* (1973), p. 25.

15 See *Mimesis as Make-Believe*, §§5.2 and 7.1, which supersede my earlier discussion in 'Fearing Fictions', *Journal of Philosophy*, 75 (1978), pp. 5–26.

16 See Bijoy Boruah, *Fiction and Emotion: Rationality, Belief and Emotional Response to Fiction* (Oxford University Press, New York, 1988), p. 66; Noel Carroll, *The Philosophy of Horror: or Paradoxes of the Heart* (Routledge, New York, 1990), pp. 69–79; and David Novitz, 'Fiction, Imagination, and Emotion', *Journal of Aesthetics and Art Criticism*, 38, no. 3 (Spring 1980), esp. p. 288, n. 2.

17 I do not claim without qualification that there are 'conventions' involved. See *Mimesis as Make-Believe*, pp. 38, 40–1, 301–2.

17

Painting, Beholder and the Self

ANTHONY SAVILE

Of the many pleasures offered by Richard Wollheim's writings on painting, one of the greatest is undoubtedly provided by their exploration of the intricate relations holding between our lived experience of that art and of its history and the conceptual assumptions underlying them. Their sure control of complex material, resisting the twin dangers of simplification in the pursuit of realism and over-elaboration in the name of sound theory, is impossible not to admire. Minded to emulation, admirers must fear missing both targets; they will be fortunate to be no more than half-way disappointed in that expectation.

It has long been customary to view the revival of dramatic history representation in French painting between the 1750s and 1780s as a largely academic and regressive return to a far grander earlier tradition. Custom has recently been challenged by Michael Fried's widely acclaimed reading of Diderot's thought about painting which presents the neo-classical attachment to the familiar dramatic genre as a uniquely apt way for the painter to satisfy the particular ethical demands of a post-Rococo conception of man.[1] Quite apart from its art-historical interest, the proposal's leading thesis embodies matter of considerable philosophical substance. This comes about because, to see how the ethical demand is met, we are invited to accept a refashioning of the general conception of the painter's subject and, with that, a new view of the work's beholder. It is only if these two interlinked renewals are in order that the proposed old wine in new casks theory of neo-classicism can displace the familiar warmed-up cabbage account. To discuss this issue, I need to outline some of the detail of the revisionary tale.

(1) We are to see the essence of Rococo, prevailing up to the mid-century, as given by the intimate, decorative and sensuous subjects that so appealed to the court of Louis XV and the society of the period. One marked feature of them is that it is so often an integral part of their aesthetic character itself that they are present on display for the beholder. It is not just that, having the character they do, they provide the beholder with delight. Rather, that they aim to do this is itself part of what the beholder is to understand as he or she comes to admire them. In consequence, the beholder is typically highly self-conscious, affectively engaged with the painter's subjects through the very diffraction to which this self-consciousness gives rise. Relations that are subsequently fostered with the surrounding world and the self that comes to be reflectively formed through them are consequently liable to detachment, estrangement and, in the end, alienation.

By contrast, progressive critics and painters of the later period are seen as motivated by a quest, not always fully conscious maybe, but real enough, for the constitution of a more natural self, unfalsified by manner and achieved through a direct, undiffracted engagement with the objects of its attention. The place that dramatic history painting comes to assume in mid to late eighteenth-century France is the locus of this quest made good. In it we find the ideal realization of the unmannered subject offering itself to the beholder, quite disarming the defensive and estranging self-conscious habit. Why this should be is explained by reflection on the antecedent stages in the art's development.

In the period up to the 1750s, after a period of desuetude, we encounter a resurgence of themes in which the depicted subjects are deeply absorbed in the activities in which they are engaged. Chardin's boy is intent on the bubble he blows or on the precariousness of the house of cards he builds, and his philosopher is quite engrossed in the book he studies. These figures and their like are presented so as to evince total obliviousness to everything but the objects of their own absorption. However, we are to notice that this oblivion does not extend to the beholder standing before the painting that depicts them, and because it does not, the theme of absorption is ultimately liable to lend itself to self-conscious apprehension. Ever ready to assert omnipotent mastery, the beholder's self will seize on this gap to deflect the invitation offered to join the painting's subject empathically in his or her engrossment. Perhaps, even those signs of the subject's forgetfulness of the world around him, the unpinned apron, the tear in the bubble-blower's jacket, or the unclosed drawer fronting the spectator, holding cards turned both towards and away from him, function as shadowy toe-holds for the beholder's self-conscious apprehension of the scene.

In the decade of the sixties, absorptive effects are intensified, most notably by Greuze, in an effort to overcome and counteract the renewed presence of the beholder. 'It is as though the presence of the beholder threatened to distract the dramatis personæ from all involvement in ordinary states or activities, and as though the artist was therefore called on to neutralise the beholder's presence by taking whatever measures proved necessary to absorb, or reabsorb, those personæ in the world of the painting' (pp. 66, 67). The 'whatever measures' alluded to cover *inter alia* the dramatization of the subject, the intensification of the absorptive state, and the strongly emphatic unification and the visual sealing-off of the pictured scene.

Why, one wants to ask, is the dramatic move so described forced on the artist? The move is one from a sort of painting in which the beholder looks on to a world in which he has no place, the world of the picture in which objective states of absorption are recorded as part of that very world, to one of a kind that insists on an emphatic ignoring of the beholder himself. Thus Fried describes Greuze's young girl as facing the beholder and sending a kiss through the window and as 'appearing to look through [him] to her lover' (p. 61). The way in which he justifies this is by saying that otherwise the illusion of absorption could not be maintained, but I very much doubt whether the viewer of the time, faced with a more restrained, Chardinesque handling of the theme, would respond by saying that this was not a persuasive representation of objective absorption in everyday scenes. Rather, what he must have in mind is that if the depicted absorption was to continue to be deeply involving for the beholder, it must go further than in Chardin's treatments of it, on pain of not being upset by self-consciousness. If this is more nearly right, we can say that unification of the picture, the dramatization of events it offers, and the intensification of the scenes it depicts all facilitated involvement, rather than illusion. This diagnosis is confirmed by the thought that it is involvement rather than illusion that is recruited to counteract self-awareness.

It is the pursuit of engrossment, too, that allegedly motivates the renewed primacy of dramatic history painting in the developed reaction against the Rococo. The leading idea is that the subjects of history are subjects of action and passion and that not only do they suppose the complete absorption of the depicted personages in these events and their related emotions, but, under one condition, are bound to involve the spectator in them too, in a way that sets at naught the spectator's awareness of himself as beholder of them. The condition in question is that the spectator should come to see the extent of the subjects' engrossment as including himself; not only must the ordinary objects of the world be banished from the spectator's consciousness, but so too must the beholder of the picture in which they figure.

'Diderot's conception of painting', writes Fried, 'rested ultimately on the supreme fiction that the beholder did not exist, that he was not really there, standing before the canvas, and that the causal and instantaneous mode of unity that came with it, provided the best available medium for establishing that fiction in the painting itself.' Speaking of paradox in the situation, he goes on to say:

> [T]he recognition that paintings are made to be beheld, and therefore presuppose the existence of a beholder, led to the demand for the actualization of his presence; a painting, it was insisted, had to attract the beholder, to stop him in front of himself, and to hold him there in a perfect trance of involvement. At the same time . . . it was only by negating the beholder's presence that this could be achieved, only by establishing the fiction of his absence or non-existence that his actual placement before and enthralment by the painting could be secured. (p. 103)

At the start, I alluded to the constitution of a new conception of the painter's object and to a corresponding new conception of the beholder. These expressions can now be made clearer. The new subject, as here envisaged, is one whose world potentially encompasses the beholder. That novelty is demanded as a condition of satisfying the requirement for spectatorial involvement that will match the moralized demand of the anti-Rococo current. However, since the satisfaction of that demand also requires the absorbed intensity of action and passion on the part of the actors, a total absorption from which nothing should escape, they come to present themselves to the beholder in the form of a fully realized, self-contained, dramatic *tableau*. The characters are potentially aware of their surroundings, even of the beholder, but they are protected from outsiders by the self-enclosed nature of the representation that involves them only with each other and with the drama in which they are engaged.

At the same time, this very involvement entrains the constitution of a new sort of beholder, '*one whose innermost nature would consist precisely in the conviction of his absence from the scene of the representation*' (p. 104). Having credited the characters with the power to be aware of him, and then convincingly represented them as totally absorbed in their own affairs, the beholder is bound to think of himself as excluded from the scene, shielded therefore from the incursions of self-consciousness and its ills. That novel conception of himself is thus implicit in his full understanding of the new sort of subject that the painter handles.[2]

(2)   So much by way of précis. The first question to ask is whether, as the matter is seen, attributed both to Diderot himself and to painters of the time, and then endorsed in exegetical commentary, these new conceptions of painting and the beholder are not even more paradoxical than is allowed. One may suspect that there is more than a sentiment of impending conflict to be felt in the contrast between the clear-minded beholder of a painting and one convinced that his presence is washed away from the scene of the representation. Is it genuinely coherent to suppose that one should recognize oneself as beholder of a represented scene and at the same time be convinced of one's absence from it, where we are explicitly told that that conviction comes to 'the fiction that the beholder did not exist, that he was not really there, standing before the canvas' (p. 103)? If one is so convinced, must one not *eo ipso* believe oneself to be absent, hence believe oneself not to be present, and thus not beholding the canvas before which one stands?

Sticking for the moment to the letter, no one should insist that there is any formal contradiction in this position. We can be convinced that P and at the same time be convinced that not P without thereby supposing the world itself to contain any sort of contradiction. The contradiction is in our minds, in our representation of the world, that is, and may lie there unchallenged until it occurs to us to put the two elements together in the form: P and not-P. Since Diderot can claim that the conviction that the beholder stands in front of the canvas recedes from the mind as he comes to think of himself as absent from the scene, there is no very great pressure on the beholder to complete any such hazardous act of association. And just as well, because if he does, and comes to recognize himself as committed to the represented conflict, he will be unable to sustain his novel way of viewing such pictures. Not, again, that their existence would, strictly speaking, be impossible; rather, they just could not have any clear-sighted admirers, and correct understanding of them could not be long sustained.

None the less, this way of handling the would-be paradox cannot be welcomed. Even if I do resist the dangerous associative act by backgrounding my awareness of my presence before the canvas, I shall still not secure the 'sympathy, absorption and self-transcendence' (p. 104) that the novel conception of the beholder is designed to achieve.

We see this by asking how Diderot envisages my conviction of absence from the scene being brought about. The answer appears to be that it is the effect of my appreciation of the states of mind of the depicted characters. I see that they are utterly absorbed in one another and in the events that have overtaken them. They are potentially aware of me, but in the event entirely oblivious of me and of my position as I look in at them. (Recall Greuze's young girl 'appearing to look *through the beholder* to her lover'). How could they be potentially aware of me standing there before the canvas, unless they thought of themselves as characters *in a picture?* Anything less than this, such as intense absorption in their own affairs, would lead me to see the picture as suggesting no more than the absence of any *internal* onlooker, and that is a long way away from persuading me of my own absence before the canvas. Yet the moment I start to attribute to the depicted personages the dispositional awareness of their place *in a picture*, I am making my interest in them theatrical, in the sense that I am regarding them as actors rather than as characters in their own right. To do this, Diderot would be the first to allow, is to undermine the goal of self-transcendence, and to undermine it from within.

Of course, it will be insisted that in a fully realized Diderotian *tableau* the personages' own sense of what lies beyond their unity is not aroused. It is not that, but the strength of that unity, that gives rise to my conviction of my non-existence. However, if it is not the occurrent conscious awareness that the beholder is absent that I am to attribute to the depicted figures and if I am not to rest content with the thought that they are simply unaware of their surroundings in their depicted world, something beyond just that must function to provide me with the thought I need. As far as I can see, it can only be the perception that the *tableau* before me has an aspect of being arranged by the characters *as if not for me.*[3] If I do not notice this, I shall not end up convinced of my own absence from the scene, but at most of the absence of an internal onlooker; yet, on the other hand, if I do notice it, any conviction I come by to this effect will be one that is self-conscious in the extreme. The very naturalness that is being pursued will inevitably be undone by my awareness of such high artifice.

To avoid theatricality then, in the pejorative sense of the term accorded it by Diderot, we are going to need an alternative way of understanding his 'supreme fiction'. It cannot be that the spectator believes that he is absent from the canvas; nor will it do to say he believes that no one observes the depicted scene. So it might seem that the sole remaining possibility is that the spectator simply take himself not to be present at it. However, the trouble here is to understand just how to do this, to find a way of reading it which does not simply amount to the beholder failing to believe that he or she is present before the canvas. For, whatever its virtues, this last does import contradiction into the world, and not just into the mind, requiring for the realization of Diderot's ideal both that the beholder be aware of himself as confronting a picture and also not aware. If, with this, we had exhausted all the alternatives, we should have to draw the conclusion that there really are no new casks waiting to receive the old wine.

(3) It might seem easy enough to avoid this danger by appealing once more to the device of foregrounding and backgrounding, not of course as applied to the two acutely conflicting positions – that would do nothing to relieve their conflict – but combined with a rewriting of the conviction that enters into the supreme fiction, the conviction that '*il n'y a personne au delà*'. For this purpose, 'conviction' might continue be read negatively to avoid the old troubles: that is, not as *conviction that not* . . . but as *not conviction that* . . . , only backed now by the stipulation that this amounts to nothing more than the denial of any foregrounded occurrence of the thought in question. The result will then be that while I dispositionally believe myself to be confronting the representation of the scene, while I admire it, I do not occurrently think of myself as doing so. However strained this reading may be, at least it embodies no contradiction; nor does it carry any suggestion of theatricality.

Patently though, the resulting position is too weak to sustain any new conception of the beholder. It is a situation no different from that which might have captured the purely classical conception, of the beholder unaware of his existence as beholder at all, except, of course, to the extent that he needs to be to make sense of his experience as of a picture having this or that meaning anyway. So, if there is nourishment in eighteenth-century theory, it is going to have to be found in a different reading of it from any attempted so far.

(4) Although I have not laboured it, the difficulty that underlies the criticisms I have raised obviously stems from an unresolved uncertainty of reference in the expressions 'the represented scene' and 'the beholder'. The first has been used indifferently to designate the events that are depicted or the depiction of the events on the canvas; the second spans an off-scene beholder of the depicted events and the beholder of the canvas itself. The train of thought I have so far pursued has basically taken the form of inviting one to consider each

in turn and of pointing out that for either one the Diderotian requirement cannot be met.

Putting it like this and stressing the way in which the neo-classical
thinker has had a sharp choice thrust upon him may move one to
wonder whether that choice might not be avoided, and a new way be
found of understanding the case. The possibility is at least discussable, and I put it like this. So far, we have followed the conventional
dichotomy of thinking that the external beholder of a picture and the
scene that he sees in the canvas are situated in different spheres, with
the consequence that the external beholder can be doubled by an
internal (not necessarily depicted) beholder of the scene, but cannot
himself be that internal beholder. On the other hand, the picture
space may extend beyond the confines of the canvas itself, although
traditionally it does not stretch out to the space in which the external
beholder finds himself.

Now, one might well ask whether it is not at least conceivable that
these conventions should be abrogated, if conventions they are, so that
in some circumstances we may come to understand paintings as depicting scenes that stretch right up to and even enclose their own
beholders. Might not, on occasion, the external beholder and the
internal beholder merge, or fuse? If this is a possibility, maybe it is one
that could be of service to the revisionary theorist, who could then put
his case by saying that while the beholder is indeed aware of his
position in front of the canvas in a dispositional way, backgrounded
by his engagement with the scene, he can also be put in a position of
understanding the scene depicted to embrace the space in which he
actually stands. Only, the beholder sees that, for the personages depicted in the scene, that very place is empty. In this way, the beholder's
understanding of the scene involves awareness of his own absence, not,
of course, by attributing a thought about himself to the figures in the
scene – that would be too extreme – but by fashioning their consciousness in a way that excludes the beholder's presence: they react to their
surroundings, which now include the beholder's place before the picture as being *vacant*. If that were permissible, we would appear to have
a way of securing Diderot's requirement of enthralment, by establishing the fiction of the beholder's absence from the scene or, slightly
misleadingly put, his non-existence.[4]

There are at least two questions here, one formal, the other substantive. The first is whether this idea is coherent at all, and the second
whether, if it is, we have any good critical ground for seeing it energe-
tically at work in our understanding of post-Rococo French painting.
Much of what follows will concentrate on the first issue, and to discuss

it I shall temporarily set aside the eighteenth-century framework of the discussion. To start with, it will be useful to render the revisionary idea at least arguably plausible. So here are three cases, each of which, in different ways, purports to demand that the world of the picture be experienced as extending to the world of the viewer, and extending continuously to his world, with the effect that we do not simply find ourselves saying that the scene we view is supposed to take place in a different part of the world that we share with it but are disjoined from by some imagined gap in space or time.

Case 1 Eager to engage viewers directly with his work, the painter aspires to situate the depicted scene in relation to the very place from which it is viewed. Conscious of the vagaries of time and chance, the painter eschews any attempt to achieve this by requiring the work to hang at this or that particular place and then recording that same place in the representation. Instead, he proposes to give the picture a content that will be correctly understood by any viewer as its taking place just in front of him, wherever that may be. The painter has, let us say, taken as his model Vermeer's canvas of the painter espied through a doorway spanned by a curtain flapping out illusionistically into our space, so that we think of the scene we see as continuous with wherever we are. I call this example *The Adjoining Room.*

Case 2 The novelist has just finished a futuristic tale. Peculiar about it is the unorthodox way it secures its character of futurity. Anxious lest some day its readers should find the lapse of time since the book's composition coming to outstrip the very futurity that constitutes its point, the writer apostrophizes the reader, instructing him that the events to be related are set some five years ahead, ahead, that is, of his reading about them. In this way, no matter who reads the tale and no matter when, it will enjoy a guaranteed futurity. Pleased with this stratagem, the author invites his friend the painter to illustrate the tale. By contagion, as it were, the content of the resulting set of illustrations comes to share an essential futurity with the written word. Let us entitle the first of this set *Tomorrow*, and in doing so recall an observation of Arthur Danto's: 'A title is more than a name or a label: it is a *direction* for interpretation.'[5]

Case 3 Imagine yourself in a new gallery with a companion looking at a traditional-seeming canvas. In it, with his back to you and straight ahead stands the painter working at his canvas. He or she – the figure is indeterminately androgynous – works from a mirror set in front of him or her. We do not see the face in the mirror, but we do have a good enough view of the portrait in progress. There the artist has drawn on resources that leave all tradition behind. However the effect is achieved, be it with mirrors or with the aid of enhanced technology, there, projected on to the almost finished canvas, you and I each see a tolerable and unmistakable image of ourself. It takes only a minute for the wit of the title to sink in: the painter has called his work *Self-Image*.

What is debatable in each case is whether the imagined artist has really managed to do what he has purported to do, to make the correct understanding of his work one that involves description of its contents in terms of the beholder's own adjacent world. *The Adjoining Room* aspires to do this by placing the depicted painter some ten feet in front of the beholder, *Tomorrow* by situating its action some time ahead of the moment at which it is viewed; and *Self-Image*, more audaciously, by having the beholder himself figure recognizably in the depicted scene.

No more than before should we think the endeavour doomed on account of some contradiction that it surreptitiously introduces. We know that the spot ten feet in front of us is in fact empty, a spot situated in mid-air some four stories up the block in which the picture is lodged, hanging on an outer wall. Yet we see the painter seated at that spot clearly, not suspended in space. How can the same spot be both? It can't: but the most that is required is that of the spot we know to be in mid-air, we think of it as being occupied by the painter we see firmly rooted to the ground. Further, it may as well be noticed that the eighteenth-century theorist, Diderot or Lessing or many another, who thinks of pictorial illusion as incomplete unless securing belief and who grants that full illusion is achieved in these cases, will still not be disconcerted. For he can say, as I have had him say before, that there is nothing unduly psychologically strenuous, let alone logically taxing, about combining the belief that the said spot is empty and the contrary belief that it is occupied. The former belief is backgrounded, and only the latter is occurrent as the picture is understood and makes its effect. As long as we are under no compulsion to associate the two opposed thoughts, which we may suppose ourselves protected from by the force of the illusion engaging us with the image, there is no puzzlement here.

(5) Another intimation of contradiction demands to be taken more seriously. If I am asked to identify the location of the painter in *The Adjoining Room*', I may be tempted to say that he is at such and such

a spot in London. If that is true, then that must exclude the painter's being situated at such and such other spot in London, or elsewhere. But shan't I be forced to say, when the picture goes on tour, that the painter is then located elsewhere, and not in London? Since the painter cannot both be in London and not be in London, can we allow his world to extend into our own?

Clearly, the painter could only be situated in London and not in London if different times were considered. So one might consider saying that we need to identify the content of the picture by reference to the occasions of its being beheld, each of which will bring its own time index to the situation. But there are a number of reasons for not doing any such thing. Perhaps the most acute is that there needs to be a way for the artist to specify the picture's content, which gives rise to the understanding each spectator has of it (when he understands it correctly, that is). At first, we might think of this standing content as one that is arrived at by abstraction from the particular ways in which it gets understood on discrete occasions of viewing. The trouble is that there is no way in which anything determinate could be abstracted from such records of token viewing as 'The painter is situated in London', when the canvas is viewed in London, and 'The painter is situated in Paris', when viewed there, and so on. As far as abstraction goes, there is nothing in common between the thoughts of these locations that could be satisfactorily filtered out. The idea of the picture having a stable content abstractable from the various occasions of its viewing must leave us thinking of it as in as miserable a case as Berkeley's *bête noire*, the abstract general triangle, right-angle, obtuse and isosceles at the same time without being any of them.

Further, the abstraction story gets things quite the wrong way round. The artist has to be able to determine the content of his work before anyone else comes to behold it, so he cannot be dependent on the occasions of viewing it by a spectator to abstract the standing content that it has as it moves from person to person, time to time, place to place. Moreover, we are bound here to respect an observation of Wollheim's to the effect that all allusion to the spectator is, as far as analysis goes, entirely hypothetical and not categorical. Unlike messages addressed to the outside world by the shipwrecked mariner, works of painting may be created in quiet indifference to their fate at others' hands (*Painting as an Art* (1987), p. 96); indeed, in indifference to whether there are others who interest themselves in them at all.[6] Any attempt to provide content by abstraction from experience of the work must consequently fail.

(6)   To avoid the still present threat then, I propose that we insist on a sharp distinction between pictures that are in their content strictly referential and those that are not. As I have proceeded so far, I have misleadingly assumed that we are to think that *The Adjoining Room* makes reference to a particular spot in our world, namely the spot at which the beholder stands, and then that we are to identify occupied positions in the painting in relation to that, with the result that we can come to say which precise spot we see the painter occupying. Similarly in the other two cases, *mutatis mutandis*. The last reflections show that this cannot be right. What we have to say is that these pictures do not introduce us to those particular places, times and people at all, but only to some such indefinitely specified counterparts. Hence, as far as its content goes, *The Adjoining Room* is at most a picture of the painter seated *ten feet or so in front of the spectator* (wherever that may be); *Tomorrow* is a picture of events taking place *so many years ahead of the picture's being viewed* (whenever that is); the identity of the painter in *Self-Image* is that of *the spectator* (whoever he happens to be). And so on. Under this quantificational interpretation, no reference is made to times, places, or people by the paintings we are concerned with. Nevertheless, as we see them, they still appear to take the figures depicted in them into a world that is utterly continuous with our own, since each occasion of viewing will supply the beholder with a highly localized identification of these items and their like.

Before moving back to neo-classicism, this is a good moment to comment on a reflection that underpins Wollheim's own rejection of any Diderot-like scenario. While it is an objection that is stated in a context that we have not yet fully faced, its broad structure would apply equally to any of these cases as long as they are thought of as genuinely referential. What worries Wollheim is that any implicit reference to the time at which the picture is observed, or the fixing of places within it by reference to the location of the observer, will open up the possibility of the painting having a different content in different circumstances, and having a different content without there being any corresponding change of marks on the surface of the canvas. This he fears to be incoherent in and of itself, though he does at one point express uncertainty as to whether the root of the incoherence may not lie deeper than at this level of description, suggesting that it will be incoherent failing the provision of a vehicle whereby any such puzzling change in content might be wrought.[7]

Now, it is certainly true that a *de re* construction of my three pictures' contents would lead one to such a shifting position, but, because that construction of them initially seemed so appealing, I doubt whether it should be dismissed without further ado as incoherent at the level of surface description. Nor, I think, is it evident that the challenge to provide a vehicle by which the shift might be effected cannot be met. In specifying the way in which my examples work, I might even be thought to have provided such a vehicle for each one: the illusion of the flapping curtain, the tie to the author's manuscript, and the directional force of title or the technological wizardry.

The root of the difficulty must lie elsewhere, not so much in the absence of a vehicle, but more surely in the impossibility of the artist determinately specifying, under this questionable conception of his work, of art, what such a vehicle is required for. It is the artist who must, in his intention, fix the content of his work, what he is aiming at and what is to count as its finished accomplishment. Consequently, he must be able to specify just which *de re* thoughts are the correct ones for the spectator to entertain when he understands the paintings in question as embracing his own world. To do this in *de re* terms, the artist would need to know who those spectators were going to be and build in genuine reference to them in the account of his work he gives (even if only for himself). Yet just because all reference to the spectator must be hypothetical rather than categorical, this cannot be done. It is fundamentally for this reason that a work with shifting content of this kind is not a possibility.

Where then does this leave our amendment to the neo-classical position? As long as we do not attempt to construe it in *de re* terms, surely, untouched. The artist can specify the thought he wants the beholder to have in terms that are not *de re*, along the quantificational lines outlined. He can require, relying on the kind of vehicle I have introduced, that the depicted painter in *The Adjoining Room* be seen as situated ten feet in front of the place whence he is viewed, painting away at the time the beholder espies him, and still deny that there is any more definite specification of the picture's content to be had than that. That is, although it is true enough that what place and what time come to be thought of by the beholder will be different on different occasions of viewing, just which those particular times and places are do not enter into the picture's content, and consequently do not need to enter into the artist's own thought. An analogy with language would be that what any two people say when they utter the English sentence 'I'm cold now' is the same; only what makes what they say true is in each case different. As far as the picture's content goes, we are concerned with only the first of these items, not the second. All threat of contradiction is thereby removed.

(7)   Can these thoughts be used to preserve the Diderotian resolution to the art-historical crux presented by the resurgence of history painting? Formally speaking, it does still remain open to say that a different sort of pictorial subject and a different sort of beholder are introduced when the sphere of the picture is, in the manner indicated, understood in its content to reach into the beholder's world. The difference in question lies in the fixing of the limits of the picture's space (and time), though whether it is a novelty in the mid-eighteenth century is open to doubt. Perhaps the claim will be that only then did this possibility come to be systematically exploited for ethical ends. To put it like that offers scope enough to save the neo-classical point, scope enough also to exonerate Diderot's criticism in the *Salons* from the charge of whimsy and sentimentality so often felt to mark it.

It is now urgent, however, to ask the substantive question whether the device is well adapted to history painting in particular. As I have argued, we are obliged to modify the proposal in order not to incur the very danger that it is designed to avoid, the incursion of theatricality. The modification proposed has been that of seeing the world of the picture as embracing the spectator's world, whoever the spectator is, without discontinuity. The events within the picture are, so to speak, brought by these means to us, not we to them. Now, one might well think that historical and biblical or mythical scenes, which make up the large part of the repertoire of dramatic painting, can only be understood if this device is disavowed. The reason is that in our understanding of what we see, we are bound to situate the depicted events precisely at a time and a place that is not our own. Hence we do not envisage them as stretching out to our world, the world of the spectator, once he is thought of as other than someone located in a space and time from which we ourselves are *de facto* shut out as we view the work. So whereas this difficulty does not directly apply to representations of events of non-historical kinds, such as are typically offered by Greuze, it does bear quite pressingly on just the sort of painting that the thesis was meant to assist us in revaluing.

Indirectly, though, it also bears on these other paintings too; for while we may think the proposed way of viewing them is not incoherent, we have to be convinced that it is in fact correct. Now much of the evidential force for applying it to Greuze lay in its possible further extension to the dramatic historical pictures not just by Greuze but in particular by the later Jacques-Louis David, whose history painting epitomizes the revisionary reading of the period. Once we hesitate to find it credible as applied there, we are less well placed than we might otherwise be to see it in play here. Something else is going to be needed to settle the issue or to tip the balance firmly in one direction or the other.

Before looking to see what offers itself, I should at least consider a possible retort to this psychologically motivated objection. May not the involvement of the spectator be achieved, and not merely with some off-scene internal onlooker, even while the spectator is encouraged to displace himself in his imagination to other climes and other times? In that case, the historicity of the dramatic works would not pose an obstacle to the application of the device under scrutiny. The idea would be that the artist invites the spectator viewing a historical scene of action and passion to imagine being displaced in time and space, and in doing so experience what he sees as taking place before him, though for the participants the place at which, in his imagination, the beholder stands is empty.

Again, I am not asserting this to be impossible. The question is not whether, through this imaginative detour, the conceptual propriety of the case can be saved, but whether it is genuinely plausible to see it motivated by the pictures in question. Earlier on, we saw the drive to involve the spectator in the work as functioning to negate his or her own self-consciousness, ever ready to assert theatricality and ever needing to be forestalled by the anti-Rococo artist. At this late stage, I am uneasy lest the very artificiality of the means on offer to achieve this end could realistically hope to attain its goal rather than simply emphasize the very self-consciousness that is presented as so threatening. The involvement that I would be invited to enjoy with the dramatic personages' actions and their passions is, after all, no longer direct; their affairs do not, so to speak, reach right up to me where I stand and as I see them. At most, they reach right up to me only when I have displaced myself in imagination appropriately enough for them to do so. Since I am supposed to understand this – indeed, have to understand this in order to make the imaginative leap – I am to all appearance free in my present consciousness to see this step as one that I am invited to undertake for my own pleasure and delight as I find myself before the canvas. Once more, it seems that the hoped for gain of immediacy and absorbed involvement with what the spectator views is slipping away from the painter's grasp as, more and more desperately, he strives to retain it.[8]

Another difficulty will also afflict the kinds of painting with which we have so far been concerned. It is that the putative annihilation of the beholder that is aimed at is to be effected through the consciousness of the depicted subjects. They see the place at which the beholder stands, whoever he or she may be, as *vacant*. What place is that for them, we have to ask? Here we cannot say that it is whatever place the beholder occupies, since for them, that could only be a place in their surroundings, and not one that stretches out into our world, and then the hypothetical spectator is no more than a possible internal onlooker, distinct from anyone who confronts the canvas. What is needed is that we should be able to attribute to the subjects a thought about the particular place beyond the canvas from which they are seen. In general, I take it, this can be done; but when it is, the circumstances permitting it are highly contrived. In particular, such pictures are designed for a particular fixed setting, and are known by all concerned to be so. That they are is what permits the artist to secure a *de re* reference to that place within the consciousness of his depicted subjects. Tiepolo's domestic frescoes at the Villa Maser are a case in point. There the subjects are clearly depicted as thinking about the particular place from which we see them and about the beholder that occupies that place. But the concrete spatial tie to the location of the image that permits this understanding of them is no feature of neo-classical history painting; so, quite apart from any self-conscious artifice that would enter into any comparable reading of them, it lies beyond their power to achieve full-scale oblivion of the spectator by the Diderotian route.

The time has come to take stock. The original reading of Diderot's criticism that is proposed and claimed to capture the anti-Rococo spirit at work is not well-defined or fully coherent as it stands. However, with amendment, the thesis has at least some claim to match our experience of the paintings in question. Here, I have said, results are at best indecisive. If my last remarks are to the point, the real possibility of intrusive self-consciousness is not forestalled by the absorptive devices lying within the artist's repertoire. In that case an alternative account of the revival of the older historical tradition than any offered by Diderot will still need to be found.

(8) It would be unsatisfactory to say nothing about one aspect of Diderot's criticism that is relied on at this point to supply further, oblique support for the now insecure reading of these pivotal dramatic works. I am alluding to the idea that in the non-dramatic pastoral genres, in landscapes, marine pictures (most notably by Vernet), scenes of ruins (by Hubert Robert), and decorative works (most notably by Fragonard), the presence of the beholder is also negated, though in an entirely different way than in their dramatic counterparts. Here it is negated not by encouraging the fiction that the spectator does not exist, but by projecting him into the world of the

painting itself. The beholder is made internal to the picture, it is claimed, even though not depicted in the canvas, and there, through his projection, he loses his self-conscious character as external beholder. If this claim can be upheld, it might do something to strengthen the credit of its dramatic pendant.

If one reads this 'pastoral' proposal in line with earlier thoughts and recalls the uncertainty as to whether 'the beholder' signifies an external spectator or a distinct internal one, there will be an immediate query as to whether this move really helps. If the suggestion merely supposes there to be an internal spectator in the picture space, one whom we do not see, it leaves open the possibility, raises the presumption even, that he is distinct from the external beholder. With that, the external beholder is not unequivocally negated, as we are invited to think, but merely doubled.

To get beyond this point, the imagined spectator who is absorbed into the world of the picture needs to be identical with the external spectator – only there is a difference between this case and the ones already discussed. There, the position of an internal beholder was merged with that of the external beholder, reaching out, as it were, into his space;[9] here, by contrast, the direction is apparently reversed, and the external beholder is allegedly transported into the picture space. This space is no longer experienced as being continuous with the space of our world, and as we look into it, we find ourselves cast there in the role of imagined internal observers. The external observer is 'negated' this time, so to speak, just by being given over to, and absorbed in, an internal identity.

At least one difficulty of the last section will not arise. There is no trouble for the artist to project the external spectator – whoever he may be – into a scene taking place far away and long ago. If the beholder makes an imaginative leap into the picture space at all, he will not be inhibited by the supposed distance in space and time from his actual location. Nor will it worry us that a determinate specification of the new content of the picture cannot be given, since we shall remain with the idea that any such projection takes place, if it does, only under universal quantification, and not *de re*. The real difficulty is that we are obliged to find an adequate ground for identifying such an internal spectator with the external one, for only if we can do this will we effect kind of oblivon of the external spectator that Diderot and his exegete are seeking to establish.

There seems no very good reason to doubt that sometimes we are obliged to understand a picture in terms of an internal spectator who is clearly *distinct* from an external spectator. Sometimes we can even identify that spectator, though this is not always the case, and then he just remains *an*, or *the*, spectator. But that is not enough here. The spectator has to be whoever is beholding the work. Can any circumstances lead to that identification?

With *Self-Image* I claimed to supply an example giving body to the idea of the external spectator being brought to the picture, strange as it may seem, precisely by depiction within it. So, we might think, if he can be found within the picture, there should be no insuperable difficulty of principle in our being able on occasion to understand him as set there, off to one side, not visible to us, though presumably potentially visible enough to others in the scene. Ultimately, I believe, this question comes down to one of interpretive force. Do we, or might we, ever find ourselves bound to such an identification in order to explain the experiential impact that some picture has for us, given that we have not found any antecedent grounds for saying that the very idea is absurd? Now, of course, it is hard enough to show that there could not be any such cases, but this may not be necessary. All that we are bound to do is to ask if the various measures that artists of the later eighteenth century are represented as taking to achieve some such identification positively require such a reading.

(9)   One effect of which much is made by Fried is the multiperspectival image that pervades the work of Vernet and which is so marked in David's earlier version of the *Belisarius*. The spectator cannot make immediate sense of these works if he adopts the traditional, central stance before them and searches for some one, centred vanishing point around which the whole can be coherently structured. Instead, we see that there are several positions that have to be adopted to integrate these works' various details, and we can only do that by projecting ourselves into the picture space to occupy them in order, one by one. So, it is said, the external beholder becomes an internal beholder.

The suggestion is hardly compelling. We need a stronger reason to say this than simply that the external beholder is required to imagine being placed (not, *nota bene*, imagine *himself* being placed) in the picture space in order to understand the picture. That is, the beholder may perfectly well be shown how the scene looks from over there, and understand what he is shown, without envisaging himself, or sharply experiencing himself, as drawn into the picture at all. The appeal of this weaker option can be brought out by noticing that in the normal course of events, when we are presented with a standardly unified picture, we are not obliged to understand the depicted scene as shown to *ourselves* at all. Such was precisely the purely classical position.

We envisage the scene as seen head on, but we do not envisage *our-selves* viewing it head on. This datum can evidently be transferred to the oblique cases. Then the support that the piecemeal character of Vernet's pastoral work gives to the general thesis will be so much diminished, unless of course there are powerful special reasons for according it privileged treatment. I do not see what they might be.

The œuvre of Fragonard supplies a second motivation for finding a projection of the spectator into the picture. Either we are visually drawn into it, as with the Besançon drawing in sanguine crayon of *Les grands Cyprès de la villa d'Este* or the *Allée ombragée* drawing in the Petit Palais, or alternatively the intended positioning of the ensemble around the beholder is designed to make him part of the scene, as with the panels constituting the *Progress of Love* in the Frick Collection. To these pointers is added the further suggestion that the canvases' unfinished appearance also invite us to complete them in our imagination by participation 'of a sort' (p. 141).

Waiving the last of these indications as no more than marginal, I doubt that either the sense of being pulled into the picture visually or the effect that flows from the disposition of the canvases sharply achieves our participation by transporting us into the picture rather than by extending the picture's world to us. Indeed, as far as the former device goes, any identification we are inclined to feel with an internal spectator most emphatically does not come from what would then need to be the case, from our recognizing that we have to understand the scene in terms of the presence of some internal, undepicted observer and then making the further discovery that we are to identify ourselves with him or her. To the extent that we do feel ourselves participant in these works – and surely it is right to respond to them in this way – we appear to have better reason to think that, unlike with the alleged Vernet effect, we do not so much project ourselves into them as find them extending up to us, somewhat as is achieved cinematographically when the camera is dollied into a scene.[10] This is of importance precisely because we now see that the pastoral genre will achieve the beholder's absorption only if it operates *in fundamentally the same way* as the dramatic history pictures are reputed to do, though without any further 'negating' or 'annihilation' or 'oblivon' of the beholder than is achieved by his being imaginatively seized by the scene before him. His consciousness as beholder here is expressively worked on so that he does not stand back from his pleasure and savour the mastery with which it is achieved; all savour is given in the engagement of his mind with what is brought before it. With the history pictures, it was said that they enthralled only by negating the beholder. Now, interestingly, oblique support for this idea is being sought in non-dramatic pictures which operate through a structurally similar transporting device – only any negation of the beholder they achieve is negation only in the attenuated sense that they engross him as he beholds them.

What is the significance of this? First, it does not force us to specify the content of these pictures in terms of their containing us (the external spectator), even if they strike us *as if* we are present at the scene. Second, it appears to be the classical mode of consciousness that fits these cases rather than its neo-classical counterpart; that is, the mode of consciousness in which the beholder *is not aware of his or her own existence.* Yet the classical mode is not one that can establish a new conception of the beholder or a new conception of the subject, either in its own right or as evidential underpinning for an otherwise open, but by itself insufficiently persuasive, account of neo-classical history painting.

The point is notable enough to bear repeating. Ancillary support for the original revisionary thesis is supplied in the pastoral mode only by the Fragonard cases, if at all. Yet when we think them through, they secure a negation of the beholder only in the entirely familiar way, by engrossing him so completely that, as he confronts them, he loses awareness of himself as their beholder. However, it was presented as a precondition of achieving the ethically motivated engrossment that the beholder should be negated in a stronger way, one typically supplied by the leading history paintings of the period and by the slightly earlier mature Greuze. However, since we are now looking to the Fragonards to hold that contention in place, they fail in their task. If anything, they seem to offer ample testimony to traditional forms of engrossment still being available. On that reading, these so-called pastoral pictures may even be thought to highlight the fragility of Diderot's conception of the dramatic genre, rather than to endorse it.

Once we set aside the multiperspectival Vernet cases, the weight that the reflections regarding Fragonard are being asked to bear in the overall structure of the argument – and keep in mind how scarce the Fragonard examples are – is disproportionate to their self-standing strength. Nothing in all this, of course, gives reason to deny the importance of the absorptive effect in this period of French painting or in particular cases. What it does do, though, is to suggest that the way in which Diderot is inclined to interpret it is better taken hyperbolically than straight. Caution here might now urge us to beware of projecting claims of his on to the practices of contemporary artists or of discerning there a new conception of their public and their subjects.

In his book Fried is careful to stress the importance of absorption in the earlier seventeenth-century tradition, in Caravaggio, in Domenichino, in Raphael, in Poussin, in Vermeer, and in Rembrandt. All in all, it must remain a question as to how late eighteenth-century history painting exploits that theme in ways that are sharply distinct from any available before that period.

(10)   Even if the revisionary case is not as strong as might initially seem, it may perhaps still enjoy some appeal. This may appear threatened by the following reflection, however. What is absolutely needed in these last cases and, I believe, in the dramatic ones discussed before, where the spectator allegedly engages himself with the scenes before his eyes, figuring, as it seems to him, as an off-scene participant and unmindful of his own real extra-pictorial presence, is that he should be able to engage his thoughts and feelings about the scene before him *in the first person*. This is brought out quite dramatically by reflecting that at the limit, the spectator's understanding of the picture may even require him to *act* in his own person, as when, confronting Alfred Leete's recruiting poster, the young men coming upon Lord Kitchener pointing outwards felt straightway impelled to join up.

If we try to put this aspect of the matter in terms of the quantificationally introduced beholder, as I have done so far, something crucial will be missing. A man who understands only that indefinite content will *not* take the next step, the step to action or to engrossed empathic feeling. For that, he has to pass from understanding the content of the work in terms of the beholder, whoever he may be, to *his own* feeling and to make this transition as part of properly understanding the work. Failing this, the whole will remain bereft of its most potent intended effect. Now this urgent demand might seem once more to bring in reference to the person of whom the painter could know nothing. Yet, if the earlier proscription of *de re* thought in this area is correct, how could these paintings and their like make their point? How could they even exist?

I believe that what we need here is to recognize that the painter has indeed to intend of any spectator who comes across his work that he do something, to wit, refer the beholder he understands as entering into the content of the work to himself.[11] Once again, the seemingly referential expressions must be understood quantificationally – only when I am such a spectator, what I have to do is to fulfil this requirement of the artist's by making a direct reference to myself, *de re*, via my further awareness that I am the beholder of his picture. This thought is naturally not one the painter himself can have. Nor need he. By contrast, in devising his work, he will, and must, envisage a general specification on which I can act, as can any other spectator when his turn comes. In conclusion, I surmise that in the end we shall not be able to give a full account of pictorial understanding without bringing in such matters, without pointing to the way in which on a particular occasion of viewing the spectator (whoever he may be) may need to refer it to himself, as I view it by referring it to me, A. S., and you to you, M. N. Nevertheless, these references to the individual do not enter into the standing content of the picture. As Wollheim points out, they cannot. It is just that what does go into its full understanding in the beholder's mind as he sees it will extend beyond, and is intended by the artist to extend beyond, the (quantificationally given) content. Happily, this is not a requirement that sets the artist at any disadvantage.

NOTES

[1] Michael Fried, *Absorption and Theatricality; Painting and the Beholder in the Age of Diderot* (Chicago, 1980). Page references in the text are to this work throughout.

[2] One might look back over the history of classicism, Rococo, and neo-classicism in this light and pick out schematically three major steps in the development of the beholder's conception of himself: (a) the classic stage of not being aware of his existence as beholder at all; (b) the Rococo stage of his being self-consciously aware of himself as beholder; (c) the neo-classic stage of his being aware of his absence (or non-existence) as beholder. If such a schema were acceptable, it would clearly furnish the materials needed to explain why what superficially looks as though it is much the same matter – dramatic history painting, for instance – should evoke different responses from beholders of these different sorts. Transferring old wine to new casks naturally lends it a distinct bouquet.

[3] By the characters, I think, rather than the artist, since the introduction of the artist here would lead even more directly to the estrangement from the scene which the early neo-classical painter seeks to avoid. It would lead me to foreground the belief that I am confronted by a picture that we are supposing to have receded. This is sharply brought out in Fried's response to the question of why Diderot was not led to extol still-life painting, whose subject-matter, being inanimate, was literally incapable of evincing awareness of the beholder. 'The answer is implicit in much that has gone before: inanimate subject matter made the artistic and presentational aspects *of the painting itself* all the more obtrusive by imposing almost desperate demands of technique and by calling attention to the fact that the objects depicted by the painter were chosen by him,

arranged by him, illuminated by him, and in general exhibited by him to
the beholder.' (p. 102)

[4] Misleadingly, because it suggests that the depicted characters think of
some particular spectator that he does not exist. But all that is needed is
that as the characters' world stretches out for them into the world that is
in fact that of the beholder, they view it as empty. Thus they do not have
to have the thought of the beholder at all, not even negatively.

[5] A. C. Danto, *The Transfiguration of the Commonplace* (Harvard University
Press, Cambridge, Mass., 1981), p. 119.

[6] This truth should encourage one to reflect on the way in which Fried
states his initial 'paradox', endorsing the inference that because paintings
are made to be beheld, they presuppose the existence of a beholder
(p. 103). I suspect that even an achieved painting could be explained in
terms of the responses of a hypothetical spectator. At most, the presupposition is made by a painting that is *recognized* to be successful. But
nothing much hinges on this adjustment, since the 'paradox' will in fact
be no less forceful when cast in hypothetical terms, only more cumber-
some to state.

[7] See Wollheim, *Painting as an Art*, ch. 3, E 3. Fried's book is reviewed in
footnotes.

[8] Any full treatment of this theme which hoped to make it work harder than
I do would need to make out that the spectator who is imaginatively
displaced might legitimately be thought of as x or y, as the case might be,
rather than merely as some indefinitely specified far-off *internal* beholder,
which would quite defeat the point of the exercise. I fancy that the
illusionistic vehicle may not be for nothing here, but even then, more will
need to be said. My own tentative and brief suggestion on this score can
be found in § 10.

[9] The *position* of the spectator, mark, not the spectator himself, since we
were to envisage the place at which we stand outside the picture as vacant.
None the less, the difference of direction is still present: in the one case
we move the pictured scene to our world, in the other we move our world
to the pictured scene.

[10] At p. 248 Fried comments on the parallel between the pastoral effect and
what is achieved in film (cf. n. 78).

[11] Compare the linguistic case in which the master says: 'The last of you lot
to leave, turn out the lights.' Jones minor, who leaves last, will have a
deficient understanding of the order unless he recognizes that he is to
turn out the lights, even though the master did not refer to him or to
anyone else in saying what he did. To manifest full understanding of his
master in the context, the boy needs to refer to himself in his own
thought.

18

Drawing from Life

ANTONIA PHILLIPS

In his essay *On Drawing an Object* (1965) Richard Wollheim makes a suggestive remark about the nature of the activity of drawing. He proposes that the techniques of representation generally, and of drawing in particular, can sometimes reveal what the draughtsman saw. This may sound like an obvious point, but it raises a number of distinctively philosophical questions.[1]

Wollheim does not mean that what a man draws in response to 'What did you see?' can reveal *which* thing he saw, but rather *how* what he saw looked to him. Of course not every drawing produced can do this, but only, he suggests, one which is 'the result of a process within which judgements of adequacy or inadequacy, of verisimilitude or distortion will have an essential place' (p. 8). Something close to this conception of drawing what we see lies, he believes, at the heart of our idea of naturalistic art as an exploration of how things look to us. If Wollheim's suggestion is true, then we want to know more about what kind of process it is that enables a competent draughtsman to produce drawings which show how what he saw looked to him. Now there is an activity which is an activity of drawing what you see *par excellence*, and it is drawing from life, or after nature. Given the rather different concerns of his essay, Wollheim does not allude to it specifically, but it must have been very much in his thoughts. In this essay, I want to pursue Wollheim's suggestion by examining what it is to draw something from life, because it is an activity widely believed to have just the potential we need for showing us what the artist saw *and* how it looked to him.[2] It may be that there are other activities which also fill the bill, for example, drawing something from memory. There are interesting issues here, such as whether drawing something from memory is a distinct activity (see below). Be that as it may, it is not a more promising candidate than drawing from life.

Drawing from life occupies a singular position in the history of, and thought about, art. Since the Renaissance, it has had an unrivalled place in the training of artists, because it is believed to be central to the development of generalizable skills which until recently were thought to be indispensable to artists and designers: specifically, in the development of skills for the achievement of naturalistic effects and hence also in the evolution of naturalism. Following Wollheim's suggestion beyond the scope of this essay, if it is indeed in the nature of drawing from life to reveal how things look, we are closer to explaining its historical connection to the ideals of naturalism in the fine arts.[3]

Pictures drawn from life have two important features. First, like photographs and portraits, they are necessarily *of*[4] some actual object, and so belong to the class of pictures which stand in some specific relation or other, possibly representational, to a segment of reality. I say 'possibly representational' because pictures can come to be *of* an object in several different but often overlapping ways, depending on how they were produced – what intentions, processes, and activity brought them into being. This means that there are a variety of factors which can underpin a relation between what a picture depicts and objects in the world, and it is an open question – and a theoretical one at that – which, if any, of these relations are *representational* relations. Fundamental differences among these relations – for example, in the way intentions operate – must be registered somehow. In some cases, pictures seem to represent objects in virtue of the artist intending to make it possible for the spectator to identify or know which object his picture is *of*. Portraiture and the representation of historical persons and events constitute main examples of this type of relation.[5] Where this kind of specific intention is lacking, however, something else must link picture and object, and the obvious alternative is to look at some special aspect of the process of production; how a picture is made can sometimes determine which object it is *of*. Photographs belong in this category. Unlike portraiture, photography does not essentially involve the intended identification of the objects they are *of*. We know there existed something – a man, a vase of flowers – that is what they are *of*, but we do not need and are not necessarily intended to know which thing it was. I believe that drawings from life are like photographs in this respect. They too are *of* their objects in virtue of how they are made (their individual causal histories) rather than in virtue of specific identificational intentions.[6] Whether or not photographs and drawings from life *represent* the objects they are *of*, and if they do, how this sense of 'represents' relates to the sense underpinned by identificational intentions, are questions beyond the scope of this essay.

Secondly, again like photographs and portraits, pictures drawn from life (by competent hands – interestingly, it is not an activity in which young children much engage) tend to be pictures which are regarded as presenting *likenesses* of their objects. What is meant by the notion of likeness here is of course highly problematic, and I shall have to rely heavily on intuition. The intuitive notion I have in mind is one of likeness holding between picture and object relativized to a perceiver, so that when I talk of a picture *x* being a likeness of an object *y*, I mean that *x* seems to a perceiver *A* like *y* (*x* strikes *A* as like *y*). It is important to see that this notion is not *merely* a case of what might be termed the perception of generic likeness, although, of course, it is that as well. What strikes the perceiver is that the picture looks like a particular instance of some kind – a particular object. The intuition here is that there are pictures – many portraits, photographs, and those drawn from life – which present likenesses of their objects in a sense which seems more specific than 'generic likeness', and this is something which must be accommodated in any account of drawing from life, as well as of the concepts of a portrait or a photograph.

In this sense, when *x* seems to *A* like *y*, it does not mean that *A* believes that there is some objective likeness between the two items; nor does *A* have to know in what respect the two items strike him as being alike. This notion of likeness also admits of degree. But there is a danger of misunderstanding here – and this is where a second unanalysed notion comes in.[7] The idea of likeness I want to invoke does not, strictly speaking, hold between picture and object, although I will continue to use this misleading form of expression in order to avoid excessive circumlocution. When I say that a picture may strike a perceiver as like the object it is *of*, I mean this: the spectator *sees* something *in* a picture which strikes him as like a particular object. We are dealing, in other words, with a three-place intentional relation of some kind between a perceiver, what that perceiver sees in a picture, and some object. What is meant by *seeing* something *in* a picture is also highly problematic; so I will rely on an intuitive understanding of the notion, which certainly exists, although it may not survive philosophical scrutiny. We speak quite freely about what we see in pictures; for example, in Titian's *Perseus and Andromeda* at the Wallace Collection, we see a naked woman chained to a rock, a youth with shield and sword flying to her rescue, the sea churned up by a gaping dragon, the woman's look of terror mixed with hope, the youth's bravery fuelled by love, and so on. The notion of likeness I am invoking applies within the scope of representation; something seen in a picture strikes the perceiver as like something else. But in this essay I leave it an open question how exactly this notion relates to the perception of likeness between objects outside pictorial representation, as when a perceiver sees a likeness between two faces. Nor do I have anything to say here about the nature of representational seeing or about the concept of depiction.[8]

A final preliminary point: the idea of a drawing done from life typically conjures up visions of an art school life class or of an artist sketching a landscape; and indeed, studies after the model or nature do constitute central cases of drawing from life. But we must not rule out the possibility that other kinds of picture are produced which may also need to be included in the category, even though the English expression 'drawing from life' may not normally be used to cover these cases. Examples might be culled from drawings of existing buildings and topographical drawings, from anatomical, zoological, and botanical drawings, and so on: *prima facie*, whenever a picture is produced by someone drawing something he sees. Even if we concentrate entirely on drawing from a model, the concept I wish to explore extends in another way beyond what ordinary usage suggests, for the activity of drawing from life is not limited to materials and media associated with *drawing* as commonly conceived: it is not restricted, for instance, by notions of linearity or independence from colour or by materials. Most pictorial media are suitable, and so pictures done from life will include water-colours, pastels, oils, as well as pencil, ink, charcoal, metal point, and so forth. They may be works on paper or vellum, but also on board, canvas, wood – on almost any surface suitable for picture-making.[9]

What we are after is a specific drawing activity capable of revealing how something the artist sees looked to him, but how is 'what the artist sees' to be understood? For drawing what is seen could be thought to include cases of hallucination or cases in which the objects seen are not present to the artist's senses when he draws them. Whether or not drawing *from life* can include drawing something hallucinated (a 'vision'), such cases would certainly be peripheral. More interesting, and potentially more threatening, is the fact that many artists represent people, things, and places they have seen from memory. Drawing from memory has many virtues to recommend it as a method of recording what is seen and of sharpening observation and visual memory. Like drawing what you see as you see it, drawing something seen from memory might issue in pictures which are both *of* some actual thing and likenesses of that thing.

Is drawing something seen as you see it essentially the same activity as drawing something seen from memory, with the latter perhaps being a subspecies of the former? The stress placed on drawing from memory by some artists might seem to suggest that it is (although no one has suggested drawing from memory as a substitute for anyone wholly untrained in drawing from life). But there are a number of interconnected considerations against thinking that the two activities are really the same. In the first place, they are subjectively very different.[10] For example, drawing from life is much *harder*, which suggests that the object plays a more complex role in the activity than it does in the case of drawing from memory. If the two activities were basically the same, one would expect drawing from life to be easier; but all the evidence points the other way. Secondly, there is a *prima facie* oddity in the idea that the presence to the artist's senses of the object to be drawn makes no fundamental difference to the nature of the activity of drawing it. (Why do artists bother with models and going out of doors?) Thirdly, when drawing something seen from memory, all the artist has are his original observations: although reflection may improve and enrich his recollection of what was seen, he cannot sharpen his observations as he works because this involves checking his perceptions.[11] One of the most important ways in which drawing from life features in the training of artists is in teaching them to look at what they see and to do so in the light of actual drawing procedures. Fourthly, there are distinctions which might not survive if the two activities were regarded as basically the same, only taking different kinds of objects (seen things and remembered things): for example, the distinction we make between life studies and the adaptation (or idealization) of them in the studio, perhaps as patterns or models for other pictures. Artists often draw or paint something from nature – for example, a landscape – and then work on the picture in the studio as well, drawing upon their memory of the scene; so there can be cases of a picture starting out as a drawing from life but ending up adulterated, so to speak, possibly with its original drawing-from-life element effaced. Of course, even if the two activities are quite distinct, it will not always be easy to separate the fruits of one from the other, but the fact that there are cases which are difficult to decide does not itself jeopardize the distinctness of the concept of a drawing from life. And it may well be that the two activities harness the same skills – indeed, just how the skills used in drawing from life relate to other representational skills is an interesting question. In this essay I will simply set aside the issue of memory to concentrate on what in any case it would be reasonable to regard as the central case of drawing from life, namely drawing an independently existing object as you see it.

If drawing from life is drawing something seen while it is seen, how does this activity produce pictures *of* the objects which were the objects perceived while the picture was being drawn? The mere fact that the artist sees a particular object while he makes a picture in which can be seen an object of the same kind does not make it a picture *of* the very object he saw. Even when we have the opportunity of watching an artist at work, we can have serious doubts.

We might have reason to doubt that the artist genuinely intends to draw what he sees; or the artist might be deluded as to what it is that he sees and intends to draw. More interestingly, it is possible that an artist intends to draw what he sees – an apple on a plate or a reclining woman or a man's face – but that he produces a picture in which we see a highly schematic or simple outline of an apple or a woman or a face. If the artist then claims that this is a drawing of that particular apple (or woman or face), we might not take him at his word. For in what way would the intention to draw *that apple* have shown itself to have been operative in the production of the drawing? Our unwillingness to take the artist at his word is not due to the picture failing to be apple-depicting; nor does it have to do with a kink in his perceptual contact with the actual apple (as it might if it were the case that, contrary to all appearances, the artist was not in fact seeing the apple itself, but was hallucinating a qualitatively similar apple). Nor does our unwillingness stem from a belief that the picture is poorly drawn, for we can imagine the problem arising in connection with a highly skilled draughtsman, whose schematic outline manifests his skill as a draughtsman.

Our doubts here as to whether the drawing is *of* the object seen are likely to arise from the feeling that the picture simply does not present a sufficient likeness of the relevant particular object (we might insist on more detail, for example). It is true that, typically, drawings done from life tend to be located towards the more naturalistic end of a naturalistic/non-naturalistic ordering of pictures, but we do not want simply to rule out a drawing from counting as a drawing *of* something done from life because of an alleged lack of likeness or detail between picture and object. For an artist might perfect a highly simplified or distilled style, and so produce highly simplified drawings from life. (Think of Matisse.)

On the other hand, we must not be over-generous either. There are many drawings purporting to be *of* something drawn while it was seen which we would hesitate to count as drawings *from life* – for example, many drawings by children and by competent draughtsmen working in what might be described as naïve or childish styles. Although there is a sense in which such pictures present a likeness of a seen object because they show it as having visual properties it is perceived to have (often to a degree sufficient to allow identification), none the less we might not judge these pictures as having captured 'how their objects look'. (The difference I have in mind is intuitive. In psychological discussions it has often been characterized in terms of the problematic distinction between concept and percept as applied to drawings; while in art history the difference is sometimes thought to be a matter of stylization: thus Giotto is stylized in some way or to a degree which Titian or Velazquez are not.) If, nevertheless, we treat such pictures as genuine drawings from life, then it would result in such a widening of the extension of the concept of drawing from life that we could not hope to account for the historical connection of drawing from life to the evolution of naturalism. If it is argued that this consequence is avoidable by regarding these children's drawings as *unsuccessful* drawings from life, it would have to be explained why children have so little success, and for so long, in doing something it is claimed that they can do: namely, draw from life. (Imagine this position being taken with regard to writing or doing arithmetic.) The better alternative is to seek out some feature of the activity of drawing from life which excludes the bulk of these problematic cases.

Although we tend to argue from what a drawing looks like to its being drawn from life and our schematic apple picture and many children's drawings fail to support such an inference, we cannot in fact ever rely wholly on the visual character of a picture. This is not just because we want to allow for the possibility that what does not seem like a drawing from life could be one none the less – even if untypical – but also because something could look like a typical drawing from life without actually being one. There can be realistic, detailed, and highly 'individualized' pictures such that what they represent, a landscape or a bowl of fruit for example, does not stand in a causal relation via thoughts, intentions, and perception to any particular landscape or bowl of fruit. Artists can represent things, from apples to mountain landscapes, naturalistically out of their heads, and such pictures are not *of* anything.[12]

There is another source of possible doubts about a picture's status as a drawing from life. Imagine a highly skilled draughtsman who can faithfully draw from life most things he sees, but who has an aberration with regard to apples: whenever he tries to draw apples from life, he produces a very naturalistic representation of a Cox apple (say) that is virtually the same from occasion to occasion, irrespective of what the particular apple he is observing looks like – it might be a red Mackintosh.[13] Clearly this artist is not producing genuine drawings from life of apples, in spite of his intentions and what he sees. But what is lacking is not a simple matter of likeness between what he sees and what he draws, for we would be no more inclined to count a particular drawing of an apple by this artist as a drawing from life when the apple he draws happens to look like the apple he sees. In his case we cannot say that had the apple he intended to draw from life been different, then his drawing too would have been different.[14] The fact that occasionally he may produce a seemingly perfect draw-ing from life of an apple is going to be set against the fact of his aberration, and so we are not going to accept any drawings of apples from him as drawn from life without some special reason.

This example shows that a picture may fail to be a drawing from life even though the artist drew the object while able to see it *and* the fruit of his efforts is a picture in which something looking like that object can be seen. Clearly, not any process of production will do. Rather than search for features distinctive of drawings done from life, we must find features distinctive of the process which produces them. The right process will be one which connects the elements of causality and likeness in drawing from life in such a way as to eliminate fortuitousness (as in the aberration regarding apples case), while re-maining flexible enough to accommodate untypical cases (as in the schematic apple case) and the variety of styles in which artists work.

Interestingly, parallel difficulties crop up in the case of photo-graphy, where abnormal production processes can discount some-thing from being a photograph despite having apparently photographic features. Here, too, it is central to an account of what it is for something to be a photograph of an object that it have been produced by certain independently specifiable, regular, physical and chemical processes involving cameras, light, lenses, photosensitive film, and so on. However, there is nothing in drawing from life quite analogous to a photographic process.

Of course, when someone draws what they see, something of a physical nature is going on, and in the hands of an experienced draughtsman from life, what is going on certainly can appear to the onlooker like a regular and 'mechanical' activity. Even so, there is not enough substance behind this appearance to solve our problem. I suggest that we shift attention from the idea of a specifiable physical process to the idea of a *skill* lying at the heart of the activity of drawing from life, and make the skill play the role which the concept of a photographic process plays in the definition of a photograph. If we can define a skill the exercise of which produces something having certain properties – this is the activity or process – then we can define a drawing done from life of an object as the result of the application of that skill to a particular object or scene. This proposal will work only if it can be shown that there is a specific skill in drawing from life which is identifiable independently of the products of the activity. A brief look at traditional artistic training offers some encouragement in thinking that these requirements can be met.

From the end of the fourteenth century until quite recently, drawing has formed the core of artistic training in the West. Schools and academies gradually formed in which the curriculum and training programme did not vary much in its fundamentals: anatomy, perspective, geometry, proportion, and so forth complemented practical lessons in drawing and painting. Many treatises were published to guide the student and craftsman, and they reinforced the basic format. The study of drawing itself for a long time followed a rigid pattern: students began by copying from the flat – that is, copying drawings and prints, often works by established masters, collected by the studio, workshop, or school; they progressed to representing static three-dimensional objects, usually antique sculptures and plaster casts; and finally to the most difficult stage, drawing from life. The three stages provided the grounding believed to be essential before painting was attempted, and many great artists continued to practise some or all the stages throughout their careers. What knowledge and skills was this training, now unfortunately abandoned in many art schools, believed to generate? Manual dexterity and discipline of course, familiarity with the works of masters and classic ideals, the acquisition of patterns, and a vocabulary of forms and schemas or stereotypes for future use. Drawing being believed to be the medium of invention, its practice would also stimulate invention. But these benefits might conceivably accrue even without the student's achieving the third stage, the practice of drawing from life. What is the special contribution of the final stage? The largest part of it stems both from its deeply empirical nature and from the problems nature herself sets for picture-making. In drawing from life, observation of the world (principally using sight and thought to gather information about it and about how it looks to us) plays a unique role, in which integrity becomes a value.[15] Drawing what is seen, observed, experienced while seeing, observing, experiencing it offers the artist the best opportunity of making as exact a representation of what he sees (and how it looks to him) as possible. But drawing from life also poses special problems for someone wishing to draw what he sees. What he sees is too much to make a picture out of, so to speak. The artist must select elements in what he sees for transcription as elements of his picture; he must decide which elements to place first on the page, where to place them, how to follow on, and so forth. Choices are made both about what of nature to take and about how the picture is to be built out of the artist's marks. All this complexity arises even from an intention to record in the simplest fashion what one sees, without any attempt at higher-order pictorial values such as expressive content.

The fact that in drawing from life there is a complex process of selection and decision explains why prior training in picture-making is necessary. It also suggests why the traditional three-stage pattern of training takes the order it does. For the order is one in which the trainee gradually progresses to tasks requiring increasing amounts of decision-making. At first he copies other pictures – he does not need to decide how his picture is to be built. When he progresses to the next stage, of drawing static three-dimensional objects, many decisions have been taken beforehand; in the case of antique sculptures, the student is presented with forms already wrought into art; in the case of a still life, the objects have been chosen and arranged already. But at the final stage, the student is faced with a model, a landscape – and everything has yet to be decided.[16]

We have seen that much of the traditional training programme does not involve the activity of drawing from life itself; but it might be wondered why the activity described in the second stage (drawing after the antique, still life) is not already one of drawing from life. After all, we have not set any restriction on the kind of objects which may be drawn from life (other than that they be visible to the artist as he draws them), so what really distinguishes stages two and three, besides mere degree of decision-making? Or to put the question more sharply, why is the student who achieves competence in this stage but goes no further in the training programme not a draughtsman possessing a full-fledged skill in drawing from life? Although it may not be possible to draw a firm line here, the description of the training programme itself suggests why the skill exercised in drawing from life may not be fully developed until the third stage is completed. It is only in the third stage that the artist tackles objects which are untouched by pictorial and artistic intentions, such as the human body, faces, and landscapes, to mention only the most difficult (hence drawing *from life* or *after nature*).[17] Competence in this stage ensures possession of a skill with a generalizable nature, one which enables the draughtsman who has it to make a picture out of *anything* he sees.[18] And, of course, once he has it, he can apply it to still-life arrangements.

So far, we have been working on the assumption of a simple characterization of drawing from life as drawing something seen while it is present to the senses, sight in particular. But this characterization leaves it unclear how visual perception contributes to the activity of drawing from life. Because of this, we are not yet in a position to see how it is that, as Wollheim proposed, drawing what is seen can reveal how things look to us, let alone how drawing something from life constitutes a good way of fulfilling the aim of showing how something looked. To achieve a better characterization (that is, one which shows how perception and the skill interlock) of drawing from life, we need, I think, to consider its paradigmatic case, namely what goes on in the art school life class.

A life class consists of students engaged in drawing a model who is placed in such a way that each student can see the model as he draws. The students are trying to capture a likeness of the model's appearance (how it looks), and that is why the model is there. But this practical function does not seem to exhaust the role played by the model in drawing from life. What further effect does its presence have? In particular, what effect does it have on the kind of picture produced?

It is a striking fact about drawing from life that the artist draws what he sees from a particular position. He may stand back, move forward, walk around his model; but however much he moves around, he comes back to a viewing position closely related to the position of his drawing surface (on an easel or on his lap), a position from which he looks at the model while drawing. The artist's gaze shifts constantly from model to support, and back.[19] What reason is there for staying in the same place? Could there be an explanation of this fact which ignored the claim that being in a particular position relative to the model has a significant effect upon the nature of the activity of drawing from life? I think the answer must be 'No', and the reason has to do with what is involved in representing how something looks.

How something appears or looks is tied to its appearing or looking thus and so *to someone*, and so it is to be expected that an artist engaged in drawing a model from life typically endeavours to capture a likeness of how what he sees – the model – looks *to him*. And indeed, as spectators we do tend to assume, when we look at a finished, successful life drawing, that we will see in it how the model looked to the artist.[20] Now, how something looks to someone is partly dependent on his position in relation to that thing while looking at it, and changes in his relative position can of course affect how what he sees looks to him. The perceiver's position relative to the object viewed yields a point of view, and this point of view is one factor among others in structuring how what the artist sees looks to him. If this is even roughly correct, then the idea of an artist attempting to represent how something he sees looks to him contains an implicit reference to his point of view. Indeed, the artist engaged in drawing something from life is acutely sensitive to the minutest shifts in his perceptual relation to his model. In representing how the model looks to him, the artist's position relative to the model will form part of the content of his representation; *somehow* the artist's viewpoint will manifest itself in his realization of how the model looks to him. This is what is distinctive about drawing from life.

If a picture of something seen is to reveal how that thing looked to the artist, then it must manifest the artist's viewpoint. But how is the idea of a point of view to be understood? Is it determined by the artist looking with his head rigid and one fixed eye? This would closely parallel the camera's viewpoint, and be consistent with strict perspectival projection; but it is too severe an interpretation to be true to normal perceptual activity and to ordinary usage of the expression 'point of view' – according to which a person's point of view is conceived as a position from which he looks in a particular direction without moving the head very much. Given actual practices, the artist's viewpoint need not be conceived more precisely than this. Thus conceived, it can be manifested pictorially by a great range of pictures, from those with strict perspectival projection to those with more intimate or impressionistic representation of space. What is ruled out by even so rough a conception of viewpoint are pictures without a viewpoint and pictures with multiple viewpoints.

It is sometimes thought that any picture depicting an object manifests point of view: all that is required to do this is that a side or face of the object is shown, and it is not possible to depict an object without showing a face of it. If this were all there is to a picture's manifesting a point of view, it would rob the notion of explanatory power. On this supposition even the Bayeux Tapestry manifests a point of view; like many children's drawings, it shows objects from one side with relative distance rendered in terms of overlap. Yet no one would claim that the Bayeux Tapestry shows us how any battle looked, let alone the Battle of Hastings.

Anyone who goes to art galleries will have experienced occasions on which he has attempted to work out a picture's point of view. One way of doing this is to imagine a place from which what one sees in the picture could look like an actual scene. (This will sometimes involve following perspectival clues.) Thus one might come to imagine oneself in that notional place from which the picture yields up a field of view. Figuring out a picture's viewpoint frequently yields the artist's viewpoint: this is how we can discover where, for example, Cézanne sat as he painted Mont Sainte-Victoire. (The possibility and extent of spectator thoughts such as these is a useful guide to how naturalistic a picture is.) In the case of the Bayeux Tapestry there is no imaginable place from which what we see in the picture could look to anyone (with our visual system) remotely like a battle at Hastings. If the idea of a pictorial point of view has no connection with the possibility of these kinds of thoughts and speculations, and if it is divorced from the idea of a perceptual point of view, then we deprive ourselves of a means of distinguishing pictures which represent how something looks from pictures (possibly of something seen), which do not (for example, many children's drawings). If, on the other hand, drawing from life is thought of as linked to the viewpoint a person has when looking at something from a particular place, then we can see how drawing what one sees could lead to representing how things look – and so to a naturalistic art. The practice of drawing from life is in this way connected to the development of naturalism.

Multiplicity of viewpoint is in some ways more problematic, and might prove difficult to distinguish from vagueness of viewpoint. There are two main forms in which such multiplicity can occur in pictures. There are cases in which the picture is built up out of two or more spatial projections, each having a distinct viewpoint. Some of Canaletto's *vedute* seem to belong to this category, because they incorporate several perspectival projections, each probably based on distinct life studies from distinct (if fairly contiguous) viewpoints (for example, from the same place, but looking in a slightly different direction). This is a familiar way of building up a panorama, and is practised by photographers too. Artists experimenting with perspective have been fond of making pictures containing several viewpoints, sometimes exploiting the tension this can create.

The second form in which multiplicity of viewpoint occurs is when there are radical breaks, interruptions, and reversals of viewpoint (for example, in some cubist Picasso pictures, some recent Hockney interiors), and also when slighter shifts in viewpoint are superimposed one upon the other (for example, *perhaps* in some of Auerbach's portraits and studies of models). If gradual shifts between contiguous viewpoints (which can easily result, intentionally or not, from slight shifts in the relative positions of artist and model from sitting to sitting) must be acceptable, given the pre-theoretical range of types of drawings from life, does this mean that we have also to accept the more extreme cases just mentioned as well? I think not, but the line will not be clear-cut. The crucial point to bear in mind is that what makes a picture a drawing from life is not so much what it looks like, but how it was produced: the activity of drawing something from life by its perceptual nature refers to a point of view from which the artist looks at a model. But the extent to which the product – the drawing – manifests or matches that viewpoint depends on many pictorial considerations other than the aim of capturing this element of how things look. Therefore we should expect cases which are difficult to decide (including those cases called untypical earlier) and a certain amount of pragmatism in respect of them when not all the facts about them are available to us.

Suppose an artist sees something which looks thus and so (a ripe lemon on a grey dish, for example) and initiates and engages in an activity of drawing it; if he possesses the skill of drawing from life, then, other things being equal (for example, use of colour in our example), he will produce a picture in which something which looks thus and so (a ripe lemon on a grey dish) can be seen. This in essence is what it is to have the skill exercised in drawing from life. By introducing elements of description referring to visual properties, this basic idea can be elaborated. In the definition which follows, the likeness required between how what the artist sees looked to him and what can be seen in the picture which is the outcome of an activity of drawing from life is captured in terms of matching properties.

This definition is not intended to be complete, and afterwards I indicate some of the refinements and details which would need to be worked in.

For any object Y and any properties $F_1 \ldots F_n$ and any time T and an activity of drawing D, D is an activity of drawing Y as looking $F_1 \ldots F_n$ from life if and only if D is the exercise of a skill such that if any artist sees Y as looking $F_1 \ldots F_n$ at time T and the artist at T exercises his or her skill in relation to Y, then by means of that skill the artist will produce a picture X such that spectators can see something $F_1 \ldots F_n$ in X.

The concept of a drawing from life now becomes definable in terms of the activity which produces it, roughly: X is a drawing from life of Y if and only if X is the outcome of an activity of drawing from life taking Y as input. (So X could be a successful or unsuccessful drawing from life of Y.)

(1)   Not any predicate can feature as a substitution instance for one of the set of properties $F_1 \ldots F_n$. As a rule, the description 'looking $F_1 \ldots F_n$' will include a sortal term and a sufficient number of predicates describing shape, colour, size, as well as spatial relations, posture, brightness, texture, and so on. The description, in other words, should comprise a fairly full description of how the object Y looks to the artist. What exactly is meant by a visual property is a difficult question. Roughly, properties detectable by the sense of sight, such as the kind just listed; but what is detectable by sight is itself problematic. In the context of this essay, I would certainly count physiognomic properties, for instance, as visual; but what about properties like being alive or dead, sick, hungry, brave, in love, all detectable by sight as well? Since the problem cannot be pursued here, I will simply assume an unanalysed notion of a visual property, in the hope that any outcome of analysis which honours intuition will be compatible with this essay's proposals.

(2)   It is also important that the set of properties $F_1 \ldots F_n$ should remain open, so that the complete definition does not imply that there must be perfect coincidence between the properties of the object as seen from the artist's point of view and the properties of the object seen in the picture. But problems arise as soon as we try to be more specific regarding which and how many properties get registered. We must dispel any suggestion that the success of a drawing from life is a simple matter of the number of visual properties a drawing from life of an object represents it as having. What counts as a sufficient number of properties will vary from case to case according to several factors, all of them deeply interwined. First, in practice the skill is not applied by each possessor of it to *any* object with equal expectation of success; not just because some objects may require a greater skill than others (for example, faces), but also because artists tend to develop 'specialities' with the result that their skills are more developed in relation to some kinds of objects than others (which kinds is a matter of talent and personal preference). Secondly, there are not some kinds of properties which are intrinsically more important than others, so that if the object in question is perceived to have one of these 'more important' properties, then a drawing from life of the object should show it as having that property. Artists differ in what they take to be salient properties, and such variations reflect what aspects of the visible world an artist is personally interested in. (Artists develop specialization with regard to visual properties.) Thirdly, there are properties which can be represented only at the expense of others,

due to limitations of the medium used, technique, and so forth. And of course, some mediums exclude certain properties; lead pencil does not register colours, for example. Lastly, the purpose for which the drawing from life is being made – portrait study, sketch, caricature, and so on – also affects which and how many properties of the object are recorded.

(3)   As it stands, the definition does not capture the selectivity of the skill. Even if it is agreed that the success of a drawing from life is not merely a matter of the number of properties it represents the object as having, and that there need not be perfect coincidence between the sets of seen properties and represented properties, yet it might be thought that the process of selection of properties to be registered in the picture is independent of the exercise of the skill upon those chosen. In other words, that the artist looks upon a scene, selects some of the properties he sees there, and then applies his skill to them so as to produce a picture in which those properties can be seen. (The artist would not have to do the choosing all at once, of course; it could be done in stages, in response to whatever he had done on the picture surface so far.)

Although it is true that while an artist is learning to draw from life, the process of selection and the effort of representation can seem as separate as this view of the matter would have it, such a characterization does not seem true of the skill when it is full-fledged. In this case, the skill seems to lie deeper, and be intertwined with other representational skills and talents, so that when an artist possesses it, it is the skill itself which in large part governs the process of selection. Artists who draw from life do not differ merely in what visual properties they happen to select and in the degree of skill they possess and have applied; the skill of each artist is itself highly individual (in the case of the best), determining what particular choices are made. Internalization probably accounts for something here: much of the training which leads to the acquisition and consolidation of the skill of drawing from life is devoted to the aim of internalizing, through habit and practice, the selective processes. (Internalization may also account for why it is that artists come to see objects and scenes as conforming to their individual skill, to see things as potential motifs.)

(4)   Clearly, two or more artists exercising their skill in drawing from life in relation to the same object or scene may produce pictures in which subsets of the set of properties $F_1 \ldots F_n$ are registered with little overlap; indeed, it is possible, although difficult, for there to be no overlap at all (perhaps two artists could set out to achieve this as

a matter of policy). Such potential variation might be thought incompatible with the idea that drawing from life can reveal how the world looks to us and to undermine our ability to judge whether a picture produced by an activity of drawing from life is successful or not. This would certainly be a consequence of a subjective interpretation of 'how something looks to the artist' – it would be merely a coincidence that a picture drawn from life happened to show to more than one perceiver how an object looks. But we can see the truth in the idea that drawing from life is representing 'a corner of nature seen through a temperament' (to borrow Zola's idea) without falling into subjectivism by making explicit an assumption of normality – perceptual and mental – on the part of the artist. We have seen how the detection of abnormality (hallucinations, aberrations) can cast serious doubts upon the status of particular products of drawing activity; it may be that there is a range of abnormalities, such as astigmatisms, which would not similarly cast doubts. But if an astigmatic artist's drawings manifesting his astigmatism are genuine drawings from life, they will not in this respect capture how the world looks to normal perceivers. (The situation could change, however, if astigmatism became the norm – in which case an 'early' astigmatic artist's pictures might retrospectively come to reveal how the world looks.)

A complete definition would need to make explicit this element of idealization – that the artist is a normal perceiver, in a normal state of mind, in normal perceptual conditions, and so on.

(5) Since drawings from life cannot be produced unmediated by a perceiver, the definition is relative to what the artist actually sees, as opposed to what might have been seen. This is in clear contrast to photography. A photograph can be *of* (and show) objects the photographer did not notice. More extremely, photographs can be produced independently of being taken by someone; for example, a camera may be set up to click at preset intervals. So one might think that in drawing from life, unlike photography, objects in the scene which are unseen by the artist cannot get registered in the picture he produces as a result of the activity of drawing from life. Assuming that the artist is a normal perceiver in a normal state of mind, what he does not see will not show up in his drawing.

Even if broadly true, this last claim needs qualification. Suppose an artist is engaged in drawing a tree upon one of whose branches an iguana is lying, naturally camouflaged; the artist does not identify the iguana, but sees the bumps of the iguana's body, which he takes to be bumps in the branch's outline, whose shape he carefully draws.

Can we, better informed than the artist about what is there to be seen, point to the relevant place in his drawing and say 'There's the iguana'? In the case of a photograph, the answer would be affirmative, but in the case of a drawing, intuition is unlikely to provide a clear answer. (It would be interesting to consider why exactly it is that we feel an asymmetry to exist between the two cases.) There is a parallel kind of case regarding unnoticed visual properties of seen objects, about which intuition is still less clear. Suppose an artist is engaged in drawing a model's face in careful detail, and later examines the finished drawing from life and notices that in the picture the model looks ill, something he had not noticed while the model was present. Is this a case of a visual property of the model being realized in the picture although it had not been noticed at the time of drawing?

Both these examples raise questions about seeing, visual experience, and about what counts as a visual property, problems that cannot be pursued here. I do not think that the definition of drawing from life is inflexible with regard to the outcome of these questions; but it seems clear that if unnoticed properties and objects can get registered in a drawing from life, this cannot be a widespread phenomenon; for what would become of our hope that drawing what we see can reveal how things look to us?

(6) The skill exercised in drawing from life admits of degree; it can be improved or lost, and it is maintained by practice. One who possesses it need not manifest it in every product of its exercise (for example, when tackling difficult or unfamiliar kinds of object). None the less, there is a level (or success proportion) below which its possession becomes questionable. In this respect, drawing from life is comparable to photography ('Is this camera working?').

In practice it may be difficult to distinguish failed or unsuccessful drawings from life from pictures that are not drawings from life. Also, because the acquisition of the skill is by training and practice, the borderline between the products of the process of acquiring the skill and the products of a full-fledged skill will never be a sharp one. It may also be difficult to tell whether a picture is an unsuccessful drawing from life or a non-standard or deviant drawing from life, because of the possibility of a genuine activity of drawing from life issuing in untypical drawings from life (as in the case of the schematic apple); and this possibility becomes more likely in the hands of real artists (for example, Matisse, Van Gogh, Cézanne). Non-standard (that is, successful untypical) drawings from life are non-standard with reference to the typical aims or expectations of the activity of drawing from life, but they are linked to the standard cases by being products of the same kind of activity. A parallel point and distinction holds in the case of photographs. In both drawing from life and photography there can be cases where doubts concerning the success or status of a particular product may evaporate when we have further information about its production – for example, who the drawing is by or what special equipment was used (special lenses, high-speed film, and so on).

(7) We have seen that the skill exercised in the production of drawings from life is one that is acquired by practice and training, and also that much of this training does not involve the activity of drawing from life itself. Dexterity with the materials of drawing, as well as experience in the construction of pictures are two of the most important prerequisites of attempts at drawing from life.[21] It might be wondered whether such a requirement of dexterity and 'picture know-how' is not far too strong; after all, do not young children draw from life? Certainly psychologists doing research on children's drawings set children tasks in which they are asked to draw objects they can see: a cup, a glass beaker half-filled with water, a cube, a model house, and the like. Many of these children are very young, without much dexterity or experience in picture-making; yet apparently they produce pictures *of* those objects arranged before them. If I am right, then the question as to whether young children's drawings of what they see are genuine drawings from life is going to depend not only on their drawing skills (representational techniques and so on), but also on whether they can be shown to satisfy the conceptual demands implicit in the exercise of the skill, including a reference to a point of view. It is often said that children's drawings fail to show how something seen looks *because* there is no viewpoint manifest. Their drawings tend to be arranged by psychologists in a progressive order according to how far their drawings approach certain canonical views of familiar objects. The schemas themselves are arranged in a progressive order: the more demanding they are, the more they include viewpoint cues.[22] It may be that the activity of drawing something from life is conceptually too sophisticated to be engaged in by small children. Again, it may be that even when children can be shown by their other behaviour to possess the relevant concepts, still they may not exercise them in drawing something they see – perhaps because their drawing skills lag behind or for other more mysterious reasons.[23]

In this essay I have tried to flesh out Wollheim's suggestion that drawing what is seen can sometimes reveal how what the draughtsman saw looked to him by exploring the activity which presents the best possible *prima facie* case for realizing this potential. That some account of how this is possible is central to any discussion of visual truth and the ideal of naturalism in the pictorial arts, including photography, is obvious enough. But there are also wider considerations motivating the discussion, which have to do with the variety of ways in which pictures can apparently be related to particular objects. The general line I have taken is that it is essential in thinking about these relations to take into account the variety of processes by which pictures can be produced. Notions of likeness and intention, even when reinforced by reference to causal connections, cannot by themselves provide for a fine-grained enough account of what it is for pictures to be *of* objects. Each of the various relations between picture and object – portrait, photograph, drawing from life, and others – are different enough to invite individual examination. Until this task is taken up, there is no way of telling how far a unitary account of the pictorial representation of particulars is possible.

NOTES

[1] Many people have been generous with comments on various versions of this paper: Ned Block, Sandra Fisher, Michael Podro, Galen Strawson, Chaim Tannenbaum, Richard Wollheim. Very special thanks to W. D. Hart and Malcolm Budd for their helpful criticism.

[2] I use the terms 'artist' and 'draughtsman' interchangeably in this essay.

[3] Indeed, the intuition behind Gombrich's (1960) thesis regarding the pattern of schema and correction – and its progressiveness in the direction of illusionistic art – might be given a stronger interpretation in terms of drawing from life.

[4] I italicize 'of' to signal a use of the expression 'picture of' in which we can make an existential generalization over what the picture represents. If X is a picture *of* Y, then X is such that $(\exists Y)$ (picture of (X, Y)). In Quine's terms, I am concerned with the *relational* use of 'picture of', rather than the *notional* use. Fictions may seem problematic here. Can there not be pictures *of* Pickwick *of* Santa Claus, *of* flying horses? Whatever we make of pictures of fictions, in this essay I am concerned only with what I take to be the basic case of a picture's being *of* an object, and shall not be concerned with fictions at all. It seems likely, in any case, that the problems posed by pictures of fictions will not be taken care of without a general theory of fiction to hand.

[5] This intention does not mean that any spectator must be capable of identifying the relevant object; nor does it mean that the artist must have someone in mind as the spectator capable of making the identification. All that is required is that the artist intend the picture to be such that if

there were a suitable spectator, that spectator could make the intended identification. For a fuller discussion, see my 'The limits of portrayal', in *Philosophy and the Visual Arts*, ed. Andrew Harrison (Reidel, Dordrecht, 1987).

6   Which is not to say that photographs and drawings from life cannot be made with the specific identificational intentions as an additional feature. The point is that a picture's being a photograph or drawn from life does not *ipso facto* make it represent the particular object it is *of* in the above sense, not even when the object it is *of* happens to be identified.

7   Unanalysed by me, that is. Wollheim has, of course, written much on the subject. For the purposes of this essay, there is no commitment to any particular account of 'seeing-in'.

8   When we get to the stage of defining drawing from life, I try to get a hold on this notion of likeness without actually using it within the definition, in the hope of thereby avoiding some of the immediate problems it presents. This strategy is entirely local to this essay's needs.

9   Sculpture raises all kinds of peculiar problems, some of them easier to see at the end of this essay; so I do not deal with it here at all.

10 This subjective difference has been widely noted by artists: for example, by Delacroix, Giacometti, Cézanne, and others.

11 It might be thought that this limitation would be overcome in the case of an artist with a perfect photographic memory, if this is conceived in terms of a perfect memory image. But it would still have to be shown that this is closer to drawing *from life* than copying an image, and that the assumption that a photographic memory registers everything there is to be seen is true.

12 Notice that these cases are quite different from cases in which an individual or object – for example, Socrates or Noah's Ark – is represented and depicted 'naturalistically' from imagination, and made identifiable 'by description'. Pictures of fictions are also a different sort of case, whether naturalistically depicted or not.

13 This example is not as fanciful as it might at first appear, for there is a curious phenomenon of which our case is an extreme example. Some artists when drawing models from life seem to draw virtually the same face every time, irrespective of the particular model's individual features. It is as if an imagined or stylized face (sometimes more like the artist's own face than his model's) is interposed. There may be various explanations of this phenomenon: faces are particularly hard to draw, especially from life; canonical and ideal facial types exert very strong influences; artists may be attracted to particular types of faces for all sorts of reasons, including that they fit the artist's personal ideal. But whatever explanation is favoured, there might be cases extreme enough to raise the question of whether the artist in such a case could be drawing the model's face from life (or only from life).

14 Actually this hypothetical is too strong. See below, § 2 after the definition.

15 The existence of blind sculptors and of painters who continue to paint despite severely weakened vision does not show that sight is not essential

to drawing from life, although in the case of sculpture, because its mediums exploit senses other than sight, notably touch, there is perhaps a stronger case for sight not being essential.

[16] First the master's and tradition's selections will dominate; then, if the student is any good, he develops his own selection from nature and from pictorial forms.

[17] The human form especially invites immediate judgements about whether the draughtsman has 'got it right'; hence the role of life classes as a heuristic method of training.

[18] Although the skill has this general nature, it does not mean that it can be applied by each possessor of it to any object with equal expectation of success. See below.

[19] In *Painting as an Art* (1987) Wollheim extracts much significance from the posture or stance the artist necessarily adopts when engaged in painting. In likewise seeking significance in the physical conditions of the more specific activity of drawing from life, I am, of course, indebted to him; but his discussion, being more general, was not concerned with features of the artist's posture which emerge when that posture is adopted in drawing something from life, with the added complexity due to the perceptual relation to an independent object, such as a model.

[20] Of course, we do not expect a perfect match here; not every feature of how the model looked to the artist will be realized in the drawing. See below.

[21] Picture-making skills include possession of what are variously called schemas, canonical figures, stereotypes, and structural descriptions, as well as the techniques for representation of spatial relations.

[22] N. H. Freeman and M. V. Cox (eds.), *Visual Order* (Cambridge University Press, 1985), is an excellent introduction to the problems surrounding children's drawings. Interestingly, the drawings of autistic children with exceptional drawing skills tend to manifest viewpoint, and are often strongly perspectival. These cases raise many questions. Are the children drawing from life or tracing eidetic images or relying on memory images? Is their skill an inborn talent (a gift), or are they advanced for their age because they do little else (for example, they do not talk or communicate) Although there is still too much confusion over these cases to be sure, it seems unlikely that they would present a problem for the account proposed here.

[23] If children's drawings of the objects displayed to them in psychologists' tasks are not drawn from life, this would not mean that they have not produced drawings of what they see in some other, perhaps weaker, sense. As suggested earlier, not all attempts at drawing something seen need be attempts at drawing from life. But if drawing from life does not exhaust pictures of what is seen drawn as it is seen, then some account of how these other pictures of seen objects come to be *of* those objects will be needed. We would want to see what in these cases could underpin the relation of *of*-ness between picture and object.

Part IV
Memory and Motive

19

Remembering Directly

Has Q-memory been so defined as to count as genuine memory? And, if so, does it not entail identity?

DAVID WIGGINS

Des expressions et formes qui ont un sens dans l'action vraie, sont excitées et employées hors de leur domaine – et perdent pied. Mais le philosophe ne s'en aperçoit pas.

Paul Valéry, *Cahiers I* (753)

I

I now remember once climbing the stairs of the Eiffel Tower. Or so I suppose. If I am right in this claim, then (a) I did once climb those stairs; (b) I can now rehearse to myself something and enough of that climbing of those stairs, as such a climbing, rehearsing it from the point of view of the climber; and finally (c) it is part of the explanation of why I can now rehearse to myself something and enough of that climbing of those stairs, as such a climbing, rehearsing it from the point of view of the climber, that I *did* once, in a manner close enough to that which I can now rehearse, climb the stairs of the Eiffel Tower.

Such an account of the matter will raise supplementary questions, both about condition (c) and about other things. I confidently expect that the proper response to these questions will be to render the explication, not less illuminating (rather the reverse), but more circular.[1] That circularity will scarcely matter very much. We are not, after all, introducing a new term, but simply reminding ourselves of our working understanding of one that we already use and possess. Circularity cannot then impede us in the pursuit of any sensible purpose we might have here. What chiefly matters is that (a), (b), and (c) constitute a sufficient basis on which to insist upon both the *directness* that Gareth Evans found in such memories[2] as this and the *plenitude, cogency*, and *egocentricity* that Richard Wollheim attributes to what he calls the standard case of event-memory, namely 'centred event-memory', or remembering experientially.[3]

There is an intimate, elusive, and philosophically notorious connection between the self and states or capacities of the self like experiential memory (or personal memory, as some prefer to call it). We may put this as William James did in his *Essays on Radical Empiricism*: 'The continuing identity of each personal consciousness is treated as a name for the practical fact that new experiences look back upon old ones, find them warm and appropriate them as mine.' Or, in due deference to Wollheim's concerns, we may say that the capacity for experiential memory is one part of what makes people the kind of thing they are, engaged as they are in leading the lives they do lead: for experiential memory is what puts their present being under the cognitive and affective influence of what they did and were in the past; and that is part of the principle of activity *par excellence* of persons. Again, more minimally (too minimally perhaps), one may simply declare, as I once did in reaction against the richer accounts suggested to some philosophers by John Locke's account of these matters, that the way in which memory is relevant to personal identity is simply that it is one highly important element among others, both in itself and in synergy with various other vital components, in the account of what it is for a person to be still there, *fully alive*.[4]

Given that some connection such as these statements are all reaching for is both conceptually founded and necessary (albeit neither analytic nor *a priori*), it may be contended that the relation between experiential memory and the continuing self is that the first is somehow constitutive of the second. This is the familiar starting point for relational (reductive or constructional) views of the self. These will habitually begin with experiences and then seek to form the self, in so far as there is admitted to be such a thing, from suitably unified sets of such experiences. But in *The Thread of Life* (1984), Wollheim rightly insists that the connection between personal memory and personal identity, so far from forming the basis for any relational view of personal identity or survival, will always subvert the relationists' attempts to derive or correct or supersede the judgements that we make of personal identity. For on a proper understanding of the connection of self and the self's capacity for experiential memory, the said connection of memory and identity will always tend to revindicate the substantial conception of the self that reductivists and constructionalists are seeking to dispense with.

At this point in the argument, reductivists and constructionalists are apt to concede that, if we take the concept of memory just as it stands, then reactionaries like Wollheim and I may be right; but then they say that there is nothing to prevent the introduction of an invented notion of quasi-memory, or Q-memory. As Wollheim describes this move, 'Q-memories are defined as being just like centred memories as we know them' except that it is not stipulated in advance, nor is it meant to follow from the definition of Q-memory, that such memories 'follow the course of a single person's life' (*Thread of Life*, p. 111).

In *The Thread of Life*, Wollheim says he 'concedes without discussion' that Q-memory, having been so defined that it positively provides for the case of the non-identity of the original experiencer and the subsequent rememberer, is 'not self-contradictory'. But, having conceded so much, he then goes on to show that the attempt to prescind from identity in the definition of Q-memory denatures the other conceptual components of experiential memory. As soon as we understand that experiential memory cannot be a purely or narrowly cognitive phenomenon, we shall be troubled that, in any case where there is Q-memory without identity, the remembering subject will lack the affective repertoire of the person whose original experience is remembered. Therefore his remembering must be expected to lack most or all of the phenomenology that it would have had if the original experiencer and the rememberer had been the same. This is a difficulty Wollheim claims we cannot rectify (as some might suppose we could) by modelling the act of Q-recollection on the act of centrally imagining how things are for someone other than ourselves or taking on for the purpose as much as we can of his affective and cognitive repertoire. Involuntary recall – an absolutely central case of experiential memory – only dramatizes the difficulty of taking this suggestion seriously.

These and all the other points that Wollheim makes serve well to remind us of some of the most central and most neglected facts about experiential memory. But, if Q-memory really is not self-contradictory when it provides for the case of non-identity, then it has to be said that the most that is strictly established by Wollheim's discussion is that, in any and every case of Q-memory that is to count (even though experiencer and rememberer are not the same person) as 'centred event-memory', the experiencer and rememberer must stand in a relation that preserves both affective repertoire and relevant phenomenology. Wollheim has indeed shown this. But the trouble is that his point is likely to be conceded by most of those whom Wollheim takes for his philosophical opponents. For the case they are interested in is the case where the rememberer is a *survivor*, in Parfit's sense,[5] of the original experiencer. And such a survivor *will* have the same affective repertoire.

Instead of unenthusiastically conceding that Q-memory, defined so as to allow for non-identity, was non-self-contradictory, ought not one with Wollheim's theoretical concerns in philosophy and psychoanalysis really to have fastened in more hostile fashion upon the definition itself of Q-memory? I believe he ought to have made the point that the only reliable, general way for memories to be 'exactly like centred event-memories as we know them' is for them to 'follow the course of just one person's life'.[6] Then (if that had been how he proceeded) the constructionalists and reductivists would have had no automatic right – still less any conceded right – to call the cases they are interested in experiential memories, or even memories. And in that case these theorists would have had to *make the argument* for their Q-cases counting as sufficiently similar to normal experiential rememberings. Meanwhile, however, on the side of conceptual reaction, perhaps we could have assembled more and more considerations of the dissuasive kind that Wollheim has rehearsed – and other dissuasive considerations of other kinds that I shall shortly enumerate.

II

To progress further, we need a more deliberate definition than the one Wollheim sketched in *The Thread of Life*. So I consider Derek Parfit's in *Reasons and Persons*:

> The objection would be this: 'It is part of our concept of memory that we can remember only *our own* experiences. The continuity of memory therefore presupposes personal identity. The same is therefore true of your Relation R. You claim that personal identity just consists in the holding of Relation R. This must be false if Relation R itself presupposes personal identity.'
>
> To answer this objection, we can define a wider concept, *quasi-memory*. I have an accurate quasi-memory of a past experience if (1) I seem

to remember having an experience, (2) *someone* did have this experience, and (3) my apparent memory is causally dependent, in the right kind of way, on that past experience.

On this definition, ordinary memories are a sub-class of quasi-memories. They are quasi-memories of our own past experiences. . . . suppose that neuro-surgeons develop ways to create in one brain a copy of a memory-trace in another brain. This might enable us to quasi-remember other people's past experience.[7]

Insofar as this makes ordinary memories into a sub-class of quasi-memories, the first question that we encounter is this: whether Q-memories that are not ordinary memories are even conceptually possible.

Looking harder at Parfit's definition, however, one is moved to raise a much more elementary question: even if ordinary memories are stipulated to count as Q-memories, are Q-memories *defined as Parfit defines them* necessarily *memories?* Surely I can seem to remember without actually remembering anything. The way in which philosophers such as Hume have insisted on subsuming misremembering under the faculty of imagination suggests strongly that this is more than a question of words.

It is easy to imagine the reply, namely that these matters can all be simply put straight by Parfit's reminding us of his further stipulation, that the apparent memory be dependent *in the right kind of way* on the experience apparently remembered. But this reply surely gives rise to the next doubt. The next doubt is the old doubt whether Q-memory, having been vindicated as memory by virtue of being causally explainable 'in the right kind of way', that is, the way proper to experiential memory, can then fall short of implying the identity of experiencer and rememberer. Is it possible to Q-remember an experience and be non-identical with the original experiencer?[8]

Such doubts can be expected to encounter some impatience among those who are still suspicious of the ordinary, unreduced substantial self and believe that reductivism *must* be right.[9] Their impatience may take two forms. They may appeal to examples where they will claim to be able to force one to admit experiential memory without the normal identity between experiencer and rememberer. Or they may say that it is simply obvious that *some* definition can do what Parfit's has set out to do. So let me respond as eirenically as I can to each of these forms of impatience.

First, a follower of Parfit will say, consider the case where everything starts as it did in your example at the beginning. Having as an adolescent done some climbing of stairs on the Eiffel Tower, you then remember this. Next, at the age of twenty, you split into two people. Each remembers the climbing. How else is this case to be truthfully described than by the use of Q-memory?

My own answer to the question would be this: that the right way to describe the case is that neither splinter strictly remembers, but that after the magical event it is (more or less) *as if* each does remember it. For each *approximates* to the condition of a proper experiential rememberer (and approximates to it in various appropriate ways under the heads (a), (b), and (c) of the first paragraph of this essay). In each case it is as if the splinter person properly remembers. But this is *not* yet to say that, by Parfit's definition of 'Q-remember', each splinter Q-remembers. The splinters approximate, I say, to the condition of ordinary rememberers. This is not to show that they remember. Nor is it to commit oneself to use 'Q-remember'.

Defenders of Q-memory will counter by saying that their description is far more natural. Each splinter seems to remember. Someone did have the experience of climbing the Eiffel Tower. The splinter's apparent memory is causally dependent in the right kind of way on that past experience. Looking at the two cases, how can I doubt that the dependence is simply the right kind of dependence? Why insist on the reservation implied by 'it is as if'?

But to this I reply that I am still in the position of thinking that *either* the definition of Q-memory is defective *or* Parfit's definition has to be interpreted by a strict identity-implying reading of 'in the right way'. The well-definedness of 'Q-remember' when 'in the right way' is *not* thus strictly interpreted cannot be judged from a simple contrast or comparison between two cases. For a definition, one needs general directions about how to go on. *What is the general explanation* of 'the right kind of way'? Of course, there is no difficulty if the explanation is guided explicitly by reference to the normal, identity-involving case. But the one who offered that sort of explanation could not possibly be *en route* to a definition of Q-memory that would help to define a relation R *which would be available to the reductivist*. The defender of Q-memory who has a reductive aim must rather suppose that one can see straight off, *without* any detour through the idea of identity, that the fission case is like the normal case in respect of causation, and can grasp thereby some *general* mode of dependence. The defender must think that what he can depend upon here is something akin to ostension. And to this I would reply that his claim leaves me in doubt, the same sort of doubt (roughly speaking) as one feels in the face of G. E. Moore's explanations of what a sense-datum is.

I am conscious that this reaction to the Q-memorist may actually increase his impatience. But let us move forward to Parfit's followers' claim that it is obvious that *some* definition can do what Parfit's was intended to do.

Surely, they will say, the sense stipulated for 'Q-memory' cannot be in worse shape than the sense of 'remember', and this last is something everybody supposes can be treated as already given. Surely the sense of 'Q-remembers' is simply fixed by saying that it is what results from the subtraction from the concept of experiential memory of the concept of identity.[10] Or am I proposing to say that the concept of identity is not clear? If I am not going to say that, then why do I raise doubts about the remainder that results from the subtraction? All Parfit has done is to seek to state what that remainder is. Even if he has not succeeded exactly, there *must* be some amendment of his account (it may be said) that will catch what is needed. If there is more to remembering climbing than being identical with the climber (as there obviously is), well, subtract the identity from the ordinary remembering and the remainder is what you are looking for.

The historical parallels for this argument in the arithmetic of concepts are scarcely encouraging.[11] To rely on such operations of subtraction leading to the identification of simpler and simpler, independent, mutually separable items, one would have to have faith in some semantic counterpart of the Axiom of Foundation or Regularity as that figures in set theory or share all the analytical enthusiasm with which Leibniz first embarked upon his *Characteristica Universalis*.[12] Of course there is no difficulty in arriving at something that *makes sense* by conjoining to 'D remembers climbing the Eiffel Tower' the words 'and D is not anyone who climbed the Eiffel Tower' – just as, at very worst, there is no difficulty in conjoining 'round' and 'square' to arrive at the perfectly significant, sense-making but unsatisfiable, predicate 'round square'. (In each case I suppose that such conjoining results in one kind of cancellation or subtraction.) The question is rather this: if the notion of remembering semantically *involves* that of identity but the semantic counterpart of the Axiom of Foundation is false, then (a) how can we, by 'cancelling' the concept of identity within the concept of remembering,[13] construct some residue concept that would, in principle, be available to Parfit's reductivist for the definition of the relation R? (b) Could this residue concept really be applied without reference to the question of the identity of experiencer and rememberer? And (c), is this residue concept itself *satisfiable*?

III

So far as I am concerned, then, *either* it remains wide open to question whether Q-memory is memory *or,* if 'the right kind of way' ensures that much, then it is still not clear whether the stipulation of 'the right kind of way', by thus ensuring memory, can fail to require the identity of experiencer and rememberer. It is unclear (no worse but no better than unclear) whether there is an explanation of the phrase that will be available to a reductivist. And it's bad for it to be even unclear, because technical terms ought not to be introduced into philosophy without demonstrably clear credentials.

How is this question to be resolved? One way to proceed would be for me to seek to multiply considerations of the kind Wollheim has adduced but across an even wider range of the mental functions that work synergetically with experiential memory in the constitution of the mental life of people; then to measure their cumulative effect on the question how we must interpret the words 'in the right kind of way', both in the definition of Q-memory and in the definition of other Q-states and occurrences such as intending and hoping and aspiring and the rest.

Pursuing a somewhat similar strategy to this, I have tried in another place to show that, if in Parfit's fashion we redescribe the concern *to survive* as the concern that certain mental events should have successors, then we cannot explain what might make anyone value his own life or make him dear to himself. We cannot even say what is so good about survival.[14] In which case, if the thought of survival cannot have the content that we attribute to it when we value our own survival, then, on the revelation of what Parfit claims is the bare truth about these things, the very concern to survive may be expected to dry up and disappear. Survival itself will seem terribly unimportant. Why bother with the question whether these experiences will have successors? It is surely not something we can simply take for granted that we shall see anything at all that matters *in the evaluative sense* in what (according to Parfit) matters in the logical sense for the question of survival. (In passing, and in furtherance of that argument, I note that there has been a tendency among reductivists to assimilate the concern for survival to something based on the dependence of one's 'projects' on 'future selves' who will remember and carry them through. Present 'projects' then carry the burden of concern for the self in the future. That this is a misdescription of the actual concern to survive will seem plainer and plainer, however – if it is not already plain – if we reflect on two things: (a) that some projects and concerns do themselves depend already upon the thought of the continuant self: for instance, the concerns to improve one's character, knowledge, ability or mastery, handicap at golf or tennis, etc.; and (b) that the reductivist account predicts, wrongly, that the more projects I have, the keener I shall be to survive. – As if overwork could not possibly lead to thoughts of suicide.)

There is this conceptual cum phenomenological way with these questions, then. One could indeed multiply considerations of the kind that Wollheim's work has already explored. It is clear that there is room for many more such conceptual cum phenomenological exercises – especially if they are invested with the sort of interest Wollheim has shown that they can have. But I fear that, with the particular reductivist audience at which they are dialectically directed, they can never succeed – if only because reductivists are always reconstructionists where phenomenology is concerned and very hard to impress by considerations of how things actually are in the life that human beings actually lead. All they can ever see here is contingency. They are not receptive to conceptual requirements that presuppose a contingency.

IV

Is there then another way to proceed? Well, one other way for one on my side of the argument to proceed is to revert to the epistemological role of memory – to revert to its *directness* or *unmediatedness* (Evans)[15] and to its *plenitude* and *cogency* (Wollheim) – and to try then to demonstrate the link between these features of memory and the feature the Q-theorist seeks to dispense with, namely its egocentricity. What I must stress, however, is that, to make these considerations work effectively, we shall have to make them register not too little and too late or at some point where exceptions have to be considered. We shall have to make them register at the most fundamental level, namely the level where the initiating conditions or constitutive terms are fixed upon which a predicate has and maintains its place in a language.

What props up the idea of Q-memory is the idea of memory. But what then sustains the idea of memory itself – the utter importance of the point is proportional to its utter banality – is not speakers' grasp of the definition of memory (if there were such a definition) or their grasp of its analysis (if there were one) into the primitive concepts of the language of thought (if there were one). What sustains it is their participation in the living use of the verb-phrase '*x* remembers (–)-ing', sustained as that use is not only by our understanding of all sorts of other predicates that are coeval with it, but by all the various assumptions and expectations that condition and regulate the use of the verb-phrase. If Q-memory rides on the back of memory, then the locutions of Q-memory must inherit all these assumptions and expectations. They can renege upon them only at risk of jeopardizing their sense or satisfiability.

What then *are* the assumptions and expectations that condition the sense of '*x* remembers (–)-ing'? Conspicuous among them is this: that it is the epistemological role of experiential remembering – as it is of direct perception, and as it is of one's memory of what one already believes (each of these three things needs the support of the other) – to help to provide us with a starting point for any further inquiry about how things are in the world. This need not be a philosophically indubitable or infallible starting point. (Obviously there is scarcely one claim I cannot in principle be proved wrong about, in the end.) What it must be is a place I can start straight out from without first making an inference from something else, which would itself have to deploy other materials which would themselves have to come from . . . Well, where would these come from?[16]

If it has started to rain and I want my umbrella, I need to be able to take it as a perceptual datum that I see that it is raining, and as a memory datum that I remember having an umbrella, that I remember last seeing it hanging on a peg, etc. Better, I have to take these states as direct presentations of those facts. (Well, I could start further back. But at some point, a point to be determined partly by context and partly by the content and nature of the judgements that are candidates to mark it, I need unmediated – which is not the same as infallible – judgements. Suppose then *exempli gratia* that *this* is the starting point.) I see it is raining. I want my umbrella. Starting there, I need to be able to say from personal memory not only 'There are pegs in the hall and by the back door' but also 'I remember seeing it on a peg somewhere', and then 'I last saw it on a peg'. From perception and memory and memory of coming in last night, etc. etc., I need to be able to say: 'I'm at home'; 'This is the hall'; 'This is the back door'; etc.

Suppose we change the normal truth-condition for the judgement 'I last remember seeing it on a peg'. Suppose we change it somehow (never mind now the difficulties I have already rehearsed of doing so) so as to relax the requirement that the rememberer did himself see it.

How would experiential memory then play the epistemological role it actually plays? The most that the recollection of seeing the umbrella on a peg could then support is '*Someone* saw it on a peg'. But then, for all that I am saying that I know, the peg could have been almost anywhere. Well, not quite anywhere. It would still no doubt be worth searching the house I am standing in. This house would be one candidate to be the resting place of the umbrella. But the search would now be a different kind of enterprise altogether – more like a police search for an umbrella that it was reported someone was trying to pawn somewhere in east Oxford. And such a police search, one notes, can only be conducted by investigators who have ordinary unmediated experiential memory of where they themselves have been and what they have done. It would not be a search effortlessly organized by someone's idea of his or her own single-tracked unitary life. We can dispense here with infallibility. What we cannot dispense with is the organization of our search by the starting points of unmediated presentations of memory and perception.[17]

V

Such then, I submit, are the terms on which the idioms of experiential memory have their point and hold their place in the language. Experiential memory must furnish unmediated starting points. And these terms on which its idioms have their sense forge in their turn an indissoluble link (a) between immediacy and egocentricity and (b) between egocentricity and a certain simple truth-condition for statements of memory. The condition delimits definitely – not indefinitely by existential generalization over people (or over entities standing in some relation to the act of remembering that the reductivist would have to try to find a way of defining) – who must have done what, and whose doing what is to explain my memory presentation, if it is to be true that I remember climbing the Eiffel Tower or seeing my umbrella on a peg. (Contrast imagination.) These links (a) and (b) are not as they are simply by convention or by accident. To seek to alter them is to deprive memory of its central place in the economy of experiential awareness. Can the operation of conceptual cancellation or subtraction alter these terms without denaturing the idea of experiential memory on which Q-memory itself depended? It is not mere conceptual conservatism, but the understanding of where memory has to fit into the life of the mind that makes one insist that if I remember

climbing the Eiffel Tower, then that gives me *all the right I could have*
to suppose that I did do so – that I *did* so and *I* did so. It gives me all
the right I could have, subject only to the condition that I hold myself
ready in principle to be shown that I never did climb the Eiffel Tower,
that I have imagined it, or that I have confused the Eiffel Tower with
Big Ben, or whatever.

VI

I suppose that someone who grasped all this might now say: 'Still it
is only a statistical contingency that links the conviction of experiential memory of climbing or seeing or . . . with its having been one's
very own self who climbed or saw . . . How can such a contingency
ground a rule that is exceptionless?'

In reply to this, I should begin by making it clear that the exceptionlessness I have claimed to derive from the epistemological role of
personal memory could never prevent one who was impressed by
thought-experiments involving fission from insisting on the striking
similarity between normal experiential memory and what would be
available to the twin products of the division of a person. It would be
absurd to seek to rule out a comparison between the cases. What the
struggle is about here is *not* how striking the similarity might be
claimed to be between experiential memory and its approximations.
It is about the reductivists' claim that the approximations reveal the
very essence – the centre of conceptual gravity, as it were – of survival,
of continuants, and of experiential memory in the life of the mind.
That – not the best way of describing bizarre cases – is what is at
issue. What is being claimed by me is that these approximations are
just that, namely approximations.

At this point, a critic may still inquire, still in good faith: 'How can
you base a semantic ruling that is exceptionless upon a contingency
that is (or could have been) merely statistical?' I am not sure that one
should in the end accept that the regularity in question is, or even
could have been (leaving everything else the same?) 'merely statistical'. But the chief thing one must point out in reply is that it is at
least equally true that it is only a contingency that those who seem to
remember climbing, seeing, or whatever have most often not *imagined*
that they did once climb, see, or whatever. And here we do *not* let the
contingency bother us or discourage us from proceeding in our normal way. Our normal way is that first we allow that the putative

rememberer has all the right he could have *to think* he did once climb or see or whatever. But secondly, if we discover that he did not after all climb or see or whatever, then we say: 'So you didn't climb [or see, or whatever]', and we try to explain how he can have fallen into error. This is our practice. There are no exceptions to it, and in this case we find nothing repressive in the exceptionlessness of the rule that informs it. For these are the terms on which memory sustains its Atlantean role in the mental life of people. The exceptionlessness of the requirement that there was a climber and the exceptionlessness of the requirement that I was that climber are for these purposes parallel and inseparable. Each reposes upon what can in a certain way be seen as a contingency. But neither can be cancelled.

In the course of the thirty years I have known Richard Wollheim, almost half of them as his colleague in London, there has been the opportunity to learn from him a rich, singular, and unpredictable variety of things. But it is a special pleasure to me to find that in these reflections stemming from his *Thread of Life*, I should emerge insisting upon a philosophical point that his work above all others has demonstrated and strikingly illustrated, both in the philosophy of art and in the philosophy of mind – namely the absolutely foundational role in everything that has to do with the mind of truths that play an organizing, conceptual role and yet repose upon contingency.

NOTES

[1] To transform the definition, in other words, into an elucidation. For the power and point of the elucidation of existing notions (and its problematical character in the case of invented notions), see my *Sameness and Substance* (Blackwell, Oxford, 1980), pp. 4, 49–55; *Needs, Values, Truth* (Blackwell, Oxford, 1987), pp. 142 n. 4, 188–9, with detailed references there to Wittgenstein and others.

[2] See Gareth Evans, *The Varieties of Reference* (Oxford University Press, Oxford, 1982), pp. 235ff.

[3] See Wollheim, *The Thread of Life* (1984), pp. 101–11.

[4] Wiggins, *Sameness and Substance*, p. 188. Cf. p. 151. Cf. *idem, Needs, Values, Truth*, p. 304.

[5] D. A. Parfit, 'Personal Identity', *Philosophical Review*, 80 (1971), 3–27.

[6] Cf. *Thread of Life*, p. 111.

[7] D. Parfit, *Reasons and Persons* (Oxford University Press, Oxford, 1984), p. 220.

[8] Cf. Frege, *Grundgesetze der Arithmetik*, § 143 (Geach and Black translation, p. 178): 'the power of creating [things by definition] is restricted by

the proviso that the properties must not be mutually inconsistent: an obvious restriction, but one very hard to observe. How do we tell that the properties are not mutually inconsistent?'

[9] For the substantial self as I intend it, see P. F. Strawson, *Individuals* (Methuen, London, 1959), ch. 3; Wiggins, *Sameness and Substance*, ch. 6, further developed in *idem*, 'The Person as Object of Science, as Subject of Experience, and Locus of Value', in *Persons and Personality*, ed. A. R. Peacocke and G. Gillet (Blackwell, Oxford, 1987). In seeking to reduce such substances to their states or eliminate them in favour of states, Parfit plays fast and loose with the idea that such substances would have to be something 'existing separately from' or as something *over and above* their states. What does 'existing separately from' or 'over and above' mean? Substances are not of course *identical* with their states. They are identical with that which is in these states. That which is in these states can scarcely be a set of such states, which is an abstract object. Nor can it be a mereological sum or fusion of such states. (We can scarcely speculate whether a sum or fusion might have had different elements.) Lest I here repeat myself yet again on the subject of substances, let me refer to Leibniz's diagnosis at *Nouveaux Essais* ii. 23 of the deep-seated confusions that always attend the polemic against substance.

[10] The prudent reader will note the crucial ambiguity of 'subtract' here. Do we subtract identity by simply stipulating the possibility of difference? Or do we subtract it by *removing* the stipulation of identity? If the first, then cf. Frege quoted at note 8 above. If the second, well how exactly do we do this? If we just scratch out all clauses that essentially involve 'I' or '=' in the definition of 'I remember', will what remains necessarily make sense? And where in any case *is* the definition of 'remember'? Where do I look for it? Maybe there *isn't* one. (My first paragraph isn't it.) What if both there isn't one *and* 'remember' is not only conceptually primitive but also *involves* identity already? This last may seem simply impossible. It will seem impossible if we think that the learning of a language is the learning of definitions. It will seem impossible if we think that definiteness of sense can only be secured to an expression by its having some unique exhaustive decomposition into semantically independent indefinables. (Cf. Wittgenstein, *Tractatus*, 5.451.) But grasping the sense of an expression cannot, in the normal or basic case, be the learning of a definition. So unique exhaustive definition into indefinables is not what normally secures definiteness of sense. See also notes 11, 12, and text below.

[11] See for instance Jennifer Hornsby, 'Arm Raising and Arm's Rising', *Philosophy*, (1980), especially Appendix. Consider also the subtle criticisms offered by J. M. Hinton, in 'Visual Experiences', *Mind*, (1967), and John McDowell, in 'Criteria, Defeasibility and Knowledge', in *Proceedings of the British Academy*, 68 (1982), of the subtraction arguments associated with the Argument from Illusion.

[12] For Leibniz's perception of what is surely no less than the difficulty of the idea of semantic Foundation or Regularity – in the sense explained in the text and note 10 – see the following passage (translated by Benson Mates, who says he doesn't know what to make of it, in the *Philosophy of Leibniz*, (Oxford University Press, Oxford, 1986), p. 60 n. 51):
Protonoemata secundum quid and *protonoemata simpliciter* are rightly distinguished . . . Certainly all things that are not explained by definition but have to be shown by example or have to be sensed in order to be known, as, e.g., heat, cold, and colours, are *protonoemata-secundum nos*; however, they can be resolved, for they have their causes. I have often given thought to *protonoemata simpliciter*, i.e. those which are conceived through themselves . . . where the question[s] can be raised, first, whether there really are any *protonoemata*, or whether there is division *in infinitum* . . . and then, assuming that there are some (for it seems that nothing at all can be conceived if nothing is conceived per se), whether there is one only or many. If there is only one, how can so many composite concepts come from it? If there are many, they will have certain things in common, e.g., possibility; also, they will have certain relations among themselves, else they will not be able to come together to make composite concepts. Therefore, in what way are these concepts simple? (Akademie 2.1.497)
The difficulty would seem to be roughly this. Either there is one protonoema or there are many. If there is only one, then no thing can be built up from it. If there are many, how can they fail to have certain common marks. (How, for instance, can a *protonoema* P fail to enjoy the mark *compossible with the concept of substance*? Surely it is not *excluded*, say, that anything that is P is a substance.) But then how can these be veritable *protonoemata*? For what cannot help but appear as some of the other difficulties, see Leibniz's unpublished exercises in analytical lexicography (e.g. those reproduced in *Opuscules et Fragments Inédits*, ed. Louis Couturat (Paris, 1901)).

[13] On the ambiguity in the idea of cancelling, cf. 'subtract' and note 10 above.

[14] Wiggins, 'The Concern to Survive', Essay 9 in *Needs, Values, Truth*.

[15] What follows is little more than an attempt to develop in one particular direction one of the points made by Evans, *Varieties of Reference*, pp. 241ff. I have to say I cannot understand Parfit's answer to Evans in *Reasons and Persons*, p. 516.

[16] It is part of the great charm of epistemological foundationalism that it sees that there have to be such starting points and that that which provides them must comprise *inter alia* the mutually sustaining states of perceiving and remembering, including personal remembering. Its fatal flaw is that it then mis-states the point as a point about immunity from error.

[17] The Q-memory theorist may react to this difficulty by suggesting that the truth-condition be modified to read 'Someone *in an R-relation to me* saw

it on a peg.' But if he is to be a reductivist, then he has no title to that explanation. Even if he can get rid of the 'me', he cannot appeal to the relation R in the explanation of Q-remember. For Q-memory is what he will use to *construct* the definition of R.

A Q-theorist may try to improve his position against this difficulty by suggesting that those with Q-memory as he defines it do best to proceed *as if* their memories were identity-involving and then to hunt down stray or wild card memories by their failure to cohere with the generality of their Q-memories. But so far from answering the procedural difficulty I am pressing on Evans's behalf, this defence seems to concede it. It concedes that we need, each of us, a kind of memory we can treat as a source of unmediated presentations of our own past. Even if we don't have such a source, he concedes that we need to proceed as if we have!

20

On the Parallelism between Theoretical and Practical Reasoning

DAVID PEARS

Many philosophers maintain that unmitigated akrasia is a conceptual impossibility: that is to say, they maintain that nobody can act freely and with full awareness against his own final value-judgement in a particular case. Some supporters of this view argue that the impossibility is exactly like the impossibility of forming a belief that contradicts one's premises when one is in full possession of one's faculties and fully aware of the contradiction. My basic claim in this essay will be that those who use this argument against the possibility of unmitigated akrasia exaggerate the parallelism between the two kinds of irrationality, theoretical and practical.

In what follows it must be borne in mind that the irrationality is internal in both cases. For the fault lies not in the principles or factual beliefs from which the person starts his reasoning, but in the use that he proceeds to make of them. It is not his material that is faulty, but his processing of it. So if, for example, someone did not know that the principle guiding an argument that he was developing about probabilities was invalid, that would be a case of external, rather than internal irrationality. I shall not be concerned with such cases in this paper. The problem that I am going to discuss arises only in cases where the reasoning violates principles, valid or invalid, which the subject himself has internalized.

Before I start my argument, there are two preliminary points that I should make. First, it is often supposed that internal irrationality always involves the subject's abstention from the conclusion that he ought to draw, and perhaps, even, his adoption of an incompatible conclusion; or, in a practical case, that it always involves his abstention from the action that he ought to perform, and usually his performance of a different action. However, that is too narrow a description of these faults. For a thinker may realize that the implication of his factual premisses is false or absurd, and so he may retrace his steps and reject one of them. Similarly, an agent may find the project to which his practical reasoning leads him unacceptable, and so he may retrace his steps and reject, or in this case more probably qualify, one of its premisses. So internal irrationality consists not simply in abstention, but in abstention without any adjustments of the original material.

The second preliminary point is one that is more easily overlooked in the dust of controversy. I am not claiming that unmitigated akrasia is possible, although, in fact, I think that it is possible. I am only claiming that one of the supposed obstacles to its occurrence is illusory. The illusion, if I am right, is produced by an exaggeration of the parallelism between theoretical and practical reasoning. But correcting this exaggeration will not neutralize other reasons for rejecting the possibility of unmitigated akrasia. My aim in this essay is only a limited defence of its possibility, designed to repel a single form of attack.

The argument that follows will be in three parts. It starts with my basic claim, that the obstacle which is taken by adversaries to block the possibility of unmitigated akrasia is not at all like the obstacle which really does block the possibility of unmitigated self-contradictory belief formation. If this claim is accepted, it destroys one view of the parallelism between theoretical and practical reasoning. However, there is another, more plausible version of the parallelism. It may be said that there is an analogy between the fit that is achieved when an action fulfils the specification in the agent's final value-judgement and the fit that is achieved when a description matches the object described. In the second part of this essay I examine this version of the analogy, and explain how it might be used to support the claim that unmitigated akrasia is conceptually impossible.

In the third and last part of the essay I develop an objection to this use of the more plausible version of the parallelism between theoretical and practical reasoning. I argue that there is an important difference between the organization of the various considerations that go to form a reason for a belief and the organization of the various considerations that go to form a reason for an action.

The difference first shows up in the fact that in theoretical reasoning the actual persuasive power of an evidential consideration tends to remain set at the level fixed by the subject's assessment of the persuasive power that it ought to have, while the actual motivational power of a practical consideration is often greater or smaller than the motivational power that the subject judges that it ought to have. Now one might just accept this difference as a fact about human nature, and one might simply claim that because of this fact we have adopted a conceptual scheme which does not force us to say that apparent cases of unmitigated akrasia are really only cases where the agent has changed his final value-judgement (as in Davidson's theory).

However, in the third part of the essay I try to advance beyond this point. I try to show that this difference between theoretical and practical reasoning is produced by a fundamental difference between the way in which the various considerations that the subject takes into account are organized in the two cases. On the theoretical side, the aim of judgement, which is truth, imposes a unified structure on reasons for belief; whereas on the practical side, though we may say if we like that the aim of the will is the good, this does not impose an equally unified structure on reasons for action.

I

Suppose that someone acts squarely against his own final value-judgement. He does not change his judgement at the last minute in the way that Davidson, who rejects the possibility of unmitigated akrasia, takes to be necessary. For this agent, we are supposing, is too honest to play any intellectual tricks – for example, in order to get his deliberation to allow him to eat the food forbidden by his diet. He just eats it. As I said earlier, I am not arguing for the possibility of such a case. My argument is only that if, perhaps *per impossibile*, a case of this kind did occur, it would not be like a case of someone drawing the conclusion not Q, from the premisses P and if P, then Q. If that were the correct model, it would be plausible to infer that unmitigated akrasia cannot occur because unmitigated self-contradiction cannot occur. It is only this argument that I am opposing.

There is, of course, a long line of possible mitigations in apparent examples of either of these two kinds. On the theoretical side, we would check for the possibility that the thinker had forgotten one of his premisses or that he did not understand that his first premiss, P, was embedded with unaltered meaning in his second, hypothetical premiss, if P, then Q, or that he did not understand *modus ponens*. On the practical side, we would check for the possibility that the agent had forgotten or had failed to understand some step in his deliberation or perhaps that he was acting in the grip of some compulsion. We need not fill in all the details, because it is obvious that at the end of the line of possible mitigations, there is something that a thinker cannot do: namely, contradict himself knowingly. So if this is the right model for deliberation and action, then at the end of that line of mitigations there will be something that an agent is equally unable to do: namely, act against his own final value-judgement knowingly and freely.

If we are going to test the appropriateness of this model, we must ask why unmitigated self-contradiction is impossible, and when we have found the reason, we must go on to ask whether a similar obstacle operates against unmitigated akrasia. Now the reason why unmitigated self-contradiction is impossible is that belief essentially aims at truth, but the three lines of the example of theoretical reasoning demonstrably cannot all achieve truth. If the conclusion is true, then demonstrably one of the premisses must be false, and if both the premisses are true, then demonstrably the conclusion must be false. The conjunction of premisses and conclusion is required to fit the world; but whatever shape the world takes, the result will demonstrably be misfit at one of the three points.

If this were the right model for unmitigated akrasia, there would have to be some property which played a role on the practical side parallel to the role of truth on the theoretical side. Just as the three statements demonstrably could not all be true, so too it ought to be demonstrable that in a case of unmitigated akrasia the final value-judgement and the action could not both possess the analogous property, whatever it might be.

However, when we look at what actually happens in a case of deliberation and action, it is immediately obvious that no property could play the parallel role. In the theoretical case, the three statements form a conjunctive representation of the world; but in the practical case, the two protagonists, the final value-judgement and the action, do not form a conjunctive representation of anything, because the direction of fit has been reversed. Consequently, the best that we could do would be to find an analogous co-operative function for them and an analogous shared property. But here we run up against an insuperable difficulty. For the function of the value-judgement is to set the standard of fit, and the action is required only to conform to that standard. Consequently, the property possessed by the action, when it does conform to it, cannot possibly be shared by the value-judgement which sets it. No doubt, there are points of similarity between truth and conformity to an action specification in a final value-judgement, but they do not extend as far as this alleged parallelism. Therefore, if there is an obstacle to unmitigated akrasia, it is not like the obstacle to unmitigated self-contradiction.

It may be objected that I am attacking a straw man. For nobody seriously supposes that there is a property analogous to truth which is possessed by both the final value-judgement and the action when the agent does what he judges it best to do but cannot be possessed by both when he deviates into unmitigated akrasia. Perhaps so; but many philosophers have made claims about the parallelism between theoretical and practical reasoning which require a property analogous to truth even if they do not pursue the consequences of the requirement.

When we do look into its consequences, it is immediately obvious that the analogue of truth in the case of actions is fulfilment of the specification in the final value-judgement, which is a property which cannot possibly be shared by the final value-judgement itself. The whole idea that the lines of practical reasoning and the action might combine to form something analogous to a representation of the world is simply not worth further discussion. The only version of the parallelism worth discussing is the one which claims that an agent's will finds the good, as he sees it, irresistible, in the same way that a thinker's judgement finds the truth, as he sees it, irresistible.

Before this version is examined, it is worth observing that it abandons the two exciting implications which made the other version attractive but incredible. First, unmitigated akrasia is no longer treated like negating a valid theoretical conclusion, and so it is no longer taken to run up against the same kind of obstacle. Second, the reason for this change is that the step taken at the end of a piece of practical reasoning, from final value-judgement to action, is no longer supposed to be like the preceding steps. The latter aim at the validity of the deliberation, and, via its validity, at the truth of its conclusion, while the former aims at fulfilment of the action specification in that conclusion, and this fulfilment is only supposed to be analogous to truth. So, though any fault in the whole process may be called 'irrational' in a broad sense, the fault committed in unmitigated akrasia is really a special kind of irrationality, which might be called 'unreasonableness'. That is what we call people who do not listen to reason. When the will of an akratic agent fails to conform to an edict of reason, that is certainly not the same kind of fault as a fault in the argumentation that led up to the edict.

II

Let us now take it as agreed that there is a certain analogy between the fit that is achieved when an action fulfils the specification in the agent's final value-judgement and the fit that is achieved when a description is true of the object described. Then the question is whether this improved version of the parallelism can be used to show that unmitigated akrasia is impossible.

As a first shot, someone might try to push the claim that has just been mentioned. Although the two cases involve opposite directions of fit, they have this much in common: an agent's will finds the good, as he sees it, irresistible, just as a thinker's judgement finds the truth, as he sees it, irresistible. The first part of this claim is only a colourful way of presenting the alleged impossibility of unmitigated akrasia, while the second part offers the improved version of the analogy in support of it. The question is whether it gives it sufficient support.

The case for saying that it does would start from a consideration of a problematical perceptual belief. For example, in the desert someone sees a distant object, and is not sure whether to describe it as a rock, a bush, or a car; but when he moves closer to it and gets a clear indication that it is a car, that is what he will inevitably believe. Similarly, on the practical side, an agent may begin by being uncertain what to do, but once he has made his final value-judgement, he will not have any difficulty choosing an action that fits the specification contained in it, and that is what he will inevitably do.

However, this way of exploiting the improved analogy is unconvincing. If the phrase 'choosing the action that fits his specification' refers to an intellectual achievement, then, of course, it does not present any difficulty for the agent. He knows what his action specification means, and he knows what would count as fulfilling it. But that is beside the point. For what has to be found on the practical side is an achievement of the will which is as inevitable as the achievement of the intellect on the theoretical side. It has to be shown that just as the traveller in the desert inevitably formed the appropriate belief that the object was a car after getting clear optical evidence, so too the man on the diet will inevitably abstain from the forbidden food after he has judged abstention best. Now, of course, the analogy may be as close as this. But it is a mistake to try to establish that it is by trading on an ambiguity in the phrase 'choosing the action'. If it refers to an intellectual achievement, it is not in dispute that the inevitability of the agent's success is as perfect as the inevitability of his forming the belief in the perceptual example. If, on the other hand, it refers to a practical achievement, the actual performance of the action, the case against the possibility of unmitigated akrasia will be resting merely on assertion and not on argument. For the question whether the parallelism is as complete as this is the same as the question whether unmitigated akrasia is possible.

We have reached the point at which the participants in this controversy usually agree to disagree. One party simply asserts that the improved analogy is perfect, because the will is inevitably drawn to the apparent good just as the intellect is inevitably drawn to the apparently true, while the other party simply denies that this is so. Of course, both sides can appeal to ordinary language, but when they do this, the result never seems to be conclusive.

So the next question is, how might we advance beyond this point?

III

We need to make a fresh start. When the controversy about unmitigated akrasia runs into an impasse, with conflicting intuitions and no clear way of adjudicating between them, it may be helpful to generalize the problem. Instead of asking whether the motivational power of a consideration which has been overridden in deliberation must remain what the agent judges that it ought to be (which would make unmitigated akrasia impossible), let us ask, more generally, whether the actual motivational power of any consideration must be what the agent judges that it ought to be. This is still not quite what we need to ask, because it is really the *comparative* version of this question that concerns us: namely, 'does the actual motivational power of any practical consideration deviate no further from its legitimate motivational power, as judged by the agent, than the actual legitimate persuasive power of a theoretical consideration differs from its legitimate persuasive power, as judged by the thinker?' Or, to put the question more concisely, is motivational power no more wayward than persuasive power?

The advantage of this strategy is that it side-steps the impasse and offers some hope that the generalization of the problem may lead to an explanation of the two conflicting intuitions. There is also the further prospect, if we can explain them, of finding out which of them is the right one. At least, if the answer to the comparative question is that motivational power is more wayward than persuasive power, we shall have set a limit to the parallelism between theoretical and practical reasoning which is based on the improved version of the analogy. We may even be able to trace the difference in waywardness back to some essential features of belief and will.

Let us start by looking at the waywardness of the persuasive power of evidential considerations. Here it must be remembered that we are concerned only with *internal* irrationality. So when the degree of persuasive power that the thinker judges to be legitimate differs from the degree that is actually legitimate, it is the former that will concern us, not the latter.

The next point that needs to be made is that the comparison between the waywardness of persuasive and motivational power must be carried out according to strict rules. We have to exclude any waywardness of persuasive power that is produced by self-deception or by wishful or emotionally biased thinking, in order to concentrate on purely intellectual processes. For we want to discover the basic degree of correlation between actual and subjectively legitimate persuasive power. Similarly, on the practical side, we have to exclude any waywardness of motivational power that is produced by cognitive errors (just as we have to concentrate on unmitigated akrasia). For here too we want to discover a basic degree of correlation, in this case between actual and subjectively legitimate motivational power.

When the lines of comparison have been drawn in this strict way, it is evident that there is not much waywardness in the persuasive power of evidential considerations. It is true that cognitive psychologists claim to have found purely intellectual distortions in the collection and use of evidence. To take a simple example, the first item on a list of evidential considerations has a salience which can bias a person in its favour. But it is not clear that this always produces waywardness. For what is biased may be the person's subjective assessment of the first item's legitimate persuasive power, and it is against this standard that waywardness for that power is subsequently judged.

On the practical side things go very differently. Suppose that a recent sufferer from hepatitis judges it best to abstain from alcohol for a prescribed period, but towards the end of it finds the prospect of taking a glass of his favourite wine increasingly attractive. In my book *Motivated Irrationality*, I concentrated on the kind of case in which he finds it so attractive that he actually takes it (if unmitigated akrasia is a possibility), and I said that he takes it because the prospect of pleasure has acquired 'emotional salience'. I meant that it had been enhanced to a point where it swayed his will without swaying his intellect, and so without causing him to change his final value-judgement, as in Davidson's theory of akrasia. But here we are concerned with the generalization of the phenomenon, and so we may suppose that, though he does not actually take the wine, the motivational power of that pleasure has become stronger than he judges that it ought to be. This is a very common phenomenon, and, without it, there would be no need for self-control. For if there were no waywardness in motivational power, the action judged best by an agent would always be performed as a matter of course.

When I developed this contrast between the minimal waywardness of persuasive power and the much greater waywardness of motivational power, I could be said to be drawing attention to very general facts about human nature. However, they are not things that might have been otherwise without far-reaching effects. For these facts, as I now hope to show, have shaped the whole conceptual scheme which we apply to theoretical and practical irrationality, because they have given our concepts of belief and will their distinctive essential features. So the limitation of the improved version of the parallelism between theoretical and practical reasoning has a very deep source, and if we trace it back to its source, we shall be in a better position to understand the phenomenon instead of being reduced to relying on blind intuitions.

Consider the concept of belief. The point was made earlier that it is essential to belief or judgement that it aims at truth, but let us now ask what follows from this. One consequence is that it is conceptually impossible to try to believe what you take to be false or even, perhaps, what you take to be equally likely to be true or false. For beliefs are imposed on us by the world, and however much ratiocination goes on at the receiving end, the reception is essentially passive (Hume's point).

Now there are exceptions to this compass-needle view of belief. It is possible to form a belief wishfully or self-deceptively, with complete indifference to its truth or falsity and even, perhaps, originally with full awareness that it is false. However, we do not need to take account of these exceptions here, because we are concerned only with purely intellectual processes. Within the restricted field of our comparison between belief and will, the truth, as it is seen by the thinker, is dominant.

This in its turn produces a further consequence. When someone is trying to work out the truth of any matter, he will treat it as an unmoving target, either P or not P and if his hypothesis is that it is P, he will assess the legitimate persuasiveness of every piece of evidence by checking its relation to P. After he has made his assessment, he may review it and change it, but such changes will not be examples of waywardness. Waywardness occurs only if his assessment of the legitimate persuasiveness of a piece of evidence remains constant, while its actual persuasiveness deviates from it.

We have seen that, when wishful and emotional thinking have been excluded, there is very little room for waywardness in the persuasive power of an evidential consideration. The consequences of the essential aim of belief can now be used to explain this fact. For the truth of any matter is a genuinely single aim, distinct from the evidence for it and giving each piece of evidence its legitimate persuasive power. Within the restricted field of our comparison, the truth of the matter has no rival which could produce a deviation in actual persuasive power as an irregularity in the local magnetic field can make a compass needle point away from standard magnetic north. To put it another way, each piece of evidence for any hypothesis derives its actual persuasive power from the same central source, so it lacks the autonomy that it would need in order to set itself up with a deviant persuasive power. Or, to put it in the way it was put earlier, evidential considerations are organized in a unified way, which largely excludes the possibility of waywardness.

On the practical side, things go very differently. We may say, if we like, that it is essential to the will that it aims at the good, just as it is essential to belief that it aims at the true. But how much substance is there behind this colourful analogy? Is the good really a single target, distinct from the various features of projects which serve as reasons for carrying it out and so are credited with legitimate motivational power? Are practical considerations really organized in the same unified way as evidential considerations? They certainly march under the flag of the good, but does the emblem on the flag represent a genuinely single and independent goal?

If these questions can be given negative answers, we shall have a convincing explanation of the fact already established, that there is more waywardness in the actual motivational power of practical considerations than in the actual persuasive power of evidential considerations. But can the questions just asked be given negative answers?

Consider an example of dietetic akrasia of the kind discussed earlier. The agent's deliberation ends with the value-judgement that it is best to preserve his health by sticking to his diet, but he chooses the path of pleasure instead. If this can be taken to indicate a certain waywardness in the actual motivational power of pleasure in his case – as I have been arguing that it can perhaps, be taken, rather than in Davidson's way – can we explain this waywardness by giving negative answers to the questions that have just been asked? To generalize the problem, is any waywardness in the motivational power of pleasure, including cases which do not produce unmitigated akrasia, attributable to the fact that practical considerations are not related to the good in the same unifying way that theoretical considerations are related to the true?

It seems to be so, but a full defence of this explanation would take too long at the end of this essay. The main point that needs to be established presents no difficulty, but there are many problems of detail. The main point is that when the good is the target of the will, it is evidently not a target which is distinct from the various features of the project which serve as reasons for carrying it out. On the contrary, these features *constitute* the value of the project. It is therefore a mistake to treat the good as a genuinely single goal which imposes on the various reasons for judging a particular project the best one the same kind of unified organization that truth imposes on the various reasons for accepting a particular hypothesis. This is the core of the explanation of the greater waywardness of motivational power, but it leaves many difficult questions of detail unanswered.

Let me end by first consolidating the position I have reached and then mentioning some of the unsolved problems. I take it as obvious that anyone who accepts the possibility of unmitigated akrasia will reject the axiom that everything desired by us is desired as good: *Omnia appetimus sub specie boni*. Similarly, anyone who explains the possibility of unmitigated akrasia by appealing to the general incidence of waywardness of motivational power will also reject a corollary of the axiom: that everything desired by us is desired to the extent that we judge it good. The aim of this part of my paper has been to support the rejection of this corollary, in order to leave room for a general explanation of unmitigated akrasia. If we start from natural sources of motivation and if it is agreed that they never completely give up their original autonomy in the federal system which we call 'the good', we can see why their waywardness is greater than the waywardness of evidential considerations. For evidential considerations never did enjoy any autonomy, because in their case the system of government was colonial, with a single centre of power, the truth. So it is not surprising that there is so much waywardness on the practical side. But why is there not more? And does true virtue require it to be reduced to zero?

Select Bibliography of the Publications of Richard Wollheim

BOOKS

1959 *F. H. Bradley*, Penguin, Harmondsworth.

1968 *Art and its Objects: An Introduction to Aesthetics*, Harper and Row, New York; Penguin, Harmondsworth, 1970.

1969 *A Family Romance*, Cape, London; Farrar, Strauss and Giroux, New York.

1971 *Freud*, Fontana, London. American edition published as *Sigmund Freud*, Viking, New York.

1973 *On Art and the Mind: Essays and Lectures*, Allen Lane, London; Harvard University Press, Cambridge, Mass., 1974.

1980 *Art and its Objects: With Six Supplementary Essays*, 2nd ed, Cambridge University Press, Cambridge.

1984 *The Thread of Life*, The William James Lectures at Harvard University, 1982, Cambridge University Press, Cambridge; Harvard University Press, Cambridge, Mass.

1987 *Painting as an Art*, The A. W. Mellon Lectures in the Fine Arts, 1984, delivered at the National Gallery of Art, Washington D.C., Thames and Hudson, London; Princeton University Press, Princeton.

PAMPHLETS AND PUBLISHED LECTURES

1961 *Socialism and Culture*, The Fabian Society, London.

1965 *On Drawing an Object*, Inaugural Lecture as Grote Professor of Philosophy of Mind and Logic, H. K. Lewis, London. Reprinted in Harold Osborne (ed.), *Aesthetics*, Oxford Readings in Philosophy, Oxford University Press, 1972, and *On Art and the Mind*.

1971 *The Art Lesson*, Byam Shaw School of Drawing and Painting, London. Reprinted in *On Art and the Mind*.

1976 *The Good Self and the Bad Self: The Moral Psychology of British Idealism and the English School of Psychoanalysis Compared*, Dawes Hicks Lecture on Philosophy, British Academy, The British Academy, London, and *Proceedings of the British Academy*, 1975.

1979 *The Sheep and the Ceremony*, Leslie Stephen Lecture, Cambridge University Press, Cambridge.

EDITED BOOKS

1963 *Hume on Religion*, with an introduction, World Meridian Books, New York; Collins, London.

1972 *The Image in Form: Selected Writings of Adrian Stokes*, with an introduction, Harper & Row, New York; Penguin, Harmondsworth.

1974 *Freud: A Collection of Critical Essays*, Anchor Books, Garden City, N.Y. Republished as *Philosophers on Freud: New Evaluations*, Aronson, New York, 1977.

1975 *John Stuart Mill: Three Essays*, with an introduction, Oxford University Press, Oxford.

1982 (with James Hopkins), *Philosophical Essays on Freud*, Cambridge University Press, Cambridge.

ARTICLES

1951 'Privacy', *Proceedings of the Aristotelian Society*, 51, pp. 83–104.

1952 'Hampshire's Analogy', *Mind* (October), 61 (244), pp. 567–73.

1954 'The Difference between Sensing and Observing', *Aristotelian Society Supplementary Volume*, 28, pp. 219–40. Reprinted in G. J. Warnock (ed.), *The Philosophy of Perception*, Oxford Readings in Philosophy, Oxford University Press, Oxford, 1975.

1954 'Historicism Reconsidered', *Sociological Review* (July), 2, pp. 76–97.

1954 'The Nature of Law', *Political Studies*, 2 (2), pp. 128–41.

1955–6 'Equality', *Proceedings of the Aristotelian Society*, 56, pp. 281–300. Reprinted as 'Equality and Equal Rights', in Frederick A. Olafson (ed.), *Justice and Social Policy: A Collection of Essays*, Prentice-Hall, Englewood Cliffs N. J., 1961.

1956 'F. H. Bradley', in *The Revolution in Philosophy*, Macmillan, London.

1957 'New Conservatism in Britain', *Partisan Review* (Fall), 24, pp. 539–60.

1957 'Sociological Explanation of the Arts: Some Distinctions', *Atti del III Congresso Internazionale di Estetica*, Edizioni della Rivista di Estetica, Turin. Reprinted in Milton C. Albrecht, James H. Barnett, and Mason Griff (eds), *The Sociology of Art and Literature: A Reader*, Praeger, New York, 1970.

1958 'Democracy', *Journal of the History of Ideas* (April), 19, pp. 225–42. Reprinted in W. J. Stankiewicz (ed.), *Political Thought since World War II: Critical and Interpretive Essays*, Free Press of Glencoe, New York; Collier – Macmillan, London, 1964, and in Anthony de Crespigny and Jeremy Cronin (eds), *Ideologies of Politics*, Oxford University Press, Oxford, 1975.

1959 'Crime, Sin, and Mr. Justice Devlin', *Encounter* (November), 13 (5) pp. 34–40. Reprinted in D. W. Hanson and R. B. Fowler (eds), *Obligation and Dissent: An Introduction to Politics*, Little Brown, Boston, 1971.

1960 'How Can One Person Represent Another?', *Aristotelian Society Supplementary Volume*, 34, pp. 209–24.

1961 'Philosophie analytique et pensée politique', *Revue Française de Science Politique*, 2.

1961 'Reflections on *Art and Illusion*', *Arts Yearbook*, 4, pp. 169–76.

1962 'Babylon, Babylone', *Encounter* (May), 18(5), pp. 25–36.

1962 Introduction to F. H. Bradley, *Ethical Studies*, Oxford University Press, Oxford.

1962 'A Paradox in the Theory of Democracy', in Peter Laslett and W. G. Runciman (eds), *Philosophy, Politics and Society*, 2nd series, Blackwell, Oxford.

1963 'Reflections on *Art and Illusion*' (expanded version of 'Reflections on *Art and Illusion*' (1961), *British Journal of Aesthetics* (January) 3 (1), pp. 13–37. Reprinted in Harold Osborne (ed.), *Aesthetics in the Modern World*, Weybright and Talley, New York; Thames and Hudson, London, 1968; and in *On Art and the Mind*.

1964 'On Expression and Expressionism', *Revue Internationale de Philosophie*, 18 (68–9, fasc. 2–3), pp. 270–89.

1965 'Art and Marxism', *Encounter* (November), 5 (5), pp. 68–71.

1965 'Minimal Art', *Arts Magazine* (January), pp. 26–32. Reprinted in *On Art and the Mind*.

1966 'Forms, Elements and Modernity: A Reply to Michael Podro', *British Journal of Aesthetics* (October), 6, pp. 339–45.

1966 'On the Theory of Democracy', in Bernard Williams and Alan Montefiore (eds), *British Analytical Philosophy*, Routledge, London; Humanities Press, New York.

1967 'Natural Law', in Paul Edwards (ed.), *The Encyclopaedia of Philosophy*, Macmillan, London and New York.

1967–8 'Thought and Passion' (The Presidential Address) *Proceedings of the Aristotelian Society*, 68, pp. 1–24.

1968 'Expression', in G. N. A. Vesey (ed.), *Human Agent*, Macmillan, London; St Martin's Press, New York. Reprinted in *On Art and The Mind*.

1969 Introduction to F. H. Bradley, *Appearance and Reality: A Metaphysical Essay*, 2nd edn. Oxford University Press, Oxford.

1969 'The Mind and the Mind's Image of Itself', *International Journal of Psycho-Analysis*, 50, pp. 209–20. Reprinted in *On Art and the Mind*.

1970 'Eliot and F. H. Bradley', in Graham Martin (ed.), *Eliot in Perspective*, Humanities Press, New York. Reprinted with alterations in *On Art and the Mind*.

1970 'Freud and the Understanding of Art', *British Journal of Aesthetics* (July), 10 (3), pp. 211–24. Reprinted in *On Art and the Mind*.

1970 'Nelson Goodman's *Language of Art*', *Journal of Philosophy* (20 August), 67 (16), pp. 531–9. Expanded version reprinted in *On Art and the Mind*.

1970 'The Work of Art as Object', *Studio International* (December), 180 (928), pp. 231–5. Reprinted in *On Art and the Mind*.

1971 'Philosophy and the Arts (Bryan Magee: Conversation with Richard Wollheim)', in Bryan Magee (ed.), *Modern British Philosophy*, St Martin's Press, New York.

1972 'On an Alleged Inconsistency in Collingwood's Aesthetic', in Michael Krausz (ed.), *Critical Essays on the Philosophy of R. G. Collingwood*, Oxford University Press, Oxford.

1973 'Bradley, Francis Herbert', in *Chamber's Encyclopaedia*, new rev. ed, vol. 1, International Learning Systems, London.

1973 'John Stuart Mill and the Limits of State Action', *Social Research* (Spring), 40 (1), pp. 1–30.

1974 'Bertrand Russell and the Liberal Tradition', in George Nakhnikian (ed.), *Bertrand Russell's Philosophy*, Barnes & Noble, New York; Duckworth, London.

1974 'Identification and Imagination', in *Freud: A Collection of Essays*, Doubleday, New York. Revised version in *On Art and the Mind*.

1975 'Needs, Desires and Moral Turpitude', in R. S. Peters (ed.), *Nature and Conduct*, St Martin's Press, New York; Macmillan, London.

1975 'Style Now', in Bernard Smith (ed.), *Concerning Contemporary Art: The Power Lectures, 1968–1973*, Clarendon Press, Oxford, pp. 133–53.

1977 'Representation: The Philosophical Contribution to Psychology', *Critical Inquiry* (Summer), 3 (4), pp. 709–23. Also in George Butterworth (ed.), *The Child's Representation of the World*, Plenum Press, London, 1977.

1978 'Aesthetics, Anthropology and Style: Some Programmatic Remarks', in M. Greenhalgh and J. V. S. Megaw (eds), *Art in Society: Studies in Style, Culture and Aesthetics*, St Martin's Press, New York; Duckworth, London.

1978 'Are the Criteria of Identity that Hold for a Work of Art in the Different Arts Aesthetically Relevant?', *Ratio* (June), 20, pp. 29–48. Reprinted as Supplementary Essay II to *Art and its Objects*, 2nd ed.

1978 'Comments', in Stanley I. Benn, *Political Participation: A Discussion of Political Rationality*, Australian National University Press, Canberra.

1979 'John Stuart Mill and Isaiah Berlin: The Ends of Life and the Preliminaries of Morality', in Alan Ryan (ed.), *The Idea of Freedom: Essays in Honour of Isaiah Berlin*, Oxford University Press. Reprinted as 'Mill: The Ends of Life and the Preliminaries of Morality', in Ted Honderich (ed.), *Philosophy Through its Past*, Penguin, Harmondsworth, 1984.

1979 'Memory, Experiential Memory and Personal Identity', in Graham Macdonald (ed.), *Perception and Identity: Essays Presented to A. J. Ayer, with his Replies*, Cornell University Press, Ithaca, N.Y.

1979 'Pictorial Style: Two Views', in Berel Lang (ed.), *The Concept of Style*, University of Pennsylvania Press, Philadelphia.

1979 'Wish-Fulfilment', in Ross Harrison (ed.), *Rational Action: Studies in Philosophy and Social Science*, Cambridge University Press, Cambridge.

1980 'On Persons and their Lives', in Amélie Oksenberg Rorty (ed.), *Explaining Emotions*, University of California Press, Berkeley and Los Angeles.

1982 'The Bodily Ego', in Richard Wollheim and James Hopkins (eds), *Philosophical Essays on Freud*, Cambridge University Press, Cambridge.

1983 'Art, Interpretation and Perception', in Dieter Heinrich (ed.), *Kant oder Hegel? über Formen der Begrundung in der Philosophie*, Klett-Cotta, Stuttgart.

1983 'Flawed Crystals: James', *The Golden Bowl* and the Plausibility of Literature as Moral Philosophy', *NLH*, 15, pp. 185–92.

1983 'Ourselves and Our Future', in Leigh S. Cauman, Isaac Levi, Charles Parsons, and Robert Schwartz (eds), *How Many Questions? Essays in Honor of Sidney Morgenbesser*, Hackett, Indianapolis.

1984 'Art, Interpretation and the Creative Process', *NLH* (Winter), 15, pp. 241–53.

1984 'On the Question "Why Painting is an Art?" ', in Rudolf Haller (ed.), *Aesthetics*, Proceedings of the Eighth International Wittgenstein Symposium, Hölder-Pichier-Tempsky, Vienna.

1988 'Crime, Punishment and Pale Criminality', *Oxford Journal of Legal Studies*, 8, pp. 1–16.

REVIEWS AND TRANSLATIONS

1950 'M. Sartre's Baudelaire', review of Jean-Paul Sartre's *Baudelaire*, *New Statesman and Nation* (27 May), 39 (1003), pp. 612–13.

1950 'Review of J. W. Gough's *John Locke's Political Philosophy*', *Mind* (October), 59 (236), p. 568.

1951 'Review of A. P. D'Entreves' *Natural Law*', *Mind* (October), 60 (240), pp. 572–3.

1953 'Review of A. C. Ewing's *The Fundamental Questions of Philosophy*', *Mind* (January), 62 (245), pp. 114–15.

1955 'Review of T. D. Weldon's *The Vocabulary of Politics*', *Mind* (July), 64 (255), pp. 41–2.

1956 Translation from French of Aleksandr Herzen's 'The Russian People and Socialism', in *From the other Shore; and, The Russian People and Socialism*, Weidenfeld & Nicholson, London. Reprinted by Oxford University Press, Oxford, 1979; and Hyperton Press, Westport, Conn. 1981.

1957 'Art as Symbol', review of Susanne K. Langer's *Problems of Art*, *New Statesman and Nation* (15 December).

1958 'Innocence and Politics', review of Dwight Macdonald's *The Responsibility of Peoples, and Other Essays in Political Criticism*, *Encounter* (January), 10 (1), pp. 71–4.

1959 'A Critic of Our Time', review of Adrian Stokes's *Greek Culture and the Ego*, *Encounter* (April), 12 (4), pp. 41–4.

1960 'The Connection', review of Jack Gelber's *The Connection*, *Encounter* (April), 14 (4), pp. 67–8.

1960 'The Consequences of Communication', *Times Literary Supplement* (15 July), 3046, pp. 450–1.

1960 'Melanie Klein', *Spectator* (30 September), 205, p. 468.

1960 'Orwell Reconsidered', *Partisan Review* (Winter), 27, pp. 82–97.

1961 'English Dream', review of Raymond Williams' *The Long Revolution*, *Spectator* (10 March), 206 (6924), pp. 334–5.

1961 'Living Like Heroes (A Conversation with Norman Mailer)', *New Statesman* (September), 62 (1594), pp. 443–5.

1962 'Action Critic', review of Harold Rosenberg's *The Tradition of the New*, *New Statesman* (31 August), 64, pp. 263–4.

1962 'London Letter', *Partisan Review* (Spring), 29, pp. 263–9.

1964 'Eliot, Bradley and Immediate Experience', review of T. S. Eliot's *Knowledge and Experience, New Statesman* (13 March), 67 (1722), pp. 401–2.

1974 'Neurosis and the Artist', *Times Literary Supplement* (1 March), 73, pp. 203–4.

1976 'Review of Daniel Bell's *The Cultural Contradictions of Capitalism*', *New York Review of Books*, 23 (11), pp. 35–8.

1978 'Adrian Stokes, Critic, Painter, Poet', *Times Literary Supplement* (17 February), 3960, pp. 207–9.

1978 'Artistic Temperament', review of Michael Levey's *The Case of Walter Pater, Times Literary Supplement* (22 September), 3990, pp. 1045–6.

1978 'Review of David Watkin's *Morality and Architecture*', *Architectural Review*, 163 (972), pp. 65–6.

1979 'Cabinet of Dr. Lacan', review of Jacques Lacan's *Écrits, Four Fundamental Concepts of Psychoanalysis*, and A. Lemaire's *Jacques Lacan, New York Review of Books* (25 January), 25, pp. 36–45.

1979 'The Psychology of Decorative Art', review of E. H. Gombrich's *The Sense of Order: A Study in the Psychology of Decorative Art, Burlington Magazine* (May), 121 (914), pp. 322–3.

1979 'Review of Frank J. Sulloway's *Freud: Biologist of the Mind*', *New York Review of Books*, 26 (17), pp. 25–8.

1981 'The Most Poetical of Painters', review of an exhibition of Poussin's works, *Times Literary Supplement*, (20 November), p. 1365.

1983 'Making and Faking', review of Denis Dutton (ed.), *The Forger's Art: Forgery and the Philosophy of Art, Times Literary Supplement* (30 December), 4213, p. 1449.

1984 'An Emphasis on Humanity', review of Leo Steinberg's *The Sexuality of Christ in Renaissance Art and in Modern Oblivion, New York Times Book Review* (29 April), 89, pp. 13–14.

1985 'Jesus Christie', review of *J. T. Christie: A Great Teacher, London Review of Books* (November), 7 (20), p. 4.

1985 'Modernism Smothered by its Friends', review of Hilton Kramer's *The Revenge of the Philistines: Art and Culture, 1972–1984, New York Times Book Review*, (17 November), p. 11.

1988 'The Mighty Father', review of Peter Gay's *Freud: A Life of Our Time, New York Times Book Review* (24 April), pp. 3, 43, 47.

1988 'Poussin, the Early Years in Rome: The Origins of French Classicism', *New York Review of Books*, (24 November), 35, p. 40.

1988 'A Wonderful Occasion for Shamelessness (Pablo Picasso, Tate Gallery, London), *Times Literary Supplement*, (15 July), p. 783.

List of Contributors

Malcolm Budd is Professor of Philosophy at University College, London. His publications include *Music and the Emotions* and *Wittgenstein's Philosophy of Psychology*.

M. F. Burnyeat is Laurence Professor of Ancient Philosophy at the University of Cambridge, to which he moved after 14 years teaching in the Philosophy Department at University College, London. He is the author of *The Theaetetus of Plato* and of articles in both classical and philosophical journals.

Marcia Cavell is currently Visiting Associate Professor of Philosophy at the University of California at Berkeley. She is the author of articles in psychoanalysis and the philosophy of mind.

G. A. Cohen is Chichele Professor of Social and Political Theory and a Fellow of All Souls College, Oxford. He is the author of *Karl Marx's Theory of History: A Defence* and *History, Labour and Freedom*.

Nicholas Dent is Professor of Philosophy at the University of Birmingham. Among his publications are *The Moral Psychology of the Virtues* and *Rousseau*.

Patrick Gardiner is Emeritus Fellow of Magdalen College, Oxford. His publications include *The Nature of Historical Explanation, Schopenhauer*, and *Kierkegaard*. He is also the editor of *Theories of History, Nineteenth Century Philosophy*, and *The Philosophy of History*.

Sebastian Gardner is Lecturer in Philosophy at Birkbeck College, London. He is the author of *Irrationality and the Philosophy of Psychoanalysis*.

W. D. Hart was Reader in Philosophy at University College, London, who escaped to the University of New Mexico. He is the author of *The Engines of the Soul* and of articles on metaphysics and logic.

Jim Hopkins is Lecturer in Philosophy at King's College, London. He edited *Philosophical Essays on Freud* with Richard Wollheim, has written articles on psychoanalysis and the philosophy of mind, and is Assistant Editor of *Mind*.

Hidé Ishiguro taught in the UK and US for many years, and is now Professor of Philosophy in Keio University in Tokyo, Japan. Her works include

Leibniz's Philosophy of Logic and Language and articles on philosophy of mind, Wittgenstein, philosophy of logic and philosophy of language.

Alexander Nehamas is Edmund N. Carpenter II Professor in the Humanities at Princeton University. He is the author of *Nietzsche: Life as Literature*.

David Pears is Emeritus Professor of Philosophy at Oxford, Fellow of the British Academy and Membre de l'Institut International de Philosophie. His most recent books are *Motivated Irrationality*, *The False Prison: A Study of the Development of Wittgenstein's Philosophy*, and *Hunt's System: an Examination of the First Book of his Treatise*.

Antonia Phillips writes reviews on art for the *Times Literary Supplement*, and is working on a book about pictorial representation.

A. W. Price is Lecturer in Philosophy at the University of York. In 1989/90 he was Junior Fellow at the Center for Hellenic Studies, Washington, D.C. He is the author of *Love and Friendship in Plato and Aristotle* and of articles on ancient and moral philosophy.

Amélie Oksenberg Rorty's *Mind in Action* discusses a range of topics on the philosophy of mind: personal identity, emotions, akrasia, and self-deception. She also writes on the history of moral psychology. Her anthology on Aristotle's *Poetics* will be published by Princeton University Press.

Anthony Savile is Reader in Philosophy at King's College, London, and Jan Hus Foundation Professor of Philosophy at the Palacky University in Olomouc, Czechoslovakia. He is the author of *The Test of Time* and *Aesthetic Reconstructions*.

Samuel Scheffler is Professor of Philosophy at the University of California, Berkeley. He is the author of *The Rejection of Consequentialism* and *Human Morality*.

Hanna Segal is a Fellow of the Royal College of Psychiatrists and a practising psychoanalyst and teacher at the British Psycho-Analytical Society. She is the author of *Introduction to the Work of Melanie Klein* (1973); *Klein* (1979); *The Work of Hanna Segal*; *Dream, Phantasy and Art* and numerous papers, mostly published in the *International Journal of Psycho-Analysis*.

Kendall L. Walton is Professor of Philosophy at the University of Michigan. He is the author of *Mimesis as Make-Believe: On the Foundations of the Representational Arts* and articles on aesthetics and the philosophy of art.

David Wiggins is Professor of Philosophy at Birkbeck College, London. He is the author of *Sameness and Substance* and *Needs, Values, Truth*.

Index

hallucinatory wish-fulfillment:
Freud on   71–2
Hampshire, Stuart   156
hearing-in   287
Hegel, G.   194, 213, 224, 225
hermeneutic process, interpretation as   4
Hobbes, Thomas   71, 250
Hoffman, Hans   283: *Pompeii*
285, 286
Hume, David   81, 94, 112, 114,
117, 129, 222, 223–4, 225,
228, 230, 232, 235, 343, 363
Hylton, Peter   221
hypothetical judgements: Bradley on   206–7, 211–13

iconic mental states   241
ideal morality   202
idealism: in Green   233; and
motions of the mind   224
idealization: in infant development   77
identity, 'is' of: in Bradley   213–
15; and personal memory
340–1, 342, 345
illusion, pictorial   261–3, 269,
283, 301
illusions: and pictorial
representation   283
imagination: and visual awareness   275
'Imagination and Pictorial Understanding' (Wollheim)   286
imaginative perception: in pictorial representation   284–5
indicative sentences   4–5
individuals: designation of, in
Bradley   208–11; existence of,
in Bradley   206, 207, 215, 218
individuation: and space-time
216–17
inductivist fallacy   21–2
interpretation   3–30:   and belief
16–19, 21; and emotion   16–
19, 21; Freud on   3, 15, 23,
25–6, 27, 29, 30; methodological short-cuts in   24, 26
interpretive hypotheses   28
introjection: archaic   66; in
infant development   77; melan-

cholic   75–6, 77; Wollheim
on   100, 102
intuition: Bradley on   198–9,
202, 204; and drawing from
life   317
Isaacs, Susan   57

James, William   40, 340
Janet   40
Johns, Jasper   284, 285
Judaeo-Christian tradition: Nietzsche on   68, 69
judgements, Bradley on: hypothetical   206–7, 211–13;
moral   196–200, 202, 204;
singular   208, 211, 212, 213;
subject-predicate   211, 213–
15; universal   206–7, 211–13
justice: in Plato's *Republic*   176,
177: Rousseau on   135,
138–9, 139

Kant, I.   162, 201, 208, 216–17,
221, 223, 225, 230:   on moral
motivation   87–92, 97–9
Kemp-Smith, Norman   222
Khrushchev, Nikita   144
Klein, Melanie   65, 100, 117,
132, 205, 222, 226:   on emotion   35; on genetic projectivism   120, 122–3; on love   81;
and morality   69, 70–1; on
mourning   77–80; on phantasy   57; on the superego
137–8; theory of envy   42–4,
45–7; on valuing   83
knowledge: Socrates on   164,
165–6; and valuing   84–5
Kripke, Saul   210

Lacan, Jacques   74
language: interpretation of   4–22
Leibniz, G.   207, 345
likenesses of objects: and drawing from life   317–18, 321
Locke, John   340
love: Freud on   81, 83–4; Klein
on   81; and moral motivation
101, 102–3, 104; Rousseau
on   131, 137, 138; and the